Comprehensive
VB .NET Debugging

MARK PEARCE

APress Media, LLC

ISBN 978-1-59059-050-8   ISBN 978-1-4302-0778-8 (eBook)
DOI 10.1007/978-1-4302-0778-8

Trademarked names may appear in this book. Rather than use a trademark symbol with every occurrence of a trademarked name, we use the names only in an editorial fashion and to the benefit of the trademark owner, with no intention of infringement of the trademark.

Technical Reviewer: Pamela Fanstill

Editorial Directors: Dan Appleman, Gary Cornell, Simon Hayes, Martin Streicher, Karen Watterson, John Zukowski

Assistant Publisher: Grace Wong

Project Managers: Sofia Marchant, Nicole LeClerc

Copy Editor: Nicole LeClerc

Compositor and Proofreader: Impressions Book and Journal Services, Inc.

Indexer: Ann Rogers

Artist and Cover Designer: Kurt Krames

Production Manager: Kari Brooks

Manufacturing Manager: Tom Debolski

Distributed to the book trade in the United States by Springer-Verlag New York, Inc., 175 Fifth Avenue, New York, NY, 10010 and outside the United States by Springer-Verlag GmbH & Co. KG, Tiergartenstr. 17, 69112 Heidelberg, Germany.

In the United States: phone 1-800-SPRINGER, email orders@springer-ny.com, or visit http://www.springer-ny.com.

Outside the United States: fax +49 6221 345229, email orders@springer.de, or visit http://www.springer.de.

For information on translations, please contact Apress directly at 2560 Ninth Street, Suite 219, Berkeley, CA 94710. Phone 510-549-5930, fax 510-549-5939, email info@apress.com, or visit http://www.apress.com.

The source code for this book is available to readers at http://www.apress.com in the Downloads section.

To Tamara: You make me whole, and in the process carve images on my soul. Thanks for civilizing me, loving me, and not killing me when I spent so much time working on this book.

To Clara Alexia: As I finished this book, you added your tiny sparkle to the 6 billion other sparkles that make up this river of humanity. Our hopes and our dreams fly with you into the future, where you'll see things that we never dreamt of.

To Martin: Your reference count finally reached zero and you sailed away into the darkness. Have some beers on me up there in the pub where the ale is real and flows forever. I'll be along soon.

Footfalls echo in the memory
Down the passage which we did not take
Towards the door we never opened
—T. S. Eliot

Contents at a Glance

Contents

Chapter 11 VB.Classic Debugging *321*

Chapter 12 SOL Server Debugging *339*

Part Four Debugging Common Scenarios *359*

Chapter 13 Error Handling
and Exception Management *361*

About the Author

Mark Pearce is a freelance consultant and developer specializing in the design and construction of investment banking systems. He specializes in software quality processes and has consulted for many blue-chip clients including Citigroup, Nomura, Barclays Capital, Lehmans, and British Petroleum. His other technical areas of interest include database design, middleware messaging, and distributed applications. In a previous life, Mark was a professional chess player who paid for his chess-playing bugs with near-starvation. His current hobbies of snowmobiling and mountain running are less energetic and more fun.

About the Technical Reviewer

Pamela Fanstill has over 20 years' experience working with information systems and holds a bachelor's degree in information systems management from the University of San Francisco. She has been focusing on Microsoft development tools since VB 3.0 and earned her first MCSD certification in 1996. For the last few years she has been teaching Visual Basic and related development technologies as a Microsoft Certified Trainer. Pam has been enthusiastic about .NET since beta 1 and is one of the charter MCADs for .NET. This is the third Apress .NET book for which Pam has served as technical reviewer. She has also been a technical contributor to the Microsoft and CompTIA certification programs. Pam lives in Northern California.

Acknowledgments

THE FIRST GROUP OF PEOPLE I want to thank is the crew at Apress. Peter Wright was adamant that I could write this book, in spite of my reservations. Gary Cornell had the guts to take a big chance on a new author, based on nothing more than a rather grandiose book synopsis. Dan Appleman didn't veto Gary's decision, for which I'm very grateful!

As the project manager, Sofia Marchant led the project to bring this book to fruition, and refused to get testy or annoyed with me, no matter how many deadlines I missed. As the copy editor, Nicole LeClerc taught me that I didn't know as much about writing as I thought, and has forever changed the style in which I write. I promise never to use the passive form again, even if I still insist that the full stop should be outside the quotes. Next, Pamela Fanstill did a very thorough job of spotting my technical mistakes, testing and fixing my occasionally dubious code, and showing me where I wasn't being clear about the points I was trying to make. Perhaps even more important than all of the technical issues and hand-holding, Sofia, Nicole, and Pam all encouraged me with my writing and gave me real moral support during the more difficult times. I would also like to thank Production Manager Kari Brooks for actually getting this book out the door and shipping it.

There's a group of people I want to thank for encouraging and helping me during the writing of this book. Rob Macdonald and Peter Blackburn had many suggestions and helped me to organize my thoughts better. John Robbins, author of the outstanding *Debugging Applications* book, gave me probably the best advice on locking myself away to do the writing—it's a shame that I didn't always follow his advice! Lawson Davies and my brother Jerome Pearce did technical reviews of some of the earlier chapters in this book. Habib Heydarian from the Microsoft .NET debugger team did full technical editing on the first few chapters before he had to step away. Finally, Gary Cornell resisted the temptation to make me rewrite my code without using Hungarian notation—sorry, Gary!

Thanks to the amazing Chris Sells for allowing me to pinch and adapt his excellent demonstration of safe multithreading in a Windows Forms application—you can see the result at the end of Chapter 14. Thanks also to Roedy Green for letting me reprint part of his very funny article on writing unclear code, which you can find in the "Interlude" section in Chapter 12. Finally, Scott Rosenberg, managing editor of online magazine Salon.com, was kind enough to let me use the results of his magazine's haiku competition, which can be found in the "Interlude" section in Chapter 13.

Einstein is reported to have said something like, "If I've seen further, it's because I've been able to stand on the shoulders of giants." If he didn't say this, he should have. In my case, if I've seen anything at all, it's because I've been able to stand on the toes of great developers. I want to thank all those great developers who've helped me develop my technical skills over the years. Bob Frankel and Brian Skinner taught me about computers and how to write code. Donald Knuth, Joe Celko, Bruce McKinney, Jeffrey Richter, Ted Pattison, Steve McConnell, Steve Maguire, and Jim McCarthy have all written truly excellent books that have improved my software development skills to the point where I'm able to claim some proficiency. Peter Morris, Mark Hurst, Lawson Davies, and Mark Sewell of The Mandelbrot Set taught me more than I care to admit about Visual Basic. The books that I've read by Dan Appleman are a model of clarity and explained many concepts that I'd previously found confusing. In fact, I came to Apress primarily because of Dan's writing and my wish to produce similar.

My Mum and Dad brought me up with certain ethical and pragmatic values. This book, and my career, simply wouldn't have been done properly without having these values to guide me. The two of you must have been worried at times, but everything seems to have turned out okay in the end. My stepfather, Donald Swift-Hook, taught me the difference between facts and opinions, and the importance of applying an objective process to my work and my life.

My wife, Tamara, supported me throughout the writing of this book, sacrificing our social life and many evenings that should have been spent together. I'm sorry for the time this project took, and I hope that you're proud of the result. I love you very much.

As for my newborn daughter, Clara Alexia, I hope the royalties from this book will be enough to pay for your diaper bill!

Introduction

THIS BOOK IS ABOUT FINDING, understanding, fixing, and preferably preventing bugs when creating desktop, network, and Web applications with Visual Basic (VB) .NET. It explores the power of the new cross-language and cross-component debugging tools, and shows you how to dig down into or tunnel across your entire application to find bugs at whatever level they live.

With the arrival of VB .NET, many of the old debugging rules have changed. This means that some ominous storm clouds are gathering on the horizon.

Well, Toto, We're Not in Kansas Anymore

Back in the personal computing Dark Ages, during a period when men were men and code was written in blood, it took some seriously hard-core work to create a viable and stable Windows application. Windows itself was still relatively immature and was being held back because of the lack of simple tools available for producing programs. Then in 1991 Visual Basic 1.0 and its successors (henceforth collectively referred to as VB.Classic) came riding to the rescue and changed the software development world in a dramatic way.

For the first time, Windows programming was made accessible, and people who had never before considered themselves to be developers could cast the spells necessary to bring their software ideas to life. Departmental business processes were automated by the thousand, often without any intervention from in-house technology departments. When these "accidental" programmers joined forces with the countless professional developers who valued the remarkable productivity that VB.Classic brought to Windows programming, the result was spectacular. Windows software applications exploded over the next decade, driven by speed of development and the greater pool of available developers. There is even a respectable argument that this ready availability of developers and their myriad applications drove the widespread adoption of Windows itself. It's entirely possible that VB.Classic was the real killer application for Windows.

One of the results of this programming explosion was many managers and even developers started to think that much of the process of software development was relatively easy and that all of the hard plumbing that VB.Classic did behind the scenes meant that applications could be designed and developed much faster. The result was another explosion—that of bug-ridden software. Windows applications have become notorious for their instability and unreliability. End users think nothing of rebooting hourly and killing errant applications.

Lacking the understanding of the types of bugs that were possible, developers have introduced many wild and wonderful defects into their programs. It has taken us a decade to understand and solve many of the typical problems that personal computing involves.

Moving forward into the future, we can see that history might be repeating itself. Where VB.Classic worked by simplifying the creation of Windows desktop applications, the common language runtime (CLR) and the .NET languages are designed to simplify the creation and deployment of desktop and especially network applications. These new applications all use a common class library and can be written in any of at least a dozen different languages. Though the learning curve is significantly steeper than that associated with VB.Classic, the payoff also promises to be much higher. The promise is that everything from XML Web services and operating system services to Web pages and desktop programs will be available with a flick of an IDE wizard's magic wand. Deployment will usually be XCOPY-simple, and DLL hell is set to retreat into ancient folklore (though it may be replaced by policy hell).

The new world beckons, dangling shiny new technology to tempt us into its embrace. The CLR and the .NET Framework have the potential to do to network applications and the Internet what VB.Classic did to Windows. A whole new wave of interesting and innovative distributed applications may be around the corner, or at least in the next town. Developers who understand the network and network applications will be at a premium.

Here Be Dragons

That's the hype . . . and now comes the reality check. One of several major problems with this rather cool technological vision is that network resources are not transparent in the same way that local resources are. Network resources do not tend to have the same availability, latency, and reliability as resources on the local machine. The software that you write must take all of this into account, and using some of the very convenient programmatic interfaces that .NET provides can even make these problems worse by concealing the hairy details from you. Furthermore, if your application reaches into the Internet cloud where thunderstorms regularly rage, it can go down faster than the *Titanic*.

Another key difficulty with this vision is that .NET's default security model grants only minimal permissions to code downloaded from the local intranet and even fewer rights to Internet-based code. Without a good understanding of this security model and the implications of changing security policies in general, debugging security and permission problems can rapidly turn into a nightmare.

So VB .NET allows developers to build software systems, especially network and Web applications, much easier than in the past. However, it also introduces many new ways of creating bugs. This leaves developers with the daunting challenge of trying to build more complex systems that are still easy to diagnose and fix when things go wrong. If we're not careful, the more distributed and more complicated our software applications become, the more we will be digging ourselves into a very large hole.

Larger systems, and especially distributed applications, have to be designed and debugged using different methods than those used for their smaller counterparts. Real-world experience has to be earned the hard way. The introduction of middleware elements in the form of firewalls, caches, accelerators, translators, gateways, and messaging infrastructures means that your software application must overcome several barriers in learning to cooperate with its surrounding environment. Software requirements seem to be increasing in complexity daily, with reliability, availability, security, and integrity becoming ever more critical to businesses.

The "programming via blunt object" school of thinking that often prevailed when using VB.Classic is no longer sufficient. If developers don't understand that the rules have changed with VB .NET and that the process of delivering reliable and low-defect software has to change likewise in order to compensate, the storm clouds will grow ever darker and more ominous. Eventually the bugs will fall like rain upon our applications. Technological progress will have merely provided us with a more efficient means for going backward.

This book is about many of the traps and dangers associated with designing and debugging software in the interesting new world of VB .NET. It is definitely not a criticism of the language or framework. Every technology has aspects that can cause problems for developers who are starting to use that technology. These dangerous aspects should not blind you to the potential benefits of this new language and class library. If you can understand and steer around the storm clouds, you will experience the benefits of a powerful and productive development environment matched with some excellent debugging tools that can work across your entire application.

How to Read This Book

This book is divided into four parts and fifteen chapters. It's advisable to start with the first four chapters, as these contain a comprehensive introduction to areas covered in the rest of the book. Apart from that, you should be able to dip in and out of chapters without having to reference backward or forward. At the end of each chapter is a short "Interlude" section, which presents some interesting stories from the debugging world.

Part One: Debugging in the VB .NET World

This part first takes a high-level, strategic look at debugging in the .NET world and then takes a much more detailed look at how the powerful new language features in VB .NET can trip you up.

- Chapter 1 is a discussion of the strategic debugging challenges of VB .NET and the new .NET world. It shows some of the challenges and danger areas that you need to understand in order to have a firm strategic base for defect prevention.

- Chapter 2 is an introduction to some of the nasty language surprises that lie in wait for the unwary. The VB .NET language has a superficial resemblance to VB.Classic, and this resemblance can deceive the developer into underestimating the dangers of switching to the VB .NET language.

Part Two: The Debugging Tools

This part covers the Visual Studio .NET debugger in some detail before investigating some other useful .NET debugging tools. It finishes with an examination of VB .NET's tracing and instrumentation facilities.

- Chapter 3 is a comprehensive introduction to the capabilities of the Visual Studio .NET debugger.

- Chapter 4 is a more detailed look at the Visual Studio .NET debugger, including a discussion of the various debugger settings and its more advanced capabilities.

- Chapter 5 investigates some useful debugging tools such as other .NET debuggers, the **Ildasm** utility, and the Performance Monitor.

- Chapter 6 looks in detail at tracing and instrumentation of desktop and network .NET applications.

Part Three: Debugging Applications

This part shows you how to configure and implement debugging for each of the most common VB .NET application types. It also includes a discussion of some advanced VB .NET debugging techniques.

- Chapter 7 investigates the debugging of Windows Forms applications, including class and control libraries.

- Chapter 8 investigates the debugging of XML Web services.

- Chapter 9 investigates the debugging of ASP.NET applications.

- Chapter 10 investigates the debugging of Windows services.

- Chapter 11 investigates cross-language debugging with VB.Classic.

- Chapter 12 investigates cross-language debugging with SQL Server.

Part Four: Debugging Common Scenarios

This part has an extensive discussion of error handling in VB .NET applications, and it also examines the debugging of multithreaded and distributed applications.

- Chapter 13 investigates VB .NET's exception mechanism and error-handling facilities, and shows you how to protect your applications effectively.

- Chapter 14 investigates the debugging of multithreaded applications, with an emphasis on the prevention of multithreading bugs by good design.

- Chapter 15 investigates the debugging and monitoring of distributed applications, with an emphasis on remote debugging, debugging remoting, and providing reliable fault diagnostics.

Who Are You?

My assumption is that you are an intermediate or advanced Visual Basic developer working with or anticipating VB .NET. This book is also very suitable for students taking advanced programming courses and recent graduates looking for a real-world understanding of debugging. Both team leaders and nontechnical managers should find it valuable for gaining an understanding of the reliability and performance problems faced by their developers working in the trenches.

This book also assumes that you have some prior knowledge and understanding of the VB .NET language, the CLR, and the .NET Framework. It isn't suitable as an introductory text for these subjects. Though I often discuss the subtleties of a specific feature and how you might (and might not) want to use it, you should read the documentation extensively and experiment in order to learn the feature being discussed. Although it would be marvelous to be able to provide computer science–level introductions to every subject, this would have resulted in a book at least three times this book's current size! So instead, the emphasis is on problem avoidance and debugging, with feature introductions that are relatively brief and only expanded where it's essential to the plot.

My final assumption is that you believe developers are responsible for fixing their own bugs, preferably before they reach the testers and certainly before they reach production. If you think that testers or end users should be the ones to find some of your bugs, then hopefully this book will change your mind or at least expose you to a very different viewpoint.

Source Code

There are many sample programs included with this book. You can download them from the Downloads section of the Apress Web site at http://www.apress.com. The source code is provided by chapter within a single ZIP file, with each of the sample programs in its own ZIP file.

The code printed in this book was tested using the last Release Candidate of Visual Studio 2003 together with version 1.1 of the .NET Framework. It has also been tested using Visual Studio 2002 with version 1.0 of the .NET Framework. The code available on the Apress Web site will additionally have been tested against the released version of Visual Studio 2003 and .NET 1.1, and will include any revisions and changes between the printed book and the latest .NET service pack. This approach is necessary given the time it takes to produce and print a book.

Part One

Debugging in the VB .NET World

"Computers let you make more mistakes than any other invention in history, with the possible exception of handguns and tequila."
—*Mitch Radcliffe*

CHAPTER 1

Strategic Debugging Issues

BACK IN A FORMER EXISTENCE as a professional chess player, I learned to differentiate between the strategic and the tactical understanding of a chess position. The strategic understanding involved appreciating the ideas and plans that underlie a chess position, whereas the tactical understanding concerned the actual implementation of these plans. In chess, these two elements have to be blended together. Strategy without tactics is mere posturing. Tactics without strategy is usually motion without progress.

When I moved into programming computers, I was surprised to find that most debugging books seem to concentrate only on the tactics of debugging. They often go directly into debugger usage and heavy debugging, and mainly discount the strategic ideas. These books tend to ignore the fact that all bugs aren't alike and that different classes of bugs have different reasons for their existence. They rarely investigate *why* bugs happen.

This chapter looks at strategic application design issues in the .NET world. Without a good understanding of these issues, all the heroic debugging in the world is not going to help you. The principle here, and a thread running through this book, is that bug prevention is much more valuable than bug finding and fixing. No matter how deftly you can wield a debugger, without understanding these issues you'll find that you're building your applications on quicksand. You may still be able to build a wonderful castle, but its brittle foundations will cause bugs that can only be fixed through a significant reengineering of the core of your application.

Later chapters go into much more detail on the tactics of bug prevention and debugging, but here I want to look at the bigger picture. While you might find it tempting to jump straight to Chapter 2 for some interesting code or to Chapter 3 for an in-depth introduction to the Visual Studio (VS) .NET debugger, please resist the temptation. The big picture presented in this chapter is invaluable for making software-quality decisions and for understanding the best methods of preventing bugs.

Visual Basic (VB) .NET will certainly be used to build a larger set of applications than is feasible with VB.Classic. These applications will typically be bigger, more complex, more distributed, and often accessed by a larger user base.

The issue from a debugging point of view is that designing for application reliability becomes much messier as an application scales up in size and complexity. As your end-user customer base becomes larger and demands ever more from the applications that you write, you need to take a serious look at your design processes to ensure that bugs don't grow in proportion with your systems.

This chapter investigates two core design issues when working with VB .NET: reliability and availability. It looks at what you need to understand in order to build systems that are both reliable and highly available to your end users. Because this is a book about software, I only take a brief look at the related hardware issues. Bear in mind, though, that hardware issues may well affect how you design your software. It's often necessary to change the design of your software in order to fix problems or errors that are hardware related.

Application Reliability

I was called in to deal with a sophisticated and highly functional trading system that was plagued with some nightmarish reliability problems. The application consisted of many megabytes of source code spread over dozens of components running on multiple machines. Its error handling and recovery was either nonexistent or deliberately suppressed errors, and its real-time interaction with external systems was frequently changing. In short, it was an application from one of the lower levels of Dante's *Inferno.*

This experience taught me more than I ever wanted to know about the reliability of complex systems and supplied some significant insights into how to approach reliability in the distributed world that VB .NET inhabits.

Understanding Reliability

Taking data from studies published by the Gartner Group, Cahners Instat, and others in the late 1990s, the typical causes of application failure can be mapped. Figure 1-1 shows this data in a chart format. Although it is unclear whether the percentages shown in the chart will change as .NET allows you to build more complex and distributed applications, it is a reasonable starting point for discussion.

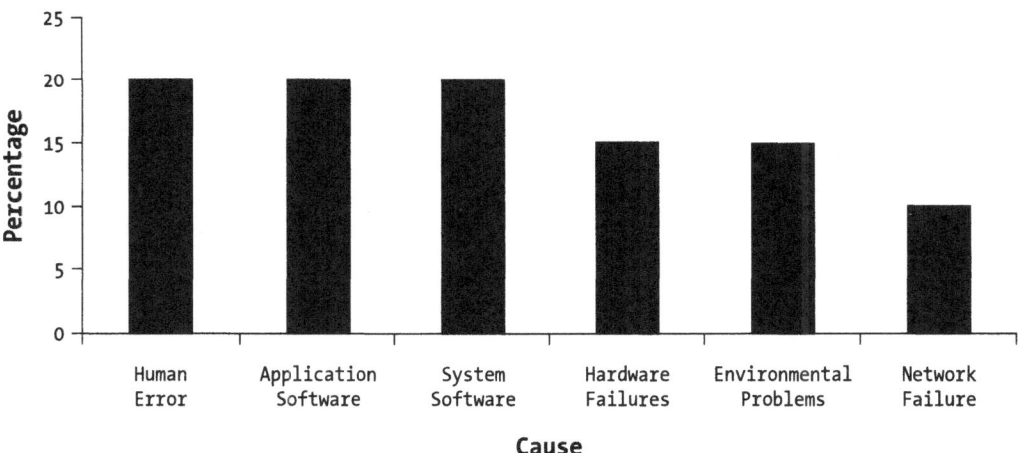

Figure 1-1. Causes of application failure

The various categories shown in Figure 1-1 deserve some explanation. Human error covers backup and restore problems—errors caused by a lack of rigorous operational procedures and failures associated with configuration problems. The hardware factor includes components such as disks, memory, and fans. The network factor covers failures in routers, switches, cabling, and network servers. System software consists of the operating system, device drivers, firewalls, Web servers, database servers, load balancers, and other sundry applications such as antivirus programs. The application software is, of course, the application that is being profiled for failure. Finally, the environment category covers power failures, cooling failures, storms, flood, and fire.

At least two interesting observations can be made about this information. The first is that the .NET Framework, here coming under the category of system software, could by itself make application reliability worse. The replacement of the relatively simple VB.Classic execution engine with a more complex class library and common language runtime (CLR) engine is unlikely to improve matters. The hope is that this extra layer is reliable and will help you to make your applications less defective than when using VB.Classic. In reality, the significant productivity boost provided by the .NET Framework may come at a high price in application reliability.

The second observation is that you need to look outside of your application for the majority of application failures. While beyond the scope of this book, it is worthwhile to understand that uninterruptible power supplies, reliable hardware, and a trustworthy network are critical in ensuring that your applications are reliable and consistently available. You also should not neglect the reliability of your Web and database servers, two very critical elements. This may involve building diagnostic utilities into your system aimed at monitoring factors that are not necessarily under your control.

Measuring Reliability

This is all very interesting, but how do you measure the reliability of your own .NET application? The first step is to establish exactly what your application's reliability requirements are and then to record those requirements for later benchmarking. If you ignore availability for the moment, as I discuss this in the next section, you need to consider at least two issues when constructing a reliability metric:

1. How well an application provides the required services

2. How well an application provides correct results

The first element, how well an application provides the required services, corresponds to a requirement something like *"The system will prevent trade entry for no more than 1 hour per year."* The second element, how well an application provides correct results, corresponds to a requirement something like *"The system will correctly report 999 out of every 1,000 trades."*

A reliability metric is often measured using something called *mean time between failures* (MTBF), which is made up of the following simple formula:

MTBF = Hours / Failures

This formula measures the average time that an application will run until a failure occurs. So if your application has six failures a year, its MTBF works out as 1,461 hours, or about 2 months. Notice that this is not necessarily the same as *mean time between bugs* (MTBB). If your application recovers properly from a bug, that bug might not even be considered as an application failure.

Unfortunately, reliability is not always as simple as this formula implies. One important element that it fails to consider is the type of error. To continue with the example application, if a trading system allows an option trade exposing the trader to literally millions of dollars of risk, it doesn't really matter how reliable the application is in all other respects. So now you need a more complex formula in order to take into account the severity of the bugs allowed:

MTBFW = Hours / (Failures × Severity Weighting)

The type of application failure also needs to be considered, because certain bugs and errors are much more damaging than others. Ask yourself the following questions:

- Is the failure permanent or transient?

- Does the failure corrupt data or not?

The preferable type of failure is usually transient and doesn't damage data, whereas at the other end of the scale is a permanent failure that corrupts data. The transient failure that corrupts data can also be nasty because its occasional nature means that a problem may not be noticed for a while. This can mean corrupted data backups and other rather scary situations.

Another element that needs to be considered is the units of time used in the MTBF formula. Each type of application has its own domain time requirements:

- *Calendar time:* Suitable for systems with regular usage patterns

- *Clock time:* Suitable for systems with peak/trough usage patterns

- *Processor time:* Suitable for nonstop systems

It can be difficult to specify a level of reliability that meets the business needs while also meeting budget and schedule requirements. This is especially true when the usage patterns and the number of users change over the lifetime of the application. There are always tradeoffs to be made in this area.

Designing for Software Reliability

Here is a list of measures to improve the reliability of your VB .NET application during the design and construction processes. They are discussed in more detail in the text that follows.

- Emphasize reliability as an explicit design goal

- Recruit designers, developers, and testers who value reliability

- Define specific reliability targets and add them to your requirements

- Test that the reliability requirements have been met

- Design monitoring and diagnostic facilities into your application

- Use assertions to document and enforce assumptions and conventions

- Design and build health checks directly into the application

- Design redundancy into your application at critical failure points

- Have a consistent error-handling and recovery scheme

- Trap and record all application bugs and failures

- Use the fail-fast principle in your designs

- Use the excellent diagnostic tools within .NET

Emphasizing reliability as a design goal and making sure that the people working on your project have reliability as one of their primary goals are essential. Without people buying into the reliability goals, all of the other measures outlined in the preceding list will not work very effectively. This means ensuring that the business sponsors and the IT managers are not allowed to be vague about reliability and quality targets. It may suit many project sponsors not to be explicit because they are worried about the schedule and resource costs of clear targets. They can always fall back to the position that good developers would understand and provide reliability without having it stated explicitly. The reality is that providing good application reliability is difficult, and providing it without a clear target is almost impossible.

Defining specific reliability targets ensures that you know how reliable your application needs to be. Performing tests against these reliability targets means that you can offer hard figures to your end users and to the application support staff. If you're happy with the reliability testing, you might even be able to offer a service-level agreement (SLA). Creating an SLA means that there's no choice except to be explicit about the SLA requirements.

Design automated monitoring and diagnostic components into your application in order to perform ongoing application analysis and to identify application faults and failures early. As your application grows, adds more users, and supports increasingly complex links to other systems, this monitoring will allow you to identify trends and to understand or even predict new problems. Another benefit this gives you is the ability to identify invisible failures. These are errors that don't stop your application from running, but may cause problems whose adverse effects wouldn't otherwise be identified until later.

In this respect, it can be useful to treat the application maintenance team as users. If this team is able to request diagnostic and other facilities to be built into the application, you are likely to find that your end users will experience a more reliable application.

Use the **Trace** and **Debug** classes, which I discuss in Chapter 5, to enforce and document all of the assumptions and conventions that every programmer makes. For example, if two methods must only be called in a specific order, an assertion can enforce this convention. Or if a variable is only supposed to have one of three values, an assertion can check this assumption. These assertions can catch many bugs automatically during development and also serve as source code documentation of the thinking of the original developer.

Automated health checks can verify that your application is working properly. For instance, a script could ping each of the components in a distributed system and report any components that failed to respond or generated an incorrect response. Another script could perform a dummy customer interaction with a Web page and e-mail or page a support technician if no response was received within a certain time. This type of checking allows you to spot problems and failures within seconds or minutes rather than hours or even days.

You can make the mission-critical parts of your application more reliable by adding redundant software. For example, you could calculate a critically important value in two or three different ways, using common validation checks to ensure success. Alternatively, you can have two or three copies of the same component, so that if one fails, its identical companion takes over. Redundant hardware components and databases are, of course, very common.

Proper error handling and recovery in distributed systems is very difficult. In some systems, as much as 80% of the code is devoted to error handling as opposed to 20% for functionality. What makes this even more difficult is that much of this code is untested during normal testing and in production, because it's only ever run when a bug or failure actually appears. A consistent pattern for building error handling and recovery is therefore invaluable. Once you've shown that the pattern works, it's then relatively simple to ensure that the same pattern is implemented properly throughout your application. You can even design schemes that will retry after failures, and in the worst case you'll at least have a reasonable postmortem trail to follow. Chapter 13 discusses ways of implementing this type of functionality.

Linked to the error handling discussed previously is the need to trap and record the full details of all bugs and failures. An unhandled error will crash your component and possibly your application. Chapter 13 contains a comprehensive discussion about implementing error handling and recovery properly in VB .NET.

You should always use the *fail-fast principle* when designing your error-recovery routines. This consists of three ideas that have consistently been found to improve reliability after a bug or failure has occurred:

1. No answer is better than the wrong answer (to the end user).

2. Fault containment is better if the task stops (but not the application).

3. Recover back to a known safe state (using **Try . . . Catch . . . Finally**).

Finally, there are some excellent diagnostic tools available with the .NET Framework SDK and the .NET Framework. For an in-depth discussion of these tools, please see Chapter 5.

Improving Software Reliability

Not all failures and bugs are created equal. Therefore, removing the bugs with the worst consequences is the most important goal. In one particular study, removing 60% of the software faults within an application only led to a 3% reliability improvement. So focus your effort where it does the most good—mainly on the failures that have the worst effects on your end users.

Defining the defects with the worst consequences can sometimes be difficult. We all know of end users who insist on marking every bug as critical. I suggest you use the following criteria for assessing the relative importance of each problem:

- Does the bug result in lost or corrupted data?

- How many people does the bug affect?

- Is there a reasonable workaround for the bug?

A second effective method of improving reliability is to fix the bugs that occur in the most frequently used parts of your software system. This will tend to give you a better result for your efforts, because fixing a single bug that occurs ten times in a day will usually be more beneficial than fixing multiple bugs that only rarely occur.

Ultimately, to build a reliable system requires that your application's requirements, its developers, and its testers all place a strong emphasis on reliability. The processes and measurements discussed in this section can help, but even with the new .NET technologies, the most important path to reliability is the people involved in the project.

Application Availability

Application availability depends to a large degree on the reliability issues discussed in the previous section, but the extra factor of failure recovery enters into the equation. I am defining *application availability* here as the system uptime required by end users in order to meet business needs.

Understanding Availability

Taking data from a study done by Dataquest in November 1999, the typical causes of unplanned application downtime can be mapped. Figure 1-2 shows this data in a chart format.

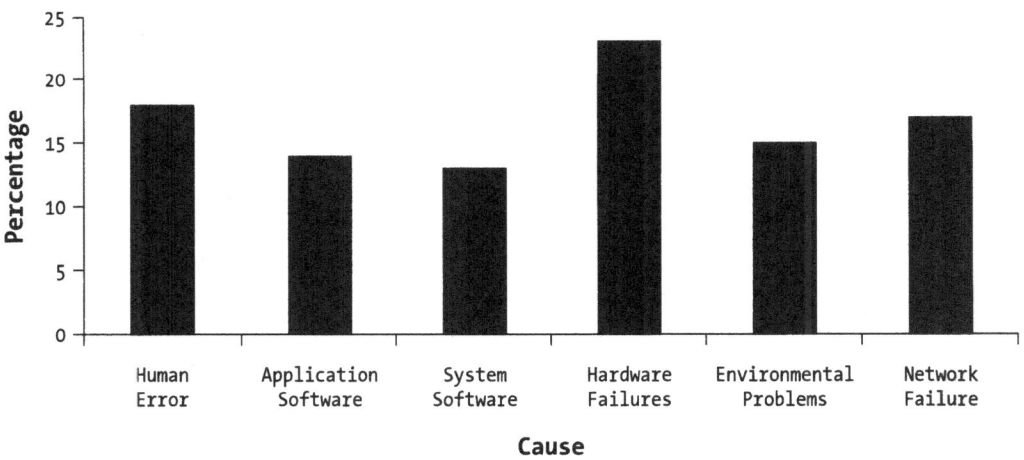

Figure 1-2. Causes of unplanned downtime

Once again, the categories shown in the chart in Figure 1-2 deserve some further explanation. Human error is a category that covers operational errors, backup problems, configuration issues, and so on. The hardware factor includes components such as disks, memory, and fans. The network factor covers failures in routers, switches, cabling, and network servers. System software consists of the operating system, device drivers, firewalls, Web servers, database servers, load balancers, and other sundry applications such as antivirus programs. Finally, the environment category covers factors such as power failures, cooling failures, flood, and fire. The application software is, of course, the application that is being profiled for failure.

Notice that the downtime profile shown in Figure 1-2 looks rather different from the failure profile shown in Figure 1-1, though it contains the same types of failure. This is because certain types of errors (for example, system software failures) may occur more often than others (for example, hardware failures). However, the former type of error is often either transient or much quicker to fix. Because the time to recovery is an important part of application availability, it skews the profile to reflect the fact that certain types of error have more side effects and are harder (and therefore slower) to fix than others.

As with the reliability profile, you can see that you need to look outside of your immediate application for the majority of the application's downtime. While beyond the scope of this book, it is worthwhile to understand that rigorous operational procedures are critical in ensuring that your applications are reliable and consistently available. The application designer should work with the likely operational procedures in mind, attempting to minimize the complexity and manual aspects of every procedure.

Measuring Availability

The most popular method of measuring availability is with a percentage figure. For example, your end users or business analysts might claim that your application must be 99.9% available, or perhaps they opt for the magical "five nines" (in other words, 99.999% reliability). In real terms, 99.9% availability implies a maximum downtime of 8.7 hours in a single year, 99.99% availability represents about 52 minutes of outage, and 99.999% means a downtime of not more than about 5 minutes in a year.

The extra factor when assessing availability as opposed to reliability is called *mean time to recovery* (MTTR). This is made up of the following simple formula:

MTTR = Hours of Downtime / Failures

This formula measures the average time that an application takes between going down and coming back up again. So if your application has six failures a year and a total of 24 hours of downtime in the year, its MTTR works out as 4 hours.

The formula to measure the percentage of application availability is therefore slightly more complex than the reliability formula discussed earlier. Mean time between failures is shown as MTBF, and mean time to recovery is shown as MTTR. Both figures are represented in hours:

Availability = (MTBF / (MTBF + MTTR)) $\times$ 100

As an example, if an application fails six times a year (MTBF = 1,461 hours) and the average recovery time is 1 hour (MTTR = 1), feeding these figures into the formula gives an availability percentage of 99.93. This in turn translates to an average downtime of about 6.1 hours per year.

It appears that most business organizations can live comfortably with 99.9% availability, which equates to about 8.5 hours service outage per year. This figure is very achievable with motivated people, good software development processes, and rigorous operational procedures.

The VS .NET documentation provides an interesting table as a guideline for the availability requirements of different business categories. This table is reproduced in Table 1-1 for your convenience.

Table 1-1. Typical Business Availability Guidelines (VS .NET Documentation)

BUSINESS CATEGORY	FAILURES PER YEAR	AVERAGE TIME TO REPAIR	DOWNTIME PER YEAR	AVAILABILITY
Noncommercial	10	10 hours	88 hours	99.00%
Commercial	5	8.8 hours	44 hours	99.50%
Business-critical	4	2.25 hours	8.5 hours	99.90%
Mission-critical	4	0.25 hour	1 hour	99.99%

Designing for Software Availability

The list of design recommendations for software availability has some similarity with the previous software reliability list, but with some added concepts:

- Emphasize availability as an explicit design goal

- Recruit designers, developers, and testers who value availability

- Define specific availability targets and add them to your requirements

- Test that the availability requirements have been met

- Design monitoring and diagnostic facilities into your application

- *Design redundancy into your application at critical failure points*

- Isolate critical applications

- Use queuing for component communication

- Have a consistent error-handling and recovery scheme

The best rewards for your effort are likely to come from designing redundant software components (the line in italic font). Doing important calculations in two or three different ways and then cross-validating the results is a very useful design concept. Having two or three copies of critical components so that one copy can take over from another in the event of failure is another important design tool.

You should also take care to isolate your business-critical and mission-critical VB .NET applications from other applications. On the server side, this means preventing other applications from competing with your critical application for resources such as CPU time, memory, network bandwidth, and database usage. On the client side, this might mean preventing the use of applications that interfere or compete with your application. As you try to attain ever-higher levels of availability, you should try to either reduce or eliminate any interference from other sources.

Designing your application to use queuing for intra-component and intra-application communication can help that application's availability. This involves using middleware such as Microsoft Message Queue (MSMQ) or TIBCO Rendezvous (TIBRV) to send and receive asynchronous messages. Queuing is useful for guaranteed message delivery, as the sender and recipient do not have to be connected together, and one or the other can even be offline without affecting the message delivery. This removes a potential failure point from your system. By increasing the number of routes for successful message delivery, your end users perceive that your application is available more consistently.

Improving Software Availability

Notice that it is possible for an application to have quite a low MTBF while still having a high availability, and vice versa. If failures are corrected quickly enough, thus reducing the MTTR, the resulting downtime is relatively low. This is important because once you have fixed the majority of the reliability problems and you're starting to work toward the higher levels of availability, it usually turns out to be cheaper to expend effort on faster failure recovery times than it is to grasp for those elusive final percentage points of reliability.

So the first step is to improve your application's reliability until the number of failures is down toward single figures per year. Then the majority of your effort should be directed at improving the recovery time from each defect. When you start to see diminishing returns in improvement on one factor, you need to concentrate on improving the other factor. So you need to balance these two factors together.

Relying on your technical support staff to keep your application available is probably a mistake. Because the support department does not usually have the skills or budget to analyze failures properly, it tends to concentrate on the quick fix, trying to get your application up and running as quickly as possible. While this is necessary, it is not sufficient. You also need to assign skilled people to analyze the root causes of availability problems. Producing a steady flow of architectural recommendations and procedural improvements is essential to the improvement of reliability and availability.

Debugging Complex Systems

As systems become larger and move ever further away from the relatively simple client/server model, you'll find that the complexity of any system grows faster than its size. The communication paths and interactions between system components grow in a factorial manner as the system grows in a linear manner. To understand the behavior of large distributed systems, and even their smaller client server counterparts, you need to understand what causes the complexity and how you can tackle the problems that complexity brings with it.

The software industry has been moving for a while toward components as a way of managing complexity. A component is a block of software that encapsulates some discrete functionality. It might be a DLL that does option pricing, a Web service that provides stock quotes, or perhaps a stored procedure that gives access to a database table. Alternatively, a component might be a middle-ware program that allows messaging between components or a third-party control that implements a grid to be displayed on a form.

These components then either interact with each other to create the software application or occasionally they are linked together with "old-fashioned" procedural code. In this way, much of the complexity of the functionality being programmed is hidden away inside each component, and is then given a friendly face through the public interface that the component exposes.

This means that a large part of managing complexity in the VB .NET world is about managing multiple components and their interactions with each other. When you understand how to build components properly and how to debug their collaboration, you will understand how to beat component complexity.

Building by Contract

In a world of distributed components, several problems have to be solved in order for these components to communicate successfully with each other. Some of these issues have been at least partially solved, but several problems remain that will cause havoc with your applications if you don't understand them properly.

The first problem that has been partially solved is the *wire protocol,* the means by which the information passes from component to component. The most common protocol in use today is HTTP, and that is proving more and more successful as developers continue to build HTTP support directly into many of their applications.

Another problem that has also been partially solved is the *communication format,* the common language understood by interacting components. Nowadays people are moving toward XML as the standard communication format, although a surprising number of applications still use HTML techniques such as screen scraping. The progress of XML has been helped because it is a format that is both machine readable and human readable.

The other nasty problem that's now well understood is *component coupling.* When designing a system, it was very common and easy to design tightly coupled components. Tightly coupled components are bad because they rely on knowledge of each other's implementation in order to communicate successfully. This means that when you change the implementation of a component or application, all the other applications talking to it will suddenly fail. Also, when you have an error in one component, the effects of this error are more likely to transmit themselves to their tightly coupled siblings. So good system designers have now learned to build applications that are loosely coupled and that don't fail or crash when component implementation changes. The applications agree on a wire protocol and a communication format, but avoid agreeing on an implementation.

So far, so good—this is a simplified description of the state of the art in distributed systems at the start of the twenty-first century. Components and applications create contracts that their clients have to understand and follow. But what happens when these contracts don't have a way of expressing certain concepts critical to normal business processes? The next section discusses some of the problems that can arise.

Understanding Communication Issues

Most applications and their individual components are what are called *finite state machines*. This means that at any one time, an application is in a particular state and can then move to one of several different states. For example, a server component that deals with e-commerce shopping carts will accept a request for a cart, handle requests to add items to that shopping cart, and finally accept a request to pay for the contents of the cart. At any one time, the server component will have a view of what's allowed and what's coming next. The problem is that there's no current machine-readable language that allows a component to express formally its possible states and therefore the contract that it supports.

This leads to several types of communication issues, which I discuss in the next few sections.

Sequencing Bugs

So what happens when your shopping cart receives a request to pay for the contents of a shopping cart without ever having received the initial cart request? In other words, what happens when a client component has got the sequence of its requests wrong, probably because there was a misunderstanding of the contract offered by the server? The result is a bug, and it's the sort of bug that can be very difficult to diagnose and fix because of the likely complexity of the interactions between the two applications.

This is a very common problem, especially when the number of transactions (and therefore states) that a server component supports is large. Persuading two different applications, each of which is a complex finite state machine, to agree on the precise sequencing of every transaction between them is very hard. Because the sequencing is not expressed in a machine-readable way, it is down to the developers of both applications to agree everything in the conversation sequence, and this process is very prone to error. Even if the original transactions are agreed properly, keeping the two state machines in step as the transactions evolve over time is still very difficult.

Latency Bugs

An illustration of the second cause of bugs is what should happen if a request to pay for the shopping cart's contents is not answered for 5 minutes. Should the payment request be abandoned and the shopping expedition ended? If you try this, maybe the payment request will eventually be accepted and the shopper's account debited! Or should the client code wait longer (how long?) for the request to be answered? The problem here is that, once again, there is no common machine-readable contract that the components can use to agree on timing issues.

The result is that both applications stubbornly stick to their own understanding of the contract, and therefore bugs caused by latency issues flourish. These types of defects are very common, especially when applications try to work together in real time.

Sequencing and Latency Interactions

In the real world, these problems are likely to be combined. During a conversation between multiple applications, you might send requests to several different applications and then receive the replies in a very fluid order. This means potentially keeping track of the state of multiple conversations and trying to coordinate the results into a coherent and sensible whole.

Semantic Bugs

When I make a verbal or written contract with you to perform a service, such as architecting your new house or performing some programming, we try to come to a common agreement about the services and payments involved. Software components have a similar problem in that they need to agree on every detail of the common contracts between them. If an XML field states itself to be the instrument price, is that net or gross? Does an XML field called "earnings" represent net earnings, earnings before interest, or earnings before interest, tax, and depreciation? The problem is that common messaging formats such as XML only push the problem of semantic meaning up by one level. The scope for communication misunderstandings is still as large as ever. If anything, the problems can be even worse because common formats such as XML appear to solve many communication issues. In fact, the problem of meaning is just suppressed and will appear at a later and potentially more expensive stage of the development cycle.

Dealing with Failure

The defining difference between local and distributed applications is the idea of failure. Communication calls between local application components normally just work, whereas the same calls made between remote components can fail in many ingenious ways. Diagnosing the failure of remote components is also much more difficult than diagnosing local failures. You need to distinguish between partial failure and complete failure if you want to ensure that your application is robust.

For a detailed treatment of this issue and some possible solutions, please see Chapter 15, which deals with the debugging of distributed applications.

Possible Solutions

Recognition and understanding of these problems is the first step toward solving them. A further step is to have good documentation for each component that expresses every transaction and every state properly, including sequencing and timing information. This documentation needs to be available to both server and client developers, and kept up-to-date as the code and the contracts change. One of the most useful, and most frequently overlooked, items in this documentation is a complete list of every known exception (error) that can be generated by the component, what each exception means, and the circumstances under which each exception is raised. This list is invaluable for a developer who needs to understand the behavior of an application component and how to use it safely.

One solution for communication issues is to create a machine-readable and human-readable document that properly expresses the contract offered by a component. This still requires that all components subscribing to the contract agree on a common contract schema, but if the schema is able to express concepts such as sequencing and timing, both integration testing and fault diagnosis become much easier. It's even possible to automate some of these processes, and human error can at least partially be removed from the enforcement of contracts between components.

Debugging Developer Psychology

Moving to the VB .NET world is going to mean leaving some of your current debugging habits behind and replacing them with new ones. You may be asked to debug a much wider variety of applications, all the way from Windows Forms applications to Web Forms applications to XML Web services, and on to Windows services, SQL Server stored procedures, and even VB.Classic code.

Although the debugging tools available to you are much more grown up than those available with VB.Classic, you are no longer working with an interpreted language. In fact, it's likely that you're no longer working with just a single language. This means that you should take some time to understand the new debugging problems that you'll have to solve.

Living Without Edit and Continue

Perhaps the first and most obvious debugging challenge for the VB.Classic developer is the loss of *Edit and Continue* (often abbreviated E&C). In the VB.Classic IDE you were able to edit your code while the program was in "break" mode, and then rerun the modified code without stopping or recompiling the program. This facility is quite addictive when you are debugging or testing code, and its loss has come as a nasty shock to the VB community. Even though VB .NET allows you to edit the source of a running program, these code changes will not actually be applied until the program is restarted.

There was some evidence buried deep in the beta documentation to suggest that the Redmondites did actually cajole E&C into working in the VB .NET environment, but then found that it was usually slower than just stopping and restarting the program. It is quite likely that E&C will be brought back in a future version of VB .NET, but until that time developers need to meet the challenge of living without it.

Developers will feel the loss of E&C deeply. It is psychologically easy to work toward a solution by progressive approximations, trying ideas and then modifying those ideas after seeing immediate results. This convenience, however, hides some problems.

E&C can be used well, but also has a dark side. Many developers find that it allows them to indulge in the rather sordid and unsafe habit of "shotgun debugging."

What typically happens is that a developer will start his or her program, put a breakpoint at the point of interest and then modify the code in ad hoc ways in order to get it working. Because it's possible to try multiple fixes and tests during a single run without having to restart the program, this approach appears to be quite productive in terms of time spent. In fact, this making of relatively undirected changes to software in the hope that a bug will be perturbed out of existence almost never works, and it often introduces more bugs.

The major problem with this ad hoc "shotgun" approach is its informality. At its heart is a misunderstanding of the tradeoff between the speed of producing a working section of code and the quality of that code. Debugging is about trying to make code work, while testing is about trying to break code. Mixing these two activities together is likely to mean that neither is done well. As debugging guru

John Robbins explains in his excellent book *Debugging Applications* (Microsoft Press, 2000), when you're in the debugger you should be debugging, not editing. Otherwise it's just as easy to add a bug as it is to remove one.

Let's take a look at some programming activities to find out how E&C can be used badly and how it can be used well. After exploring the E&C issues, I show you what workarounds are possible in its absence.

Bad Debugging with E&C

In this first scenario, a developer makes several attempts during a single run to fix a problem. He repeats a cycle of altering code and then resetting the current execution point to run through the altered code. For example, a developer believes that a bug is caused by an off-by-one error in a loop. So he first puts a +1 in the loop and then checks the result. If that doesn't work, he puts a –1 in the loop instead, still hoping to get the right result.

Proponents of this debugging approach say that it is more efficient because there is no need to restart the program after every code change. The problem, though, is the indisputable fact that in this case the developer doesn't actually understand the problem. If he did understand the problem, there would be no need to make multiple attempts at a fix—he would be able to go straight to the problem area and fix it in one attempt.

While E&C makes it very tempting to try many potential solutions until something seems to work, this is akin to poking a jellyfish with a stick to see if it moves; it doesn't actually teach you very much. A quality solution is much more likely to come from some deep thinking about a problem rather than ad hoc attempts at a fix.

More Bad Debugging with E&C

In the second scenario, a developer starts by finding and fixing a single bug, but then attempts to fix more defects that appear. These defects are often related to or hiding behind the first bug. The temptation when using E&C is to find and fix as many bugs as possible during a single run—this can be very satisfying and at first sight seems to be an efficient method of working.

Unfortunately, this approach also has problems. First, the developer once again probably doesn't understand the original defect at a deep level. If she understood the original bug properly, it is unlikely that her original fix would have exposed the multiple new issues. Even if she did understand the bug, it is debatable how well the new issues and subsequent fixes were understood. As before, E&C makes it far too tempting to fix bugs as they arise, rather than taking time to think about the issues away from the heat of the battle.

Another problem with this approach is that if there are multiple issues being exposed within a block of code, it is likely that the code itself is fundamentally flawed. Such code always benefits from taking a step back from the situation rather than fixing the bugs in an ad hoc manner. Using E&C to push multiple fixes is unlikely to improve the code's quality.

The next problem is that several programming experiments have been done that collectively show that the average developer introduces one new bug for every two bugs that he or she fixes. Even the best developers produce one new bug for every four that they fix. Making multiple concurrent fixes, some of which might potentially interfere with each other, is not conducive to producing high-quality solutions.

Perhaps the final nail in the coffin of "shotgun debugging" is that many of the E&C fixes made are small ones, often affecting only a few lines of code. These are made because they are the type of changes that look manageable without having to perform desk-checking or proper review. Unfortunately, the literature shows that the chances of creating a bug significantly increase when making such small changes. Specifically, as the number of lines changed increases from one to five lines, the chance of making a bad change is high and increases. With more than five altered lines, the chance of making a bad change decreases, probably because the developer becomes more careful as the fix becomes larger.

Bad Unit Testing with E&C

In this third scenario, a developer edits code several times within a single run in order to run multiple unit tests on a procedure or component. For example, a VB .NET program that executes an embedded SQL script sees the developer correcting, tuning, and reexecuting the SQL script many times until he is happy that everything is working properly. The typical argument for this approach is that it is much faster to run these multiple edit-and-test cycles in one hit rather than having to restart the program every time a change is made.

There are several problems with this type of ad hoc testing. The first is that any tests done in this manner are not going to be as comprehensive as a manual or automated unit test harness that has been implemented beforehand. It's hard to invent several good unit tests on the fly, especially when the psychological mindset is aimed at making the code work rather than proving that the code doesn't work. The temptation is always to fix the code in-flight when each test fails rather than running a test suite, collating the results, and then thinking about the fixes as a single, well-controlled patch to the program. Simultaneous mixing of the unit testing mindset with the quite different mindset of fixing code that fails the unit tests is very dangerous.

A second problem with this approach is that it makes it very difficult to perform unit regression testing on future versions of the code. Even if the developer could manage to remember the entire unit test suite that he had performed, repeating a set of interactive regression tests every time the code changes is very boring and therefore prone to mistakes.

Another trap that many developers fall into with E&C in this context is changing code on both sides of the interface being tested. It is just too easy to make a change to the calling code that makes the interface being tested appear to work. What might actually be happening is that two errors, one on either side of the interface, could compensate for each other and result in the interface appearing to work. Once again, the psychological need to get the code working can interfere with the unit tests being performed. In effect, this makes it easier for the developer to fool himself into believing that everything is working correctly through an artificial test case created by manipulating two sets of code.

Good Debugging with E&C

One appropriate way of debugging with E&C is when you find an obvious coding error, often while looking at something completely different, and change the code for an obvious fix. While it is a fine line between an "obviously correct" fix and a "subtly wrong" fix, most developers know when they've found a glaringly obvious problem. In this case, it can be good practice to fix the problem, test the fix immediately, and then proceed on your way with your original mission.

Another reasonable way of using E&C is when you've found an error and managed to reproduce it successfully. The next step is often to reproduce the error in several different ways in order to learn more about it. E&C can be very useful in allowing multiple code changes and tests during a single run in order to triangulate the bug and learn more about it. The proviso, of course, is that you must put the code back into its original state once you have completed your investigation.

Good Unit Testing with E&C

E&C can prove very useful when you perform graphical user interface (GUI) unit testing. Although it's still better to create a proper test harness if possible, this task can be rather difficult to automate because you have to simulate a very unpredictable component (the end user), and also it's difficult to validate the unit test results. For this reason, many developers prefer to test interactively, so I'll reluctantly grant that this can be a reasonable use of E&C.

Good Prototyping with E&C

In this scenario, a developer makes multiple code changes during a single run in order to prototype, typically when investigating the behavior of a class, a control, or some other component. With E&C, it is much faster to perform this type of testing, and because it is only prototyping, there is much less danger of bugs running rampant. This scenario is one of the genuinely useful ways of using E&C.

Workarounds for "Bad" E&C

Viewed in the light of the numerous problems mentioned previously, losing the ability to use E&C in "shotgun" mode is a blessing in disguise. You can wean yourself away from the E&C addiction and instead produce better bug fixes and unit tests.

If you have previously been tempted to use "shotgun debugging," you can now try a more formal approach that might be called *think and restart* (T&R). With T&R, you sit back and take the time to understand the problem at a deep level before introducing the fix. After restarting the program and testing the fix, you should be very surprised, even shocked, if the fix didn't work. In this case, stop the program and figure out where you don't understand the problem before making another fix and restarting the program for some tests. The pain of frequent program restarts may even help by tempting you into making the correct fix on the first time around.

To replace ad hoc unit testing, you should think seriously about creating a *test harness*, otherwise known as a *debugging scaffold*. Constructing a test harness before building your program is like erecting a scaffold before building your wall. For small projects, it makes life much easier. For large projects, it is essential. A test harness makes it possible to repeat your unit tests and regression tests at will to ensure that fixed bugs stay fixed and that no new bugs have been introduced. It also makes it feasible for you to create a thorough and more thoughtful test suite than is possible with "shotgun testing." So you can write the test harness, start your application, and then apply all of your unit tests in one hit. After analyzing the test results, you can try to understand any resulting problems by setting breakpoints and looking at the flow of data within the code. Finally, you will have to stop the program before you can apply all of the necessary fixes and start a new test cycle.

Although the two alternative approaches outlined previously may be more formal and seem to take longer than using E&C in shotgun mode, the payoff is that your fixes and tests will be much higher in quality. Your understanding of the code is likely to be better and it will have been through some comprehensive testing.

At the root of this clash between formal and informal debugging and testing are two different mindsets. The classic VB mindset often values a solution that is produced fast to meet immediate business needs for an application that may not even be needed tomorrow. The resulting solution may not be of the highest quality, but is produced fast—it is considered fit for its purpose. Up until recently, this type of application was the typical domain of many VB.Classic programming shops.

The VB .NET mindset is perhaps more applicable to bigger departmental or enterprise-type solutions where the application is likely to have a longer life, be subject to more maintenance, and where quality is more important than speed of result. In this mindset, the quality required tends to rule out the use of E&C in shotgun mode because it often produces solutions with more bugs that are harder to maintain.

Workarounds for "Good" E&C

That still leaves you with finding an alternative to the reasonable uses of E&C mentioned previously. If you want to modify code within the IDE during program execution, this is still possible. After you select Tools ➤ Options ➤ Debugging ➤ Edit and Continue, you should select the "Allow me to edit VB files while debugging" box. You also should select the "Always ignore changes and continue debugging" option.

The problem is that these changes won't be applied until you restart the program, and unless you identify changes made since the program was last restarted, it's possible to become confused about which code is actually executing. My advice is to put the new code within a region by using the region directive with a suitable heading. You can then collapse this region within the IDE code window so that you don't see the new code, but you can use the region heading to identify what change you made and why you made it. To remember this code change, add a bookmark linked to it in the Task window. When you decide to review your changes, double-clicking the bookmark in the Task window will take you straight to the related region or lines of code.

For GUI unit testing, you should create one or more procedures that can throw tests against the GUI. Because you are able to change data at will during a run, and you can also execute your test procedures from the Command window, it is then trivial to modify the data in the Command window and invoke your test procedures. This gives you an E&C unit test framework without having to change code.

This still leaves you trying to find a replacement for E&C during prototyping. While you can prototype code at will from the Command window by just changing data values, this isn't really a complete solution. Until E&C is added to VB .NET, it's the best solution that you have.

Psychological Factors

From the point of view of the CLR or any other runtime engine, the most error-prone component of any computer application is the actual programmer. The problem is that nearly every developer finds it extremely difficult to maintain the level of precision necessary to program a complex software system successfully. It's not just that the tools and plumbing have idiosyncrasies, implementation subtleties, unfamiliar levels of abstraction, and outright defects. The main issue is that human brains are unsuited to handling the level of detail required and to spanning levels of abstraction ranging from bits up to gigabytes. Add into this volatile mix a compiler that has to understand the lovingly crafted code and then translate it into goo that the processor can understand, and you are left with enormous potential for mistakes and misunderstandings when writing a computer application. It's hardly surprising that studies report most projects spend around 50% of their schedule in the debugging phase.

COM is a good example of a reasonable development technology that has proved difficult to implement in the real world because of developer frailties. Dealing with the separation of components from their registry entries and keeping the two in step for every version of every component interface on every user's machine is a nightmare in a world of constantly changing business requirements and code. It's not that COM technology doesn't work, it's just that even clever people find it very hard to cope with the detail involved in orchestrating their components and corresponding registry entries into a coherent whole on every user's machine and then maintaining that orchestration over the lifetime of an application. Countless numbers of VB.Classic developers have struggled with implementing binary compatibility on a daily basis.

Faced with an almost new language and completely new ways of interacting with the core of Windows, developers must ensure that they learn effectively and don't create bugs due to their initial inexperience with the .NET world.

Learning the .NET Framework

The first learning challenge is rather large. There are over 5,600 classes in over 90 namespaces within the .NET base class library—an enormous amount of functionality by anybody's standards. Understanding and implementing these base classes within your applications without creating bugs is not a task for the faint-hearted. The average VB.Classic developer will have to put much more effort into learning the .NET Framework than into learning the VB .NET language itself. As opposed to just learning a relatively familiar language, with the .NET Framework you're faced with that scary "I don't know what I don't know" feeling.

If you're already an expert in a particular part of the Win32 API, relearning the .NET Framework approach to that area may not be so hard. Much of the .NET class library simply wraps the Win32 API in an object-oriented wrapper for your convenience. There are some exceptions to this, such as in the graphics area, but in general the Win32 API is still at the core of the .NET Framework. If, however, you're an expert in VB.Classic's approach to your specialist area, now is the time to start thinking about doing some serious homework.

The first step is probably the most important: Read the framework documentation thoroughly! In the past, we VB.Classic developers have traditionally been spoiled. The language concealed much of the complexity from us—it just worked. We often didn't need to read the documentation, and when we did we found that it often wasn't that great. Sometimes the documentation had been written for C programmers and was unintelligible to your average VB.Classic developer. At other times the documentation looked as though it was thrown together by a Microsoft intern on some very heavy medication. So the end result was that we became accustomed to ignoring the documentation. Because VB.Classic successfully hid many of the nasty details, we were often able to get away with this approach.

Now we're in a different and more complex world. So when you need to use a framework class, the first place to go is its documentation. The problem of dodgy documentation and flaky code samples is still present, but to a much lesser degree than in VB.Classic. VB .NET is a first-class citizen of the new world, and the documentation has in most cases been upgraded to match this new position. Nearly all of the code samples are written in both C# and VB .NET, another reflection of the fact that VB is no longer a second-class citizen. Finally, there is a vast amount of documentation available on other resources such as MSDN, and this extra information is sometimes quite good at showing you the "when" and the "why," in addition to the "how." To avoid bugs in your implementation, it is important to have a broad, as well as a deep, understanding of the specific class that you're using.

I would also advise taking some time away from coding to just read through the class library documentation in general. Even though you're reading casually and often looking at classes about which you have no specific interest, your mind will absorb the information by osmosis; it will just seep in without any great effort on your part. You don't have to be able to keep all of this information at a conscious level—even at an unconscious level it will help you to avoid bugs.

One final tip is to take the time to become an expert about either a single namespace or just a set of classes within that namespace. Learn everything you can about the namespace, and experiment with it until you understand it at a deep and broad level. Twist it into knots so that you understand all of the designer's conventions and where things can go wrong. Answer questions about it from your colleagues and even in public newsgroups. Every question that you answer about that namespace is likely to teach you more about avoiding bugs when you use it. Once you've learned a namespace or even a single class in great detail, this knowledge will also help you in learning other areas of the .NET Framework.

Sharing Knowledge Between Developers

VB .NET looks and feels enough like VB.Classic to cause some confusion. As an example, you can if you want ignite a moderately sized flame war in any VB .NET newsgroup by asking innocently whether **<Object> = Nothing** is useful or required in VB .NET. Developers moving to VB .NET need to go back to school for a while if they want to create software that is relatively bug-free and easy to modify and debug.

One major cause of bugs is likely to be the "top geek" syndrome. This occurs when a developer who is highly paid for his expertise is faced with a situation where his current knowledge no longer applies. Lacking the knowledge to use his new tools safely, the response is to charge ahead anyway, with unflattering results on the reliability of his new application.

The sensible response would be to admit his ignorance and not produce designs or code without a better understanding of his tools. In reality, this is unlikely to happen because both his ego and his compensation are usually directly linked to his ability to appear as a guru.

One approach to this problem is to adopt a discipline taken from the Extreme Programming (XP) process called Pair Programming (PP). While the XP process has its critics, PP can be very useful when applied to situations where simultaneous learning and programming is taking place.

The idea is for two developers to pair up and program together. The two developers take it in turns either to drive the keyboard or to sit and observe. The idea is that the driver handles the small details by writing and talking about the code while the observer watches for problems either in the code or at a higher, more strategic level. The driver tends to the trees while the observer considers the whole forest.

If done carefully, this pairing technique can be very useful when operating in a new environment such as VB .NET. The driver is likely to make lots of small and mostly silly errors that will be corrected by the observer, while the observer learns from the driver's experience of actually writing the code. The two learn together at a faster rate than either one could do individually, each contributing his or her share of the knowledge.

The trick is to make sure that the pair chemistry is right. For instance, it is not recommended to pair a guru with a novice. The novice is soon likely to be out of his or her depth and the guru will become bored and frustrated, especially when the novice has his or her turn as the driver. It is better to keep the pairing reasonably close in ability.

Apart from the bug prevention and detection benefits, another benefit of PP is through taking a developer who has to use an unfamiliar component and pairing her together with the author (or experienced user) of that component. The author can then guide the developer rapidly through the component's public interface and explain the component's conventions and usage subtleties. This can save a lot of time and effort, and prevent bugs arising from accidental misuse of the component.

A final benefit from PP is that having to discuss your code with another developer often means that you find yourself refactoring your code to make it simpler because it is then easier to explain. Simpler code means less opportunity for bugs, and many of the bugs that do creep in are easier for the observer to spot.

Murphy's Law Is Wrong

There is one final, perhaps rather philosophical, factor that I want to discuss. You've undoubtedly come across Murphy's Law, which states, "What can go wrong, will go wrong." Unfortunately, analysis of real-life bugs and system failures shows that Murphy's Law is completely wrong—what *can* go wrong usually goes *right*. In most applications, there are usually many defects hiding within the software when it goes into production. Most of the time, these bugs stay silent and the application works successfully. Only occasionally is a bug actually triggered, whereupon the application goes wrong or crashes.

The implication is that developers are usually wrong when they assume that because their application has been running successfully in a testing or production environment for a while, the software doesn't have many remaining defects. In reality, the bugs are biding their time and waiting for the most opportune moment to strike. This mindset can be compared with the technical culture at NASA before the 1986 explosion of the space shuttle *Challenger*. O-ring worries were put to one side because there had been so many successful launches with these exact O-rings.

There is another clue here. It becomes clear that some errors in complex distributed software systems *will* happen, and it is impossible to prevent all errors. So as well as working to prevent errors, you should also place serious emphasis on limiting their negative consequences and on detecting them when they do occur.

Summary

This chapter examined some of the more strategic issues in the war against VB .NET bugs. You learned about how typical applications fail and how to make your application more reliable and more available. After understanding that the loss of Edit and Continue is actually a blessing in disguise, you learned about some of the "softer" issues dealing with developer psychology when faced with a new and strange environment such as .NET.

INTERLUDE

THE FOLKLORE OF DEBUGGING

Over the years developers have swapped stories around the virtual campfire about weird bugs and wonderful debugging techniques. I thought it might be entertaining and even instructive to gather a few of these stories in one place.

The Phase of the Moon Bug

Developers are prone to blaming their bugs on freak occurrences or unusual conditions. Anything that can direct the blame away from their code is fair game for a developer frantic to explain away a tenacious bug. The cry goes up: "I can't reproduce the bug, so it must have been a full moon/cosmic rays/in an older version/already fixed/a problem between the keyboard and chair."

One such bug struck two MIT researchers who were writing some code that generated comments into a file of LISP forms. Normally the code worked fine, but at regular times in each month the resulting LISP forms would fail to compile. The *Twilight Zone* feeling arrived when it became clear that the program only failed during certain phases of the moon!

The cause of the bug was that the comments being written included the phase of the moon as part of their text. This meant that the comment lines were of variable length. At certain times of the month, the comment line length would exceed the page width of the LISP form. This automatically ran the comment onto a new line, which was then no longer perceived as a comment but as executable code, thus causing the compilation failure.

So there you have it: Finally a bug that really *can* be blamed on the full moon.

The 49.7 Bug

This bug was originally thought to be mythical, but it is now recognized as a real bug in a device driver that is part of Microsoft Windows 95. The rumor was that the maximum number of days that Windows 95 could operate continuously was 49.7 days. This was not verified for a while, possibly because uptimes of longer than a month are rare in the wild. However, this has now been confirmed as a timing problem in an obscure device driver.

For those of you who are curious and still have access to this rapidly fossilizing operating system, the details of the offending device driver are as follows:

Date	Time	Version	Size	File name
6/23/98	2:44pm	4.00.951	18,570	Vtdapi.vxd

The Musical "Bug"

This next curiosity is actually a feature rather than a bug. Microsoft started receiving the occasional support call about users complaining that their computer was randomly playing classical music! Heavy medication was the obvious diagnosis, or perhaps even a virus, but this "bug" turns out to have an interesting origin.

From 1997 onward, the Award/Unicore company produced several PC BIOSs and motherboards containing an electronic hardware-monitoring component. This component was designed to detect whether the CPU fan was failing or had failed, and whether power supply voltages had drifted out of tolerance. If the component spotted any such problem, it signified the discovery by playing either "Fur Elise" or "It's a Small, Small World."

If you're having a hard time believing this, take a look at the Microsoft Knowledge Base article number Q261186.

Deliberate Excel Bug

If you type the formula **=DATE(1900,2,29)** into any version of Excel, this date will be accepted even though it's actually invalid—1900 is definitely not a leap year. In case you're interested, the rule is that all years divisible by 4 are leap years, except those years divisible by 100; the exception is that all years divisible by 400 are leap years.

The reason for this Excel bug appears to be a deliberate compatibility decision by the Excel team. Back when Lotus 1-2-3 was by far the most popular spreadsheet application available, the Lotus developers accidentally created this leap year bug. In order to maintain compatibility with the Lotus spreadsheet application and to be able to use the same date serial number scheme, the Excel developers decided to copy the same bug. In fact, all days of the week prior to 1 March 1900 are reported by Excel as one day earlier than they actually are. Microsoft claims that fixing this bug would create many more problems, presumably in existing spreadsheets.

The Margarita Bug

At an appliance company that builds blenders, a small group of developers is responsible for testing the blenders, which the lucky fellows do by making margaritas. For a while, in a politically correct environment, they only used virgin margaritas (those made without any alcohol). This changed rapidly after the first of a new series of blenders all failed. Apparently, the alcohol depresses the freezing point of the mix, which loaded the electric motor more heavily, which in turn burned out the drive transistors. So now the poor fellows are forced to test using real margaritas.

The Lunch Game

I don't know who invented this game, but several developer shops now play it. The idea behind the game is rather simple. Whenever somebody creates a new procedure, that person has to add a random day of the week in the header comments of the procedure.

After the procedure has been deployed into production and a bug has been found in it, the person finding the bug looks at the day of the week in the header. If somebody other than him- or herself wrote the offending procedure, and the day in the header is the current day, the person who wrote the procedure has to buy lunch for the developer who fixes the bug.

This has two interesting results. First, it encourages extensive testing for bugs, and second, it encourages you to fix any bugs that you find as soon as possible. This is because if the bug is in a procedure that you wrote, fixing it means that you avoid having to buy lunch for somebody else. If the bug is in somebody else's code, fixing it means that somebody buys lunch for you.

Language Surprises in VB .NET

THIS CHAPTER DEMONSTRATES that the relatively familiar face of VB .NET conceals a quite different beast underneath than the one to which you are accustomed. The examples in this chapter show unintuitive and sometimes surprising behavior ensuing from some of the new and changed features in VB .NET. The result of executing each of the code samples in this chapter often violates the important principle of "least surprise." Because surprises are one of the major causes of bugs, it is worthwhile to take the time to analyze and understand these examples.

Many of the examples mentioned in this chapter are surprises associated with implementation inheritance. This is no accident. Inheritance is a complicated subject fraught with difficulties, and without a good understanding of the issues it is very easy to create both design and implementation bugs when coding base or derived classes.

The True Value of True in VB .NET

I start with something simple. VB.Classic was always prone to taking a contrary view of the world, usually in order to make life simpler for its users. For instance, while most languages considered **true** to equate to 1, VB.Classic stated that **true** was really –1. When moving VB forward to .NET, the language team faced a dilemma. Should they redefine **true** to be the value used by the common language runtime (CLR) and the other .NET languages, or should they keep the same value to remain compatible with gigabytes of VB.Classic code that already exist? Listing 2-1 shows that they decided to have their cake and eat it too.

Listing 2-1. What Is True Really?

```
Option Strict On
Module Test
    Sub Main()
        Console.WriteLine("CInt(True) = " + CInt(True).ToString)
        Console.WriteLine("Convert(True) = " + Convert.ToInt16(True).ToString)
        Console.ReadLine()
    End Sub
End Module
```

This code returns the following result:

```
CInt(True) = -1
Convert(True) = 1
```

So the value of **true** in VB .NET is not fixed—it depends on which view you take. If you use VB.Classic functions such as **CInt**, then **true** will be –1. On the other hand, VB .NET functions such as **Convert** will return **true** as 1. As long as you have **Option Strict On** so that no implicit conversions are performed, and as long as you always compare to **true** or **false** rather than to –1 or 1, you will be okay.

Class Member Overloading

Class member overloading allows you to keep a consistent interface by calling a single logical method regardless of the type of data that will be passed in that method. When you use class member overloading, it is relatively easy to create situations where the physical procedure that will be invoked is not clear at first glance.

Ambiguous Overloading

The code in Listing 2-2 shows a base class member that is overloaded both within its own class and within a derived class. The task is to determine which procedure is going to be invoked by each of the test calls and also why.

Listing 2-2. Ambiguous Overloading

```
Option Strict On

Class Test
    Public Shared Sub Main()
        Dim objMyTest As New Derived()
        With objMyTest
            .WriteLine(10)
            .WriteLine(10.5)
            .WriteLine("11")
        End With
        Console.ReadLine()
    End Sub
End Class
```

```
Class Base
    Public Sub WriteLine(ByVal AnyString As String)
        Console.WriteLine(AnyString + " called Base:String")
    End Sub

    Public Sub WriteLine(ByVal AnyInteger As Integer)
        Console.WriteLine(AnyInteger.ToString + " called Base:Integer")
    End Sub
End Class

Class Derived : Inherits Base
    Public Overloads Sub WriteLine(ByVal AnyDouble As Double)
        Console.WriteLine(AnyDouble.ToString + " called Derived:Double")
    End Sub
End Class
```

Whereas the answers to the last two tests are easy to anticipate correctly, the first test is more difficult. The literal number 10 could be considered to be either an **integer** or a **double**, so therefore which of the two possible procedures will be invoked? If the compiler looks through the methods in the derived class first and uses any one that is found to be suitable, then the derived class method that accepts a **double** will be used. Alternatively, the compiler could look across all of the possible methods in the inheritance tree and then make a decision about the most appropriate method to call, which means that the base class that accepts an **integer** is the most likely candidate.

C# (and C++) developers normally know the answer to this question. The compiler performs overload resolution at each level of the inheritance hierarchy, starting with the most derived class. This breadth-first scan means that it will pick the most derived method that is suitable. Therefore, the result will be

```
10 called Derived:Double
10.5 called Derived:Double
11 called Base:String
```

Unfortunately, this is the wrong answer when using VB .NET. The VB .NET compiler (unlike the C# compiler) looks across the whole inheritance tree before making a decision about which of the overloaded methods is most suitable. Because **Overloads** actually means hide by name and signature, the compiler takes the view that you are essentially adding a new member to the base class in this case. So the preceding code will produce the following result:

```
10 called Base:Integer
10.5 called Derived:Double
11 called Base:String
```

C# vs. VB .NET Overloading

As demonstrated in the previous section, C#'s way of resolving overloaded methods is different from VB .NET's. If you want to confuse a C# developer, examine the VB .NET code in Listing 2-3 and try to predict the result it will produce.

Listing 2-3. Member Overloading in VB .NET vs. C#

```
Option Strict On

Class Test
    Public Shared Sub Main()
        Dim objDerived As New Derived()
        Dim objTest As New MyTest()
        objDerived.DoSomething(objTest)
        Console.ReadLine()
    End Sub

End Class


Class MyTest
End Class


Class Base
    Public Overridable Sub DoSomething(ByVal NewValue As MyTest)
        Console.WriteLine("Base:DoSomething(MyTest) called")
    End Sub
End Class

Class Derived : Inherits Base
    Public Overloads Overrides Sub DoSomething(ByVal NewValue As MyTest)
        Console.WriteLine("Derived:DoSomething(MyTest) called")
    End Sub
    Public Overloads Sub DoSomething(ByVal NewValue As Object)
        Console.WriteLine("Derived:DoSomething(Object) called")
    End Sub
End Class
```

This VB .NET program resolves the method overloading by showing what most developers would probably intuit as the most reasonable result given the ambiguous circumstances:

```
Derived:DoSomething(Object) called
```

Now translate the VB .NET code in Listing 2-3 into C#, and ask a C# developer to predict what this program will produce (see Listing 2-4).

Listing 2-4. C# Translation of Listing 2-3

```
class Test
{
    public static void Main()
    {
        Derived objDerived = new Derived();
        MyTest objMyTest = new MyTest();
        objDerived.DoSomething(objMyTest);
        System.Console.ReadLine();
    }
}


class MyTest {}

class Base
{
    public virtual void DoSomething(MyTest NewValue)
    {
        System.Console.WriteLine("Base:DoSomething(MyTest) called");
    }
}


class Derived : Base
{
    public override void DoSomething(MyTest NewValue)
    {
        System.Console.WriteLine("Derived:DoSomething(MyTest) called");
    }
    public void DoSomething(object NewValue)
    {
        System.Console.WriteLine("Derived:DoSomething(Object) called");
    }
}
```

This is an exact C# translation of the VB .NET code in Listing 2-3, so many developers will predict the same result. Unfortunately, C# produces the following different—and maybe somewhat surprising—result:

```
Derived:DoSomething(Object) called
```

In spite of the fact that the class instance passed exactly matches the parameter type of one of the members of the **Derived** class, the other more general member is the one actually chosen.

The reason for this is buried deep in the C# language specification. Any method marked as **Override** in C# is not added to the list of members considered as candidates for the resolution of an overload. Because of quirks like this, you should take some care when switching between VB .NET and C# to avoid the creation of quite subtle bugs.

The Overload That Broke the C# Developer's Back

This, however, is not the end of the member overload saga. Once again, I present a VB .NET program and its C# equivalent, and then attempt to predict the results of running each program. Listing 2-5 shows the VB .NET code.

Listing 2-5. More Member Overloading in VB .NET vs. C#

```
Option Strict On

Class Test
    Public Shared Sub Main()
        Dim objDerived As New Derived()
        objDerived.DoSomething(CLng(8))
        Console.ReadLine()
    End Sub
End Class


Class Base
    Public Overridable Sub DoSomething(ByVal NewValue As Long)
        Console.WriteLine("Base:DoSomething(Long) called")
    End Sub
    Public Sub DoSomething(ByVal NewValue As Double)
        Console.WriteLine("Base:DoSomething(Double) called")
    End Sub
End Class
```

```
Class Derived : Inherits Base
    Public Overloads Overrides Sub DoSomething(ByVal NewValue As Long)
        Console.WriteLine("Derived:DoSomething(Long) called")
    End Sub
    Public Overloads Sub DoSomething(ByVal NewValue As Integer)
        Console.WriteLine("Derived:DoSomething(Integer) called")
    End Sub
End Class
```

Just as in Listing 2-3, this VB .NET program resolves the method overloading by showing what most developers would probably intuit as the most reasonable result given the ambiguous circumstances:

The code shown in Listing 2-6 is a direct C# translation of the VB .NET program in Listing 2-5. Given that you have learned that members marked with **Override** are excluded from any C# member resolution group, what would a C# developer expect this program to produce?

Listing 2-6. C# Translation of Listing 2-5

```
class Test
{
    public static void Main()
    {
        Derived objDerived = new Derived();
        objDerived.DoSomething((long) 8);
        System.Console.ReadLine();
    }
}


class Base
{
    public virtual void DoSomething(long NewValue)
    {
        System.Console.WriteLine("Base:DoSomething(Long) called");
    }
    public void DoSomething(double NewValue)
    {
        System.Console.WriteLine("Base:DoSomething(Double) called");
    }
}
```

```
class Derived : Base
{
    override public void DoSomething(long NewValue)
    {
        System.Console.WriteLine("Derived:DoSomething(Long) called");
    }
    public void DoSomething(int NewValue)
    {
        System.Console.WriteLine("Derived:DoSomething(Integer) called");
    }
}
```

Just as in Listing 2-4, there is a member marked with **Override** here (the line in bold), and according to the C# language specification, that member won't be included in the group of members considered for overload resolution. So what will be the result of running this program?

```
Derived:DoSomething(Long) called
```

Now our hypothetical C# developer might be justified in feeling really confused! Why is this program resolving the method overload in a different manner to the program in Listing 2-4, and why is the member that is being called not removed from the group of members considered for overload resolution?

The reasoning behind this is quite obvious once you've seen it, but it's rather subtle. Just as the C# language specification states, the **Derived.DoSomething(long NewValue)** member is not considered for the method resolution because it is marked with **Override**. In fact, **Base.DoSomething(long NewValue)** is the only member in the group of possible overloads, so unsurprisingly that is the member actually chosen. But of course a derived member overrides that base member, so the derived method is the one executed. The trick here is to remember that the overload resolution process is just one step in the process of deciding which method is executed.

Contrast this with Listing 2-4. In that case, there is a derived method that is suitable, and C# will always use a derived method if it is considered suitable, even if a base method might seem more appropriate.

As stated earlier, you should take some care when switching between VB .NET and C# to avoid these types of bugs.

Understanding Inheritance Issues

One of the objectives of the VB .NET compiler team was to avoid a situation where adding a new method to a base class would result in an unexpected change of behavior within the inheritance tree. This would be a definite route to some nasty bugs and is classified academically as the "fragile base class" problem.

Shadowing by Accident

VB .NET's way of resolving an overloaded method (i.e., searching through the entire inheritance chain) was demonstrated in the previous sections and has an interesting side effect. Consider what should happen if you define a new base class method that happens to have the same name as a previously defined derived method. The derived method has, of course, no inheritance qualifier specified, as there was not previously a base method to inherit.

In the perfect world, current code should carry on using the derived method, even if normal method resolution would suggest that the base method is more appropriate. Likewise, new code should always invoke the base method, even if polymorphism suggests that calling the base method should result in the derived method being invoked.

If the compiler defaulted the derived method to **Overloads**, the normal overload method resolution might result in current code calling the new base method instead of the derived method. Likewise, if the derived method had defaulted to **Overrides**, the rules of polymorphism might result in new code calling the derived method when the base method was expected.

So the VB .NET team decided that where the author's intent was not specified, the default inheritance qualifier for a member should be **Shadows**, which hides any base class methods with the same name and results in unchanged behavior in the situation discussed previously. This decision avoids this type of fragile base class problem very well, but it needs to be treated carefully. If a base class author defines a method as **Overridable**, but a derived class author forgets to use the **Overrides** keyword, the derived method will instead default to **Shadows**, which is unlikely to be what the derived class author intended when he or she wrote the base class shown in Listing 2-7. The only saving grace is that the compiler does issue a warning about a potential mistake.

Listing 2-7. Don't Forget to Override

```
Option Strict On

Class Base
    Overridable Sub DoSomething
        'The method definition goes here
    End Sub
End Class


Class Derived : Inherits Base
    Sub DoSomething
        'This method will actually shadow its base method rather than Override it,
        'because the developer forgot to add the Overrides keyword
    End Sub
End Class
```

Making **Shadows** the default is more conservative, and probably safer, than using **Overrides**. In this way, changes to third-party libraries will not break your existing code or change its behavior. However, the result can be surprising, so perhaps it would have been better for the IDE to insert the **Shadows** keyword automatically in these circumstances so that the actual behavior would be obvious.

More Shadowing Issues

You should also realize that using the **Shadows** keyword could seriously degrade the maintainability of your code. For instance, you might create a **Cat** class that subclasses an **Animal** class; here the assumption is that **Cat** is an **Animal** and therefore behaves like an **Animal**. If you then use the **Shadows** keyword within the **Cat** class, you can alter the behavior of your **Cat** class so that it no longer behaves like an **Animal**. If you want the maintenance programmer who supports your code to go psychotic and come after you with a loaded AK-47, this is probably one of the better ways of doing it.

Listing 2-8 shows an example of a normal **Cat** inheritance hierarchy, without using the **Shadows** keyword. You can see that the **objNormalCat** object is declared and instantiated as a **Cat**, the **objLameCat** object is declared and instantiated as a **LameCat**, and finally, the **objUglyCat** object is declared as a **Cat** but instantiated as a **LameCat**.

Listing 2-8. Normal Inheritance Hierarchy

```
Option Strict On
Module CatTester

    Sub Main()

        'NormalCat
        Dim objNormalCat As New Cat()
        With objNormalCat
            Console.WriteLine("NormalCat is a " + .GetType.Name)
            Console.WriteLine("It has " + .Legs.ToString + " legs and " _
                                        + .Feet.ToString + " feet")
            Console.WriteLine()
        End With

        'LameCat
        Dim objLameCat As New LameCat()
        With objLameCat
            Console.WriteLine("LameCat is a " + .GetType.Name)
            Console.WriteLine("It has " + .Legs.ToString + " legs and " _
                                        + .Feet.ToString + " feet")
            Console.WriteLine()
        End With

        'UglyCat
        Dim objUglyCat As Cat
        objUglyCat = New LameCat()
        With objUglyCat
            Console.WriteLine("UglyCat is a " + .GetType.Name)
            Console.WriteLine("It has " + .Legs.ToString + " legs and " _
                                        + .Feet.ToString + " feet")
            Console.WriteLine()
        End With

        Console.ReadLine()
    End Sub
```

```
End Module

Class Cat

    Overridable Function Feet() As Int16
        Return 4
    End Function

    Overridable Function Legs() As Int16
        Return Me.Feet
    End Function

End Class

Class LameCat : Inherits Cat

    Overrides Function Feet() As Int16
        Return 3
    End Function

    Overrides Function Legs() As Int16
        Return Me.Feet
    End Function

End Class
```

As expected, this will show the following results:

```
NormalCat is a Cat
It has 4 legs and 4 feet

LameCat is a LameCat
It has 3 legs and 3 feet

UglyCat is a LameCat
It has 3 legs and 3 feet
```

Now change the **Overrides** modifier of the **LameCat.Feet** member (the line marked in bold) to **Shadows**, and suddenly you are looking at a quite unexpected mutant and nonsensical cat:

```
NormalCat is a Cat
It has 4 legs and 4 feet

LameCat is a LameCat
It has 3 legs and 3 feet

UglyCat is a LameCat
It has 3 legs and 4 feet
```

The **Shadows** keyword (which is the default) makes a huge difference in this code. The slightly unusual situation here exists because you are cheating the compiler by declaring an object as a **Cat** but actually instantiating it as a **LameCat**. This is allowed because inheritance rules dictate that a subclass can always be substituted for its superclass. Wherever you use a **Cat**, you can also use a **LameCat**.

The result of using **Shadows** is that **LameCat.Feet** is accessible when viewed from within the class, for instance via the **LameCat.Legs** member, but hidden completely from the inheritance chain. This mixing of paradigms can be very confusing for maintenance programmers. Whenever you see the **Shadows** keyword, be on the lookout for unintended side effects.

Understanding Equality

If you shift the **Shadows** keyword back to **Overrides**, you can investigate another nasty side effect of declaring an object as a superclass but instantiating it as a subclass. In an attempt at political correctness, you want a lame cat to be the equal of any other cat. In order to do this, you need to overload the **Equals** member of the **LameCat** class to return **true** whenever a lame cat is compared to a normal cat. You're going to ignore the **Equals** member of the **Cat** class, as you're only concerned here with lame cats. This looks like it should be relatively trivial (see the lines marked in bold in Listing 2-9).

Listing 2-9. Lame Cat Equal to Any Other Cat?

```vb
Option Strict On
Module CatTester

    Sub Main()

        'NormalCat
        Dim objNormalCat As New Cat()
        With objNormalCat
            Console.WriteLine("NormalCat is a " + .GetType.Name)
            Console.WriteLine("It has " + .Legs.ToString + " legs and " _
                                    + .Feet.ToString + " feet")
            Console.WriteLine()
        End With

        'LameCat
        Dim objLameCat As New LameCat()
        With objLameCat
            Console.WriteLine("LameCat is a " + .GetType.Name)
            Console.WriteLine("It has " + .Legs.ToString + " legs and " _
                                    + .Feet.ToString + " feet")
            Console.WriteLine("Equal to a cat? " + .Equals(New Cat()).ToString)
            Console.WriteLine()
        End With

        'UglyCat
        Dim objUglyCat As Cat
        objUglyCat = New LameCat()
        With objUglyCat
            Console.WriteLine("UglyCat is a " + .GetType.Name)
            Console.WriteLine("It has " + .Legs.ToString + " legs and " _
                                    + .Feet.ToString + " feet")
            Console.WriteLine("Equal to a cat? " + .Equals(New Cat()).ToString)
            Console.WriteLine()
        End With

        Console.ReadLine()
    End Sub

End Module

Class Cat
```

```
    Overridable Function Feet() As Int16
        Return 4
    End Function

    Overridable Function Legs() As Int16
        Return Me.Feet
    End Function

End Class

Class LameCat : Inherits Cat

    Overrides Function Feet() As Int16
        Return 3
    End Function

    Overrides Function Legs() As Int16
        Return Me.Feet
    End Function

    'Add an overload only for cat comparison purposes
    Overloads Function Equals(ByVal AnyCat As Cat) As Boolean
        Return True
    End Function

End Class
```

Once again, you see a surprise when you look at the ugly cat:

```
NormalCat is a Cat
It has 4 legs and 4 feet

LameCat is a LameCat
It has 3 legs and 3 feet
Equal to a cat? True

UglyCat is a LameCat
It has 3 legs and 3 feet
Equal to a cat? False
```

The explanation for this behavior is subtle. The **Equals** member of **LameCat** does not actually overload the **Equals** member for **Cat**, because **Cats** inherit from

Object, whose **Equals** member takes an **Object** parameter. Note that this will seem to work correctly in most circumstances, such as in the **LameCat** case shown in the preceding code. The problem is dangerous because it is only likely to appear under circumstances that will probably never be tested by the original developers of the **Cat** or **LameCat** classes.

Ironically, you can work around this problem by not checking your types so carefully. You can override the default **Equals** by using an **Object** parameter, and then use runtime type checking to identify whether any equality exists. So the new **Equals** member of **LameCat** might look as shown in Listing 2-10.

Listing 2-10. Corrected LameCat.Equals Member

```
Overloads Overrides Function Equals(ByVal Obj As Object) As Boolean
    If Object.ReferenceEquals(Obj.GetType, New Cat().GetType) Then
        Return True
    Else
        Return MyBase.Equals(Obj)
    End If
End Function
```

This runtime type checking is obviously more error-prone than compile-time checking, and it might also have a performance overhead.

One lesson that can be learned from this confusion is that when you're adding or changing an inherited method, it isn't sufficient just to test that specific method. You also need to retest every related method in the inheritance tree to ensure that your modifications didn't cause any unwanted side effects. This is the result of linking classes together within a model operating on implementation inheritance.

Better Equality

If you implement your own version of **Equals** for your reference and value types, you must ensure that you keep to the four major principles of equality:

- *Reflexivity:* a.Equals(a) must always return **true**.

- *Symmetry:* a.Equals(b) must return the same as b.Equals(a).

- *Transitivity:* If a.Equals(b) is **true** and a.Equals(c) is **true**, then b.Equals(c) must also be **true**.

- *Consistency:* a.Equals(b) must always return the same value until either a or b has been changed.

If you fail to keep to one or more of these principles, your code is likely to encounter horrible bugs that are difficult to reproduce. You have been warned!

Inheritance and Method Visibility

The previous examples showed that predicting which method will be called in some inheritance situations can be challenging and sometimes surprising. When you add method visibility into the mix, things can become even more confusing. The code in Listing 2-11 instantiates a **Man**, a **Feline**, and a **Cat**, all from within an **Animal** class. It then attempts to call the **ClassName** member belonging to each of the three objects and prints the results.

Listing 2-11. Using Protection with Inheritance

```
Option Strict On

Class Animal
    Public Shared Sub Main()
        Dim objMan As New Man(), objFeline As New Feline(), objCat As New Cat()
        Console.WriteLine(objMan.ClassName("This Man"))
        Console.WriteLine(objFeline.ClassName("This Feline"))
        Console.WriteLine(objCat.ClassName("This Cat"))
        Console.ReadLine()
    End Sub


    Protected Overridable Function ClassName(ByVal CallingType As String) As
String
        Return CallingType + " appears to be an Animal"
    End Function
End Class


Class Man : Inherits Animal
    Protected Overrides Function ClassName(ByVal CallingType As String) As
String
        Return CallingType + " appears to be a Man"
    End Function
End Class


Class Feline : Inherits Animal
    Protected Overridable Shadows Function _
                    ClassName(ByVal CallingType As String) As String
        Return CallingType + " appears to be a Feline"
```

```
        End Function
End Class

Class Cat : Inherits Feline
    Protected Overrides Function ClassName(ByVal CallingType As String) As
String
        Return CallingType + " appears to be a Cat"
    End Function
End Class
```

Many developers, even some quite experienced ones, will predict the following output:

```
This Man appears to be a Man
This Feline appears to be a Feline
This Cat appears to be a Cat
```

Some developers, usually those who are looking more carefully, will predict the following output:

```
This Man appears to be an Animal
This Feline appears to be an Animal
This Cat appears to be an Animal
```

So both groups of developers are surprised when the following output appears:

```
This Man appears to be a Man
This Feline appears to be an Animal
This Cat appears to be an Animal
```

This looks peculiar. Each method is being invoked directly from the correct type of variable, and at first glance it's hard to see what's going wrong. The key lies in the **Protected** keyword and the way in which it interacts with the **Overrides** and **Shadows** keywords.

A protected member without a **Friend** qualifier can only be accessed from within its own class or a derived class. Clients of the base class or the derived class cannot access it. So in each of the previous tests, the member within the

Animal class is the only method that is ever invoked directly. The **ClassName** member within the **Man** class is simply an **Override**, so it is visible from within the **Animal.ClassName** member and can be called. However, the combination of the **Protected** and **Shadows** qualifiers on the **ClassName** member within the **Feline** class blocks access from the base class to that member and any associated member above it in the inheritance chain.

If all of the members had been qualified with the **Friend** keyword as well as the **Protected** keyword, the prediction given by the first group of developers would have been correct. The combination of the **Protected** and **Friend** keywords allows complete member accessibility within an assembly, as well as accessibility from derived classes in other assemblies. Therefore, the behavior of the code would have been more intuitive to most developers.

You will be looking at the benefits and dangers of implementation versus interface inheritance in more detail as part of a later chapter. For the moment, make a mental note that when you use implementation inheritance, you should use the **Overridable**, **Shadows**, and **Overloads** keywords with great care. Because they can cause confusion and inconsistent behavior depending on the type of variable being referenced, they have the potential to catch developers by surprise, and surprises often lead to bugs.

Navigating the Inheritance Tree

Sometimes even perfectly straightforward code can conceal a surprise. For instance, attempting to locate your position in an inheritance chain looks like exactly the task that **MyClass** is designed for. **MyClass** is similar to the familiar **Me** keyword, except that **MyClass** identifies the class member to call at compile time (sometimes known as *static binding*). The keyword **Me**, on the other hand, identifies the class member to invoke at runtime in any situation where the method being called is declared as **Overridable** (sometimes known as *dynamic binding*). So **MyClass** looks like a useful keyword to have when writing the code shown in Listing 2-12.

Listing 2-12. Where Am I?

```
Option Strict On

Class Test
    Shared Sub Main()
        Dim objDerived As New Derived()
        Console.WriteLine(objDerived.ClassName())
        Console.WriteLine(objDerived.BaseName())
        Console.ReadLine()
```

```
        End Sub
End Class


Class Base
    Public Overridable Function ClassName() As String
        Return MyClass.ToString
    End Function
End Class


Class Derived : Inherits Base
    Public Overrides Function ClassName() As String
        Return MyClass.ToString

    End Function    Public Function BaseName() As String
        Return MyBase.ClassName()
    End Function
End Class
```

Many developers, knowing that the use of **MyClass** results in a static (i.e., compile time) decision about which method to invoke and therefore is not subject to polymorphism and runtime decisions, expect this code to print the following:

```
ProgramExample.Derived
ProgramExample.Base
```

The actual result is not so intuitive:

```
ProgramExample.Derived
ProgramExample.Derived
```

The key to understanding this particular result is to look at what **ToString** is doing internally. If you substitute **ToString** with **GetType.FullName**, you will see exactly the same result. It appears as though **ToString** is calling **GetType.FullName** under the hood. **GetType** is using the type of the declared variable—and the type of the variable is of course always **Derived**, even when the call to **MyBase** is performed. In fact, the documentation states specifically that **Type** always returns the derived class runtime type. You can verify this by instantiating a new variable of type **Base** and then calling its **ClassName** member. This time you will see the **Base** class type appearing in the result.

Instead of using **GetType.FullName** in the base class method, you could try using **GetType.BaseType.FullName**. This would return the desired result in this specific case, but it is still not useful in the general case where you want to know the type of the current class instance regardless of where it is in the inheritance chain. To achieve this, you can perform a little trick. Try adding the following function to the **Test** class:

```
Public Shared Function ImmediateClassName() As String
    Dim objStackFrame As New Diagnostics.StackFrame(1)
    Return objStackFrame.GetMethod.DeclaringType.FullName
End Function
```

Then replace each **MyClass.ToString** with a call to **Test.ImmediateClassName** and run the program again. This time you will see the desired result:

```
ProgramExample.Derived
ProgramExample.Base
```

This works by getting access to VB .NET's method call stack. The parameter of 1 means look at the stack frame one above the current stack frame—namely, the frame that invoked the **ImmediateClassName** method. The **GetMethod** function then returns the method within which the specified stack frame is executing. Finally, the **DeclaringType** property returns the actual type that declared the method, as opposed to the base or derived type.

Miscellaneous Gotchas

In this section I've included various problems that can bite you but that don't fall under any clear categories of their own.

Confusion Between Developer and Compiler

It can sometimes be difficult to be sure that what you code is what the compiler sees. The code in Listing 2-13 demonstrates a nasty bug that arises from a classic confusion between developer and compiler: The intent in this code is to verify that a specific path is actually a folder, rather than a file. Once the file's attributes have been retrieved, they are compared with attributes that a folder should have, thus returning **true** or **false**. There is only one problem with this line of code: It doesn't work. If you specify any file that exists, this line will return **true** regardless of whether it is actually a folder.

Listing 2-13. What the Developer Writes

```
Option Strict Off
If GetAttr(Path + FolderName) And _
    FileAttribute.Directory = FileAttribute.Directory Then
```

The problem here is operator precedence. When the compiler sees two or more operators and the order of execution has not been explicitly stated by the programmer, it uses precedence rules to determine the order of execution. In this case, because the = operator has a higher precedence than the **And** operator, the compiler understands that the line of code actually means the code shown in Listing 2-14.

Listing 2-14. What the Compiler Sees

```
If GetAttr(Path + FolderName) _
   And (FileAttribute.Directory = FileAttribute.Directory) Then
```

This order of operand execution means that the test will always return **true** for any file or folder. What the developer really intended is shown in Listing 2-15.

Listing 2-15. What the Developer Sees

```
If (GetAttr(Path + FolderName) _
    And FileAttribute.Directory) = FileAttribute.Directory Then
```

So what should the developer have written instead? The first point is that the original code in Listing 2-13 would give a compiler build error if **Option Strict On** had been specified. Because the compiler is being asked to compare an **Integer**— the result of **GetAttr(Path + FolderName)**—with a **Boolean**—the result of **(FileAttribute.Directory = FileAttribute.Directory)**—**Option Strict** grumbles because this involves an implicit conversion that it dislikes. The compiler warning is perfect in this case and is just one of many reasons why you should always use **Option Strict** in your programs.

With **Option Strict** now turned on, you need to compare like with like. So your first try at fixing this line might be to try the solution shown in Listing 2-16.

Listing 2-16. Is This Better?

```
Option Strict On
If GetAttr(Path + FolderName) And FileAttribute.Directory Then
```

However, the compiler will still complain, this time about the implicit conversion from **VisualBasic.FileAttribute** into **Boolean**. Because there is an implicit "**= True**" at the end of this line, the compiler doesn't want to perform this conversion implicitly. In fact, if you add the "**= True**" to the end of the line, you can see the squiggly underline showing the location of the error move from under the whole line to under the **True** keyword. So to really get this right, you need to perform the conversion explicitly, as shown in Listing 2-17.

Listing 2-17. This Is Best

```
Option Strict On
If CBool(GetAttr(Path + FolderName) And FileAttribute.Directory) = True Then
```

Now what would be really nice is if the VB .NET IDE automatically inserted any missing brackets where necessary to show what will actually happen when a line of code is run. In other words, the IDE could show clearly what the compiler will do in terms of operator precedence and associativity rather than just showing what the developer wrote. For those people worried about using more disk space due to the extra brackets, I would suggest using a smaller font.

Confusion Between VB .NET and C#

The code in Listing 2-18 shows interesting confusion between the developer and compiler, and between the VB .NET and C# compilers. Unlike the previous example, both of the operators here have identical precedence—obviously, because they're both the same operator. So the question is, which assignment will happen first, and therefore will the variable **A** contain 1 or 2?

Listing 2-18. What the Developer Writes

```
Option Strict Off
Dim A As Integer = 0, B As Integer = 1, C As Integer = 2
A = B = C
```

Because the precedence rules don't help here, the compiler instead uses associativity. The associativity protocol explains the real precedence among all operators that have the same precedence level. Its only use is to avoid confusion when an expression contains two or more equal-precedence operators.

The protocol for all assignment operators is that they have right associativity. This means that the rightmost operation in the expression is evaluated first, and evaluation proceeds from right to left. Given this, you might assume that **C** is first assigned to **B**, and then **B** is assigned to **A**, thereby leaving **A** with the value of 2.

In fact, you are probably thinking that it works in the manner shown in Listing 2-19.

Listing 2-19. What the Developer Sees

```
Option Strict Off
Dim A As Integer = 0, B As Integer = 1, C As Integer = 2
B = C
A = B
```

In fact, **A** will actually have the value of 0! A clue to this behavior becomes clear when you set **Option Strict On**. The compiler now complains because it doesn't like the implicit conversion from **Boolean** to **Integer**. It is interpreting the second = operator as a conditional test resulting in a **true** or **false** value, and the first = operator as an assignment operator that converts the **true** or **false** to an integer. The integer equivalent of **false** is, of course, 0. To verify this, you can set the value of **C** to 1 and **A** will then contain the value of –1, the integer equivalent of **true** (because **B** now equals **C**).

This is not always a surprise to VB.Classic developers because that language behaves in exactly the same way. In both languages this kind of statement involves an ambiguity; does = mean assign or test? The = operator does double duty—it can be said to be overloaded. It can mean either assignment (**B** takes the value of **C**) or equivalence (**B** is the same value as **C**).

So what the VB .NET compiler is seeing is the code in Listing 2-20.

Listing 2-20. What the VB .NET Compiler Sees

```
Option Strict Off
Dim A As Integer = 0, B As Integer = 1, C As Integer = 2
A = CInt(CBool(B = C))
```

This becomes more interesting when you translate the code in Listing 2-18 directly into C#. Listing 2-21 shows this translation.

Listing 2-21. The C# Translation of Listing 2-18

```
int A = 0; int B = 1; int C = 2;
A = B = C;
```

Assuming that the C# developer understands operator precedence and associativity, he or she will expect the code in Listing 2-21 to work like the code shown in Listing 2-22. Sure enough, the C# compiler sees exactly what the developer sees, and **A** will actually contain the value of 2.

Listing 2-22. What the C# Developer (and Compiler) Sees

```
int A = 0; int B = 1; int C = 2;
B = C;
A = B;
```

There is a fairly obvious reason behind the fact that the C# compiler sees this code differently from the VB .NET compiler. Unlike in VB .NET, in C# there are separate operators for assignment and for conditional test. Assignment is represented by the = operator, whereas equivalence is represented by the = = operator. This means that there is never an ambiguity in C# between assignment and equivalence.

The Dangers of Boxing

There are two types of type in VB .NET and the CLR. Examples of value types include any type defined as **boolean, int32,** or **struct**. When you assign a value-type variable to another value-type variable, the value of the first variable is copied to the second variable. So in the following code, **TestVar1** has the value of 2 after the assignment:

```
Dim TestVar1 As Int32 = 1, TestVar2 As Int32 = 2
TestVar1 = TestVar2
```

Examples of reference types include any type defined as **object** or as **string** or as a class. When you assign a reference-type variable to another reference-type variable, you're assigning the reference to the variable, not the value of the variable. So in the following code, both variables will have their **Name** property set to "Martin" after the second assignment because they both reference the same instance after the first assignment:

```
Dim Person1 As New Person("Mark"), Person2 As New Person("Tim")
Person1 = Person2
Person2.Name = "Martin"
```

Given the preceding example, you might be wondering what happens if you assign a value-type variable to a reference-type variable. When you do this, the CLR performs an automatic type conversion calling *boxing*. A boxing conversion implies making a copy of the value being boxed. Listing 2-23 shows what happens in a typical boxing operation and compares it with a similar operation that doesn't involve boxing.

First a **boolean** and an **object variable** are declared, and both are set to the value of **false**. The two variables are then passed in turn as a **ByRef** argument to the **SwitchBoolean** method. The **boolean** variable is automatically boxed to a reference value type because the method argument is of type **object**. The argument value is then changed inside the method from **false** to **true** and passed back out of the method via the **ByRef** argument. Then the two results are printed to the console. What would you expect to see shown as the results?

Listing 2-23. Boxing Can Be Dangerous

```
Option Strict On
Module BoxingTest
    Sub Main()
        Dim MyBoolean As Boolean = False
        Dim MyObject As Object = False

        SwitchBoolean(CType(MyBoolean, Boolean))
        Console.WriteLine("MyBoolean = " & MyBoolean.ToString)

        SwitchBoolean(MyObject)
        Console.WriteLine("MyObject = " & MyObject.ToString)

        Console.ReadLine()
    End Sub

    Private Sub SwitchBoolean(ByRef TestBoolean As Object)
        TestBoolean = True
    End Sub

End Module
```

The **MyBoolean** result shows as **false**, but the **MyObject** result shows as **true**. What's happened is that the automatic boxing that took place when **MyBoolean** was converted to the argument of type **object** meant that a new reference-type variable was created. Changing the reference-type variable inside the method had no effect on the **ByRef** argument because the boxing that was performed meant that a copy of the original variable was passed to the method rather than the original variable. Changing the copy of the method argument obviously had no effect on the original argument.

This is not intuitive, but the good news is that you probably won't encounter this type of situation very often. As long as you understand which types are value types and which are reference types, and then try not to mix the two, you should rarely have the sort of problem shown here.

When Is a Number Not a Number?

VB.Classic is fairly strict about dividing by zero. Anywhere that you try it, it's going to result in an error. VB .NET does something rather different. The following code is divided into five separate tests: The first two tests perform integer divisions, and the final three tests perform floating-point divisions. The challenge is to predict which of the five tests laid out in Listing 2-24 will throw an exception and what exceptions will actually be thrown.

Listing 2-24. Division by Zero

```
Option Strict On
Module Test

Sub Main()
    Dim intTest As Integer, dblTest As Double
    Dim intZero As Integer = 0, blnExceptionThrown As Boolean = False

    'First test
    Console.WriteLine("Integer division by zero assigned to integer:")
    blnExceptionThrown = False
    Try
        intTest = 5 \ intZero
    Catch objException As Exception
        Console.WriteLine(objException.Message)
        blnExceptionThrown = True
    Finally
        If blnExceptionThrown = True Then
            Console.WriteLine("Result: not available")
        Else
            Console.WriteLine("No exception was thrown")
            Console.WriteLine("Result: " + intTest.ToString)
        End If
        Console.WriteLine()
    End Try

    'Second test
    Console.WriteLine("Integer division by zero assigned to double:")
    blnExceptionThrown = False
    Try
        dblTest = 5 \ intZero
    Catch objException As Exception
        Console.WriteLine(objException.Message)
```

```
            blnExceptionThrown = True
    Finally
        If blnExceptionThrown = True Then
            Console.WriteLine("Result: not available")
        Else
            Console.WriteLine("No exception was thrown")
            Console.WriteLine("Result: " + dblTest.ToString)
        End If
        Console.WriteLine()
    End Try


    'Third test
    Console.WriteLine("Float division by zero assigned to integer:")
    blnExceptionThrown = False
    Try
        intTest = CInt(5 / intZero)
    Catch objException As Exception
        Console.WriteLine(objException.Message)
        blnExceptionThrown = True
    Finally
        If blnExceptionThrown = True Then
            Console.WriteLine("Result: not available")
        Else
            Console.WriteLine("No exception was thrown")
            Console.WriteLine("Result: " + intTest.ToString)
        End If
        Console.WriteLine()
    End Try


    'Fourth test
    Console.WriteLine("Float division by zero assigned to double:")
    blnExceptionThrown = False
    Try
        dblTest = 5 / intZero
    Catch objException As Exception
        Console.WriteLine(objException.Message)
        blnExceptionThrown = True
    Finally
        If blnExceptionThrown = True Then
            Console.WriteLine("Result: not available")
        Else
            Console.WriteLine("No exception was thrown")
            Console.WriteLine("Result: " + dblTest.ToString)
```

```
        End If
        Console.WriteLine()
    End Try


    'Fifth test
    Console.WriteLine("Float division of zero by zero assigned to double:")
    blnExceptionThrown = False
    Try
        dblTest = intZero / intZero
    Catch objException As Exception
        Console.WriteLine(objException.Message)
        blnExceptionThrown = True
    Finally
        If blnExceptionThrown = True Then
            Console.WriteLine("Result: not available")
        Else
            Console.WriteLine("No exception was thrown")
            Console.WriteLine("Result: " + dblTest.ToString)
        End If
        Console.WriteLine()
    End Try


    Console.ReadLine()


End Sub


End Module
```

Developers accustomed to using VB.Classic might predict the following results:

```
Integer division by zero assigned to integer:
Attempted to divide by zero
Result: not available

Integer division by zero assigned to double:
Attempted to divide by zero
Result: not available

Float division by zero assigned to integer:
Attempted to divide by zero
Result: not available
```

```
Float division by zero assigned to double:
Attempted to divide by zero
Result: not available

Float division of zero by zero assigned to double:
Attempted to divide by zero
Result: not available
```

What actually happens is that VB .NET integer division by zero behaves in the same way as any zero division does in VB.Classic: An exception is thrown. Floating-point division by zero, however, results instead in no exception and a result of either **Infinity** or **NaN** (the acronym for "Not a Number"). These results can be held and expressed in a variable of type single or double, but not in an integer. So the code in Listing 2-24 produces the following results:

```
Integer division by zero assigned to integer:
Attempted to divide by zero
Result: not available

Integer division by zero assigned to double:
Attempted to divide by zero
Result: not available

Float division by zero assigned to integer:
Arithmetic operation resulted in an overflow.
Result: not available

Float division by zero assigned to double:
No exception was thrown
Result: Infinity

Float division of zero by zero assigned to double:
No exception was thrown
Result: NaN
```

The results from the first two tests are understandable: integer division by zero is not allowed. The result from the third test is interesting: The floating-point division causes a special floating-point value called **Infinity** to be generated, and since an integer cannot hold this value, an overflow exception is generated. The fourth test also produces **Infinity**, but no exception is thrown because this value can be held in a variable of type **Double**. The final test, where zero divides zero, produces another special floating-point value called **NaN**; once again no exception is thrown. One final surprise: If you check, **Infinity** is not equivalent to **NaN**.

You can check for these floating-point values using the shared boolean members **System.Double.IsInfinity(x)** and **System.Double.IsNaN(x)**, along with their **Single** counterparts.

Why is this happening? It's because the VB compiler is finally exposing you to the real nature of the underlying processor. The X86 floating-point instruction set has always generated the nonfinite floating-point values **Infinity** and **NaN** in the case of division by zero. These values are part of the Institute of Electrical and Electronics Engineers (IEEE) standard for floating-point operations. To simplify matters, VB.Classic added extra instructions that caused these nonfinite values to throw the same error as thrown by an integer division by zero. Although you were able to turn off the generation of these instructions by manipulating the compiler optimization flags, few developers ever bothered. But now that VB has to interact with other .NET languages and with the underlying .NET base classes, the decision was made to admit that these floating-point values do actually exist and so developers are required to deal with them.

More Trouble with NaN

NaN and **Infinity** have some other peculiar properties. Listing 2-25 shows a console application performing some tests on these two values whose results might surprise you.

Listing 2-25. Seeing Double

```
Option Strict On
Module Test

    Sub Main()

        Console.WriteLine(Single.NaN = Single.NaN)
        Console.WriteLine((Single.NaN - Single.NaN) = 0)

        Console.WriteLine(Single.PositiveInfinity = Single.PositiveInfinity)
        Console.WriteLine((Single.PositiveInfinity - Single.PositiveInfinity) = 0)

        Console.WriteLine(1.0 < Single.NaN)
        Console.WriteLine(1.0 >= Single.NaN)
```

```
            Console.ReadLine()
        End Sub

End Module
```

The six equality tests in this code return the following results:

```
False
False
True
False
False
False
```

The first result shows that **NaN** doesn't equal **NaN**! Once again, this is part of the IEEE floating-point standard, if somewhat nonintuitive. Given the first result, the second result then makes some sense. Although subtracting a number from itself normally gives a result of zero, you already know that **NaN** doesn't equal **NaN**.

The third result shows that, unlike **NaN**, **PositiveInfinity** does equal **Positive-Infinity**. But when you try to subtract **PositiveInfinity** from itself, the result isn't zero! In fact, the result is actually **NaN**.

The final two results look fine as long as they're taken one at a time, but they're rather peculiar if you look at them together. Combining these two tests shows that 1.0 is neither less than, equal to, or greater than **NaN**. As **Single.NaN** can be used wherever a normal **Single** value is expected, you therefore need to be careful whenever you perform comparisons on **Single** (or **Double**) values. Listing 2-26 shows two different ways of coding a function that takes an argument of type **Single**. Only one of these two functions works as you might expect when passed **Single.NaN** instead of a normal number.

Listing 2-26. Trouble When You Don't Cater Properly to NaN

```
Option Strict On
Module Test

    Sub Main()

        Try
            Console.WriteLine(CalcTotalOne(Single.NaN))
            Console.WriteLine(CalcTotalTwo(Single.NaN))
        Catch ex As Exception
```

```
            Console.WriteLine(ex.Message)
        Finally
            Console.ReadLine()
        End Try


    End Sub


    Function CalcTotalOne(ByVal PurchaseAmount As Single) As Single
        If PurchaseAmount < 0.0 Then
            Throw New ArgumentException("PurchaseAmount must be >= zero")
        End If
        Return PurchaseAmount * 1.08F
    End Function


    Function CalcTotalTwo(ByVal PurchaseAmount As Single) As Single
        If PurchaseAmount >= 0.0 Then
            Return PurchaseAmount * 1.08F
        Else
            Throw New ArgumentException("PurchaseAmount must be >= zero")
        End If
    End Function



End Module
```

The **CalcTotalOne** function returns **NaN** and doesn't throw the exception that you might expect from reading the code. This is because comparing a number (in this case, 0.0) with **NaN** will always return **false**. The **CalcTotalTwo** function, on the other hand, throws the exception that you would expect. When you're using floating-point calculations, you should always be aware that you might be dealing with **NaN** or **Infinity**.

Seeing Double

There are some other interesting side effects resulting from floating-point issues. One problem results from the rounding that VB .NET performs when using floating-point **Double** variables. The code in Listing 2-27 assigns a very large value to a variable of type **Double** and then assigns this to a second variable of type **Double** and adds 1. Of course, any developer can see that these two variables are therefore not equal.

Listing 2-27. Seeing Double

```
Option Strict On
Module Test
    Sub Main()
        Dim X As Double, Y as Double
        X = 10 ^ 18
        Y = X + 1
        Console.WriteLine("X = Y? " + (X = Y).ToString)
        Console.ReadLine()
    End Sub
End Module
```

This code returns the following result:

```
X = Y? True
```

This behavior occurs because both 10 ^ 18 and (10 ^ 18) + 1 are represented with the same 64-bit floating-point **Double** value. 10 ^ 18 is in fact the largest value that can be expressed in 64 bits, and adding 1 to it will make no difference.

Converting the same code to VB.Classic normally returns the correct value of **false**. Specifically, this happens if you're running in interpreted mode or as compiled p-code. If, however, you compile to native code, you will also see **true**. The solution to this issue when using VB.Classic with native code is to use the Advanced Optimization compiler dialog box to turn on the "Allow Un-rounded Floating Point Operations" option. This option usually allows VB.Classic to reuse the 80-bit values already on the math coprocessor stack, instead of using the 64-bit values stored in variables (memory locations), and once again you will see the correct value of **false** returned. Unfortunately there does not appear to be any equivalent compiler optimization when using VB .NET.

In this type of situation, you should really be using the **Decimal** datatype. As explained in the next section, this datatype is not subject to floating-point issues.

Double Trouble

There is another common floating-point issue missed by many developers, especially those doing financial calculations. This issue is also found in VB.Classic, but I'm discussing it here anyway because it has claimed so many victims. The problem occurs when you work with floating-point numbers that can only be represented approximately in binary. In the code shown in Listing 2-28, it seems obvious that both variables should have the same value at the end of the calculation.

Listing 2-28. Double Trouble

```
Option Strict On
Module Test
    Sub Main()
        Dim X As Double = 2.45, Y as Double = 245
        X *= 100
        Console.WriteLine("X = Y? " + (X = Y).ToString)
        Console.ReadLine()
    End Sub
End Module
```

This code returns an interesting result:

```
X = Y? False
```

This behavior occurs because just as 1/3 cannot be represented exactly as a decimal (0.3333...), 2.45 and many other numbers cannot be represented exactly in binary, the notation used by the CLR for floating-point numbers. If you use the **Ildasm** utility to examine the Common Intermediate Language (CIL) produced by the assignment of 2.45 to the variable X, you will see that the value actually assigned is 2.4500000000000002.

Financial calculations, the most common type of calculations affected by this issue, should always be done with **Decimal** variables rather than floating-point numbers. The **Decimal** datatype uses scaled integer arithmetic and isn't affected by this representation problem. If you have to compare **Single** or **Double** variables for equality, you should check that the absolute value of the difference between the two variables is less than **Single.Epsilon** or **Double.Epsilon**.

Summary

Many of the issues mentioned in this chapter are subtle, and you may not find them until well into your build-test-release development cycle. The ideal approach is to prevent these types of bugs from appearing by ensuring that you have a good understanding of the new VB .NET language concepts and of the underlying .NET Framework classes that your application uses. At the very least, developers should take note of the debugging challenges mentioned in Chapter 1 and learn those design and programming concepts that are necessary for their development responsibilities.

As you find code or design errors, decide whether any of the bugs are unusual or tricky enough to catch other developers. If so, try writing about each of your discoveries in a short document so that your colleagues and others in your organization can learn from your experiences. Whereas explicit knowledge is definable and usually documented, this tacit knowledge normally lives only in developers' heads and in their day-to-day practices. It shows itself only through the practice in which it is used, in this case inside streams of code. Codifying such knowledge is not a panacea. Describing certain programming techniques can be as difficult as describing how to ride a bicycle. But even an attempt to pass this information on to other developers is better than leaving them to walk through the same minefields.

Finally, be wary of the new VB .NET language, no matter how wonderful Microsoft claims it to be. You will need to unlearn some of your VB.Classic habits as well as learn some new VB .NET habits. Much of the folklore that built up around VB.Classic is no longer useful, and this unlearning can be more difficult and dangerous than understanding the new concepts. To paraphrase a somewhat cynical conclusion drawn by Chris Hoare during his 1980 Turing Award lecture, there are at least three ways of designing a software language. You can make it

- So simple that there are *obviously* no deficiencies—VB.Classic

- So complicated that there are no *obvious* deficiencies—C++

- *Look* simple yet be complicated enough to conceal *obvious* deficiencies—VB .NET

INTERLUDE

With the increasing software automation of modern society, there are some hard questions coming about how much we should trust the software that runs our mission-critical systems. Do we trust the software more than its human minders? Should the software monitor and prevent human error or should human flexibility be put at a premium over and above software's rigidity?

When the Airbus A320 commercial airliner was introduced in the early 1990s, it had extensive computer-controlled aviation systems, including the first fly-by-wire system on a commercial aircraft. The on-board computers also had preprogrammed restrictions on what the pilots were allowed to do with the plane. This "guardian angel" behavior, known more formally as the Flight Envelope Protection System, is actually considered to be more revolutionary than the fly-by-wire controls. The A320's designers decided that their judgment about the plane's limits was more important than any pilot's judgment.

Imagine, for instance, that the A320 pilot has to perform a violent avoiding maneuver upon seeing another plane nearby. No matter how hard the pilot manipulates the sidestick, the computers will not allow the airframe to sustain a stress of greater than 2.5G. This allows the pilot to perform the evasion maneuver as fast and as violently as possible, knowing that the software will prevent his or her inputs from actually damaging the plane. This is similar to an automated braking system on a car that allows you to brake as hard as you wish, because the software prevents the wheels from locking up and sending your car into a skid.

While the 2.5G stress limit allowed by the A320 appears to be generous and allows some quite violent maneuvers, there is at least one precedent for exceeding this figure. In February 1985, China Airlines flight 006 was cruising at 41,000 feet some 300 miles northwest of San Francisco. A combination of power loss and undue reliance on the autopilot led to a sideways roll followed by a near-vertical dive and an inverted spin. For 3 minutes the plane plunged nearly 6 miles before the captain was able to pull out of the dive at 9,500 feet. In doing so, he measurably warped the wings and caused several million dollars of other structural damage. But he saved the airplane and its passengers at the cost of pulling an estimated 5.5G, well beyond the 747's safety limits. The evidence is that if the plane had been an A320, the software might have prevented the pilots from pulling out of the dive. On the other hand, it is possible that the computer software might have prevented the problem in the first place.

Part Two

The Debugging Tools

"Too many errors on one line (make fewer)."
—*Error message emitted by Apple's MPW C compiler*

CHAPTER 3

The Visual Studio .NET Debugger

IF YOU WERE GIVEN A BRIEF to design the Ultimate Debugger, what goals would you aim for? For me, there would be one goal above all else: the ability to single-step through my entire application, no matter what languages are involved and where the code is running. While the Visual Studio .NET debugger does not quite reach this state of nirvana, it comes fairly close.

This chapter is a detailed introduction to some of the features offered by this rather complex system, investigating how it works, what it is capable of, what debugging modes are available, and how to use some of the new debugging windows. This is a necessary precursor to future chapters that will go into more detail on configuring and using the Visual Studio .NET debugger.

Introduction to the Visual Studio Debugger

For developers accustomed to the VB.Classic debugger, this new version can come as something of a shock. Up until now we've only had the ability to debug a single interpreted language, and even that came with some frustrating limitations. Now we've been gifted with a debugger that is considerably more versatile and more complex. Here are some of the Visual Studio debugger highlights:

- A single user interface for all of the languages

- Three different debugging modes

- Simultaneous debugging of multiple processes across multiple machines

- Advanced breakpoints across multiple components

- Knowledge of every loaded component, including version and load path

- Remote debugging

- Direct access to low-level assembly code and to memory

- Debugger automation

To give you a taste of these capabilities, I briefly discuss each of them in the sections that follow, before going into more detail later in the chapter.

Single User Interface

If you use multiple languages in your application—for instance, C#, VB.Classic, or SQL in addition to VB .NET—a single user interface across all of these languages can boost your productivity significantly. It means that you can use the same debugging windows, the same keystrokes, and almost the same debugging facilities wherever you go. There is no need to learn a different debugging environment every time you make a language switch. This reinforces the part of the .NET philosophy that says your programming language choices are not as critical in the new world as they were in the old.

The list of languages that the Visual Studio debugger can handle is long, and it includes a couple of surprises:

- Any .NET language (e.g., VB .NET, C#, J#, C++ managed extensions)

- Native Win32 languages (e.g., VB 5.0 and upward, C++, C)

- Transact-SQL (SQL Server 7.0 and upward)

- Any ASP.NET language (e.g., VB .NET, C#)

- Any ASP language (e.g., VBScript, JScript)

The capability to step seamlessly from one language to another within the same application is one of the more impressive features of the Visual Studio debugger.

Different Debugging Modes

The VB.Classic debugger allowed you just one debugging mode. The Visual Studio debugger gives you more choices, and therefore you have more decisions to make. There are three major debugging modes:

- Start one or more programs from within the Visual Studio IDE.

- Attach the debugger to one or more already-running processes.

- Use the Just-In-Time debugger to attach to your application when it crashes.

Distributed Debugging

Because Visual Basic (VB) .NET makes it feasible to build and deploy large distributed systems, the Visual Studio debugger gives you the ability to debug multiple processes running on multiple machines simultaneously. This means that you can sit at a single machine and debug the interactions of every component in your application, no matter where that component lives. If you were trying to find a bug that might be hiding in any part of a distributed application, testing and debugging each part of that application separately would be a nightmare. Now you can analyze and debug your application as a single entity.

This facility also allows you to attach to a program running on an end user's machine, assuming that you have been given the right permissions. In this way you can investigate an end user's program bug as it happens, without having to replicate the problem on your own machine.

Advanced Breakpoints

The Visual Studio debugger is much more flexible in its use of breakpoints than VB.Classic. The following breakpoint types are available when you use VB .NET:

- *File:* Stops at a line within a specified source file

- *Function:* Stops at the start of a specified function

- *Address:* Stops when instruction at a memory address is reached

Any of these breakpoint types can have additional modifiers whereby it is only triggered when it has been executed a specified number of times or when a specific expression evaluates to **true** or has changed its value. Other enhancements are the automatic saving of breakpoints from session to session in the solution's .suo file and the ability to disable breakpoints without removing them. Finally, the debugger can generate any necessary child breakpoints automatically; if, for instance, you set a breakpoint on an overloaded method, every overload of that method can be given the same breakpoint.

Application Knowledge

Many nasty bugs can be traced to versioning problems. The Modules window is designed to show you as much information as possible about every .dll, .exe, and other module loaded by your application. This information includes the module's name, memory address, version, load path, and whether its debug symbols were located. Even the load sequence of the modules is shown.

Remote Debugging

There are many times when it is very convenient, or even essential, to debug an application running on another machine. This could be on a production machine where Visual Studio cannot be installed locally, a machine whose configuration you don't want to upset, or perhaps you want to debug some window painting code where using a GUI-based debugger locally would be impossible. To do this, you can install a small set of remote debugging components that will allow you to attach and debug remotely while sitting at your own machine. This allows you to debug most problems in place, which is a major step forward for VB.Classic developers.

Low-Level Access

Some bugs can only be solved with the use of "heavy" debugging, where you have to dive down into low-level code. For this purpose, the Visual Studio debugger provides the Disassembly, Memory, and Registers windows.

The Disassembly window shows you the processor-native code side by side with your source code. You can single-step this native code and even set breakpoints. With an advanced technique, the Disassembly window can also show the native code with its matching Common Intermediate Language (CIL) rather than your source code. This technique is useful if you want to understand how CIL works or if you are trying to solve a CIL problem.

The four Memory windows allow you to peer deep into the memory used by your application and play with what you find there. My suspicion is that most managed code developers will rarely use this window, but it's there for that once-a-year occasion when you really do need it.

The Registers window allows you to examine (and change if you dare) the contents of the CPU's physical registers. Managed code doesn't use the physical CPU registers directly, but instead accesses a set of registers that are maintained by the common language runtime (CLR). These CLR registers can also be viewed and edited.

Debugger Automation

The Visual Studio debugger has a set of interfaces that can be accessed programmatically. This means that you have access to the debugging state of your application, and therefore you can write macros that use this information. If you open the Macro Explorer window, you can see some sample macros that perform useful tasks such as dumping the call stack of every thread in every program within the current application.

How the Visual Studio Debugger Works

The Visual Studio debugger has some powerful capabilities, but the tradeoff is that it can be more complex to set up and use than the VB.Classic debugger. This section explores how the debugger is able to work its particular brand of magic and aims to give you an understanding of its basic mechanics.

Figure 3-1 is a slightly simplified view of the process that occurs when you press F5 within the VB .NET IDE. The language compiler and Just-In-Time (JIT) compiler together have to turn your lovingly crafted code into instructions that the processor can understand. The debugger then has to reverse this process in order to map back from the processor-native code to the corresponding source code. You should read the diagram in Figure 3-1 going counter-clockwise.

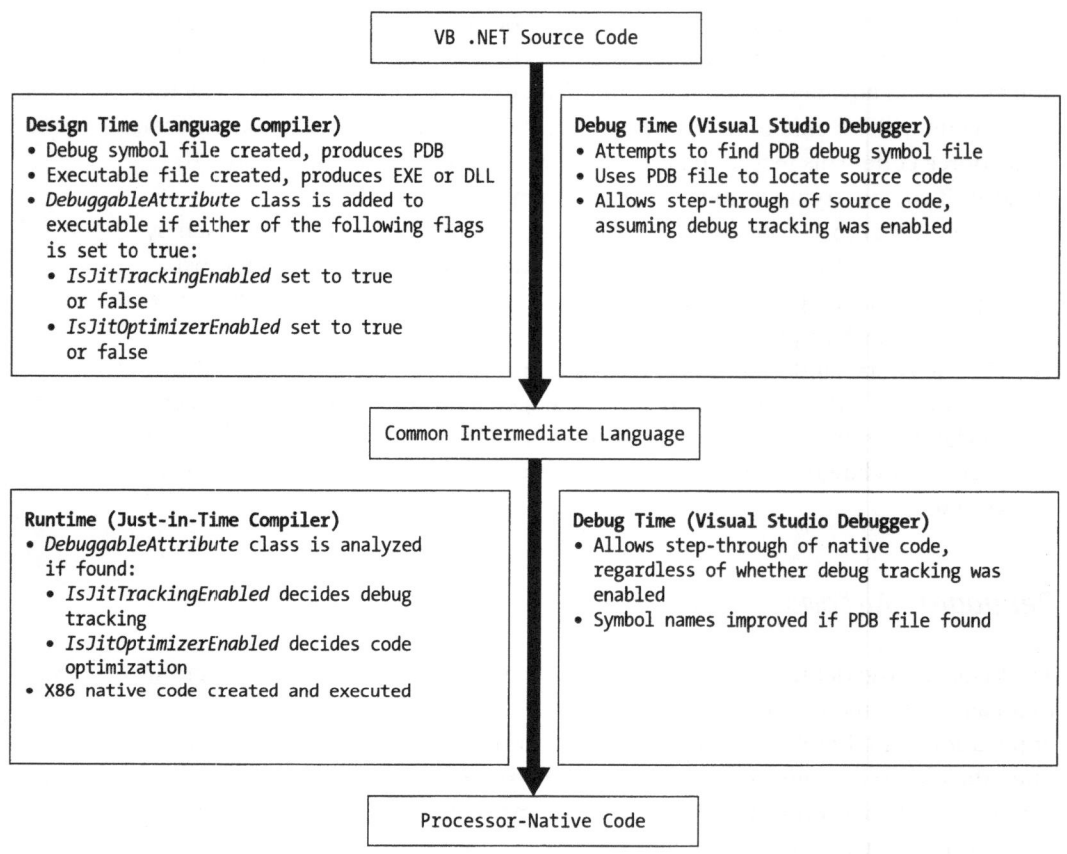

Figure 3-1. How the compilers and the Visual Studio debugger work together

Figure 3-1 shows that compiling your program is now a two-stage process, rather than the single stage offered by the VB.Classic interpreter. Because compiling your application is now a two-stage process, the mapping done by the Visual Studio debugger is more complex.

The first stage is design-time compilation, when the language compiler converts your source code into an intermediate format called Common Intermediate Language (CIL), along with some metadata that describes your program in detail. The CIL and metadata together form the physical executable, which is stored in an .exe or a .dll. This compilation stage also produces debug symbols for each component, in a file with a .pdb suffix. These debug symbol files help the debugger with its code mapping.

The second stage is runtime compilation, when the JIT compiler converts the CIL code to native code that the processor can execute. If you've chosen to enable code optimization, this is when most of the optimization happens. Once the JIT compiler has converted a method, it caches the native code for that method in memory so that the method doesn't have to be compiled again.

It's also important to notice that you're now always executing and debugging a compiled program. This is a change from the VB.Classic IDE, which ran your code using an interpreter rather than a compiler.

Understanding the DebuggableAttribute Class

The **DebuggableAttribute** class and its two associated flags determine how well you can debug your application. The VB .NET language compiler sets these flags automatically depending on the build settings you specify when compiling your program. The JIT compiler then reads these flags and decides its actions depending on their values. Therefore it's important to know what these two flags represent.

Debug Tracking Flag

If the *IsJitTrackingEnabled* flag is set to **true**, the JIT compiler creates tracking information to help the debugger work its way back from the native code to the CIL. This tracking information is a mapping between the native code and the CIL, in the form of what are called *offset tables*. This mapping is part of the process used by the debugger to show you what's happening in your VB .NET source code during program execution.

Code Optimization Flag

If the *IsJitOptimizerDisabled* flag is set to **true**, the native code produced by the JIT compiler is not optimized to run as fast as possible. If it's set to **false**, the native code produced is optimized to run as fast as possible while still producing the same results. This latter setting can affect debugging because native-code optimization can confuse the debugger when it's trying to map from native code back to source code.

What the VB .NET Language Compiler Does

When you press F5 to start running your program from within the Visual Studio IDE, the VB .NET language compiler translates your VB code into CIL. This produces an executable file that has an .exe or .dll suffix and also an associated debug symbol file with a .pdb suffix. This debug symbol file contains information about your program that helps the debugger to match your source code to the corresponding CIL and native code.

The language compiler also decides whether to inject the **DebuggableAttribute** class into each assembly within your program. If the *IsJitTrackingEnabled* and *IsJitOptimizerDisabled* flags contained within this class are both set to **false**, this signifies a release build where tracking is not needed and code optimization is allowed. In this case, the **DebuggableAttribute** class is not added to the assembly and in its absence both flags are understood to have the value of **false**. On the other hand, if either flag is set to **true**, the **DebuggableAttribute** class is added to the assembly.

What the JIT Compiler Does

After the program has been compiled, it obviously has to be executed. This is done by the JIT compiler, which translates the CIL for each invoked procedure into processor-native code that the CPU understands. If the **DebuggableAttribute** class was added to the assembly by the VB .NET compiler, the JIT compiler looks at the two flags discussed previously and uses them to decide whether to add debug tracking information for the debugger and whether to optimize the processor-native code.

What the Visual Studio Debugger Does

Provided that the *IsJitTrackingEnabled* flag is **true**, the tracking information that this generates together with the information in the debug symbol file allow the debugger to work backward from the native code through the CIL and into your source code. This means that you can see what your program is doing at the VB .NET source code level even though the code being executed is processor-native code.

Build Configurations and Their Effects on Debugging

How you compile and run each of the projects within your application determines how easily it can be debugged. Both Visual Studio and the command-line compilers have facilities for controlling this process.

Building in Visual Studio

Within Visual Studio, there are two build configurations for a project, the **Debug** configuration and the **Release** configuration. Each of these configurations has a set of properties that affect the way your program runs and is debugged. The default settings for the two configurations are shown in Table 3-1.

Table 3-1. Default Build Configuration Settings in Visual Studio

CONFIGURATION	DESCRIPTION
Debug configuration	Generates PDB file
	Sets *IsJitTrackingEnabled* to **true**
	Sets *IsJitOptimizerDisabled* to **true**
Release configuration	Does not generate PDB file
	Sets *IsJitTrackingEnabled* to **false**
	Sets *IsJitOptimizerDisabled* to **false**

You can alter the default settings shown in Table 3-1 using the Visual Studio project properties dialog window. To control the setting of the *IsJitTrackingEnabled* flag and the generation of the debug symbol file for a Visual Studio project, right-click that project in Solution Explorer and select Properties ➤ Configuration Properties ➤ Build. There you can see and set an option called "Generate debugging information". Within Visual Studio, there is no way of controlling the .pdb generation and the *IsJitTrackingEnabled* flag independently.

Setting of the *IsJitOptimizerDisabled* flag is similarly controlled for a project under Properties ➤ Configuration Properties ➤ Optimizations. The relevant option is "Enable optimizations".

One point of interest is that if you run your project under the Visual Studio debugger, the *IsJitTrackingEnabled* and *IsJitOptimizerDisabled* flags are both temporarily set to **true** so that you can debug your project regardless of any of the Visual Studio build settings.

Building from the Command Line

If you build from the command line, the two flags that control how easily you can debug your programs are */debug* and */optimize*. As shown in Table 3-2, they correspond directly to the two flags that I have been discussing.

Table 3-2. Command-Line Flags

FLAG	DESCRIPTION
/debug:full /optimize- (equivalent of Visual Studio debug mode)	Creates PDB file Sets *IsJitTrackingEnabled* to **true** Sets *IsJitOptimizerDisabled* to **true**
/debug- /optimize+ (equivalent of Visual Studio release mode)	Does not create PDB file Sets *IsJitTrackingEnabled* to **false** Sets *IsJitOptimizerDisabled* to **false**
/debug:pdbonly (no equivalent mode in Visual Studio)	Creates PDB file Sets *IsJitTrackingEnabled* to **false** Sets *IsJitOptimizerDisabled* to **true**

The /debug Compiler Option

The */debug:full* setting tells the compiler to generate all of the information necessary to debug your program fully. It ensures that the debug symbol file is created and that the *IsJitTrackingEnabled* flag of **DebuggableAttribute** is set to **true**.

The */debug:pdbonly* setting tells the compiler to generate the debug symbol file, but sets the *IsJitTrackingEnabled* member of **DebuggableAttribute** to **false**. If you debug your program from within the Visual Studio IDE, this won't make any difference—this setting is then equivalent to the */debug:full* setting. If, however, you debug a program running outside the IDE, you will see only assembly code during debugging and you won't be able to step through the source code.

The */debug-* setting tells the compiler not to generate the debug symbol file and sets the *IsJitTrackingEnabled* member of **DebuggableAttribute** to **false**. This means that you will only be able to debug by stepping through the processor-native code.

Because the */debug* flag has an extra setting that has no Visual Studio equivalent (i.e., generating the debug symbol file without tracking information), the command line is slightly more flexible. This is most useful when you're building a production release of your application. By default, you don't necessarily want the debug tracking information, as this can be generated at runtime if necessary—for more about this, see the "Debugging Production Applications" section in Chapter 4, which covers overriding debug settings at runtime. However, you must have the debug symbol files available if you ever want to debug your production programs.

The /optimize Compiler Option

The */optimize+* setting tells the compiler to optimize both the CIL code and the x86 code. This optimization process gives permission to the language and JIT compilers to rearrange code as they see fit in order to generate the fastest code possible. One minor problem with this is that it can cause confusion when source code shown in the debugger is not executed as you expect because of the compiler optimizations. Because the native code is optimized, there is no longer any guarantee of a direct match with the source code. You can see this discrepancy in the source window when certain source statements appear to be skipped or executed in a strange order. For a good example of this, see the "Debugging and Optimization" tutorial in the .NET Framework SDK documentation.

The */optimize-* setting tells the compiler not to mess with the code. This means that you won't see any strange behavior when stepping through your source code, but the tradeoff is that the code may run slower.

Locating Debug Symbol Files

A .pdb file contains debug symbols and is essential for most debugging, unless you are happy to wade through pure assembly code. Even for modules or third-party components where you have no access to the source code, having a .pdb file means that you can see proper function names in the Disassembly window.

The .pdb files for your application need to be located by the Visual Studio debugger. Normally, the debugger searches for a program's debug symbol files in the same folder that the executable resides, which is where the build process places them by default. If this is not the right location, you need to tell the debugger where to find the symbols. To do this, go to the Solution Explorer window, right-click your solution, and select the Properties menu item. Under Common Properties ➤ Debug Symbol Files, add any required paths.

Whenever you build a production release of your application, you *must* build the associated .pdb files and store them under version control with the corresponding source. Trying to debug a production application with out-of-date or mismatched debug symbol files is usually impossible. You can use the **dumpbin** utility to find the debug symbol file associated with an .exe or .dll. The following command line searches for the debug symbol file related to the executable JitTest.exe and reports a list of the folders that it searched:

```
dumpbin /PDBPATH:VERBOSE C:\Test\JitTest.exe
```

The **dumpbin** utility with the */PDBPATH* flag searches the following folders:

- The folder where the executable is placed

- The location of the debug symbol file written into the executable, which is usually the location at the time that the executable was built

- The search path configured within the Visual Studio IDE

- The paths contained in the _NT_SYMBOL_PATH and
  _NT_ALT_SYMBOL_PATH environment variables

- The Windows folder

This utility can be very useful when your breakpoints aren't being triggered and you need to verify that the executable file and debug symbol file are properly matched.

Locating Source Files

If you're debugging a solution that was started within the Visual Studio IDE, the debugger will normally have no problem in locating any source files that it requires. If, however, you're attaching to a process or doing remote debugging, you can tell the debugger where to find any necessary source files by using the Solution Explorer window. There you can right-click your solution, select Properties ➤ Common Properties ➤ Debug Source Files, and add any required paths to allow Visual Studio to find the source file. If Visual Studio makes a guess about the name or location of the source file that it needs to use, you can ask it to confirm its choice by going to Tools ➤ Options ➤ Debugging ➤ General and selecting the "Confirm correct file was found when finding source" option. Of course, these source files don't need to be held locally—you can use them even if they're on a remote machine.

Three Debugging Modes

The VB.Classic environment allowed only one way to debug a program. You loaded the source code into the IDE and the VB interpreter executed the *p-code* (packed code, an intermediate format between source and native code). This was a simple concept and therefore easy to understand, even for a VB neophyte. From version 5.0 onward, you could also compile your source code into processor-native code, but then you were on your own if you wanted to debug the result.

The .NET environment gives you no less than three ways of debugging your application, and each of these ways has some variations. As happens so often in the .NET world, you now have more choices, more flexibility, and more complexity.

- *IDE debugging:* You start an application within Visual Studio, and the Visual Studio debugger automatically attaches to the processes within that application.

- *PROCESS debugging:* You manually attach a debugger to a process that's already running.

- *JIT debugging:* The CLR prompts you to attach a debugger to an application that has crashed.

The first method is similar to the VB.Classic way of doing things, although it has its own quirks. The other two methods will be unfamiliar to many VB.Classic developers, but they're useful because of the extra debugging facilities that they make possible. In fact, all three methods work the same way under the hood in that they all involve a debugger being attached to the process that you want to debug. Visual Studio does the process attachment automatically with the first method, you do the process attachment manually with the second method, and the final method requires you to tell the CLR which debugger you want to attach to a crashed process. The next three sections discuss how each of these three methods works when using the Visual Studio debugger.

IDE Debugging

This is relatively familiar territory to a VB.Classic developer. You load the solution that contains your application into Visual Studio, set your breakpoints, and press F5. Visual Studio automatically attaches its debugger to your application's processes, and as long as your debugging doesn't step outside of the projects that make up your Visual Studio solution, you can step through your code and debug in comfort.

A twist on this process is the ability to start more than one of the projects in your solution simultaneously. If you're executing components that need to run side by side and cooperate with each other, this is now very easy. In the Solution Explorer window, right-click your solution, select Set Startup Projects ➢ Common Properties ➢ Startup Project, and click the Multiple Startup Projects option. This allows you to specify which of the projects that make up your solution need to start together. If you examine the Solution Explorer window, a solution with a single startup project shows that startup project in bold. If you use the Multiple Startup Projects option, the solution itself is shown in bold instead.

An important point is that you can combine the debugging of your current Visual Studio solution with the "attach to process" method of debugging explained in the next section. Assuming that a project within your Visual Studio solution calls into another process to which you've attached the debugger, you can step seamlessly back and forth between your code in your solution and the code in the process that you've attached to manually.

You can also use the IDE to debug an application that was built outside of Visual Studio or one for which you have no source code. If you don't have a solution open, or you don't want to add the application to an existing solution, select File ➤ Open ➤ File and find and select the .exe file. To add the application to an existing solution, choose File ➤ Add Project ➤ Existing Project and then select the .exe file. Once the .exe file is loaded and shown in the Solution Explorer window, right-click the imported .exe file and select Debug ➤ Step into new instance, and Visual Studio attempts to find any associated source and debug symbol files so that you can start debugging. Alternatively, you can use the menu option File ➤ Open ➤ File to select the source file manually and import it into your solution.

In this situation, if both the source code and debug symbol files are available, you can debug using the source code. Otherwise, you can only debug by observing and setting breakpoints in the assembly code within the Disassembly window.

There are some limitations to debugging applications within the IDE, such as effective debugging of a Windows service. When faced with these limitations, you can opt to debug by attaching manually to a process that's already running, as described in the next section.

Process Debugging

You'll often encounter situations where you want to debug programs that you can't, or don't wish to, load into the IDE. Some examples of these situations include the following:

- Debugging a program that was not created with Visual Studio, such as a VB 6.0 component

- Debugging a production component that's already running

- Debugging any program running on another machine, such as a Web service

- Debugging a program running in another process, such as an ISAPI DLL

- Debugging a program difficult to run in the IDE, such as a Windows service

In these cases you need to attach the debugger manually to the process or processes that you want to debug. To attach to a process, you simply tell the debugger which process you wish to debug and the debugger will jump on its back, in a manner of speaking. Once the debugger is attached, you can break into the process and debug it just as though it was running within the IDE. After you've finished debugging the process, you tell the debugger to detach from it and the debugger will climb off its back.

Attaching to a Process

You can find the dialog window that controls attaching to, and detaching from, a process by selecting the Processes menu item on the Debug menu. Understanding the subtleties of this dialog window is important because you are likely to use it frequently, and because you should treat attaching to a process and detaching from it with some care. The Processes dialog window is shown in Figure 3-2.

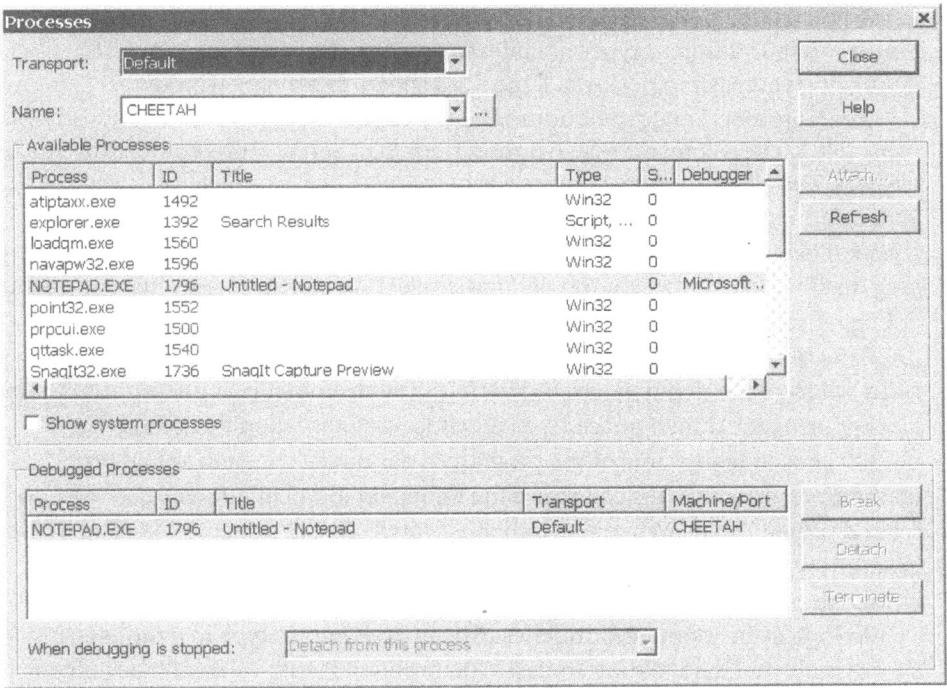

Figure 3-2. The Processes dialog window

The Available Processes subwindow shows the processes executing on the machine specified in the Name combo box. If you choose the option to show the system processes, you can view processes running under the system account, such as Windows services. The Refresh button is useful because this window is not updated in real time and therefore may not reflect the true state of processes that have started and stopped while the window was showing.

The Transport combo box controls the transport protocol used for remote debugging. By default, the Visual Studio debugger uses the Distributed Component Object Model (DCOM) protocol for remote debugging. If DCOM is not available for some reason, and then only if you're debugging native Win32 applications, you can specify the Native-only TCP/IP transport. If you've upgraded to Visual Studio 2003, you have the additional option of using the Native-only Pipe transport protocol, which is more secure than TCP/IP, but slower. You use the Name combo box to specify the machine that you wish to debug remotely. Choosing a valid machine name shows the processes running on that machine. Please see Chapter 15 for more information about these options and about remote debugging.

When you click on a process in the Available Processes subwindow, the debugger enables the Attach button. Clicking this button prompts the debugger to ask you which types of application you wish to debug. A process can be running up to four different types of code, so you can choose which types of debugging you wish to perform. Figure 3-3 shows this dialog window.

The Common Language Runtime option is for debugging applications built using .NET. The Microsoft T-SQL option is for SQL Server stored procedures and triggers. The Native debugger option is for native Win32 applications, and the Script debugger option works for debugging VBScript or JScript pages. A neat shortcut is to Ctrl-click the Attach button. Provided that you have native debugging installed, this bypasses the debugger selection page and uses just the native debugger without asking.

Attaching the Visual Studio debugger to a process can lead to issues, especially when you're debugging remotely. This means that it isn't uncommon to see errors during the attach phase. Typically this happens when the debugging components necessary for one of the program types haven't been installed or configured correctly. This can cause the debugger to fail in attaching to the related program type. When this happens, you'll see a message explaining which program types the debugger attached to successfully and which program types caused the debugger attach to fail.

As long as the debugger attaches to a single program type in a process, it's successfully attached to that process. The problem is that you won't be able to debug the other program types running within that process. If you wish to receive a more detailed error message about an attach error, you should detach from the partially attached process and then attempt to attach to the process again, but only using the program type that failed. You should then see a better explanation of what went wrong with attaching to that program type.

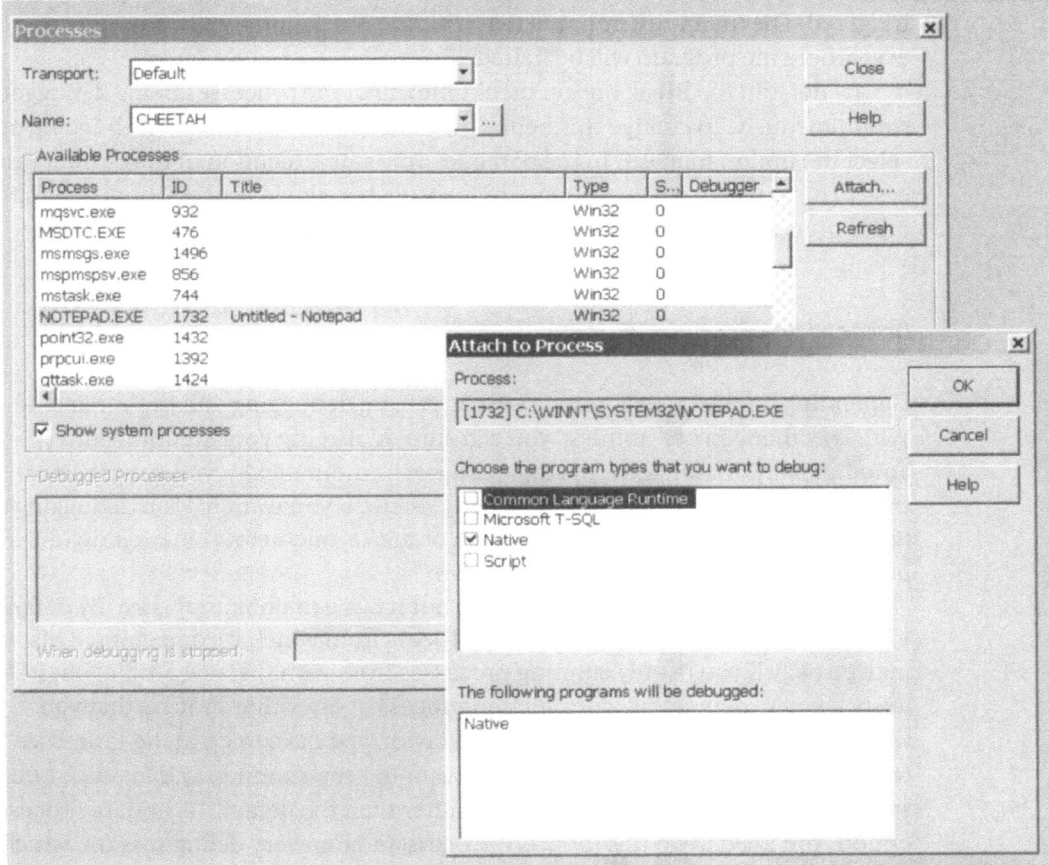

Figure 3-3. The Attach to Process dialog window

If the debugger completely fails to attach, you'll also see an error message—for example "Access denied" because of a permissions problem. In this case, it isn't uncommon for the process to be shown as attached even though it isn't. Clicking the Refresh button will show you the real status of the process.

For a more detailed understanding of the debugging components and setup required for each of these program types, you should read the chapter appropriate for each of the program types in which you are interested.

Breaking into a Process

You can break into any of the processes being debugged by clicking the Break button on the Processes dialog window. This is the manual equivalent of setting a breakpoint and performing a program action that causes the breakpoint to be triggered. The major difference is that with the Break button you have no control over where the program will be halted.

By default, the Break button breaks into all of the processes being debugged simultaneously. To change this behavior, go to Tools ➤ Options ➤ Debugging and select the option marked "In break mode, only stop execution of the current process". This is useful when you want to investigate a single process, but keep the other processes in your application running normally.

Detaching from a Process

Depending on the type of processes that you are debugging and the version of Windows that you are running, you can stop debugging your solution either automatically or manually. To stop debugging automatically, you simply select the Stop Debugging option on the Debug menu. If you want to stop debugging manually, you can use either the Detach or the Terminate button on individual processes shown in the Processes window.

The automatic option is the easiest, but it has a major annoyance. By default, Visual Studio always terminates every process from which it's detaching. This may be okay if you're only running processes from within Visual Studio, but it's nasty if you're debugging a production process or any other process that you want to keep running. To change this behavior, you have to go to the Processes window, choose the processes that you want to keep running, and for each one select the Detach from Process option rather than the default Terminate process option. You need to do this for every process and for every debug session, which rapidly turns into a major pain.

You can stop debugging a process manually by using the Detach button in the Processes window. If you're using Windows XP, this button is always enabled, and using it stops debugging without any harm to the process from which you're detaching. If, however, you're using Windows 2000 or Windows NT, and you're debugging a native Win32 process (one not created using .NET technology), the Detach button may not be enabled and you then have to use the Terminate button instead. This has the unfortunate property of doing exactly what its name implies: It kills the process that you've just been debugging. This isn't always what you want to happen. For obvious reasons, you should be especially careful about terminating a production process, a system process, or any process that other users are likely to be depending on.

This process termination happens because Win32 processes were not really designed to cohabit with a debugger; if you've ever used the Visual C++ debugger, you'll know that it never gave you the choice of detaching from a process without terminating it.

The key to fixing this problem with Win32 processes under Windows 2000 or Windows NT is to find and start the Visual Studio Debugger Proxy Windows service before debugging. This service then sits between the Visual Studio debugger and the native Win32 process being debugged, and allows you to detach from the process without terminating it. The debugger proxy service does have a few restrictions. It won't work on Windows 98 or Windows ME, and also doesn't work when you're debugging COM Interop applications. Finally, you can't use the debugger proxy service when you're debugging under Terminal Server. Whether or not you're using the proxy debugger service, Visual Studio doesn't allow you to detach from a process if you're debugging more than one project type within that process. For instance, if you're debugging a Web service together with a non-Web client of the Web service, the option to detach won't be available. I don't know why this restriction exists.

JIT Debugging

Just-In-Time (JIT) debugging shouldn't be confused with JIT compiling. It is instead an exotic variant of the process debugging discussed previously. It's designed to attach a debugger at the point that a managed or unmanaged program crashes due to an unhandled error. Without the presence of a JIT debugger, a crashed program simply closes down and vanishes.

JIT Debugger Settings with Managed Code

For a crash in managed code, and depending on the JIT debugger settings, the CLR can perform one of the following actions:

- Terminate the program after displaying some diagnostic information

- Launch a debugger and break at the point where the crash occurred.

- Give the user a choice between the two preceding options.

This gives you some choices about handling a program crash. On a developer's machine, you probably want to use the second or third option. On an end user's machine, a better choice would probably be the first option.

The two registry settings that control this behavior are both under HKEY_LOCAL_ MACHINE, abbreviated as HKLM. The first registry setting controls how the crash is handled. The second registry setting specifies which debugger to launch if one is needed. Both settings and their possible values are shown in Table 3-3.

Table 3-3. Registry Settings for JIT Debugging of Managed Code

REGISTRY SETTING	POSSIBLE VALUES
HKLM\Software\Microsoft\.NetFramework\ DbgJITDebugLaunchSetting	0: Show a message giving the user a choice of OK (dumps the call stack and terminates the process) or CANCEL (launches the listed debugger). 1: Dump the call stack and terminate the process. 2: Launch the debugger that is specified under the **DbgManagedDebugger** registry setting.
HKLM\Software\Microsoft\.NetFramework\ DbgManagedDebugger	The default debugger is cordbg.exe, the SDK command-line debugger. You can change this value to **dbgclr.exe** to invoke the SDK graphical debugger or **devenv /debugexe** to launch the Visual Studio debugger.

JIT Debugger Settings with Unmanaged Code

For a crash in unmanaged code, you have fewer options. The two choices are as follows:

- Launch a debugger and break at the point where the crash occurred.

- Give the user a choice of launching a debugger or terminating the crashed program.

On a developer's machine you can use either option, but on an end user's machine a better choice would probably be the second option.

Once again, the two registry settings that control this behavior are both under HKEY_LOCAL_MACHINE. The first registry setting controls how the crash is handled. The second registry setting specifies which debugger to launch if one is needed. Both registry settings and their possible values are shown in Table 3-4.

Table 3-4. Registry Settings for JIT Debugging of Unmanaged Code

REGISTRY SETTING	POSSIBLE VALUES
HKLM\Software\Microsoft\Windows NT\ Current Version\AeDebug\Auto	0: Show a message giving the user a choice of OK (terminates the process) or CANCEL (launches the listed debugger) 1: Launch the debugger that is specified under the **Debugger** registry setting.
HKLM\ Software\Microsoft\Windows NT\ CurrentVersion\AeDebug\Debugger	The default debugger is Dr. Watson, and the default behavior is to show a message giving the user a choice (in other words, *Auto* is set to 0).

An alternative way of managing these settings is from within Visual Studio. Here you can set the Visual Studio debugger to handle crashes in managed code, native code, and even script by going to Tools ➤ Options ➤ Debugging ➤ Just-In-Time and setting the appropriate options. If you didn't install the Visual C++ .NET section of Visual Studio, you may not see the native code switch in this dialog window. This is, in my opinion, a bug because you may still want to JIT-debug native code such as VB.Classic even if you're ignoring C++. If you fell into this trap, you should either install Visual C++ .NET or use the registry settings mentioned previously.

Using the Visual Studio Debugger IDE

Now that you have a good understanding of how the Visual Studio debugger works, it's time to introduce you to some of the Visual Studio debugging windows. As you'll see, there is much more debugging functionality in Visual Studio .NET than in VB.Classic.

Using the Immediate/Command Window

This window is the equivalent of the VB.Classic Immediate window, but it now operates in one of two modes. The *Immediate* mode is for controlling your application. It gives you facilities similar to those provided in VB.Classic's Immediate window, allowing you to execute VB statements, evaluate expressions, and view variable values. The *Command* mode is for controlling Visual Studio. It allows you to execute Visual Studio commands directly, and even gives you access to commands that aren't on any Visual Studio menu. The current window mode, either *Immediate* or *Command*, is always displayed in the window title.

Switching Modes

To switch from *Immediate* to *Command* mode, enter **>cmd**. The greater-than (>) character is an instruction telling the window that what follows next is a Visual Studio command, not a VB expression. Once you are in *Command* mode, you will see the **>** character preceding all of your commands, in a similar manner to a DOS window.

To switch back from *Command* to *Immediate* mode, use the **>immed** command. At this point, the **>** character will disappear. If you want to issue a Visual Studio command while remaining in *Immediate* mode, simply prefix the Visual Studio command with the **>** character.

Using Immediate Mode

If you're using Visual Studio 2002, one of the first things you may notice about *Immediate* mode is that IntelliSense has disappeared. This is a disappointing regression from what was possible with VB.Classic. The good news is that if you upgrade to Visual Studio 2003, codenamed Everett during its beta phase, IntelliSense is back again. Even better, the IntelliSense prompt in Visual Studio 2003 tracks the most recently used member and defaults to that member. So if you type **?TextBox1.Text**, then **.Text** will be the default text box member that pops up the next time that you use IntelliSense on **TextBox1**. This can save you a surprising amount of time, especially because it's also implemented in the Source window.

One other major difference between the Visual Studio and VB.Classic Immediate windows is that when your program is in design mode, the Visual Studio .NET Immediate window can't evaluate any expressions. So whereas in the VB.Classic Immediate window you can enter the design-time expression **? 1+2** and expect to see the answer **3**, all you would see with Visual Studio is a helpful error message saying "The expression cannot be evaluated while in design mode". This happens because the VB.Classic Immediate window supports the VB interpreter when in design mode, but the Visual Studio Immediate window doesn't support the VB .NET language compiler unless your program is already running.

Provided your application is in break mode, the Immediate window operates in a very similar fashion to the VB.Classic Immediate window. You can print variable values and evaluate expressions using the question mark (?) character. For example, typing **? [object instance]** gives you a tremendous amount of information about the object in question. Figure 3-4 shows the Immediate window during a debugging session.

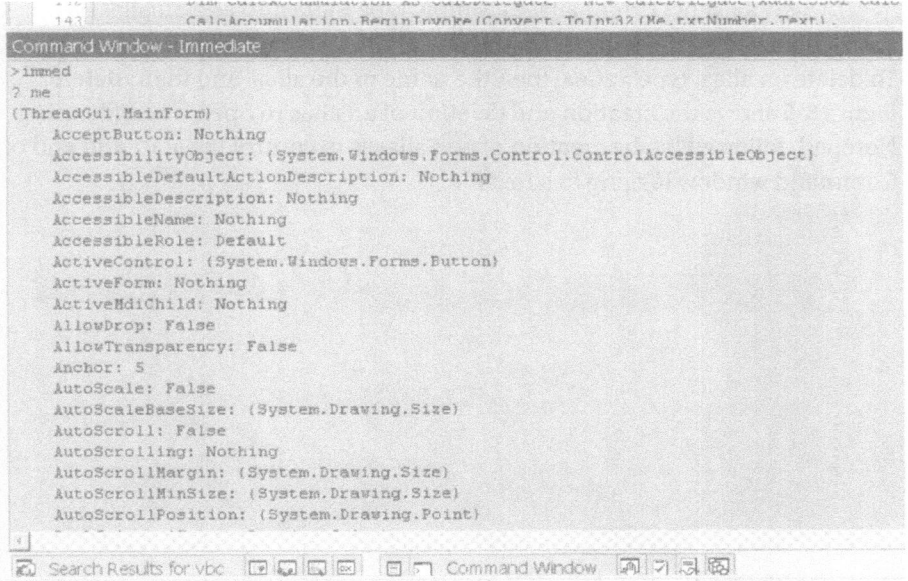

Figure 3-4. The Immediate window during a debugging session

You can also call any functions that are within scope, which gives you ample opportunity to add debugging hooks into your application. For instance, if you want to check the validity of the items within a collection, it's trivial to write a function to walk the collection and print any problems, and then call this function directly from the Immediate window.

This can be a very useful debugging aid, although there is a minor caveat. You should beware of invoking functions that call into unmanaged code or that block in some way, or that create a deadlock with code that is currently executing. In these cases you're unlikely to see correct function evaluation and you may cause Visual Studio itself to become unstable.

Using Command Mode

In *Command* mode, you have access to Visual Studio menu commands and macros. While this is very helpful for the keyboard-centric developer, perhaps the best feature is that you can alias commands down to a few letters. Visual Studio comes with its own predefined list of aliases; for instance, **nf** is the alias for the menu option **File.NewFile**, which brings up the New File dialog window. Another example is **>immed**, which is actually an alias for **Tools.ImmediateMode**. These aliases are a major help for those repeated lengthy commands that would otherwise need a fair amount of mouse movement or typing.

To view a list of current aliases, simply type **>alias**. To add an alias, type **>alias** followed by the command and any arguments taken by the command. To delete an alias, type **>alias**, then the name of the alias, and then **/delete**. Figure 3-5 shows the creation and deletion of an alias to open a text file using Notepad, followed by the creation of two aliases to control the start and end of Command window logging to a text file.

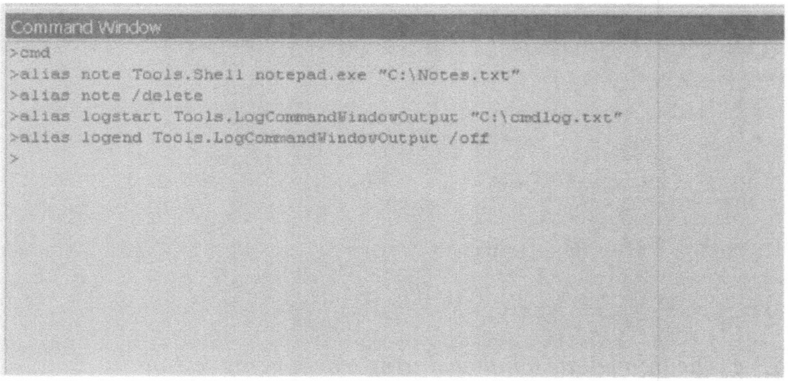

```
Command Window
>cmd
>alias note Tools.Shell notepad.exe "C:\Notes.txt"
>alias note /delete
>alias logstart Tools.LogCommandWindowOutput "C:\cmdlog.txt"
>alias logend Tools.LogCommandWindowOutput /off
>
```

Figure 3-5. Aliasing in the Command window

Navigating the Immediate/Command Window

You can use the up arrow and down arrow keys to scroll through previous commands, but these keys do not move the cursor to previous commands like they did in the VB.Classic Immediate window. Instead, they repeat the previous command at the current cursor position, in a similar fashion as the up arrow and down arrow keys work in a console window. You can also select, copy, and paste text into the window (the documentation refers to this rather confusingly as *Mark mode*). To do this, simply click a previous line in the window and perform the select, copy, or paste.

As a final tip, you can clear the Command/Immediate window with the **>cls** command.

Using the Output Window

The Output window is useful for recording the results of various Visual Studio operations. It is divided into multiple panes accessed from a drop-down menu at the top of the window. The most commonly used panes are likely to be the Build pane, which records the result of program build operations and any errors, and the Debug pane, which records output from the **Debug** and **Trace** commands, assertion failures, and module load/unload information. Figure 3-6 shows some of the information written to the Build pane after compiling a program.

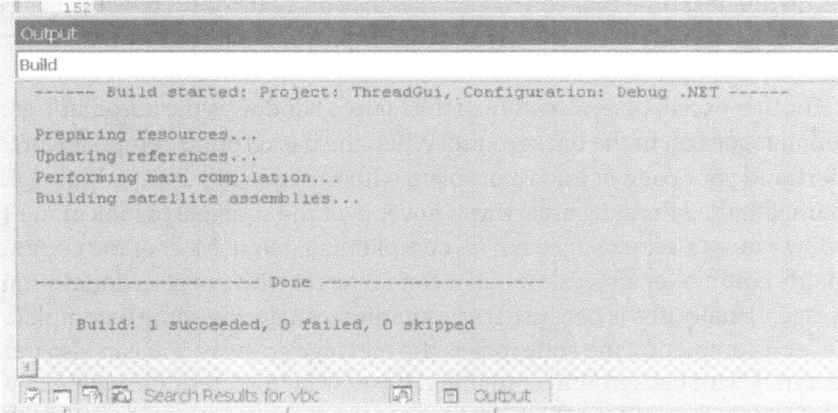

Figure 3-6. The Output window showing program compilation information

You can also tell batch files and other external tools that normally send results to the DOS window to instead send their output to custom panes in the Output window. You do this with the Tools ➢ External Tools ➢ Use Output window option. If you use SQL Server as part of your applications, the output from stored procedures that you call interactively using Server Explorer is also displayed in the Output window.

You can even use the Visual Studio automation facilities to write code to create your own Output window pane and then add to it any text you want. This could be useful, for example, when dividing your debug/trace reporting into different levels of severity.

Using the Source Window

VB .NET's Source window may look superficially similar to its VB.Classic ancestor, but this similarity conceals many new features.

DataTips in the Source window have been improved somewhat over their VB.Classic counterparts. In debug mode, if you hover the mouse over a variable, you can see its current value if it's in scope and its declaration if it's out of scope. You can also see a function's current return value, but only while that function is actually executing. Just as with VB.Classic, you can select and highlight any valid expression and see its value using a DataTip. This also works when evaluating properties, but not for function evaluations.

Just as with the Immediate window, the IntelliSense prompt in Visual Studio 2003 tracks the most recently used member and defaults to that member. So if you type **?TextBox1.Text**, then **.Text** will be the default text box member that pops up the next time that you use IntelliSense on **TextBox1**. This can save you a surprising amount of time, although this improvement is unfortunately not available in Visual Studio 2002.

Another excellent new feature of the Source window is the automatic compilation that goes on in the background. When the background compiler can't understand your code or finds a problem with the code, it puts a red squiggle underneath the offending area. If you hover over the squiggle or look in the Task window, you can see exactly what it's complaining about. Most of the comments are fairly comprehensible, although it can come up with the occasional strange message. Usually this is because it's prematurely analyzing some incomplete code, and completing the code makes the message go away. You can also perform a neat trick with background compiling. If you want to determine where in your code a certain method is called, simply comment out the method and you'll then see a red squiggle under every statement where that method is invoked. If you're using Visual Studio 2003, you can also set the Source window to show procedure line separators just like VB.Classic by going to the Tools menu and selecting the Options ➢ Text Editor ➢ Basic ➢ VB Specific property page, then selecting the "show procedure line separators" option. Unfortunately, this option isn't available in Visual Studio 2002. If you're confused by the new Visual Studio keystrokes for all of the old favorites such as single-stepping, jumping to and from a procedure, and so on, it's very easy to set all of these back to their VB.Classic equivalents. Go to the Visual Studio Start page (the House icon on the Navigation toolbar), select "My profile" and set the Profile setting to Visual Basic Developer.

Another improvement helps you to view source code easier. Pressing Ctrl-R twice toggles the line wrap in the Source window as well as several other IDE windows. This is very convenient when the automatic source indenting forces a line of code too far over to the right side of the window. If you really want to devote the maximum possible screen real estate to viewing and typing source code, the keystroke Shift-Alt-Enter maximizes the Source window and removes all of the other IDE windows. Repeating the keystroke returns the IDE back to its normal display. Figure 3-7 shows the maximized Source window.

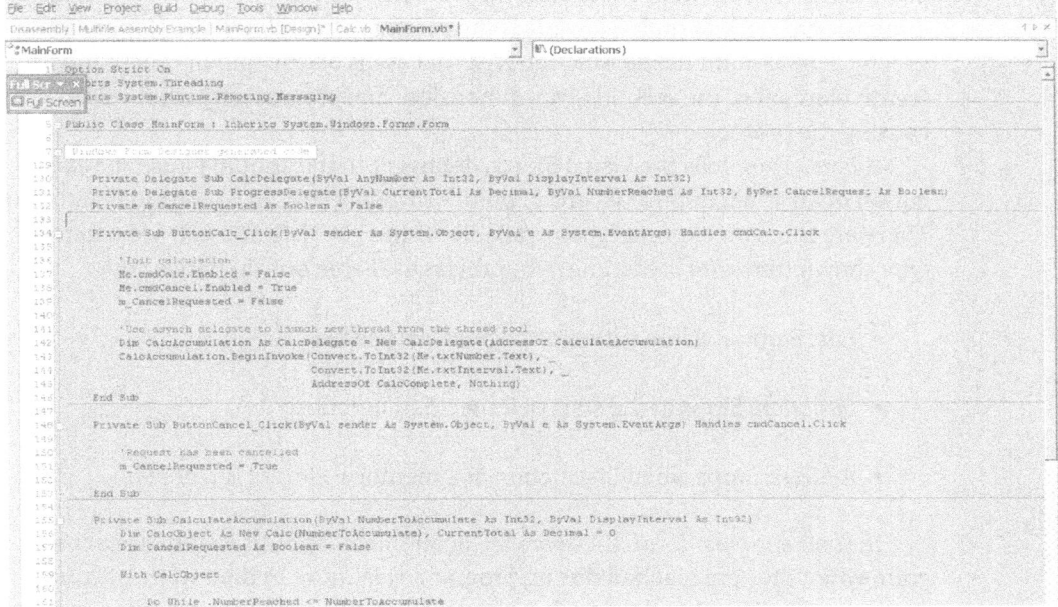

Figure 3-7. Source window maximized using Shift-Alt-Enter

It's easy to show line numbers for any source module. Simply go to Tools ➢ Options ➢ Text Editor ➢ Basic ➢ General and check the "Line numbers" option.

You can store fragments of source code for later copying and reuse by selecting the source you want to copy and simply dropping it onto the Visual Studio Toolbox. The source code is stored in the toolbox as a text item, and you can then easily paste it into another location.

Finally, you can create your own customized source comments. Go to Tools ➢ Options ➢ Environment ➢ Task List and you can add to the system-defined TODO, HACK, and UNDONE comments. When you add one of these custom comments to your source code, it will show up automatically in the Comments view of the Task window. You can use the Task window together with the Source window to synchronize code with associated notes and tasks that need to be done. Typically you're juggling many mental tasks as you code and debug a program, and the Task window helps to reduce some of this mental workload.

Using Breakpoints and the Breakpoints Window

Breakpoints are at the heart of debugging and really bring the practice out of the Dark Ages. In olden times, a developer had to debug a program by sprinkling trace statements liberally through the source code and then indulging in fanciful postmortem speculation about how function XYZ coped with processing a three-dimensional array of nulls. Nowadays the modern streamlined developer can specify a breakpoint inside function XYZ that stops on the population of the fifteenth element of the second array dimension, and view exactly what value is causing the problem.

A *breakpoint* tells the Visual Studio debugger that it should pause the execution of an application at a certain point or when a certain condition is satisfied. There are three breakpoint types available within VB .NET. You will see a fourth type shown (the *data* breakpoint), but this is available only in native code.

- *File:* Stops at a line within a specified source file

- *Function:* Stops at the start of a specified function

- *Address:* Stops when instruction at a memory address is reached

In their simplest form, these are all location breakpoints that pause a program when they are reached during program execution. In their more advanced form, the conditions under which breakpoints cause a halt in program execution can be modified to allow fine-tuning of your debugging.

You can set a *file* breakpoint by clicking to the left of a line of code in the Source window, or by pressing F9 when positioned on a source code line, or finally by right-clicking a line and selecting the Insert Breakpoint menu option. To set a *function* or *address* breakpoint, go to the Debug menu and select the New Breakpoint menu option. Figure 3-8 shows the New Breakpoint dialog window when a new function breakpoint is being added.

You can also disable breakpoints without actually removing them. This is very useful when you don't want to trigger a breakpoint at the current moment, but don't want to lose that breakpoint's position in case it's needed later.

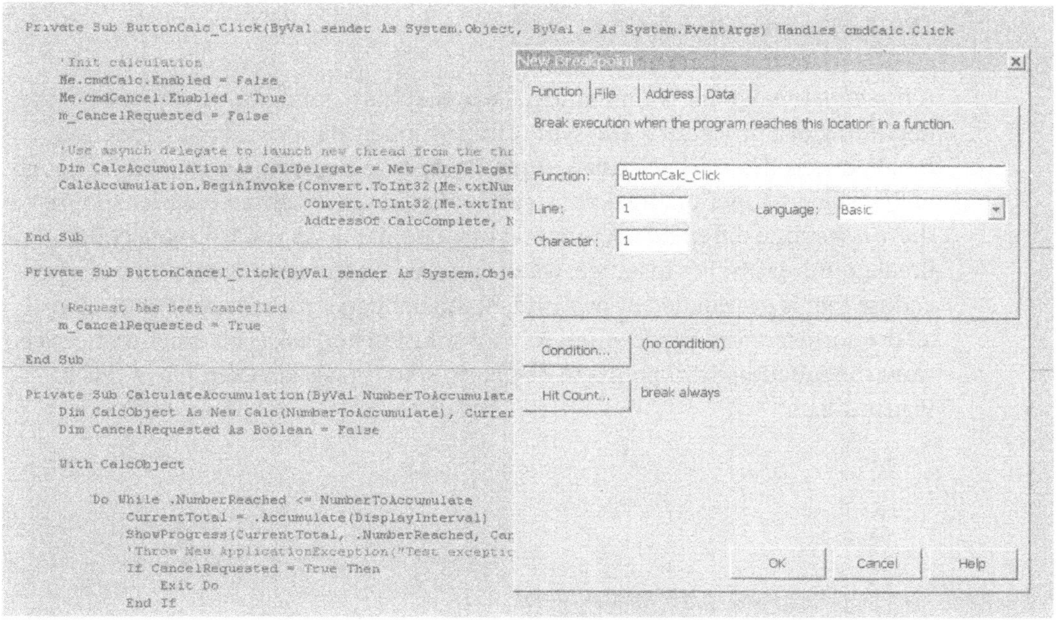

Figure 3-8. Adding a new function breakpoint

Using Simple Breakpoints

The simplest types of breakpoint are location breakpoints, of which there are three types.

Using a File Breakpoint

A *file* breakpoint specifies a break at a line and character position within a source file, and it is the only sort of breakpoint available to VB.Classic developers. The syntax that uniquely defines a simple file breakpoint is **[Pathname and Filename, line xxx character x]**. The pathname, filename, and line number are self-explanatory. You can normally leave the character number at the default of 1, but you could set it to a different number if there are multiple statements on a single line. You would then specify the character number that marked the beginning of the statement where you wanted the program to pause.

Using a Function Breakpoint

A *function* breakpoint is similar to a file breakpoint, but it is always placed at the beginning of a procedure. The syntax that uniquely defines a simple function breakpoint is [**Namespace.Class name.Procedure name and signature**]. Though at first sight, a function breakpoint just looks like a specialized file breakpoint, there is a subtle difference. A function breakpoint allows you to create child breakpoints easily. For instance, when you create a function breakpoint in a procedure that is overloaded or overridden, the debugger presents you with a list of all the corresponding procedures in your solution and asks you exactly where you want the function breakpoints to be placed. You can see an example of this in Figure 3-9.

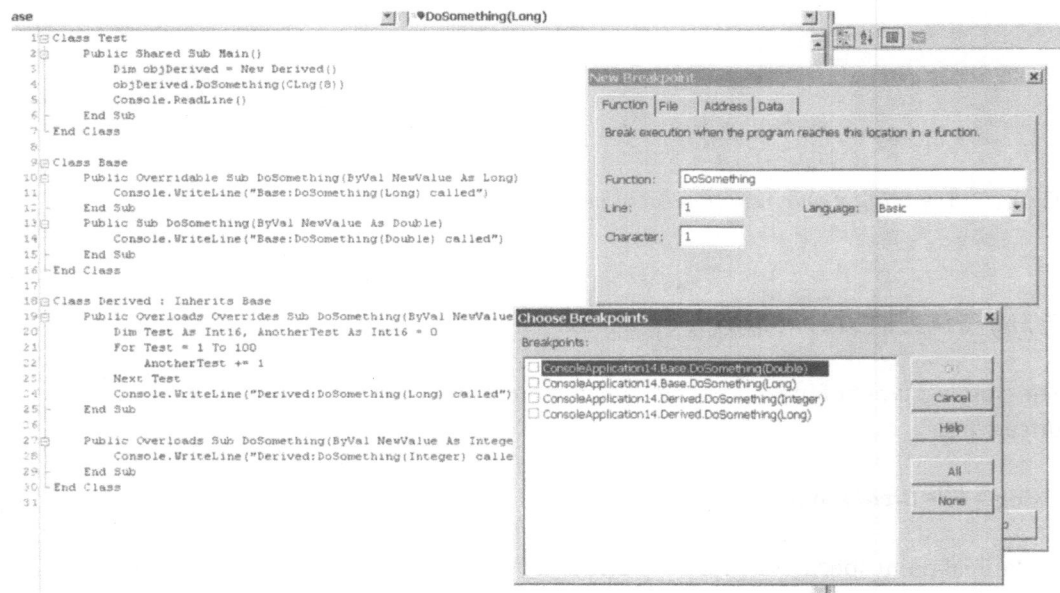

Figure 3-9. Adding a function breakpoint to an overloaded class member

Using an Address Breakpoint

You can set an *address* breakpoint from the New Breakpoint menu option on the Debug menu, which launches the New Breakpoint dialog window. An address breakpoint is a way of asking the debugger to break into your program when it hits an instruction at a specific memory address. Most VB .NET developers won't do any assembler-level debugging. My advice is that if you're trying to solve a problem that requires using one or more address breakpoints, you're probably going too deep. The problem with these forays into the darkest depths of memory is that they can take an inordinate amount of time and often raise more questions than they answer.

In most cases, it's significantly quicker and cheaper to work around the problem at the source level. Try using a different source construct or rewriting the code in question to work in a different manner, and resist the temptation to embark on a potentially endless chase through recursive rabbit holes. There's no way to make this type of quest sound like a good thing.

Using Advanced Breakpoints

You can set advanced breakpoints by adding one or two modifiers to the location breakpoints discussed previously. These modifiers allow you to fine-tune the exact behavior of a breakpoint so that you can go straight to a bug without having to track it down by laboriously single-stepping through your code.

Using the Hit Count Modifier

When the problem that you're investigating is happening inside a loop or in a procedure that's called many times, the hit count modifier allows you to specify that a breakpoint will only trigger after it's been hit a certain number of times. You can specify the number of times by clicking the Hit Count button in the New Breakpoint dialog window or the Breakpoint Properties dialog window. This button gives you a choice of selecting to break after a breakpoint has been hit exactly x times, x times or greater, or finally a multiple of x times. When the debugger stops at the breakpoint, the Breakpoints window will tell you how many times the breakpoint has been hit. Figure 3-10 shows this in action.

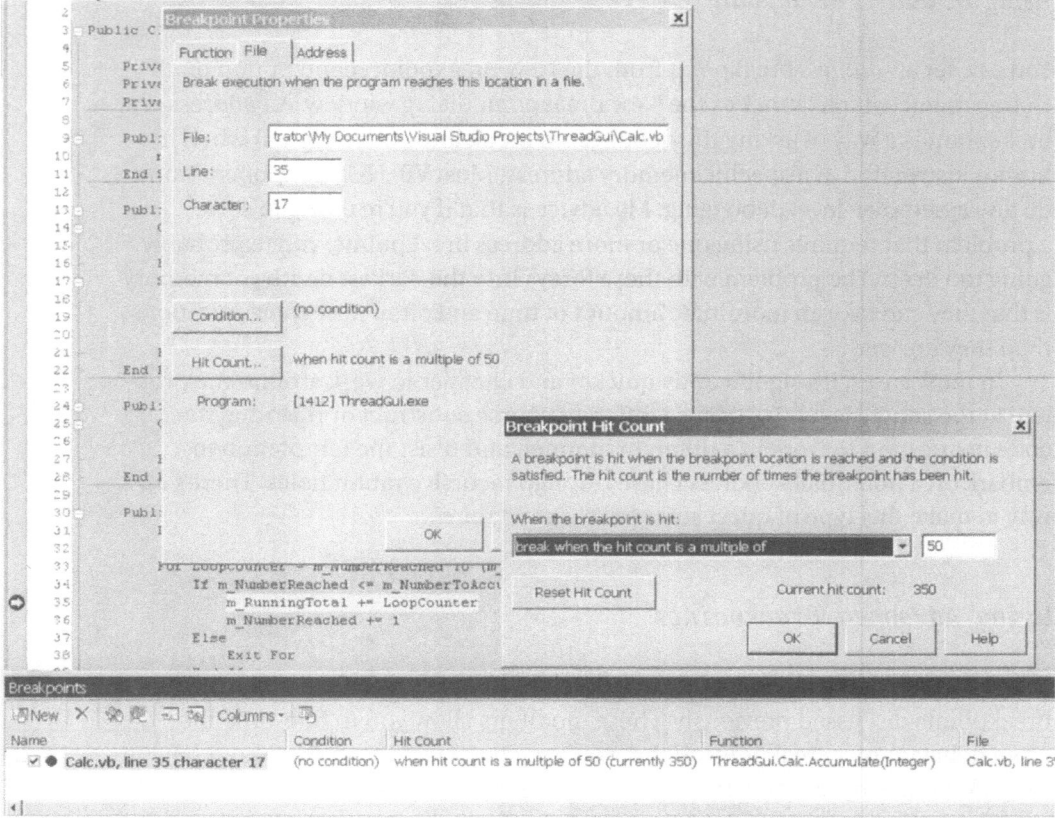

Figure 3-10. A breakpoint with a hit count modifier

This adds several tricks to your debugging arsenal. For instance, if you have a loop that's crashing but you don't know on which iteration the exception is occurring, simply set the hit count to a number larger than the maximum loop index. When the exception happens, looking at the Breakpoints window will tell you the number of times that the breakpoint was hit and therefore the loop iteration. Another tip is that if you always want a break to happen, but you still want to keep track of the hit count, set the hit count to break when it's a multiple of 1.

If you were accustomed to using skip count in the Visual Studio 6.0 debugger, you should note that single-stepping over a breakpoint now increments the hit count—this behavior has changed since version 6.0.

Using the Conditional Expression Modifier

The second type of modifier for a location breakpoint is the conditional expression. This type of breakpoint is useful when you want the breakpoint to trigger only when the conditional expression that you specify evaluates to **true**, or alternatively when the evaluation of the conditional expression has changed since the last time the breakpoint was hit. One important caveat to be aware of is that the conditional expression is evaluated only when the breakpoint is actually hit—some developers find it more intuitive to think of the expression being evaluated after every statement, but this of course is not correct.

You specify the conditional expression that you want the debugger to evaluate by clicking the Condition button in the New Breakpoint dialog window or the Breakpoint Properties dialog window. This button shows a dialog window that allows you to enter a conditional expression and specify whether the breakpoint should trigger when that expression evaluates to **true** or when the evaluation changes. Figure 3-11 shows a breakpoint that will only trigger if the Shift key is held down when the breakpoint is hit. This particular conditional breakpoint is useful when debugging events that contain drawing code, as discussed in Chapter 7.

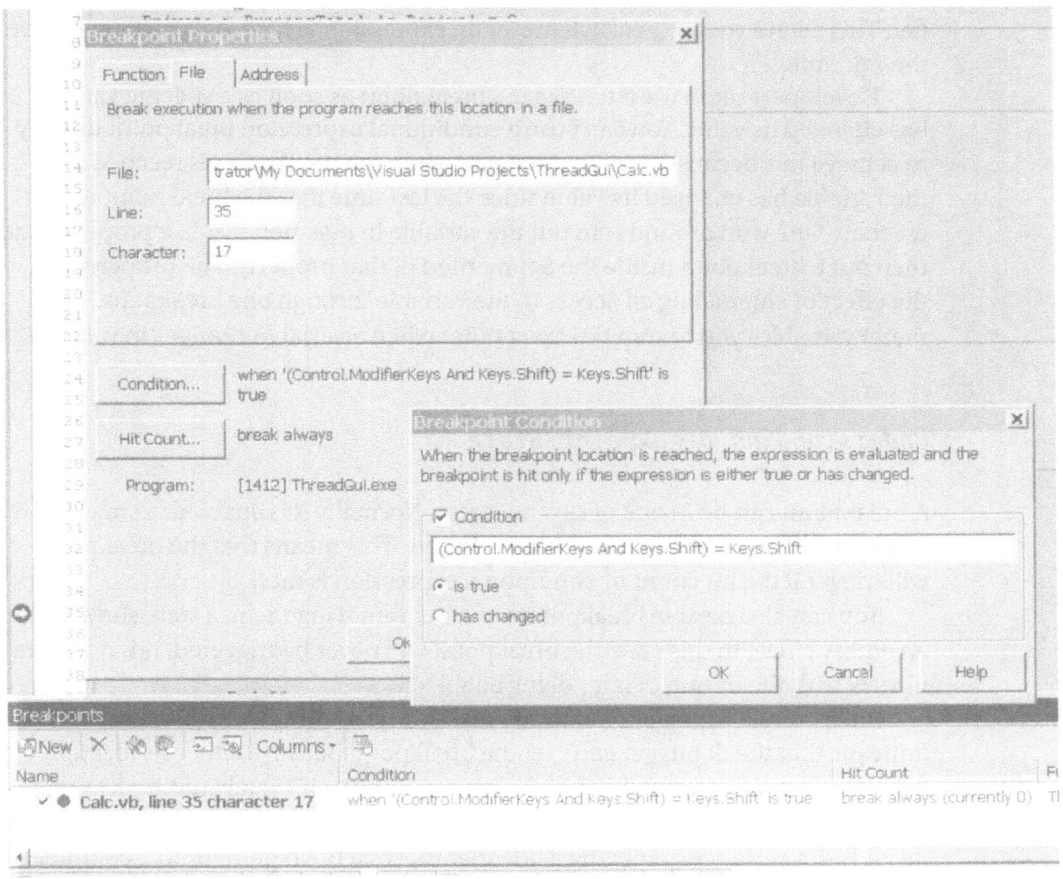

Figure 3-11. A breakpoint with a conditional expression modifier

All variables and functions within the current scope can be used in the conditional expression, including overloaded functions. Inheritance trees are fully supported within conditional expressions. So if you have an object **Tiggles** of type **PersianCat**, derived from type **Cat**, the expression **Tiggles.Color** will return the correct value for an object of type **PersianCat**.

There are some restrictions on conditional expressions. Local constants aren't supported for some reason. You should also be careful about including a function, as the function will actually be executed and any side effects of that function, such as changing a global variable, will be triggered. This can lead to your program changing state and producing unexpected results. The Visual Studio documentation provides a list of keywords that aren't supported in conditional expressions—the most notable of these is probably **AddressOf**. Although you can use simple casts, casting using **CType** isn't supported. Using properties is supported, but as with functions, you should beware of causing unintended side effects. The final restriction is that you can't call a Web service method in a conditional expression.

You can combine a hit count modifier with a conditional expression modifier. This allows you to break whenever an expression is **true**, or has changed, for the nth time.

Developers often want to trigger a breakpoint as soon as a specific variable has changed its value. You can't use a conditional expression breakpoint directly to achieve this because it will only trigger when the breakpoint is reached and the variable has changed its value since the last time that the breakpoint was reached. One workaround is to put the variable in question inside a property, and then put a breakpoint inside the **Set** method of that property. The property has the effect of channeling all access to the variable through one breakpoint, and thereby enables you to trap the exact point when a variable changes in value.

Understanding Breakpoint State

A breakpoint can be in one of several states. Normally it is enabled, a state shown as a dark red circle in the appropriate window. This means that the breakpoint will trigger if the hit count or conditional expression is met.

You can also disable breakpoints without removing them, a state shown with an empty circle. In this state the breakpoint will never be triggered, but it will stay in view with the option of later being enabled.

A dark circle with an exclamation mark (!) symbolizes an invalid breakpoint. It means that the debugger can't set the breakpoint because either its location or its conditional expression is invalid. This can happen if Visual Studio picks up source file changes made outside of Visual Studio that make a current breakpoint invalid—for instance, removing a line that moves a breakpoint onto a comment. It also happens if you specify an invalid conditional expression for that breakpoint.

A dark circle with a question mark (?) is warning you about a breakpoint that won't currently be hit. This usually happens when you set a breakpoint in source belonging to a DLL that won't be loaded until some point after the program has started. The debugger allows you to set these breakpoints in the source, but it isn't able to validate and set the actual breakpoint in the executable until the DLL in question has actually been loaded during the program run.

Finally, a full circle with a diamond inside stands for a mapped breakpoint. This is where you have set a breakpoint in ASP code and the debugger has set a corresponding breakpoint in the generated HTML page.

During a debugging session, the breakpoint marked in bold in the Breakpoints window is the one that caused the current pause in program execution. Figure 3-12 shows the Breakpoints window in action.

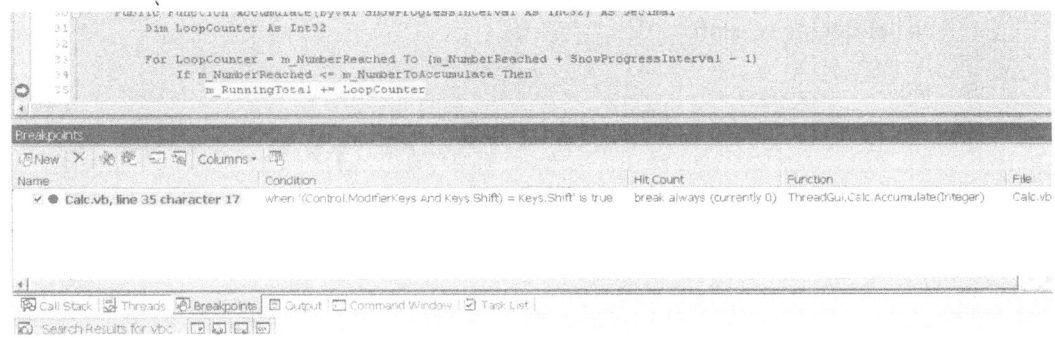

Figure 3-12. Using the Breakpoints window

Breakpoints are carried forward from session to session because they're stored in the solution's .suo file. This is a big improvement over VB.Classic, where you lost your breakpoints as soon as the current debugging session was closed.

Using the Watch Windows

A Watch window allows you to keep a close watch on variables or expressions that you think are important for whatever problem you're investigating. It's more specific than the Me, Locals, and Autos debugging windows that I discuss later, because you have full control over which variables and expressions are displayed in the window.

After breaking into an executing program or pausing it at a breakpoint, you can drag either a variable or a highlighted expression from the Source window to a Watch window, or you can type a variable name or expression directly into a Watch window. From this point on, the debugger continuously monitors and evaluates everything that you place in the Watch window. This is useful because many bugs can be tracked down to the execution of multiple interacting statements rather than just a single statement, so the Watch window helps you to keep an eye on important data as it flows through your code.

If a variable or expression in a Watch window drops out of scope during debugging, the Value column displays a message to this effect because it can't display the actual value. When you've finished debugging, all Watch variables and expressions are saved in the .suo file associated with a solution, which enables you to carry over your watches from one debugging session to the next.

There are four Watch windows available to you, which means that you can logically separate different parts of your debugging problem as you see fit. You can also use a Watch window to edit variable values directly, a facility that's very useful for checking multiple scenarios during a single testing run. Figure 3-13 shows some variables and expressions being evaluated in a Watch window during a debugging session.

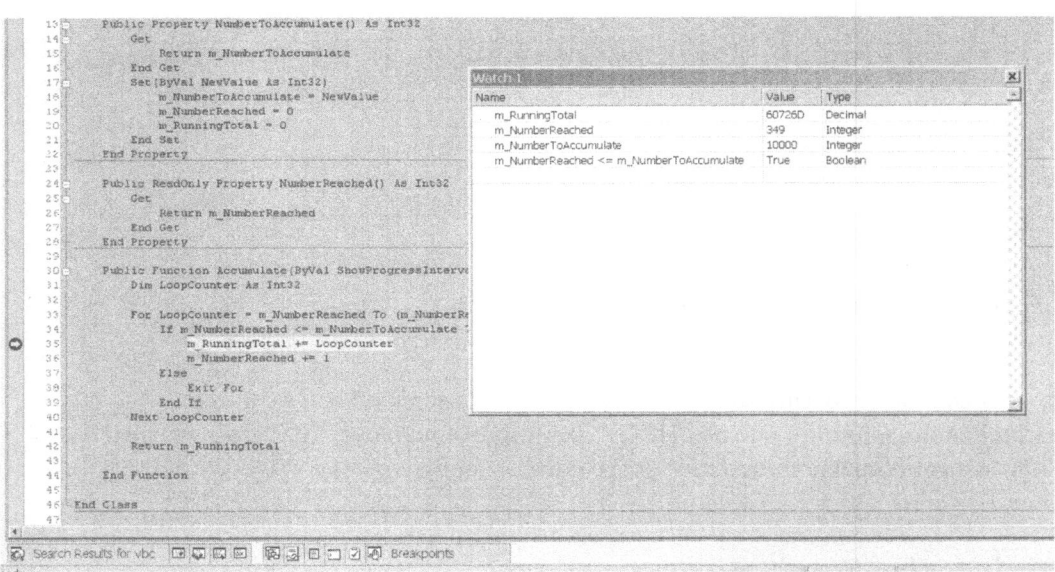

Figure 3-13. Using a Watch window

Be wary about the side effects of placing an expression into a Watch window, because it will be executed every time you step from one line to the next and the debugger re-evaluates the expression. If an expression, property, or method performs an action that you don't want to happen repeatedly, you should avoid placing it in a Watch window.

Using the QuickWatch Window

The QuickWatch window is the baby brother of the Watch window. It's a modal window suitable for evaluating just a single expression or variable, though it has a history list that you can use to repeat previous quick watches. Figure 3-14 shows this window in action.

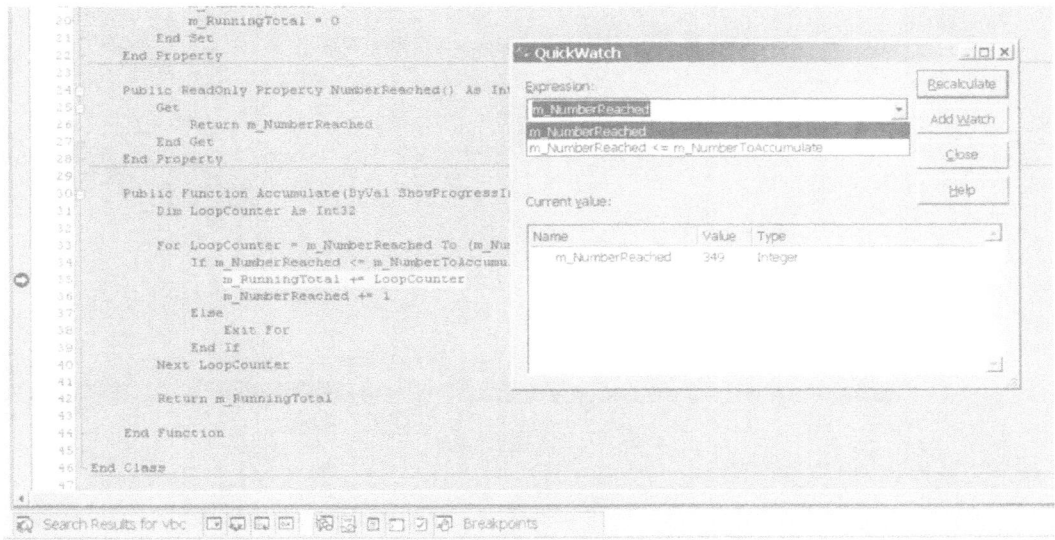

Figure 3-14. Using the QuickWatch window

Using the Locals Window

The straightforward and boring functionality of the Locals window is to display all variables local to the current context. Its more interesting functionality is to switch the current context temporarily so that you can look at other parts of the program.

You can switch context either by using the Debug Location toolbar to select a different function, thread, or stack frame, or by double-clicking a thread in the Threads window or a stack frame in the Call Stack window. To resume the current context after examining other contexts, simply step forward in the debugger and the Source window will switch back to the current context and continue execution as normal. It's fairly common for other parts of the program to be critical to the current context, so this ability to switch contexts while inspecting your program is very useful. Figure 3-15 shows the Locals window during a debugging session.

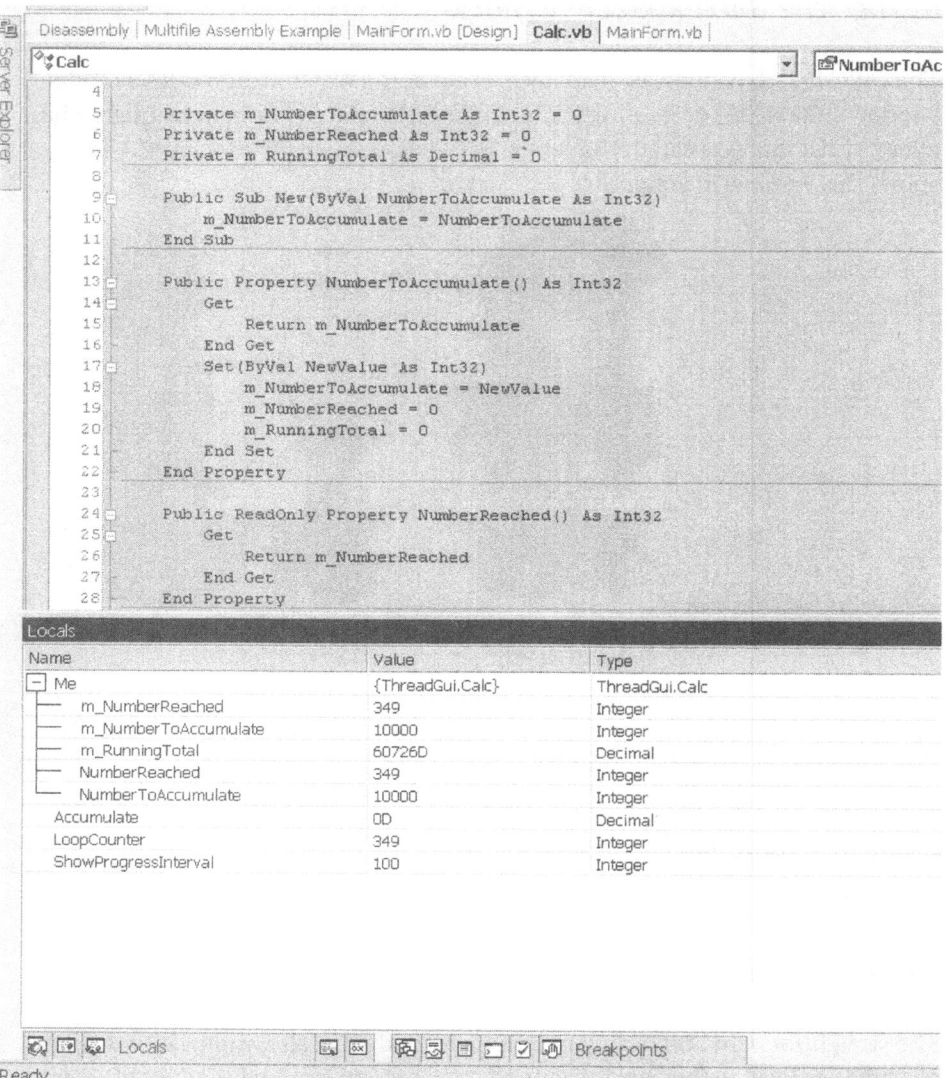

Figure 3-15. Using the Locals window

To view and modify variables in the Locals window requires the debugger to be in break mode. Although information does appear in the Locals window during program execution, this information won't be current until the program stops on a breakpoint or you choose to break the program using the Break All command on the Debug menu. The Locals window in Visual Studio 2002 shows any type of object member, but in Visual Studio 2003 the private members of an object instance are hidden.

One feature of the Locals window is that when stepping through your application, the value of any variable that has changed since the last debugger step is shown in red. You can also double-click a variable's value to modify it. This is useful when you want to test a scenario or correct a value without having to change code and restart your application.

Using the Autos Window

The Autos window is a minimal version of the Locals window. It displays variables that are part of the current statement and three statements before and after the current statement. You can edit the value of variables shown in this widow by double-clicking the Value column, but you should be careful about entering a valid value for the variable type and also about entering floating-point values that might be subject to decimal-to-binary conversion inaccuracies. Just like the Locals window, the Autos window in Visual Studio 2002 shows any type of object member, but under Visual Studio 2003 it doesn't show an object instance's private members. Figure 3-16 shows the Autos window during a debugging session.

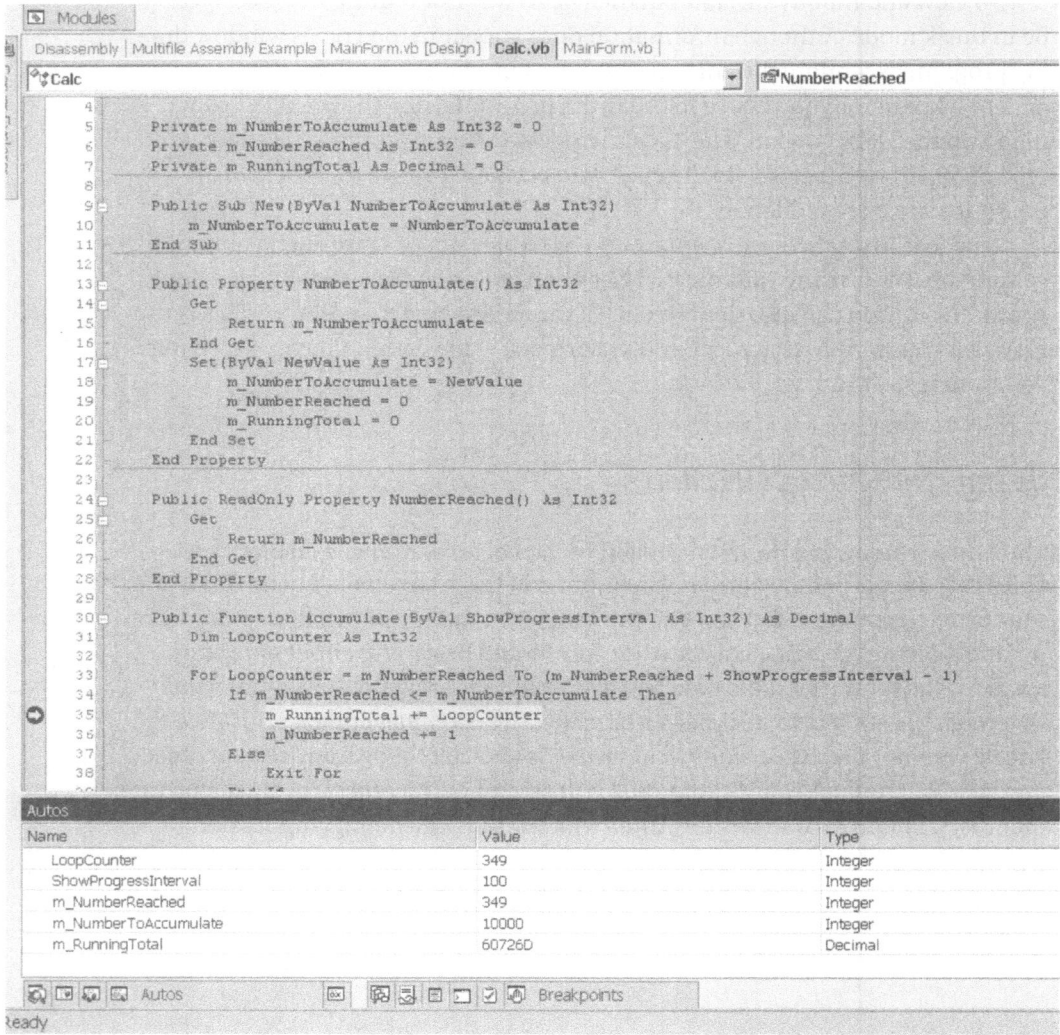

Figure 3-16. Using the Autos window

One useful feature of the Autos window is that when stepping over a function call, it shows the return value of that function and any other functions called by that function.

Using the Me Window

This is a convenient window that automatically displays the members of the current object instance. Like the Autos window, it allows you to edit the values of these members, with the same validity restrictions. Figure 3-17 shows the Me window in use during a debugging session.

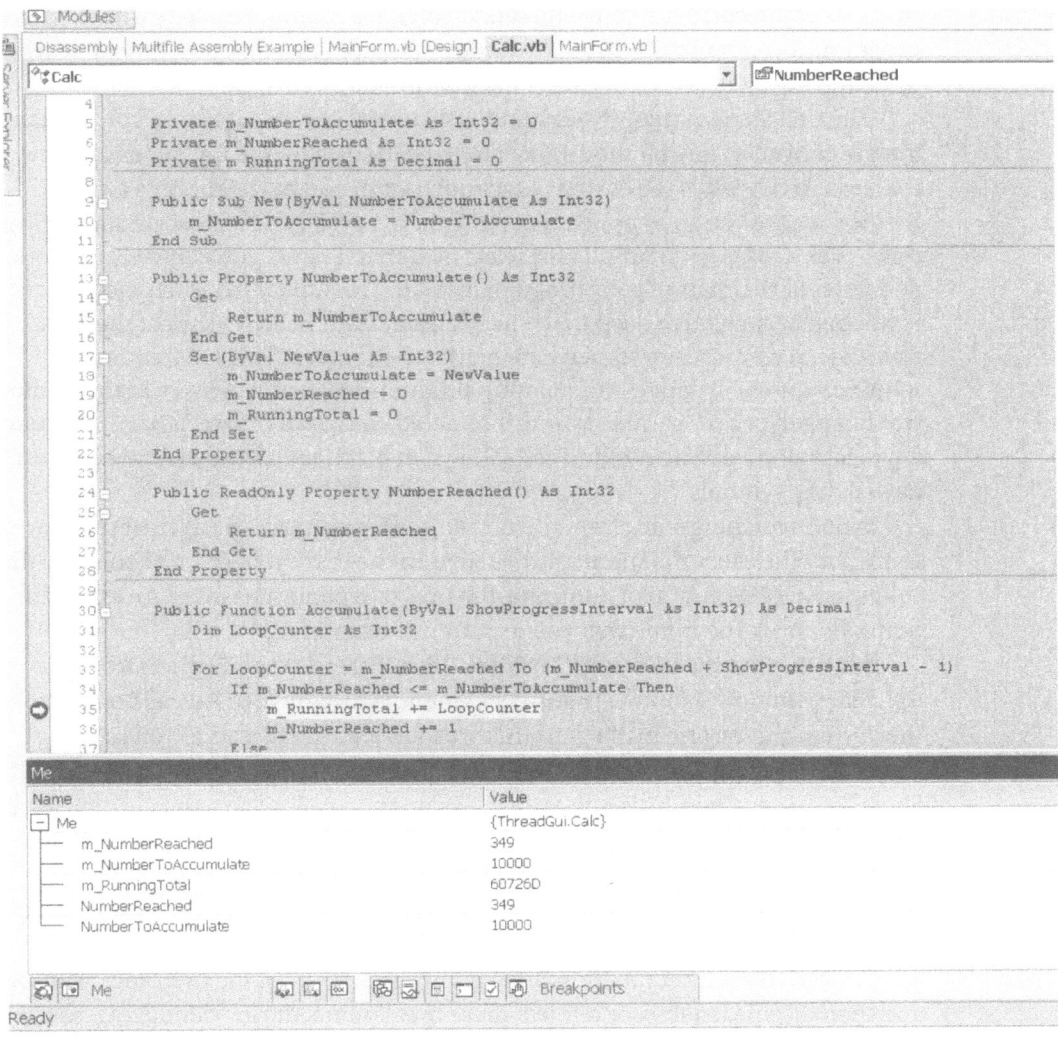

Figure 3-17. Using the Me window

Using the Call Stack Window

The Call Stack window shows you the list of active procedure calls within the thread that's currently executing. It's called a "call stack" because every time a method is called in your code, that method is pushed onto a stack held in memory. When that method finishes execution, it's popped off the stack, and so on for every method called within your application. Therefore, the call stack at any period in time always shows the list of procedures (otherwise known as stack *frames*) for the currently active thread. If you have multiple threads within your program, you can use the Threads window to switch to a different thread, whereupon the Call Stack window shows the new thread's active call stack.

The Call Stack window is tremendously useful because it allows you to examine the context of any method shown in the call stack. In the Call Stack window, a yellow arrow shows the current execution point, and by default this is the method whose variables appear in your Watch, Locals, and Autos windows. If you right-click a different method and select Switch to Frame, you can view the code and data for that part of your program instead. This ability to switch methods is invaluable when you're deep down in a call stack but need to inspect the data and state of a procedure somewhere higher in the stack. This is a frequent requirement when you're investigating situations such as where a variable's value was changed or how various events interacted with each other. Figure 3-18 shows a typical call stack. The method calls shown in black are methods for which you have debug symbols.

When switching stack frames, you can see a green triangle against the new frame, but the execution point always stays in the current frame, as shown by the yellow arrow. If you step or continue, the program continues from the execution point, not from the frame that you're currently examining.

Selecting the Include Calls To/From Other Threads menu option from the Call Stack window's context (right-click) menu adds any method calls made to the current thread and by the current thread to another thread. If you're using Visual Studio 2003, the context menu also gives you an additional option called Show Non-user Code. This option displays method calls within the current stack for which you have no debug symbols, such as .NET Framework class methods. These method calls are shown in gray rather than the normal black. Other context menu options allow you to view method line numbers together with method parameter types, names, and values.

Finally, you can set function breakpoints directly from the Call Stack window, and then disable, enable, or remove these breakpoints during debugging. An active function breakpoint in the Call Stack window shows as a solid red dot in the left margin next to the method name.

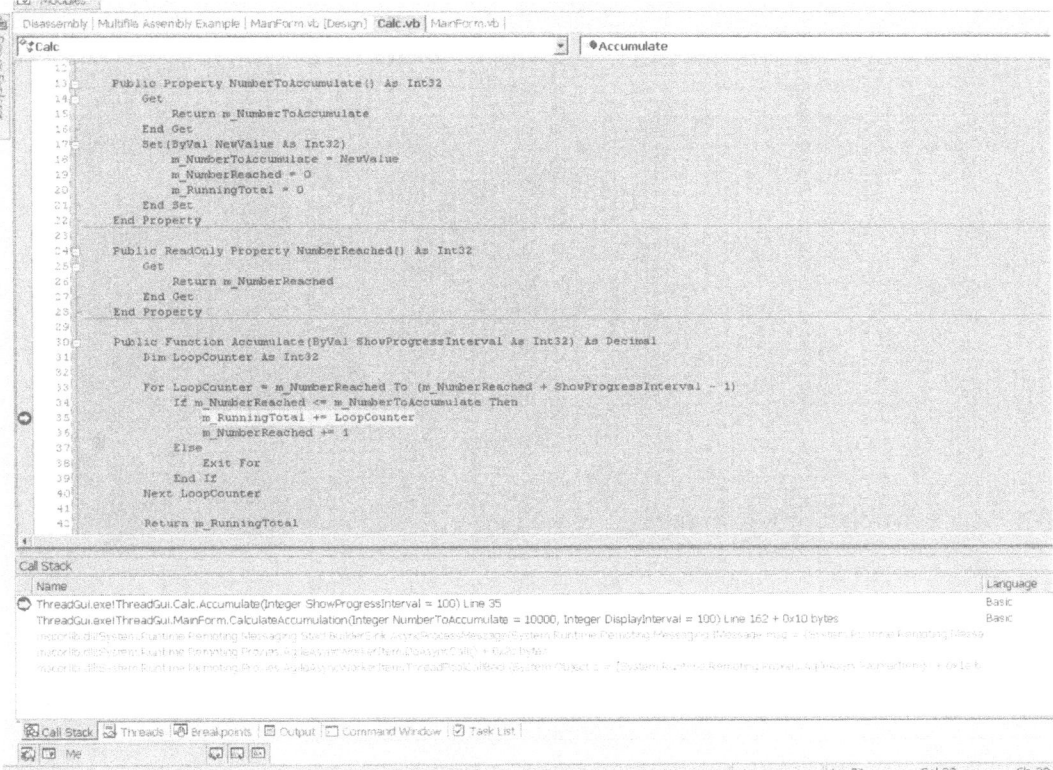

Figure 3-18. Using the Call Stack window

Using the Modules Window

The Modules window shows you extensive information about each of the components loaded by your application. Modules in this context include your application's executables, class libraries, control libraries, and dynamic link libraries (DLLs). Both managed and un-managed modules appear in the Modules window, in the order that they're loaded by your application.

This information is invaluable for finding component location and version issues. Because the Modules window shows the version, load path, and time-stamp for every loaded module, it's easy to diagnose when the wrong module is being used, especially if you adopt the useful practice of assigning an identical version number and timestamp for every module in a release of your application. Because .NET can run different versions of the same component side-by-side, debugging version and location issues is likely to be more important than in the COM world. Figure 3-19 shows the Modules window in action.

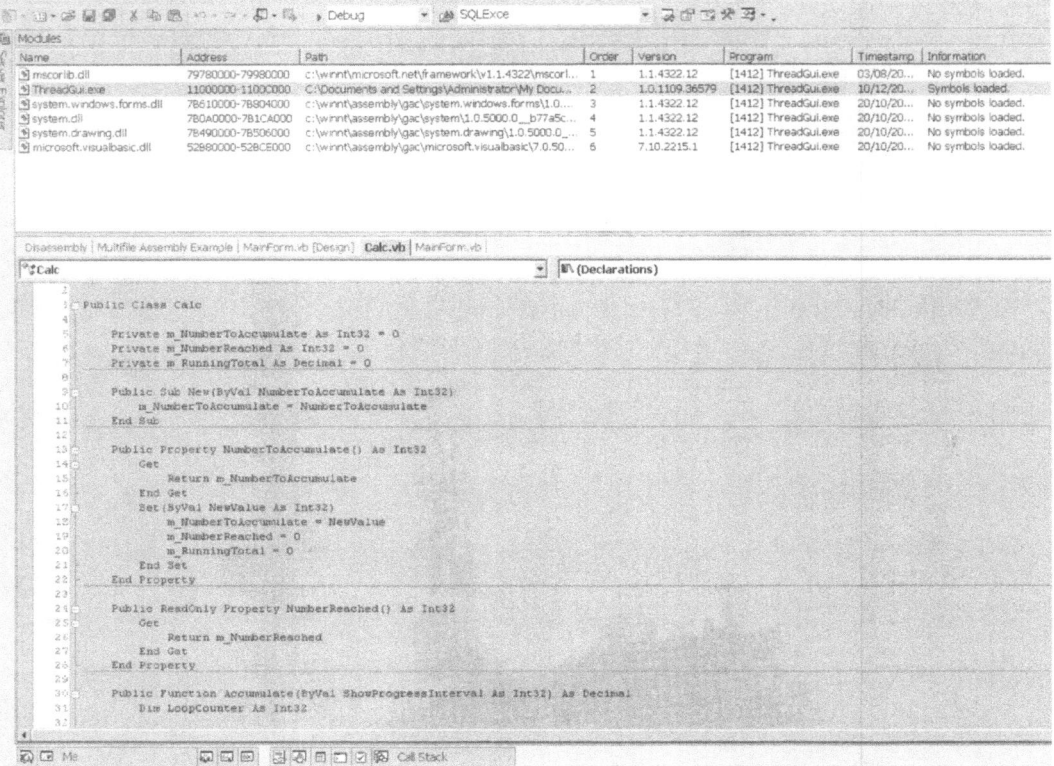

Figure 3-19. Using the Modules window

Perhaps the most useful information, especially when you do remote debugging, is the column showing whether a module's debug symbol file was loaded. As discussed previously, debug symbols are produced during language compilation and written to a file with a pdb suffix. Without matching debug symbols for each component in your application, your breakpoints won't be triggered and you won't be able to do any real debugging. If the Modules window shows that the debugger hasn't loaded a module's debug symbols, you can tell the debugger where to find the correct .pdb file by right-clicking the relevant module and selecting the "Reload symbols" menu option. If you have a set of modules whose debug symbol files are all located in the same folder, you can select multiple modules together and go to "Reload symbols". At this point, the debugger asks you for a folder and then tries to match each of the modules with a corresponding debug symbol file.

To switch between looking at just the modules loaded for the current assembly and looking at the modules for every assembly in your application, you can toggle the "Show modules for all programs" context menu switch by right-clicking in the Modules window.

Using the Disassembly Window

The Disassembly window shows you the processor-native code being executed for each statement in your source code. Although this window is rarely useful for most VB .NET developers, it can come into its own if you're investigating a particularly low-level problem such as one related to code optimization. Figure 3-20 shows this window in action.

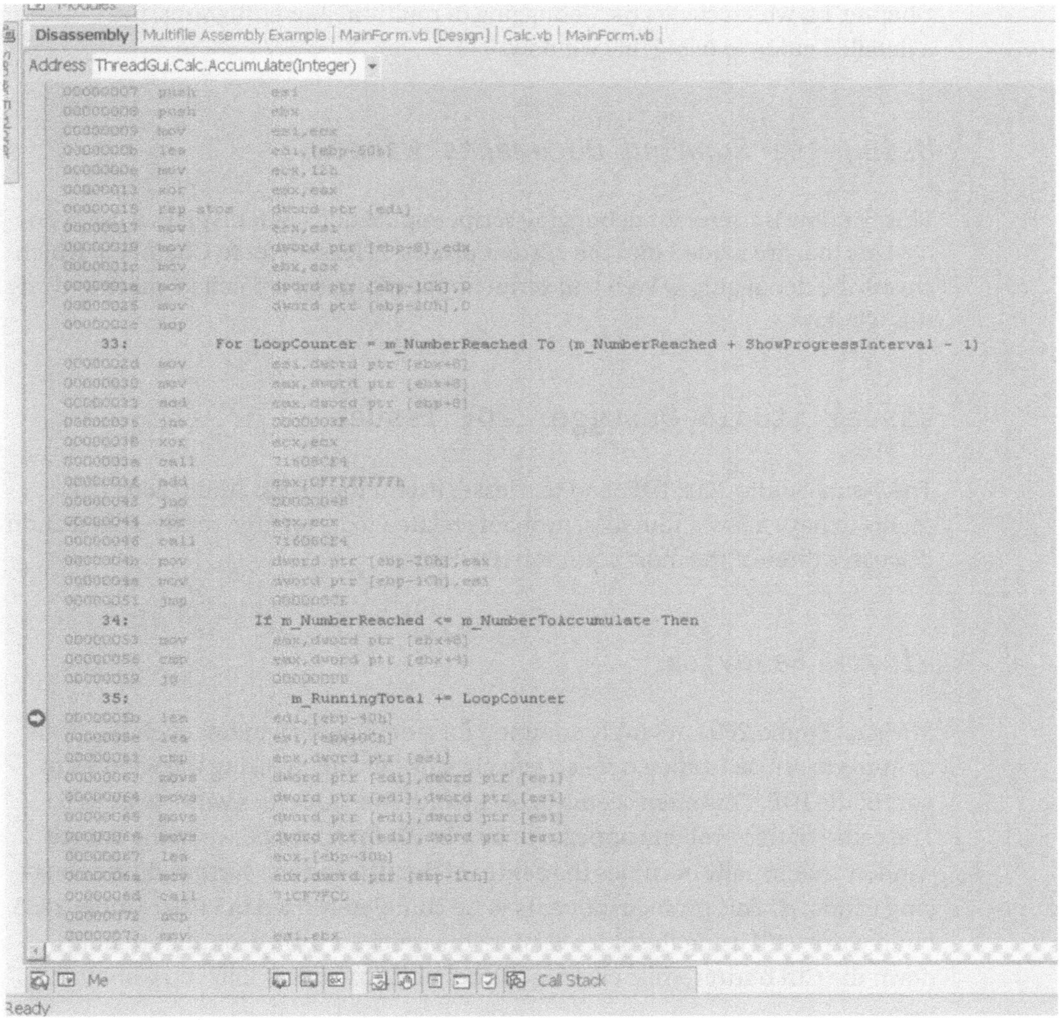

Figure 3-20. Using the Disassembly window

In my opinion, the Disassembly window would be more useful if it showed source code with corresponding CIL rather than native code. If you really want to do this, Chapter 4 presents a trick that makes it possible.

Using the Threads Window

When you debug a multithreaded program, the Threads window allows you to view, stop, and start each of the threads in your application. Please refer to Chapter 14, which covers the debugging of multithreaded programs, for a detailed guide to using this window.

Using the Running Documents Window

This window is useful for debugging script applications as it displays a list of documents that are loaded into the current process. Please refer to Chapter 9, which covers the debugging of Web and script applications, for a detailed guide to using this window.

Visual Studio Debugger IDE Issues

The Visual Studio 2002 IDE, and to a lesser extent the Visual Studio 2003 IDE, seems to have a few anomalies, probably related to its relative youth. This section discusses three of the most common IDE issues.

Window Behavior

In Visual Studio 2002, it's fairly common for a debugging window such as Locals or Autos to refuse to appear when you click its tab after docking the window to part of the IDE. This often seems to occur with the Properties window as well. The cause of this problem appears to be a battle for space between the Source window that usually occupies the center of the IDE and the surrounding debugging windows. This problem appears to be completely fixed in Visual Studio 2003, but if you're still using the older version, the quickest fix I've found is to hold down the Ctrl button while clicking the debugging window that you want to display.

Another rather more laborious way of fixing this problem is to unpin all of the other windows docked on that side of the IDE. Then hover the mouse pointer over the offending window and slowly move the pointer toward the edge of the Source window. As you cross the edge of the Source window, you should see the mouse pointer turn into a double-headed arrow, at which point you can drag the edge of the offending window toward the center of the screen, whereupon it will magically appear.

Yet another fix is to find and delete a file called devenv.xml. This file controls many of the IDE settings, including the positioning of the IDE windows. After you delete this XML file and restart Visual Studio, the file is rebuilt automatically and the data corruption within it that caused the window sticking disappears. Suddenly all of your debugging windows will come to life again.

The final fix that I've found for this problem is simply to reboot Visual Studio, although this can be annoying if you have to do it too often because startup speed can be quite slow. If you want Visual Studio to start as fast as possible, there's a trick to this too. First dock the Properties window and autohide it. Then, if you use the Dynamic Help window, dock that too and autohide it. Next, close Server Explorer and the Toolbox window. Finally, on the Start page set the switch marked "Show empty environment". Now when you reboot Visual Studio, you should find that it starts almost instantaneously, because it doesn't have to load the CLR during startup. From a clean desktop, you can press Ctrl-Esc, press R, type **devenv**, and press the Enter key—from zero to Visual Studio loaded in 2 seconds or less.

Interpreting Chr(0)

Debugging windows, such as the Immediate and Watch windows, can become confused about how they represent the values of certain variables. The windows sometimes seem to be marooned somewhere between the native and managed views of the world, and this occurs in both Visual Studio 2002 and Visual Studio 2003.

For example, VB.Classic developers have long had to be careful about how they handle strings containing Chr(0), such as those returned by many Win32 API calls. Chr(0) is the character that C, and therefore Windows by default, uses to terminate strings. So what happens if you create a couple of these strings and then look at them in the Immediate window?

```
Dim strTest1 As String = "123" & Chr(0) & "456789"
Dim strTest2 As String = Chr(0)
```

If you run some tests on these two strings, you can see the following results:

```
? strTest1.Length
10
? strTest1="123"
True
? strTest1
"123
? strTest2.Length
1
? strTest2=""
True
? strTest2=Chr(0)
True
```

The first test result, showing the string's length, looks reasonable. The second test result looks rather strange. The third test result isn't a misprint—printing of the string really does stop as soon as it hits the null terminator, and even the closing quotes are ignored. In a similar fashion, the fifth test contradicts both the fourth and sixth tests.

Debugger Single-Stepping

The Visual Studio 2002 debugger has a nasty habit of sometimes stepping onto a line of code that isn't actually being executed. Although this is irritating, it's thankfully the debugger that's showing you the wrong information and not a problem with the code itself. Often, rebuilding the project or the entire solution fixes the problem. At other times, even this doesn't work and you just have to ignore the debugger's eccentric behavior. This is a known bug caused by the debug symbols information in the .pdb file being emitted incorrectly, and it appears to have been fixed in Visual Studio 2003.

Summary

This chapter introduced you to some of the capabilities of the Visual Studio .NET debugger. After you received an introduction to some of its significant features, you learned about how build configurations and flags affect your ability to debug your programs. Following this, you saw how you can use the debugger to debug processes running both inside and outside of Visual Studio. This flexibility allows you to deal with almost any debugging situation that you're likely to experience.

Finally, you embarked on a comprehensive introduction to the various debugging windows and how you can use them to make your debugging easier. The conclusion that I hope you're drawing is that the power and range of the Visual Studio debugger will allow you to find and fix problems much easier than is feasible with VB.Classic. In later chapters you'll take a more detailed look at some of the Visual Studio debugger features mentioned in this chapter.

INTERLUDE

A DEBUGGING WISH LIST

While investigating the capabilities of the VB .NET IDE in preparation for writing this chapter, I created a wish list of the sort of capabilities that a truly grown-up IDE ought to have to help developers diagnose and fix their bugs. While this wish list might not help with every type of bug, it will certainly give you a deeper insight into your code and probably highlight some problems that would pay for the work involved many times over.

- *Add the ability to step* backward *through code.* Good developers tend to work backward when they debug anyway, and adding debugging support for this would be very cool. Saving every change in state and applying each one in reverse would be fiendishly difficult and probably use much more memory, but think how much easier it would be to track down an incorrect value if you could step backward.

- *Add a tool that would automatically compare trace logs of a program's execution with UML activity diagrams.* This would be an effective way of validating the documentation against what an application is actually doing.

- *Show source code colored by author.* We all know some developers whose code we trust and other developers whose code needs to be handled like a live grenade.

- *Show source code colored by age, with the developer able to specify the date ranges that are of interest.* This helps because old code is usually more reliable than new code, especially new code that's only just gone into production.

- *Use color to show the path of executed code.* This means that during a debugging run, you would easily be able to view the execution path through the entire program. Because a procedure might be executed many times, with a different path each time, there would need to be some sort of color sequence for examining the different paths.

- *Add all of the default brackets and default keywords to make clear the compiler's understanding of what is going to happen when a VB .NET statement is executed.* It seems strange that developers still have to remember all of the language defaults. Making sure that the compiler sees exactly what the developer sees would be invaluable in some cases (see Chapter 2 for some examples of the misunderstandings that can occur).

- *Use lines or background shade variations to delineate clearly the boundaries of Ifs, loops, and other code blocks.* This would be especially useful with nested statements where it can be quite difficult to match up the start and end statements.

- *Apply developer-preferred notation or color to show variable scope.* This is now needed more than ever because VB .NET variables can be local to a block of code as well as to a whole procedure.

- *Have the JIT compiler use color to show the hotspots in executed code.* This could help with subtle (and not-so-subtle) performance bugs, without the need for an intrusive third-party profiler.

CHAPTER 4

Using the Visual Studio .NET Debugger

Now that you've seen the mechanics of the Visual Studio debugger and gained a good idea of its capabilities, in this chapter you'll examine this debugger in more detail and look at some of its more advanced capabilities. The Visual Studio debugger is a complex and powerful beast, so it's worthwhile spending some time investigating its capabilities if you want to exploit its power.

Before you can start debugging any managed or native code that's running under your own user account, you must be a member of either the Debugger Users group or the Administrators group. To do this, go to the Control Panel, choose Administrative Tools ➢ Computer Management ➢ System Tools ➢ Local Users and Groups ➢ Groups, and add yourself to the relevant group.

If you want to debug managed code running under a different user account, you must be a member of the Administrators group. To debug native code that's running under another user account, you must have the SE_DEBUG_NAME permission in the local security policy. By default, the Administrators group has this permission.

Visual Studio Preparation

Visual Studio has a set of debugging options that affect all types of projects. You can find these options by selecting Tools ➢ Options. There are four pages of options, most of which you can leave at their default settings. However, you should understand some of these options in detail, because they can have a big effect on the efficiency of your debugging sessions. This section looks at the more important options.

General Debugging Options

From the Tools ➢ Options menu item, you can find the major settings that control the debugger's behavior on the Debugging ➢ General property page. Figure 4-1 shows the options that you can manipulate from this page.

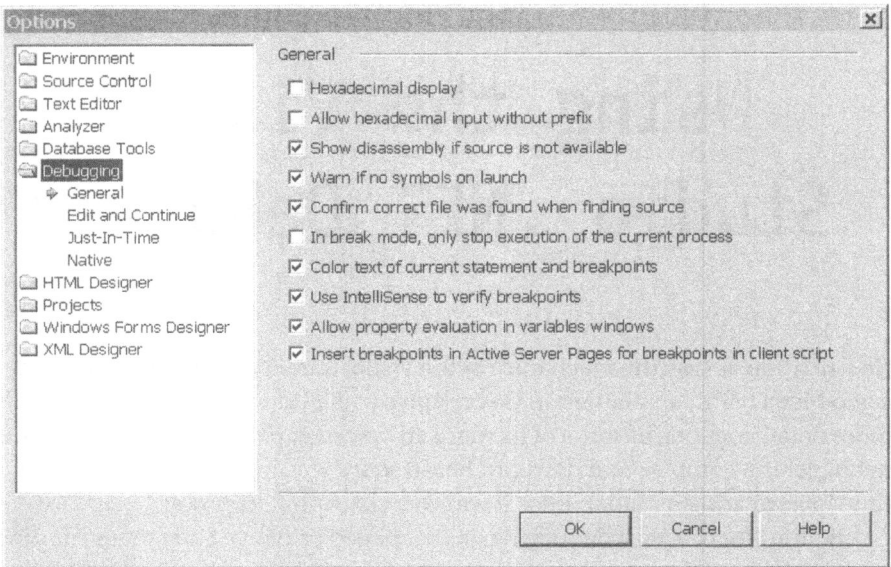

Figure 4-1. The General debugging property page

The "Hexadecimal display" option allows you to display variables in hexadecimal format in the debugging windows such as Locals and Autos. Normally, you won't want to select this option, but it might be useful if you're doing a lot of mathematical work.

"Allow hexadecimal input without prefix" is another setting that you probably don't want to select unless you're doing some significant hexadecimal work. When selected, this option allows you to enter values as direct hexadecimals, without using the ampersand (&) prefix.

There are many reasons why the debugger might not be able to locate source code during a debugging session. One reason occurs when you don't actually have available source code for part of your application, perhaps for a process written by another developer. Another possibility is a security problem, such as when you don't have the right permissions to access a Web application's virtual directory. Whatever the cause, you can ask the debugger to "Show disassembly if source is not available" by selecting the option of the same title. For some reason that's unclear to me, this option is disabled by default. You should also be aware that there are some circumstances where the debugger can't even display the disassembly—for instance, when you're debugging a script and stop on a breakpoint while there are no threads in your program.

You should usually select the "Warn if no symbols on launch" option. It's most useful when you mistakenly try to debug a version of your program that was built in release mode. Without this warning, you can become rather confused when none of your breakpoints are hit.

When you debug your application, the Visual Studio debugger tries to find a source file for each of the binary executables being debugged. The first place it looks is the folder containing the binary, and then it searches through the paths defined on your solution's Common Properties ➢ Debug Source Files page. Because it's possible for the debugger to find ambiguously named or versioned files, it sometimes prompts you to confirm that it's found the correct source files. If you select the "Confirm correct file was found when finding source" option, the debugger has permission to confirm its guesses. If you don't select this option, the debugger just keeps quiet and hopes for the best. Selecting this setting is especially useful when you're debugging in a test or production environment, where the source is unlikely to live in the same folder as the binary.

Many of your applications, especially the distributed ones, are going to contain multiple execution processes. So when you break into an application with a breakpoint or by using the Break button, you want to either pause all of the processes in the application or pause just the single process that you're interested in. Selecting the "In break mode, only stop execution of the current process" option means that just the active debugger process is paused, leaving the rest of the application to continue normally. This can be very useful when one of the processes, such as a Web service, might be used by another application that would otherwise be frozen. Alternatively, you can choose to pause the whole application, which is most likely to be useful when you're investigating a problem that crosses multiple processes.

You should always leave the "Color text of current statement and breakpoints" option selected, as the colors are a great help in finding your way around the source window when you're stopped on a breakpoint.

Another option you should always select is "Use IntelliSense to verify breakpoints." This option allows you to hover over a breakpoint glyph in order to see information about that breakpoint, including the reason why the breakpoint won't be hit if that's applicable.

The "Allow property evaluation in variables windows" option tells the debugger to evaluate all object properties (i.e., members) in the Autos, Locals, and Watch windows so that you can see their values. Although this option is shown as enabled in Figure 4-1, there are two good reasons to keep the option disabled during normal debugging. First, enabling this option can cause unexpected side effects when you have any of the previously mentioned debugging windows open. This is because the debugger automatically evaluates any property displayed in a debugging window by invoking it. This can have the effect of changing the normal execution path of your program, because the code in the property might not have been invoked if the program wasn't running under the Visual Studio debugger. It's really not advisable to have your program behave differently when it's running inside the debugger compared to when it's not. The second reason for disabling this option is when you're doing mixed-mode debugging with both managed and unmanaged code. Making multiple property evaluation calls across into unmanaged code can be very expensive in performance terms.

When you set a breakpoint in a client script, you normally want that breakpoint to be reflected in the corresponding Active Server page that is generated. Selecting the "Insert breakpoints in Active Server Pages for breakpoints in client script" option ensures that this behavior happens.

Edit and Continue Options

From the Tools ➤ Options menu, the options on the Debugging ➤ Edit and Continue property page allow you to control what the Visual Studio source editor does when you edit code during a debugging session. Figure 4-2 shows the options available on this page.

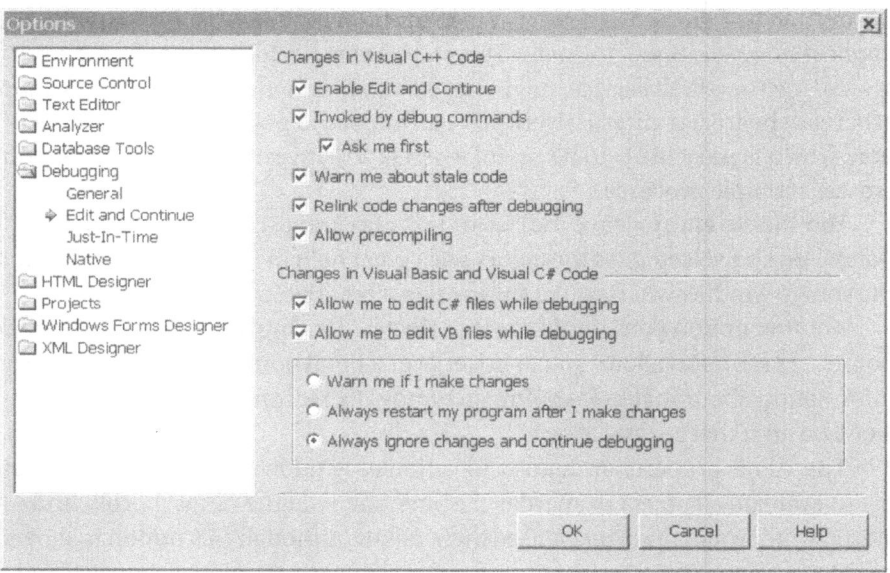

Figure 4-2. The Edit and Continue property page

Most of the options on this page aren't applicable to VB .NET programmers because Edit and Continue hasn't been implemented for the first version of VB .NET (or C#). However, you're allowed to edit your code, with the proviso that your program will continue running with its current code and will completely ignore any new code that you add until you restart the application. Selecting the "Allow me to edit VB files while debugging" option gives you this facility. Bear in mind that this can lead to some really confusing results because the code shown in the source window will no longer match the code being executed. I discuss a workaround for this in the "Coping Without Edit and Continue" section later in this chapter.

In the final frame on this page, you can choose what you want the debugger to do when you edit your VB source code during a debugging run. I recommend using the "Always ignore changes and continue debugging" option because this avoids the annoying message stating that changes won't be applied until after the application is restarted. If you're happy dealing with this message, select instead the "Warn me if I make changes" option.

Just-In-Time Debugging Options

From the Tools ➤ Options menu, the Debugging ➤ Just-In-Time property page shows you some options that affect the behavior of the Just-In-Time debugging process that I discussed in Chapter 3. Figure 4-3 shows this property page.

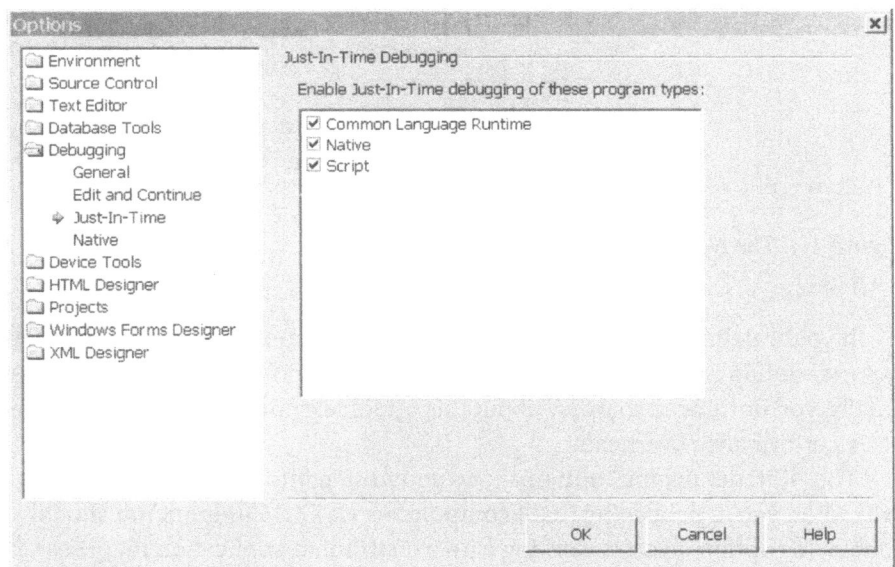

Figure 4-3. The JIT debugging property page

The options on this page allow you to enable or disable the types of code that can be debugged when a program crash is caught by the Just-In-Time debugger. You can specify the setting for managed code and for script. As I pointed out in Chapter 3, you need to have installed Visual C++ .NET in order to specify the setting for native code.

Native Debugging Options

From the Tools ➤ Options menu, the Debugging ➤ Native property page (see Figure 4-4) shows you the debugging options available when you're debugging native Win32 code.

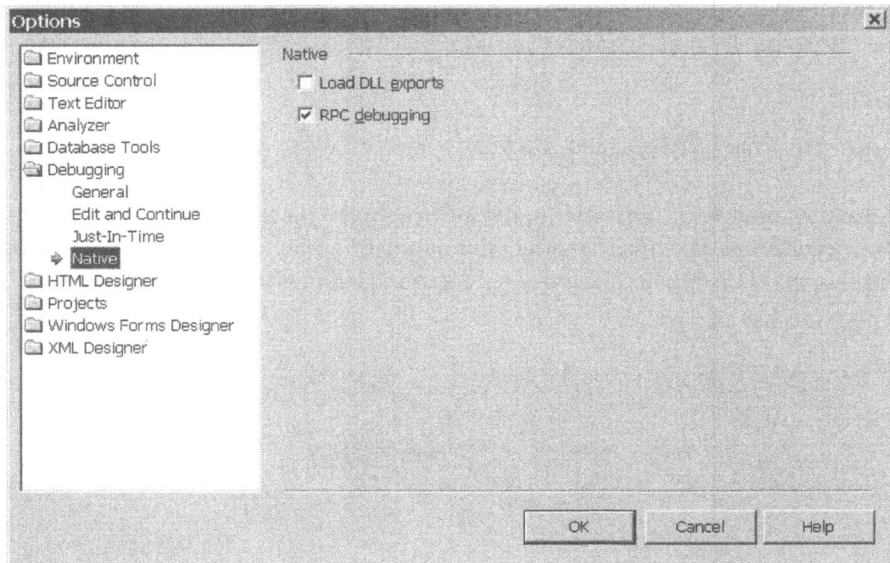

Figure 4-4. The Native debugging property page

If you're debugging Win32 objects that contain export tables, the "Load DLL exports" option will load those export tables. If you don't understand what this entails, you don't need to worry about this option except to deselect it because it has a performance overhead.

The "RPC debugging" option allows you to step into COM remote procedure calls when you're debugging COM components via COM Interop. You should enable this option if you're working with a distributed application that uses COM Interop.

Project Default Options (Visual Studio 2003 Only)

From the Tools ➤ Options menu, the Debugging ➤ Projects ➤ VB Defaults property page shown in Figure 4-5 is only applicable if you're using Visual Studio 2003. This page allows you to specify the default **Option Explicit** and **Option Strict** settings for each new VB .NET project.

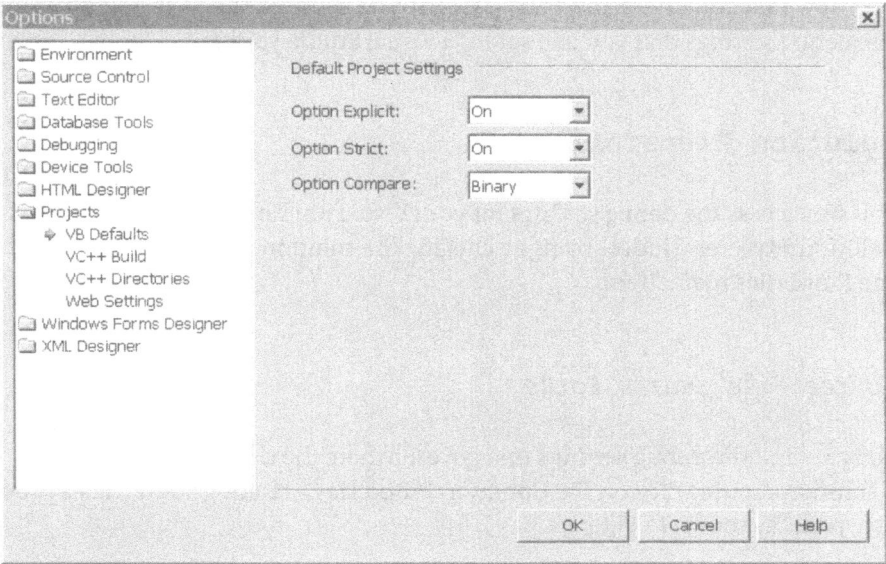

Figure 4-5. The VB Defaults property page

The first option on this property page allows you to specify the default **Option Explicit** setting for every new VB .NET project. Setting this option to "On" requires you to declare every variable in your code before you use it, and I recommend that you always use this setting. It behaves identically to **Option Explicit** in VB.Classic.

The second option allows you to specify the default **Option Strict** setting for each new VB .NET project. I advise you to ensure that this option is *always* set to "On" for absolutely every VB program you ever write. The "On" setting is applied to every new project and finds many type coercion and code ambiguity problems at compile time, as opposed to you having to wait for a runtime error.

The "Project Preparation" section later in this chapter has more detailed information about the effects of these settings.

Other Useful Visual Studio Settings

The final Visual Studio setting to enable is not really debugging related, but it displays line numbers within every source file. This is very useful for locating assertions and exceptions, both of which give you a line number, and it generally makes it easier for you to follow the setting of breakpoints and source code. To enable this setting, select Text Editor ➤ All Languages ➤ General from the Tools ➤ Options menu item, and select the "Line numbers" option in the Display frame.

Now that you understand the Visual Studio settings, the next step is to look at the debug settings that you can set for a Visual Studio solution.

Solution Preparation

You can access the debug settings for your Visual Studio solution from the Solution Explorer window by right-clicking the solution and choosing the Properties menu item.

Source File Search Paths

You can find the debug settings that govern where the debugger searches for a solution's source files on the Common Properties ➤ Debug Source Files property page, as shown in Figure 4-6.

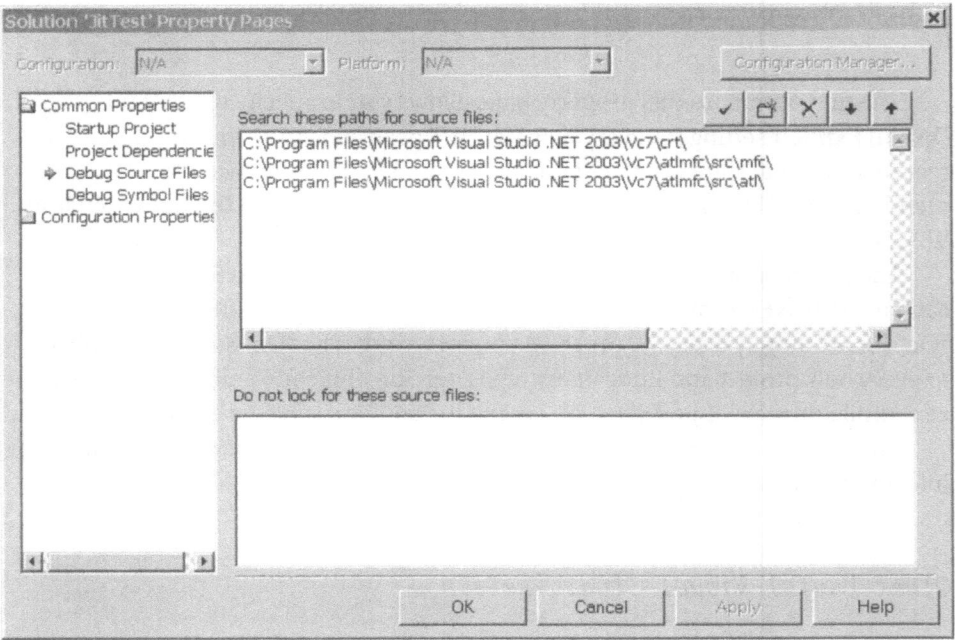

Figure 4-6. The Debug Source Files property page

Using this page, you can specify the paths that the debugger should use when it tries to locate source files for the projects within your solution. If you're debugging your application solely within Visual Studio and with the source code already loaded, you won't have to add any path in this page. If, however, you're debugging any projects where the source code isn't readily available, such as when you're attaching to a process that's already running or when you're debugging software that wasn't created within Visual Studio, you should add every path that the debugger needs to find the solution's source files.

Symbol File Search Paths

You can find the debug settings that govern where the debugger searches for your solution's debug symbol files on the Common Properties ➤ Debug Symbol Files property page, as shown in Figure 4-7.

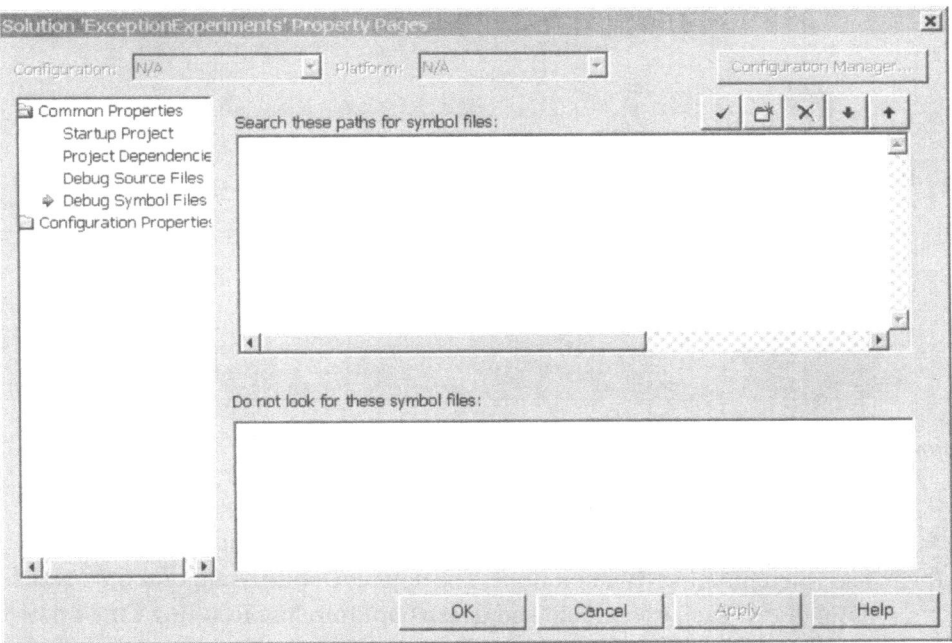

Figure 4-7. The Debug Symbol Files property page

Using this page, you can specify the paths the debugger should use when it tries to find the debug symbol files (those suffixed with .pdb) for each of the projects within your solution. The same criteria apply for specifying paths as those that I just discussed with the Debug Source Files page. For more information on debug symbols and how they work, please see the "Debug Symbols Management" section later in this chapter.

Solution Build Configuration

You can find the settings that govern how your solution is built, and therefore
how easily it can be debugged, on the Configuration Properties ➤ Configuration
property page, as shown in Figure 4-8.

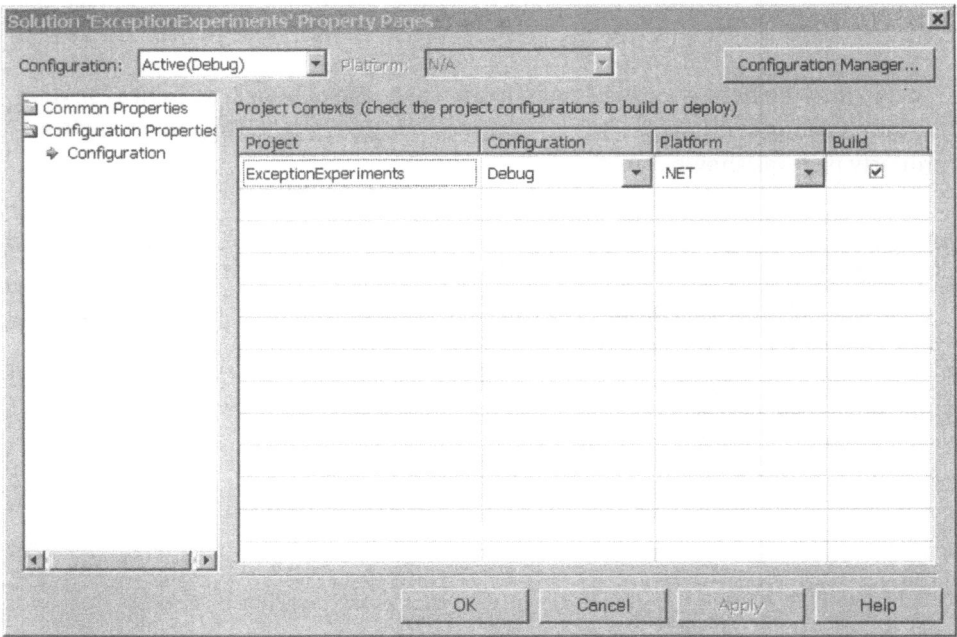

Figure 4-8. The solution Configuration property page

As I described in Chapter 3, there are two standard configurations that you
can use when building your solutions. The default **Debug** configuration creates
a symbol file for each executable and doesn't optimize the resulting CIL or native
code, whereas the default **Release** configuration doesn't generate symbol files
and optimizes the compiled code. This page allows you to alter the behavior of
each of these configurations or to create your own custom configuration. If you
create a custom configuration, you should go to each project's Configuration
page to define what your custom configuration represents for each project.

As an example, I always create a custom release configuration for each of my
solutions. Then I go into each project in the solution and specify that for this custom release configuration, the project should be built with code optimization
and with full debug symbols. This lets me create and release a production program that can be debugged in-place rather than having to go back to the debug
version of the program.

The other useful setting on this page is the Build option. You should uncheck this option for each project in your solution that doesn't need to be rebuilt every time you start a debugging run. I tend to concentrate on changing just one project per session, and therefore I normally use this setting to tell the compiler not to bother with rebuilding the other projects.

Project Preparation

You can reach the debug settings that apply to each of your solution's projects from the Solution Explorer window by right-clicking a project and choosing the Properties menu item.

Project Build Options

You can find some build settings that affect your ability to debug a project on its Common Properties ➤ Build property page, as shown in Figure 4-9.

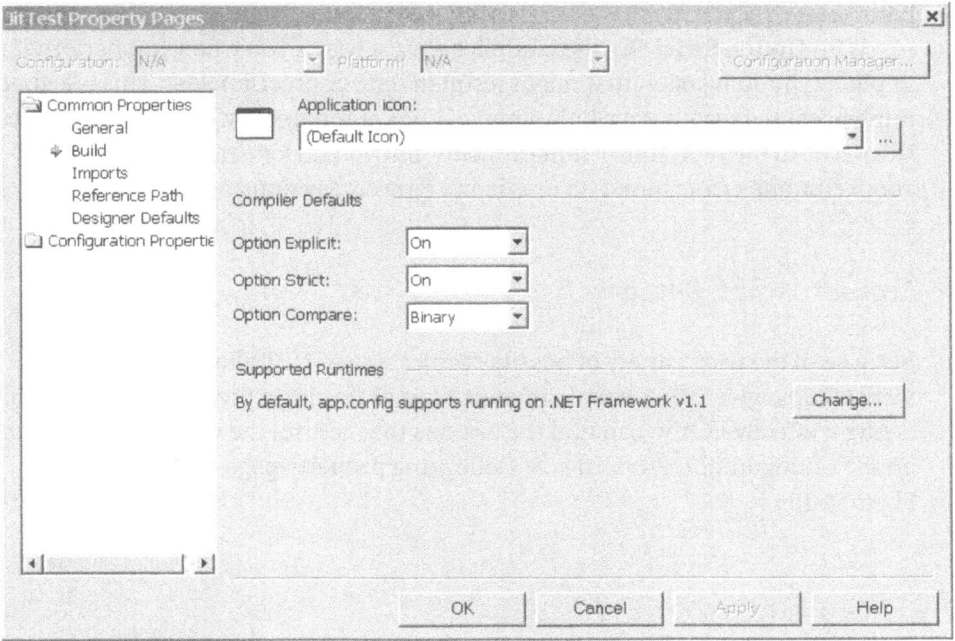

Figure 4-9. The project Build property page

On the Common Properties ➤ Build page, you should ensure that **Option Explicit** is specified as "On" for every project in your solutions. When **Option Explicit** is switched on, you're forced to declare every variable that you use. This prevents you from mistyping the name of a variable in your code and thereby accidentally creating a new variable—with **Option Explicit On**, any mistake like this is automatically flagged by the compiler as an error. **Option Explicit On** can also help you to avoid scoping mistakes. If you try to use a variable outside its scope, the compiler again flags this as an error instead of simply creating a new variable. This becomes especially important now that VB's block scoping rules have changed with the arrival of .NET, and you're able to have two variables with the same name within the same procedure.

On the same property page, you should always switch on **Option Strict** for every project in your solutions. **Option Strict** goes a step further than **Option Explicit** by adding automatic type-conversion checking to your applications. Without this setting, VB .NET allows the implicit conversion of one type to almost any other type, a "feature" that was often called *Evil Type Coercion* in VB.Classic. Examples of this behavior include data loss when converting a numeric variable to another variable of lesser size or precision, nonintuitive results when adding a numeric variable to a string variable that just happened to contain a number, and a runtime error when passing a string argument to a numeric procedure parameter.

With **Option Strict On**, the compiler always warns you when you perform an implicit type conversion that might result in data or precision loss. This is a good thing because it catches a whole genre of bugs automatically. You can, of course, still perform the type conversion explicitly, but you no longer have to worry about runtime errors based on accidental type conversions.

Project Start Options

Because of the wide variety of possible projects that .NET allows you to create, Visual Studio gives you several different ways of starting a project so that you can debug it effectively. You can find the options that control the way a project starts on the Configuration Properties ➤ Debugging property page, as shown in Figure 4-10.

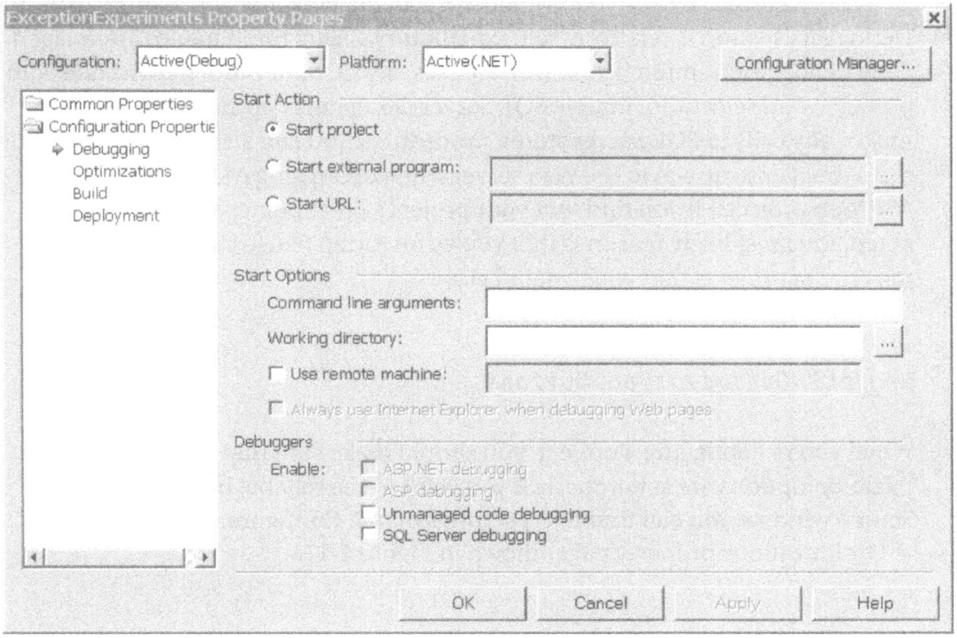

Figure 4-10. The project Debugging property page

On this page, you have the option to start the debugging of your project by using an external program or a URL. An example of when this is useful is for debugging a class library, otherwise known as a DLL. Because class libraries and certain other project types can't be run without being loaded by some other component, this page gives you the chance to specify that component. By default, it assumes that the starting component is already contained within your solution, so you can specify that component with the "Start project" option. Alternatively, you can specify some prebuilt component to start your debugging by using the "Start external program" option. If your project is invoked from a Web site, you can specify the URL by using the "Start URL" option. Finally, if your project is a Web application or a Web service, you are given the option to use the "Wait for an external process to connect" option. This causes the debugger to attach to any process that calls into your project, and any breakpoints that you've created in your project can then be triggered.

The Start Options section allows you to specify any command-line parameters that your project needs. You use the "Use remote machine" setting when you're debugging a program on a remote machine (for more about remote debugging and how to use this option, please see Chapter 15). If you don't select the "Always use Internet Explorer when debugging Web pages" option, Web pages will be loaded into the default Windows browser for debugging.

This page also allows you to choose the debuggers that you want to use—the Debuggers section is relatively self-explanatory. Select the "Enable unmanaged code debugging" option if your project uses any COM or other native code components, and select the "Enable SQL Server debugging" option if your project makes any calls to SQL Server stored procedures. You can also set options that tell the debugger to attach to the Web server when debugging ASP.NET or old-style ASP Web projects. If you find that your project's breakpoints are not being triggered, the most likely reason is that you've forgotten to use this page to specify the type of projects that you're debugging.

Project Optimization Options

When you're debugging a project, you should make sure that the project optimization options are set properly if you want to see reliable behavior in the Source window. You can find these settings on the Configuration Properties ➤ Optimizations property page, shown in Figure 4-11.

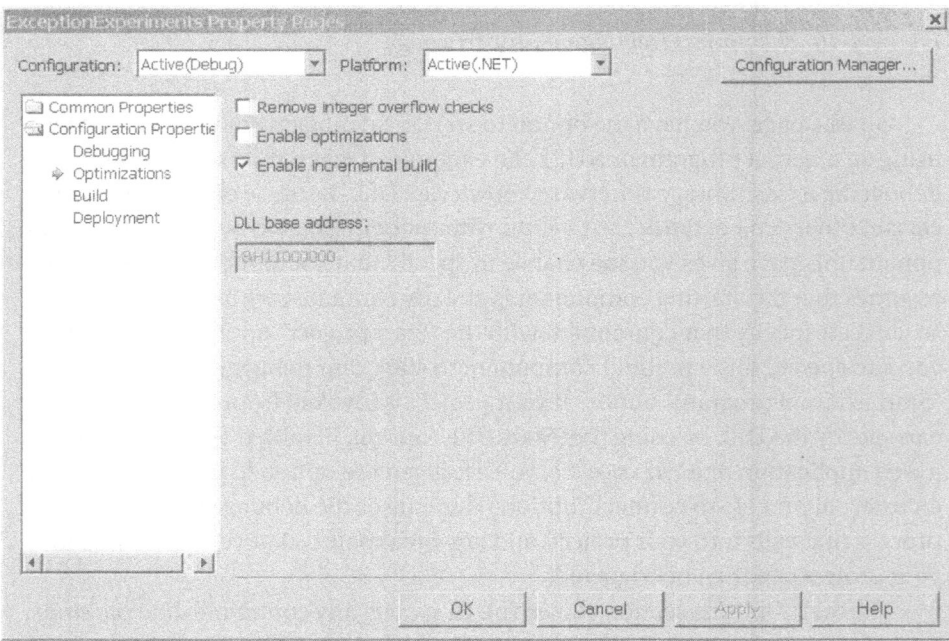

Figure 4-11. The project Optimizations property page

On this page, you can specify the optimizations that you want the VB .NET language compiler to make when building your program. When building in debug mode, you should normally uncheck the "Remove integer overflow checks" and "Enable optimizations" options. Both of these options, if checked, ask the compiler to optimize the generated processor-native code as aggressively as possible. This can cause major problems for the debugger as it tries to work back from the optimized native code to the original source code. The effect of this is that the execution point displayed in the Source window during a debugging run can jump around erratically and be unreliable, which is why it's best to leave both of these options unchecked. For more information on the effects of these settings, please see the "Understanding Code Optimization" section later in this chapter.

Project Build Configuration

You can find the final project properties that you need to consider on the Configuration Properties ➤ Build page, as shown in Figure 4-12.

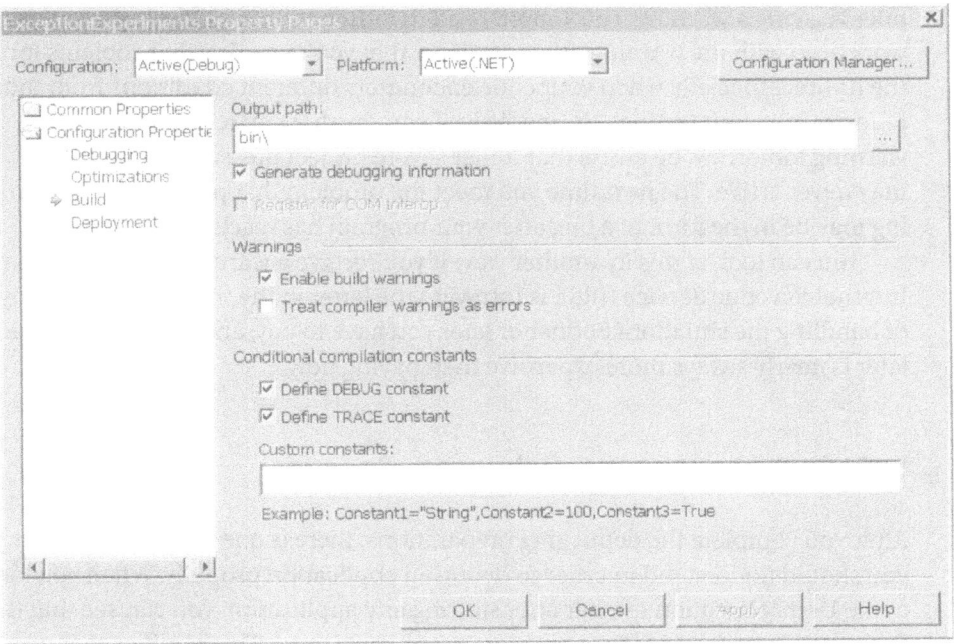

Figure 4-12. The project Build Configuration property page

Regardless of the build configuration you're using, you should always, and I emphasize *always*, select the "Generate debugging information" option. This guarantees that the project's debug symbols (.pdb) file is built. Even with a fully optimized production release, you can debug the resulting assemblies provided you have the correct debug symbols available. You don't need to release the debug symbols to the end user, but you do need to have them available and under source control if you later want to do any debugging. Please see the "Debugging Production Applications" section later in the chapter for more details on how to do this effectively. A second benefit of having debug symbols is that any exception thrown by your application will include the exact line number where the exception was thrown. Without debug symbols, you usually have to resort to guessing which line of code actually caused the exception.

For a **Debug** build configuration, you should also select the DEBUG and TRACE conditional compilation constants to activate your debug and tracing code, such as statements that use the **Debug** and **Trace** classes.

You should also select the box marked "Treat compiler warnings as errors". Checking this option stops you from ignoring any compiler warnings. Some developers tend to ignore any compiler warnings on the basis that either the compiler is too dumb to understand what the developer is doing or the warning can be fixed at a later stage. Both of these assumptions are dangerous. If the compiler is giving a warning, you should heed it. Although your code may seem to work even with the warning, it's quite likely that you're storing up problems for the future, especially when your code encounters different conditions from those found during unit testing. Alternatively, if you say that you're going to fix the warning tomorrow, be aware that under severe project pressures "tomorrow" may never arrive. The next time you meet the problem that produced the warning may be in the form of a bug after your program has reached production.

You can look at this in another way: If you receive a warning letter from the Internal Revenue Service (IRS), is throwing the letter in the trashcan a good way of handling the situation? Sooner or later you have to pay, and in this case paying later is nearly always more expensive than paying now.

Setting the Active Debugger Process

After you complete the debugging preparations, there is one final concept that you should understand in order to debug an application properly. When you look at the Debug Location toolbar after starting any application, you can see that the Program, Thread, and Stack Frame areas are grayed-out. This signifies that no process is currently active in the debugger. The concept of an active debug process is important. The debugger can handle multiple processes simultaneously, but only a single process is actually active within the debugger at any one time. In addition, unless the debugger is actually stopped on a breakpoint, there is no active debug process. This lack of an active debug process is shown by the fact that the Debug Location toolbar has all of its areas grayed-out.

Once the application is running, you can manually set the active debugger process by using the Break All option on the Debug menu or by selecting the relevant process in the Processes window and clicking the Break button. This is the manual equivalent of setting a breakpoint and performing a program action that causes the breakpoint to be triggered.

To break into an application automatically, you add a breakpoint in the program's Source or Disassembly window and then perform a program action that causes this breakpoint to be hit. This program containing the breakpoint then becomes the active debug process. If you examine the Debug Location toolbar of a program that's hit a breakpoint, you'll see that it's no longer grayed-out—its Program drop-down shows the name of the executable and its process ID, the Thread drop-down shows the ID of the program's active thread, and the Stack Frame drop-down shows the current call stack.

Debugging Production Applications

Because there are now two distinct phases—the first when the language compiler creates the .exe or .dll, and the second when the JIT compiler executes the program at runtime—an intriguing possibility becomes available.

Normally, you want a production program to execute fast during normal execution. Because enabling debug tracking lowers performance a little and disabling code optimization can lower performance significantly, you usually want to turn off debug tracking and turn on code optimization. But when you need to investigate a production problem, you want the ability to turn debug tracking on and code optimization off. If you could manage both of these settings on a per-execution basis without having to recompile your program, you could have the best of all possible worlds.

Step forward a configuration file called *MyApp*.ini, where *MyApp* is the name of your program. If you place this file with this name in the same folder as your .exe or .dll, it allows you to configure these two JIT compiler settings on a run-by-run basis. The lines in the INI file that control these settings are as follows, where 1 = true and 0 = false:

```
[.NET Framework Debugging Control]
GenerateTrackingInfo=1
AllowOptimize=0
```

This allows you to override the debug tracking and optimization settings that were specified when the .exe or .dll was built. It's ideal for investigating those troublesome production problems that you're unable to duplicate on your own machine. As long as you make sure that the correct debug symbol (.pdb) file is available, you can step through source code and do full debugging without having to recompile your production program or having to revert back to a debug version of your code.

Debug Symbols Management

When you start serious debugging of your VB .NET applications, and especially when you have to support multiple versions of your software, you'll find life much easier if you have a good debug symbols management process.

When you look in the Call Stack window, any methods for which debug symbols aren't available are shown in gray. The Modules window tells you the modules of your application for which the debugger was unable to locate debug symbols. If this happens and you know where a specific module's symbols can be found, try right-clicking the module and specifying the path by using the Reload Symbols menu item.

Symbols for Your Applications

You should always keep matching binaries, source, and symbol files under tight source control for every production and test version of your application. Of course, you normally won't distribute either the source or symbol files to your end user, but you need them available in case you have to reproduce a problem that occurs with just the version of the application that your pesky end user is running. It's then a relatively simple matter to use Visual Studio's remote debugging facilities to hop onto the end user's machine while still keeping the source and symbol files on your own machine. See Chapter 15 for more details on exactly how to do this.

Symbols for Windows

Every version of Windows comes with its own set of debug symbols. You can find the debug symbols for the various Windows operating systems on the Microsoft Web site at http://www.microsoft.com/ddk/debugging/symbols.asp. You should place these files in a folder on a path where the Visual Studio debugger has access to them—by convention, this folder is normally C:\Windows\Symbols\Dll. Be careful after patching or service-packing your Windows installation, or even updating a Microsoft application, as you may need to download a new set of symbol files. If this happens, you'll see an error message that says "No matching symbolic information found."

Unfortunately, these Windows symbols are of limited use when debugging VB .NET code, as most of the calls are done into managed code rather than native Windows code.

Symbols for the Framework SDK

There are also some limited .NET Framework debug symbols installed as part of the .NET Framework. For version 1.0 of the .NET Framework, you can find these symbols in a folder called

```
C:\Program Files \Microsoft.NET\FrameworkSDK\symbols
```

For version 1.1 of the .NET Framework, you can find the same symbols in a folder called

```
C:\Program Files \Microsoft Visual Studio .NET 2003\SDK\v1.1\symbols
```

To allow the Visual Studio debugger to locate these symbols, you should add the appropriate path to your solution's Common Properties ➤ Debug Symbol Files page. An alternative is to copy each debug symbol file to the folder containing its corresponding framework binary.

Unfortunately, at the time of this writing, Microsoft doesn't release debug symbols for most of the interesting binaries, such as mscorlib.dll and system.dll. This situation may have changed by the time that you read this book, as Microsoft is known to be working on this project.

Because even the Framework binaries for which symbols are available are retail builds, you won't gain much information just by having the debug symbols available. If you recall from Chapter 3, a typical release build turns off the JIT tracking attribute, without which the symbols aren't nearly so useful. Fortunately, you can use the same trick described in the previous section on debugging production applications. You need to create an .ini file for each of the appropriate framework binaries (for instance, one called mscoree.dll.ini), and place it in the same folder as the binary. This .ini file would contain

```
[.NET Framework Debugging Control]
GenerateTrackingInfo=1
AllowOptimize=0
```

This should allow the debugger to load the debug symbols and at least give you access to the assembly's complete call stack.

Symbol Server

Keeping track of all of the binaries and symbols needed to debug every version of your applications can turn into a full-time job. So Microsoft has come up with a solution that shows promise, even though unfortunately it doesn't yet work with the managed world.

A *symbol server* is designed to store all of the debug symbols for a public build in a single known location. Then all that's needed is a debugger smart enough to know where to find the symbol server and which versions of the stored files should be used.

To set up a symbol server, you need the symbol server binaries, a symbol server location, and a symbol server store. You can retrieve the binaries by downloading the Debugging Tools for Windows package (sometimes called *WinDbg*) from http://www.microsoft.com/ddk/debugging. After installing the package, you need to place the symbol server binaries SYMSRV.DLL and SYMSTORE.DLL somewhere where they can be found and used by the Visual Studio debugger.

Then you need to specify the symbol server where the debug symbols are stored. For the Windows symbols, this is http://msdl.microsoft.com/download/symbols. For your own symbols, this would be any local or network folder that you care to specify.

Next, you need to designate a symbol store where you want to store the debug symbols once they've been downloaded from the symbol server. This symbol store might be simply a folder on your local machine if you're the only developer on the team. Alternatively, a bigger team should find a network folder that everybody on the team can access. The only caveat is that everybody on the team should have both read and write rights to this folder.

Finally, you need to tell the Visual Studio debugger where the symbol store and symbol server are located. With this information, it can download the correct version of the debug symbols from the symbol server to the symbol store and then use them during debugging sessions. To do this, use the Control Panel System applet to create an environment variable called _NT_SYMBOL_PATH and place the following value in it (where c:/localstore is replaced by the location of your symbol store):

```
SRV*c:/localstore*http://msdl.microsoft.com/download/symbols
```

Now when the Visual Studio IDE is next loaded and the debugger starts, it should locate the appropriate debug symbols on the symbol server and download them to the symbol store where it can use them. This is a once-only operation unless, of course, the binary versions change and the revised symbols therefore need to be downloaded.

Unfortunately, you should remember that this currently only works with Win32-native code, not with managed code. Also, at the time of this writing, this is an undocumented procedure and might well change with the next release of Visual Studio and the .NET Framework.

Improving JIT Debugging

Chapter 3 investigated how you can use JIT debugging to intercept a program crash and launch a debugger automatically. When a crash occurs, the CLR presents you with a list of debuggers and asks you to choose one. If your favorite debugger isn't on the list, there's an undocumented and unsupported way to add it to that list. For example, if you sometimes like to use WinDbg, the following command line registers WinDbg for JIT debugging:

```
vs7jit.exe /RegisterOld "c:\Windbg\windbg.exe" "WinDbg"
```

To unregister WinDbg for JIT debugging, you can use the following command line:

```
vs7jit.exe /UnregisterOld "c:\Windbg\windbg.exe"
```

As I've already stated, this switch is undocumented so I don't know for how long it will continue working.

Coping Without Edit and Continue

As I discussed in some detail during Chapter 1, perhaps the most noticeable loss within the Source window is the inability to edit your code during a debugging run and then continue execution of the new code without restarting the program (a feature sometimes referred to as Edit and Continue, or E&C). If you select the option Tools ➢ Options ➢ Debugging ➢ Edit and Continue ➢ Allow me to edit VB files while debugging, you'll be able to edit your source code during program execution, but this revised code is ignored by the compiler until you restart the program. This is actually rather dangerous, as it's very easy to become confused about what code you've changed and what code is actually executing.

If you do want to take advantage of this ability to change code during a program run, I suggest adding all new and revised code into one or more separate procedures that you can then enclose within a collapsible region using the **#Region...#End Region** directive. The **#Region** directive allows you to remove the new code from your view so that it doesn't interfere with your view of the code that is currently executing.

Placing the new code into separate procedures, maybe including revised copies of current procedures, is necessary because the **#Region** directive can only be used at a class or namespace level. Unfortunately, you can't place a region directive within a procedure or function. An alternative to creating a new dummy procedure just for gaining the benefits of a collapsible region is to place the new code into a comment code, as a comment block is automatically created as a collapsible region.

Having placed the code into one or more regions and collapsed these regions so that new code can't be seen, you should mark each region with a bookmark by right-clicking the left column of the source window and selecting "Add task list shortcut". You can see and reference these bookmarks in the Task window by opting to show "All tasks" (or just "Shortcuts" if you prefer) from its context menu.

After the current debugging run has finished, double-clicking each of these shortcuts in the Task window takes you directly to the associated region where new code is stored. You can then amend your code to incorporate all of the new changes before restarting your program.

Debugging Common Intermediate Language

One frequent query from new .NET developers is how to view and debug Common Intermediate Language (CIL). The Source window only allows you to step through source code, and the Disassembly window only shows you the source code together with the processor-native code. Although your .exe or .dll contains the CIL, it seems to be impossible to get at it in any useful way.

There is a neat trick that allows you to both view and step through CIL. It's based on using the CIL disassembler utility to dissect your executable into CIL source and then rebuilding the executable again so that the CIL code is bound to the VB .NET source. This may sound a little complicated, but the command-line steps are simple:

1. VBC **MyProgram.vb** /debug:full /optimize- /out:**MyProgram.exe**

2. ILDASM **MyProgram.exe** /source /out:**MyTest.il**

3. ILASM **MyTest.il** /debug /out:**MyTest.exe**

The first step builds your executable as normal, in full debug mode, and without code optimization. The second step disassembles the resulting binary into a CIL source file—the /source flag adds the original VB .NET source code as CIL comments. The final step builds a new executable from the CIL source, once again in debug mode.

Having completed these command-line compilation steps, load the original project into Visual Studio. In my case this was a console application called DoubleTrouble.sln containing a single project called **DoubleTrouble** that, in turn, contained a source code file called Module1.vb. Choose the Add Existing Item option from the File menu, change the files filter to be "All files," and select the source code file that was produced by the **Ildasm** step mentioned previously (the one with a .il suffix). Double-click this CIL file in Solution Explorer to see it displayed in Visual Studio's Source window. If you scroll down past the initial code preamble, you should see your VB .NET source code shown as comments (prefixed with //) and the CIL statements shown as executable code. Figure 4-13 shows how this looks with my selected project.

Figure 4-13. Single-stepping and debugging CIL code with VB .NET source

Debugging the new executable that you've just created is simple. First, you place a breakpoint on one of the CIL statements shown in the Source window. Then you need to tell Visual Studio to launch your new executable. To do this, you should right-click your project in Solution Explorer and use the option under Properties ➢ Configuration Properties ➢ Debugging ➢ Start external program to specify the executable that you created in the final command-line step mentioned previously. Now when you press F5, the breakpoint that you set should be hit. If you then jump to the Disassembly window, you can see the CIL code together with its corresponding native code. This is an instructive way of learning about CIL and how it functions.

Understanding Code Optimization

Many developers take the approach of turning off the optimization switch during development and testing, and turning it on when compiling for a production release. This should in theory give you faster production code, but there is some risk with this approach. If the compiler is overzealous in its optimization or makes assumptions that are different from those made by the developers, you run the risk of seeing a bug that only appears in production code, but not during development or testing. This means you have to weigh the relative risks of an optimization bug that appears only in production versus the speed of your application. Here's a good example of this behavior:

```
Option Strict On

Module Module1

    Sub Main()

        Dim dblOne As Double = Math.Log(8, 2)
        Dim dblTwo As Double = Math.IEEERemainder(dblOne, 1)

        'DEBUG or RELEASE configuration
#If Debug = True Then
        Console.WriteLine("DEBUG configuration")
#Else
        Console.WriteLine("RELEASE configuration")
#End If
        'Started with F5 or Ctrl-F5?
        Console.WriteLine("Debugger attached? " &
                                Debugger.IsAttached.ToString)
        Console.WriteLine("dblOne = " & dblOne.ToString)
        Console.WriteLine("dblTwo = " & dblTwo.ToString)
        Console.WriteLine("dblTwo = 0? " & (dblTwo = 0).ToString)

        Console.ReadLine()

    End Sub

End Module
```

Investigating this small program is very instructional. First you should build the program in Visual Studio using the default **Debug** configuration, in other words without code optimization. If you then execute the program under the Visual Studio debugger, by pressing F5, you'll see a result of **true** printed to the console. If you try executing the program without a debugger, by pressing Ctrl-F5, you'll see a result of **false** instead!

Then build the program using the default **Release** configuration, in other words using code optimization. Once again, execute the program under the Visual Studio debugger by pressing F5. Just like before, you'll see a result of **true** printed to the console. If you now try executing the same program without a debugger, by pressing Ctrl-F5, you'll see a result of **false**.

So regardless of whether code optimization was used, running this program under the Visual Studio debugger always produces a result of **true** and running the same program without a debugger always produces a result of **false**. Is this really a code optimization issue or is it an issue related to running under the debugger? Or is it a combination of the two? It's worth noting in this context that the Visual Studio debugger always turns off code optimization, regardless of whether code optimization was specified when the program was originally compiled.

To investigate this interesting issue further, I used the console debugger **Cordbg**. I discuss how to use this powerful low-level debugger in Chapter 5, but one useful trick that **Cordbg** can do is switch code optimization on and off at will. You can't do this with the Visual Studio debugger, because it always switches off code optimization. When I ran this program under **Cordbg** and experimented with the code optimization settings, I got some interesting results.

The first realization was that code optimization, just like code compilation, is a two-stage process. When you *build* a program with code optimization, the resulting CIL is optimized. When you *run* a program with code optimization, the resulting native code is optimized. By default, the design-time code optimization setting for the language compiler is carried forward and used as the runtime code optimization setting for the JIT compiler (see the discussion of the **DebuggableAttribute** class in Chapter 3). However, **Cordbg** can operate to switch the JIT code optimization on and off at will, regardless of the code optimization setting used to build the program.

When I ran a default **Debug** build of the program under **Cordbg** without JIT code optimization, I saw a result of **true**, just like the corresponding test with the Visual Studio debugger. When I ran the same build with JIT code optimization, I saw the result of **false**, just as though I was running without any debugger. I got exactly the same results when I ran a default **Release** build of the program with and without JIT code optimization.

After the dust has settled from this experiment, it's clear that CIL code optimization (by the VB .NET compiler) doesn't affect the result produced by this program, but native code optimization (by the JIT compiler) definitely does. This is the sort of tricky issue that code optimization can produce, and you're still left with trying to understand why the native code optimization makes such a difference in this case. My guess is that it's something related to numeric precision and the use of the **Double** type, but this would need further investigation.

The initial results of this experiment were rather confusing, and it needed some deeper investigation to find out what was really happening. This is a good example of the sort of subtle optimization problems that can trap you. The real "gotcha" here is that this code is likely to run as expected during development and unit testing, but start producing a different result during integration testing and production.

Optimization Is Your Enemy

My advice is that before you turn on optimization automatically in your release build, you should study the performance effects of optimization on your application. Before you start sharpening your Outlook in preparation for a critical e-mail, hear me out for a minute. The odds are that allowing the compiler to optimize your code may not always result in a significant performance boost. This is because much of the code being executed is within the .NET Framework library, which is already optimized. Additionally, unless your application is performing numerically intensive work, it is quite likely that it's spending much of its time waiting for users or other resources, and there's little advantage to be gained by asking the compiler for optimization. Finally, the compiler is quite likely to optimize parts of your code that have no significant effect on the overall performance of your application. Performance bugs are notorious for being difficult to find and understand, and trying to gain a performance boost by using compiler optimizations without a prior in-depth understanding of the performance profile of your application is a recipe for nasty bugs.

If you do insist on optimizing your production build, I suggest that you then use a profiling tool in order to establish that your application is really receiving a significant performance boost in exchange for the extra risk of optimization defects. You might be surprised by what you see.

A Code Optimization Test

You can use the sorting application to test the effects of optimizing the code performance. If you run four tests for each of the four sort algorithms, you can see the performance effects of running in normal debug mode, then in debug mode but with code optimization, next in debug mode but removing integer overflow checks, and finally testing a fully optimized build with code optimization and without the integer overflow checks. You can find all of these settings on each project's Properties ➢ Configuration properties ➢ Optimizations page.

Table 4-1 shows the results of performing these four tests on each of the four sort algorithms, using an unsorted array containing 30,000 items, each array item containing a value between 1 and 30,000. The test hardware was a Pentium III 800 MHz laptop with 256MB of RAM, and all times shown are in seconds.

Table 4-1. Testing Code Optimization Effects on an Array with 30,000 Items

ALGORITHM	DEBUG	OPTIMIZED	NO CHECKS	OPTIMIZED/NO CHECKS
Bubble sort	10.5	9.8	9.3	5.0
Selection sort	8.0	6.1	3.7	3.1
Quick sort	1.1	1.1	1.1	0.9
Counting sort	0.0	0.0	0.0	0.0

The most interesting observation here is that the performance benefits of each of the code optimizations varies widely depending on the type of algorithm. Just turning on code optimization, as you might normally do when building in release mode, improved the bubble sort by about 7%, the selection sort by 25%, the quick sort not at all, and the counting sort was too fast to measure.

Removing the integer overflow checks improved bubble sort performance over a default debug build by 12%, but the selection sort improved by a whopping 55%. Going to full optimization finally has a performance effect on the quick sort, but this time the bubble sort benefits the most. As you can see, the benefits of code optimization vary dramatically depending on the code that's being optimized and which optimization measures are taken. Before indulging in potentially risky code optimization, you should benchmark your code to see that you're really gaining a decent benefit.

To investigate the effects of code optimization further, Table 4-2 shows the same tests, but this time done on an array containing 60,000 items, each array item having a value between 1 and 60,000.

Table 4-2. Testing Code Optimization Effects on an Array with 60,000 Items

ALGORITHM	DEBUG	OPTIMIZED	NO CHECKS	OPTIMIZED/NO CHECKS
Bubble sort	41.8	40.1	34.3	20.5
Selection sort	20.0	25.0	15.1	12.6
Quick sort	2.2	2.2	2.2	1.7
Counting sort	0.02	0.02	0.02	0.01

The shock is seeing the effect of code optimization on the selection sort—it actually decreases performance by 25%! This isn't a freak result—the test was run many times, and the numbers didn't vary by much. I haven't investigated the reason for this, but it's very strange that code optimization produces a performance gain of 25% when selection sorting an array of 30,000 items but a loss of 25% with an array of 60,000 items. You really should test any benefits that your application expects to see from code optimization before you start using it.

Summary

This chapter looked in some depth at the Visual Studio .NET debugger. You learned how to prepare Visual Studio for a debugging session and how to debug production programs. I discussed debug symbols and the importance of keeping them matched with their corresponding sources and binaries. Then you saw how to compensate at least partially for the loss of Edit and Continue, and how to examine and debug CIL. Finally, you learned about some of the dangers of code optimization.

INTERLUDE

There are some peculiar developers out there who love writing *obfuscated* code—in other words, programs where it's almost impossible to work out what the code is doing. Although there are regular language competitions that give prizes for writing obfuscated programs, Visual Basic has never been an obvious candidate for this kind of treatment. With no peculiar syntax or fancy programming constructs, it seems to be the ugly stepsister when placed alongside its more complicated and confusing language cousins. So I thought I would address this sad state of affairs by writing an obfuscated VB .NET program. See if you can work out what this console application produces without actually running it:

```
Option Strict On
Module Obfuscation

    Sub Main()
      Dim x As Integer, x1 As String, x2 As String

      For x = 0 To 5
        x1 = x1 & Chr(CInt(x * (x * (x * (x * (-0.75 * x + 7.2917) - 22.5) _
             + 16.708) + 28.25) + 72))
      Next x

      For x = 0 To 6
        x2 = x2 & Chr(CInt(x * (x * (x * (x * (x * (0.425 * x - 6.8667) _
             + 40.833) - 109.58) _+ 122.24) - 23.05) + 87))
      Next x

      Console.WriteLine(x1 & x2)
      Console.ReadLine()

    End Sub

End Module
```

CHAPTER 5

Other Debugging Tools

Now that you've been introduced to the Visual Studio .NET debugger, it's time to look at some other tools that can help you to make sense of what's going on inside your applications. The CLR, the .NET Framework, the compilers, and Visual Studio itself are all vast and imposing beasts, which means that you're going to need some powerful weapons to tackle them properly. This chapter introduces some useful tools, shows you when and how you might want to use them, and warns you about any potential problems that they have.

Cordbg: The Console Debugger

Cordbg is a framework command-line debugger for managed code only. Whereas the Visual Studio debugger has an easy-to-use graphical interface and swaggers along with the power to debug almost any situation it encounters, **Cordbg** is its ugly sibling lurking in a corner. There are, however, some situations where you will want to dispense with the all-dancing cool gadget and instead get to know some more primitive and usually hidden details about your application.

Why Use Cordbg?

Cordbg ships with the .NET Framework SDK, so you can use it in situations where Visual Studio can't be installed or would consume too much memory. **Cordbg** consists of only four components, namely Cordbg.exe, msdis130.dll, msvcp70.dll, and msvcr70.dll. This means that **Cordbg** is small enough and has few enough dependencies that even paranoid management can be persuaded to allow its installation on a production server.

You can also use **Cordbg** to debug window painting and drawing code that a graphical debugger chokes on because of interference from its own windows. Another benefit is that **Cordbg** has some low-level functionality that isn't available from within Visual Studio. For instance, attaching the Visual Studio debugger to your managed code automatically disables JIT optimization, which can make it very difficult to debug a problem that appears in a release build, but not in a debug build. With **Cordbg**, you can switch JIT optimization on and off at will, even in the middle of a debug session.

The two major caveats with **Cordbg** are that it can only debug managed code and it's less straightforward to use than the Visual Studio debugger. **Cordbg** also has a few minor bugs—see the Microsoft Knowledge Base article Q307169 for more details about these.

Using Cordbg

If you create a simple "Hello, VB .NET World" program and then compile it, you can then load it into **Cordbg** and show its source code. It's important that you have debug symbols available during debugging, so you should either compile the program as a debug build or compile it as a release build, but change the **Release** configuration to produce debug symbols, as explained in Chapter 3. Figure 5-1 shows such a program after it's been compiled and loaded into **Cordbg**. Note the **run** command that loads and starts the specified executable and the **show** command that shows you the program source. The asterisk (*) next to line 003 shows the current execution point, where the program has been paused by the debugger.

```
VS.NET Command Prompt - cordbg                                    _|□|×|

C:\Demo\HelloWorld>cordbg
Microsoft (R) Common Language Runtime Test Debugger Shell Version 1.0.3705.0
Copyright (C) Microsoft Corporation 1998-2001. All rights reserved.

(cordbg) break helloworld.vb:3
#1      <UnknownModule>!helloworld.vb:3 [unbound]
(cordbg) run helloworld
Process 120/0x78 created.
Warning: couldn't load symbols for c:\winnt\microsoft.net\framework\v1.0.3705\ms
corlib.dll
[thread 0x5ec] Thread created.
Breakpoint #1 has bound to C:\Demo\HelloWorld\helloworld.exe.
break at #1     C:\Demo\HelloWorld\helloworld.exe!helloworld.vb:3        Main+0x0
(il) [active]
Source not available when in the prolog of a function(offset 0x0)

[0000] mov         ecx,dword ptr ds:[01BA086Ch]
(cordbg) show
001: Module HelloWorld
002:
003:*      Sub Main()
004:
005:          System.Console.WriteLine("Hello VB.Net world")
006:
007:      End Sub
008:
(cordbg)
```

Figure 5-1. Loading and showing the HelloWorld program with the Cordbg debugger

You can ignore the warning message in this case—the debugger is just informing you that it can't locate the debug symbols for mscorlib.dll, the CLR's primary runtime library. If you want to load debug symbols for the .NET Framework, you should copy them from C:\Program Files\Microsoft.Net\ FrameworkSDK\symbols and put them into the same folder used by the Windows symbol files, normally C:\Windows\Symbols\Dll, although the path might be different on your computer.

Cordbg Commands

Cordbg has many commands, all of which are fully documented. Typing **/?** at a **Cordbg** command line shows you these commands and their usage. One of the most useful commands is **mode**, which allows you to set various debugger features. For example, **mode AppDomainLoads 1** (or **mode app 1** for short) tells the debugger to inform you about every application domain and assembly load event. Another useful mode command is **mode JitOptimizations 1** (or **mode jit 1** for short), which tells **Cordbg** to turn the JIT compiler code optimization on. You can use this and another command called **wt** to see what effect code optimization has on the HelloWorld program.

First type **wt**. This command steps through the entire program, printing the call tree as it goes. At the end of the trace, when the return instruction is reached for the function in which the **wt** command was executed, you will see a line showing the total number of native instructions executed. As the program is currently running with the JIT optimizer off, you can see that this number is very substantial for such a simple program—3,385 native code instructions with my version of Windows 2000 Professional and the .NET Framework. Now type **go** to continue and finish program execution.

So what happens if the JIT optimizer is turned on and you run the same test? If you look at Figure 5-2, you can see the results. Note that you need to add a breakpoint on line 3 first to make sure that the program halts; otherwise, the optimization causes the program to run straight through without stopping.

As you can see, the difference between nonoptimized code (3,385 native instructions) and optimized code (374 native instructions) is quite dramatic. This type of information is much more difficult to retrieve when you use the Visual Studio debugger.

Before I leave **Cordbg**, one final tip. You can prefix most **Cordbg** commands with an asterisk (*), which causes the command to execute once for every managed thread in the process. If you want to explore **Cordbg** and its commands further, you can view both the documentation and the complete source code of this debugger, as it comes as one of the sample programs.

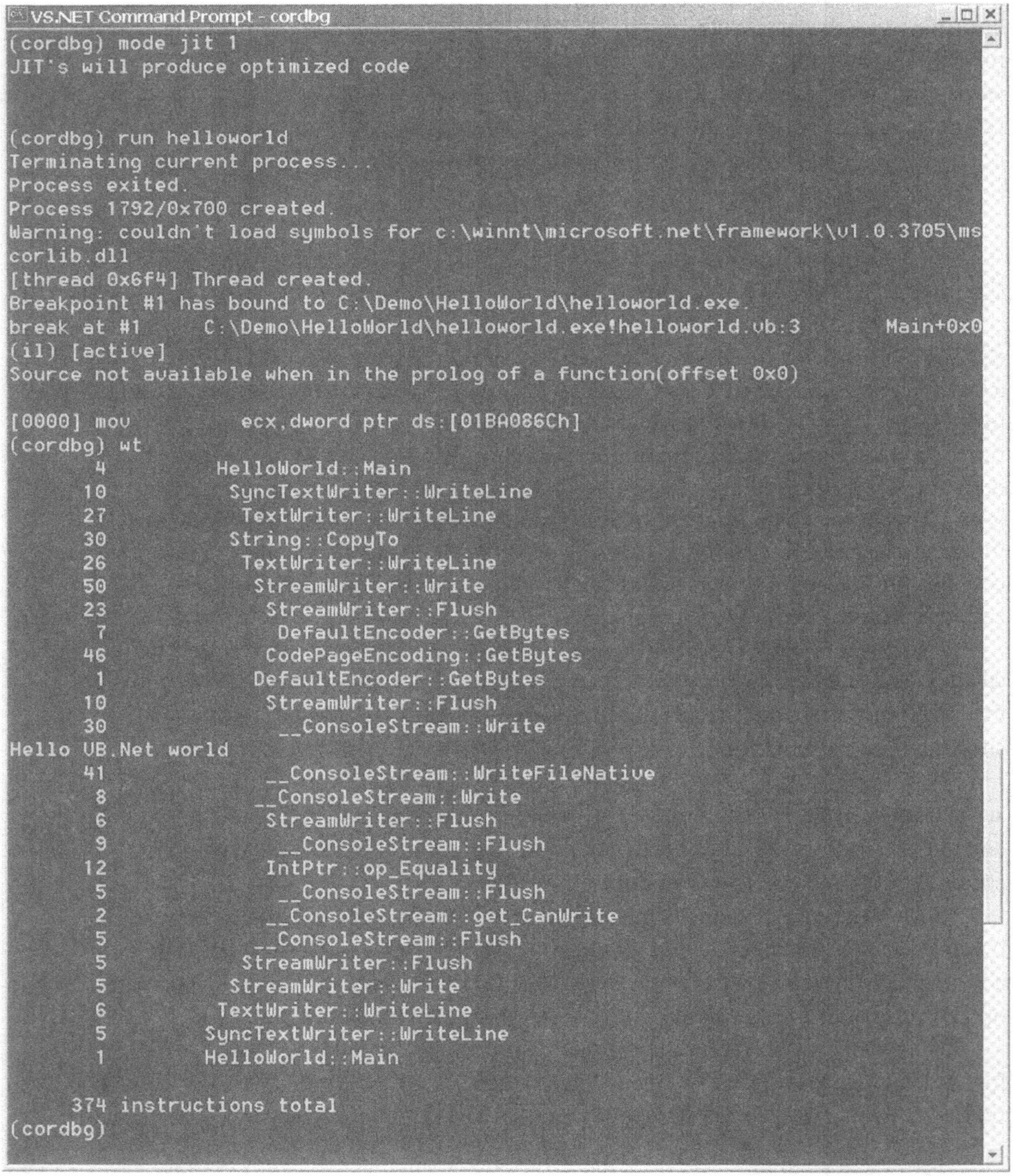

```
VS.NET Command Prompt - cordbg                                    _ |□| ×|
(cordbg) mode jit 1
JIT's will produce optimized code


(cordbg) run helloworld
Terminating current process...
Process exited.
Process 1792/0x700 created.
Warning: couldn't load symbols for c:\winnt\microsoft.net\framework\v1.0.3705\ms
corlib.dll
[thread 0x6f4] Thread created.
Breakpoint #1 has bound to C:\Demo\HelloWorld\helloworld.exe.
break at #1     C:\Demo\HelloWorld\helloworld.exe!helloworld.vb:3        Main+0x0
(il) [active]
Source not available when in the prolog of a function(offset 0x0)

[0000] mov          ecx,dword ptr ds:[01BA086Ch]
(cordbg) wt
        4             HelloWorld::Main
       10             SyncTextWriter::WriteLine
       27             TextWriter::WriteLine
       30             String::CopyTo
       26             TextWriter::WriteLine
       50              StreamWriter::Write
       23               StreamWriter::Flush
        7                DefaultEncoder::GetBytes
       46               CodePageEncoding::GetBytes
        1              DefaultEncoder::GetBytes
       10               StreamWriter::Flush
       30                __ConsoleStream::Write
Hello VB.Net world
       41                __ConsoleStream::WriteFileNative
        8                __ConsoleStream::Write
        6              StreamWriter::Flush
        9                __ConsoleStream::Flush
       12              IntPtr::op_Equality
        5                __ConsoleStream::Flush
        2                __ConsoleStream::get_CanWrite
        5                __ConsoleStream::Flush
        5             StreamWriter::Flush
        5             StreamWriter::Write
        6            TextWriter::WriteLine
        5           SyncTextWriter::WriteLine
        1           HelloWorld::Main

    374 instructions total
(cordbg)
```

Figure 5-2. Viewing the optimized code call tree

Dbgclr: The GUI Debugger

Dbgclr is a framework debugger with a GUI that's similar in many ways to the Visual Studio debugger. In fact, it's largely based on work done for its bigger brother. Like **Cordbg**, it can debug only managed code. Unlike the Visual Studio debugger, it can't do remote debugging. Another restriction is its Registers window, which isn't very functional compared to its Visual Studio counterpart. **Dbgclr** also doesn't have any built-in help, and there isn't much information about it in the .NET Framework documentation.

Like **Cordbg**, **Dbgclr** ships with the .NET Framework. Its main use is for situations where Visual Studio can't be installed or would consume too much memory.

Using Dbgclr

You can find Dbgclr.exe in the GuiDebug subfolder under your .NET Framework installation. Remember that, like **Cordbg**, **Dbgclr** is simply a debugger, so it won't launch the VB .NET language compiler like Visual Studio does. I find it useful to think of **Dbgclr** as a lightweight version of the Visual Studio debugger combined with a runtime-only version of the Visual Studio IDE. This avoids mental confusion because the two IDEs look very similar.

Dbgclr doesn't understand Visual Studio solutions directly, but it will build its own solution (suffixed with .dln) once you've specified an executable that you want to debug. To debug a program, you first need to compile it in debug mode, either using Visual Studio or the command-line compiler. Then you run **Dbgclr** and choose the "Program to debug" option from the Debug menu. When you've located your program executable, this will be added to a new **Dbgclr** solution. Next, you add the corresponding source file(s) to the solution using the File ➤ Open ➤ File menu option. Once you've done this, you can set breakpoints and start debugging your program using F5 or F11, just as you would do within Visual Studio.

Debugging within **Dbgclr** is very similar to debugging within Visual Studio. You have access to the same debugging windows and you can manipulate the same breakpoints. You can even attach to and detach from processes just like you can in **Dbgclr**'s bigger brother, although you can't attach to a process on a remote machine.

One little trick that can save you some time is to add a **Dbgclr** shortcut to your Send To menu. Assuming that the .NET Framework is installed in the default location, the shortcut to add is

```
C:\Program Files\Microsoft.NET\FrameworkSDK\GuiDebug\DbgCLR.exe
```

Then you can right-click any .NET executable in Windows Explorer and launch **Dbgclr** directly.

Ildasm: Viewing CIL

Ildasm is the Common Intermediate Language (CIL) disassembler—it parses any .NET assembly and shows a graphical or textual representation of the CIL, name-spaces, types, and interfaces within the assembly. If you want to know what's really going on inside your code, **Ildasm** is the tool that will tell you. As well as analyzing your own assemblies, you can point **Ildasm** at assemblies belonging to other developers or even at the .NET Framework assemblies themselves.

Ildasm Within Visual Studio

The easiest way to check CIL on a regular basis is to create a new item on Visual Studio's Tools menu. You can do this by going to Tools ➤ External Tools and completing the External Tools dialog window with the following entries:

Title: CIL (or whatever title you want)

Command: C:\Program Files\Microsoft.Net\FrameworkSDK\bin\ildasm.exe

Arguments: $(TargetPath) /adv /source

Initial directory: $(TargetDir)

This creates the new item on the Tools menu. Selecting this new item invokes **Ildasm** in graphical mode on the current assembly, allowing you to dig down to each method and examine the CIL. Notice the two switches that I have chosen to specify. The */adv* switch adds some useful extra options to the **Ildasm** View menu (such as access to statistics), and the */source* argument causes source code to be embedded into the CIL display as comments.

Ildasm from the Command Line

Invoking **Ildasm** from the command line is just as easy. The following command line tells **Ildasm** to create a disk file named MyAssembly.il containing the CIL extracted from the assembly MyAssembly.exe. Once again, note the use of the */source* argument to embed source code as comments within the CIL listing.

```
Ildasm MyAssembly.exe /source /out=MyAssembly.il
```

Investigating Ildasm Code

To give you a good idea of **Ildasm**'s capabilities, I'm going to investigate an example that compares two different VB .NET error-handling techniques. When you wrote VB.Classic code, you were required to use the **On Error Goto...** form of error handling. VB .NET still allows you to keep this legacy method of error handling, but it offers a more modern alternative in the form of **Try...Catch...Finally**. Now VB developers have to make decisions about which form of error handling is best, and even whether it is advisable to mix the two modes within an application.

Error handling is a large subject that will be investigated in depth as part of Chapter 13. Here I want to investigate a small subset of the problem. Should you replace the **On Error Resume Next** method of suppressing unwanted errors with **Try...Catch...Finally**? Listing 5-1 shows the simple program that I'm going to use for experimentation. This program sets up a database connection string and then performs two database connection tests. The first test uses the **On Error Resume Next** form of error handling to suppress any connection error, clean up the connection, and then return **true** or **false** depending on whether the connection was made successfully. The second test is almost identical, but it instead uses the **Try...Catch...Finally** form of error handling.

Listing 5-1. Error Handling Comparison

```
Option Strict On
Imports System.Data.SqlClient


Module ErrorTest


    Sub Main()
        Dim strConnection As String
        'Set up database connection
        strConnection = "Initial Catalog = Northwind;"
        strConnection += "Data Source = CHEETAH;"
        strConnection += "Integrated Security = SSPI"
        'Try old and new error-handling functions
        MethodOld(strConnection)
        MethodNew(strConnection)
    End Sub
```

```
Function MethodOld(ByVal ConnectString As String) As Boolean
    Dim objSqlConnect As SqlConnection
    'Test database connection with old error handling
    On Error Resume Next
    objSqlConnect = New SqlConnection(ConnectString)
    MethodOld = CBool(Err.Number = 0)
    objSqlConnect.Close()
    objSqlConnect.Dispose()
End Function

Function MethodNew(ByVal ConnectString As String) As Boolean
    Dim objSqlConnect As SqlConnection
    'Test database connection with new error handling
    Try
        objSqlConnect = New SqlConnection(ConnectString)
        objSqlConnect.Close()
        objSqlConnect.Dispose()
        Return True
    Catch
        Return False
    Finally
    End Try
End Function
End Module
```

If you compile this program as a debug build, remembering to replace CHEETAH with your own data source, and then disassemble the resulting executable using **Ildasm**, it is possible to compare the CIL generated for each of these two methods and make some sort of comparison of their relative efficiency.

Examining the CIL

Now you can examine the CIL generated for each of the two test methods. As before, the */source* flag means that the VB .NET source code is added as comments to the CIL code. Listing 5-2 shows the CIL generated for the legacy method of error handling, and Listing 5-3 shows its more modern counterpart. The VB .NET source lines are highlighted in bold.

Listing 5-2. CIL Produced by On Error Resume Next

```
.method public static bool  MethodOld(string ConnectString) cil managed
{
    // Code size       174 (0xae)
    .maxstack  2
    .locals init ([0] bool MethodOld,
                  [1] class
 [System.Data]System.Data.SqlClient.SqlConnection objSqlConnect,
                  [2] int32 _Vb_t_CurrentStatement,
                  [3] class [mscorlib]System.Exception _Vb_t_Exception,
                  [4] int32 _Vb_t_Resume,
                  [5] int32 _Vb_t_OnError)
//000017:
//000018:      Function MethodOld(ByVal ConnectString As String) As Boolean
    IL_0000:  nop
//000019:          Dim objSqlConnect As SqlConnection
//000020:
//000021:          'Test database connection
//000022:          On Error Resume Next
    IL_0001:  call       void
[Microsoft.VisualBasic]Microsoft.VisualBasic.CompilerServices.
ProjectData::ClearProjectError()
    IL_0006:  ldc.i4.1
    IL_0007:  stloc.s    _Vb_t_OnError
//000023:          objSqlConnect = New SqlConnection(ConnectString)
    IL_0009:  ldc.i4.1
    IL_000a:  stloc.2
    IL_000b:  ldarg.0
    IL_000c:  newobj     instance void
[System.Data]System.Data.SqlClient.SqlConnection::.ctor(string)
    IL_0011:  stloc.1
//000024:          MethodOld = CBool(Err.Number = 0)
    IL_0012:  ldc.i4.2
    IL_0013:  stloc.2
    IL_0014:  call       class
[Microsoft.VisualBasic]Microsoft.VisualBasic.ErrObject
[Microsoft.VisualBasic]Microsoft.VisualBasic.Information::Err()
    IL_0019:  callvirt   instance int32
[Microsoft.VisualBasic]Microsoft.VisualBasic.ErrObject::get_
Number()
    IL_001e:  ldc.i4.0
    IL_001f:  ceq
    IL_0021:  stloc.0
```

```
//000025:          objSqlConnect.Close()
     IL_0022:  ldc.i4.3
     IL_0023:  stloc.2
     IL_0024:  ldloc.1
     IL_0025:  callvirt    instance void
[System.Data]System.Data.SqlClient.SqlConnection::Close()
     IL_002a:  nop
//000026:          objSqlConnect.Dispose()
     IL_002b:  ldc.i4.4
     IL_002c:  stloc.2
     IL_002d:  ldloc.1
     IL_002e:  callvirt    instance void
[System]System.ComponentModel.Component::Dispose()
     IL_0033:  nop
     IL_0034:  leave.s     IL_00a3

     IL_0036:  ldloc.s     _Vb_t_Resume
     IL_0038:  ldc.i4.1
     IL_0039:  add
     IL_003a:  ldc.i4.0
     IL_003b:  stloc.s     _Vb_t_Resume
     IL_003d:  switch      (
                                IL_0001,
                                IL_0009,
                                IL_0012,
                                IL_0022,
                                IL_002b,
                                IL_0034)
     IL_005a:  leave.s     IL_00a1

     IL_005c:  isinst      [mscorlib]System.Exception
     IL_0061:  brtrue.s    IL_0065

     IL_0063:  br.s        IL_0070

     IL_0065:  ldloc.s     _Vb_t_OnError
     IL_0067:  brfalse.s   IL_0070

     IL_0069:  ldloc.s     _Vb_t_Resume
     IL_006b:  brtrue.s    IL_0070

     IL_006d:  ldc.i4.1
     IL_006e:  br.s        IL_0073
```

```
      IL_0070:  ldc.i4.0
      IL_0071:  br.s       IL_0073


      IL_0073:  endfilter
      IL_0075:  castclass  [mscorlib]System.Exception
      IL_007a:  dup
      IL_007b:  call       void
[Microsoft.VisualBasic]Microsoft.VisualBasic.CompilerServices.ProjectData::
SetProjectError(class [mscorlib]System.Exception)
      IL_0080:  stloc.3
      IL_0081:  ldloc.s    _Vb_t_Resume
      IL_0083:  brfalse.s  IL_0087


      IL_0085:  leave.s    IL_00a1


      IL_0087:  ldloc.2
      IL_0088:  stloc.s    _Vb_t_Resume
      IL_008a:  ldloc.s    _Vb_t_OnError
      IL_008c:  switch     (
                              IL_009b,
                              IL_009d)
      IL_0099:  leave.s    IL_009f


      IL_009b:  leave.s    IL_009f


      IL_009d:  leave.s    IL_0036


      IL_009f:  rethrow
      IL_00a1:  ldloc.3
      .try IL_0001 to IL_005c filter IL_005c handler IL_0075 to IL_00a1
      IL_00a2:  throw

//000027:
//000028:       End Function
      IL_00a3:  ldloc.0
      IL_00a4:  ldloc.s    _Vb_t_Resume
      IL_00a6:  brfalse.s  IL_00ad


      IL_00a8:  call       void
[Microsoft.VisualBasic]Microsoft.VisualBasic.CompilerServices.ProjectData::
ClearProjectError()
      IL_00ad:  ret
    } // end of method ErrorTest::MethodOld
```

Listing 5-3. CIL Produced by Try...Catch...Finally

```
.method public static bool   MethodNew(string ConnectString) cil managed
{
  // Code size        56 (0x38)
  .maxstack  1
  .locals init ([0] bool MethodNew,
           [1] class
[System.Data]System.Data.SqlClient.SqlConnection objSqlConnect)
//000029:
//000030:      Function MethodNew(ByVal ConnectString As String) As Boolean
    IL_0000:  nop
//000031:        Dim objSqlConnect As SqlConnection
//000032:
//000033:         'Test database connection
//000034:        Try
    IL_0001:  nop
//000035:            objSqlConnect = New SqlConnection(ConnectString)
  .try
  {
    .try
    {
      IL_0002:  ldarg.0
      IL_0003:  newobj      instance void
[System.Data]System.Data.SqlClient.SqlConnection::.ctor(string)
      IL_0008:  stloc.1
//000036:            objSqlConnect.Close()
      IL_0009:  ldloc.1
      IL_000a:  callvirt    instance void
[System.Data]System.Data.SqlClient.SqlConnection::Close()
      IL_000f:  nop
//000037:            objSqlConnect.Dispose()
      IL_0010:  ldloc.1
      IL_0011:  callvirt    instance void
[System]System.ComponentModel.Component::Dispose()
      IL_0016:  nop
//000038:            Return True
      IL_0017:  ldc.i4.1
      IL_0018:  stloc.0
      IL_0019:  leave.s     IL_0036

      IL_001b:  leave.s     IL_0035
```

```
//000039:          Catch
        }   // end .try
        catch [mscorlib]System.Exception
        {
            IL_001d:  call        void
[Microsoft.VisualBasic]Microsoft.VisualBasic.CompilerServices.
ProjectData::SetProjectError(class [mscorlib]System.Exception)
            IL_0022:  nop
//000040:               Return False
            IL_0023:  ldc.i4.0
            IL_0024:  stloc.0
            IL_0025:  call        void
[Microsoft.VisualBasic]Microsoft.VisualBasic.CompilerServices.
ProjectData::ClearProjectError()
            IL_002a:  leave.s    IL_0036

            IL_002c:  call        void
[Microsoft.VisualBasic]Microsoft.VisualBasic.CompilerServices.
ProjectData::ClearProjectError()
            IL_0031:  leave.s    IL_0035

//000041:          Finally
        }   // end handler
      }   // end .try
      finally
      {
        IL_0033:  nop
        IL_0034:  endfinally
//000042:          End Try
      }   // end handler
      IL_0035:  nop
//000043:
//000044:     End Function
      IL_0036:  ldloc.0
      IL_0037:  ret
    } // end of method ErrorTest::MethodNew
```

The most obvious result is that the older form of error handling produces 125 lines of CIL, including 9 comment lines containing VB .NET source. The newer form of error handling generates 76 lines of CIL, including 14 comment lines containing VB .NET source. Although it's true that the more compact (by 40%) CIL may not necessarily mean better or faster code, a deeper investigation of the longer CIL routine shows some rather peculiar gyrations. There are some clear signs that, at least in this particular instance, the more modern form of error handling is better.

As you can see from the preceding experiment, **Ildasm** is very useful for deeper investigations. When you want to be sure of what the code is really doing under the hood, seeing the CIL can be very instructive. If you want to delve further into CIL itself and how it works, see the "CIL Instruction Set Specification" document, which you can find in the Partition III CIL.doc file in the FrameworkSDK\Tool Developers Guide\Docs folder.

Performance Monitor: Viewing Performance Information

Performance Monitor (**PerfMon**) is an operating system application built into Windows NT 4.0 and upward. On Windows XP and .NET Server, it's called System Monitor. It allows you to monitor and graph both predefined and customized performance information about your .NET applications. Although **PerfMon** doesn't aim to show you exactly how your application performs from a high-level point of view, it does give you detailed information about what's happening inside your application that you can use to diagnose performance and resource problems.

PerfMon is actually a combination of four separate utilities. Each utility is a different view of selected counters that measure the performance of the hardware and software on a particular computer.

- **Alert** shows a list of counters to monitor and a log of counters that have exceeded a specified limit.

- **Chart** displays selected performance data on a chart in real time.

- **Log** shows a list of counters that are logging data to a file, for monitoring over an extended period.

- **Report** displays the current values of the selected counters.

You can create and customize your own performance data programmatically, a technique that I examine in the next chapter during an investigation of instrumentation and tracing. In this section, I'm going to look at some of the information automatically provided for you to monitor the performance of your

.NET applications. This information provides statistics and performance data about the following categories:

- Exceptions

- COM Interop

- The JIT compiler

- Application loading

- Locking and threading

- Memory

- Networking

- Remoting

- Security

Copious information about the performance counters within each of these categories is available in the .NET documentation. Rather than just rehash this documentation, I thought it would be better to write and then monitor a small program so that you can see why the Performance Monitor is so useful.

Testing String Performance

To put together a comparison of repeatedly modifying a string versus using the **StringBuilder** class, I wrote a program to perform each of these tasks and then used **PerfMon** to monitor the internal behavior of these two programs. Listing 5-4 shows the code for repeatedly modifying a string, in this case 20,000 times.

Listing 5-4. Modifying a String Manually

```
Option Strict On
Module StringPerfTestOne
    Sub Main()
        Dim strTest As String = "Coming up: ", intTest As Integer = 0
        System.Console.WriteLine("Starting...")
        For intTest = 1 To 20000
            strTest += "another test "
```

```
        Next
        System.Console.WriteLine("Finished")
        System.Console.ReadLine()
    End Sub
End Module
```

Listing 5-5 shows the same code, but now using the **StringBuilder** class. The documentation is adamant that the **StringBuilder** class is a huge improvement over VB.Classic's string handling, so now I'm going to look at what actually happens internally.

Listing 5-5. Modifying a String Using StringBuilder

```
Option Strict On
Module StringPerfTestTwo
    Sub Main()
        Dim sbTest As New System.Text.StringBuilder("Coming up: ")
        Dim intTest As Integer = 0
        System.Console.WriteLine("Starting...")
        For intTest = 1 To 20000
            sbTest.Append("another test ")
        Next
        System.Console.WriteLine("Finished")
        System.Console.ReadLine()
    End Sub
End Module
```

Comparing the execution of these two programs should give you some idea about the relative performance of these ways of manipulating strings. The crude way of measuring this is simply to time the two samples. If you do this, you'll find that using the **StringBuilder** class is much faster than modifying the string manually.

But I want to investigate further and find out what's happening underneath the hood. There's a performance counter supplied by .NET that monitors the percentage of time a process spends in the .NET garbage collector (GC). To start the ball rolling, you should run the program shown in Listing 5-4 after adding a breakpoint on the line marked in bold. This breakpoint gives you a chance to switch to **PerfMon** and set up the monitoring process.

Once you've started the program and hit the breakpoint, you should start **PerfMon** by typing **PerfMon** at the Start ➤ Run command. Go to the System Monitor page and add a new performance counter by clicking the Add toolbar button, which is the one marked with a plus sign (+). Under the "Performance Object" heading, choose ".NET CLR Memory" and under the "Select counters from list" heading, select the "% Time in GC" counter. Then select the **StringPerfTestOne** process as the one to monitor.

Now switch back to the program being monitored and continue from the breakpoint. You should see a graph being drawn in Performance Monitor that shows you the percentage of time that the **StringPerfTestOne** process is spending doing garbage collection. This should look something like the graph shown in Figure 5-3.

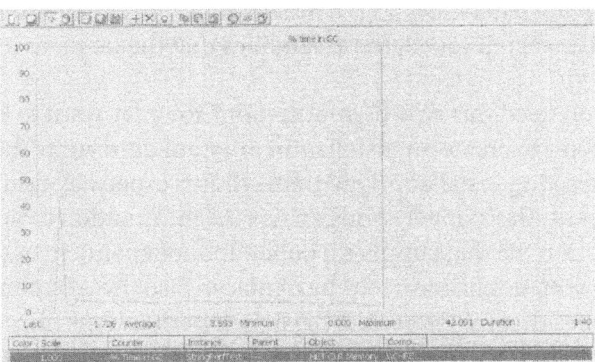

Figure 5-3. Garbage collection for the StringPerfTestOne process

As you can see, the program spends most of its time in the control of the garbage collector! The percentage of time used by the GC on my machine peaks at over 40% percent before dropping back to around 5% as the program runs. The

PerfMon profile shown on your machine may differ in quantity from mine, but the overall profile is still likely to resemble a small mountain.

So what happens if you perform the same test, but this time on the application that uses the **StringBuilder** class? I haven't bothered to include a screenshot of the result, because there's nothing to see. In addition to finishing much faster, the **StringBuilder** sample program shows a completely flat line in terms of garbage collection.

There are many other .NET performance counters available for investigating your applications, and I urge you to play with a few of them in order to understand how to monitor your programs effectively. VB .NET even comes with a sample program that illustrates how to create your own Performance Monitor. In the next chapter you'll meet **PerfMon** again when I look at the creation and use of performance counters that are customized for your application.

ADepends: Viewing Assembly Dependencies

ADepends is a useful utility buried in the \FrameworkSDK\Tool Developer Guide \Samples\ADepends folder. It's a C# sample program. Once you've compiled it using the supplied batch file and the **nmake** tool, you can point it at any .NET assembly and it will tell you all the assemblies that the target assembly depends on.

Why do you need this type of information? You may want to know the assembly dependencies to create an installation program or to verify the dependencies shown by an existing installation program—this is especially useful for checking version numbers. Alternatively, you can use the information to help create a custom configuration file that supplies a policy about dependent assembly version numbers that your application requires. You can also use **ADepends** to identify those assemblies that might need to have their permissions traced in the case of a security exception. Security exceptions are often caused by a permission problem somewhere deep within a call stack rather than by the assembly that actually raised the exception because, by default, a specific permission is required by every assembly within a call stack.

If you point **ADepends** at itself, you can see a good example of the sort of information available (see Figure 5-4). The first line shows the name, version, culture, and public fingerprint of the assembly under analysis. Then you can see the list of assemblies and modules used directly. The assemblies in this case are **mscorlib**, **System.Windows.Forms**, **Accessibility**, **System.Xml**, **System.Drawing**, and **System**. The analysis then continues recursively, showing all of the lower assembly dependencies.

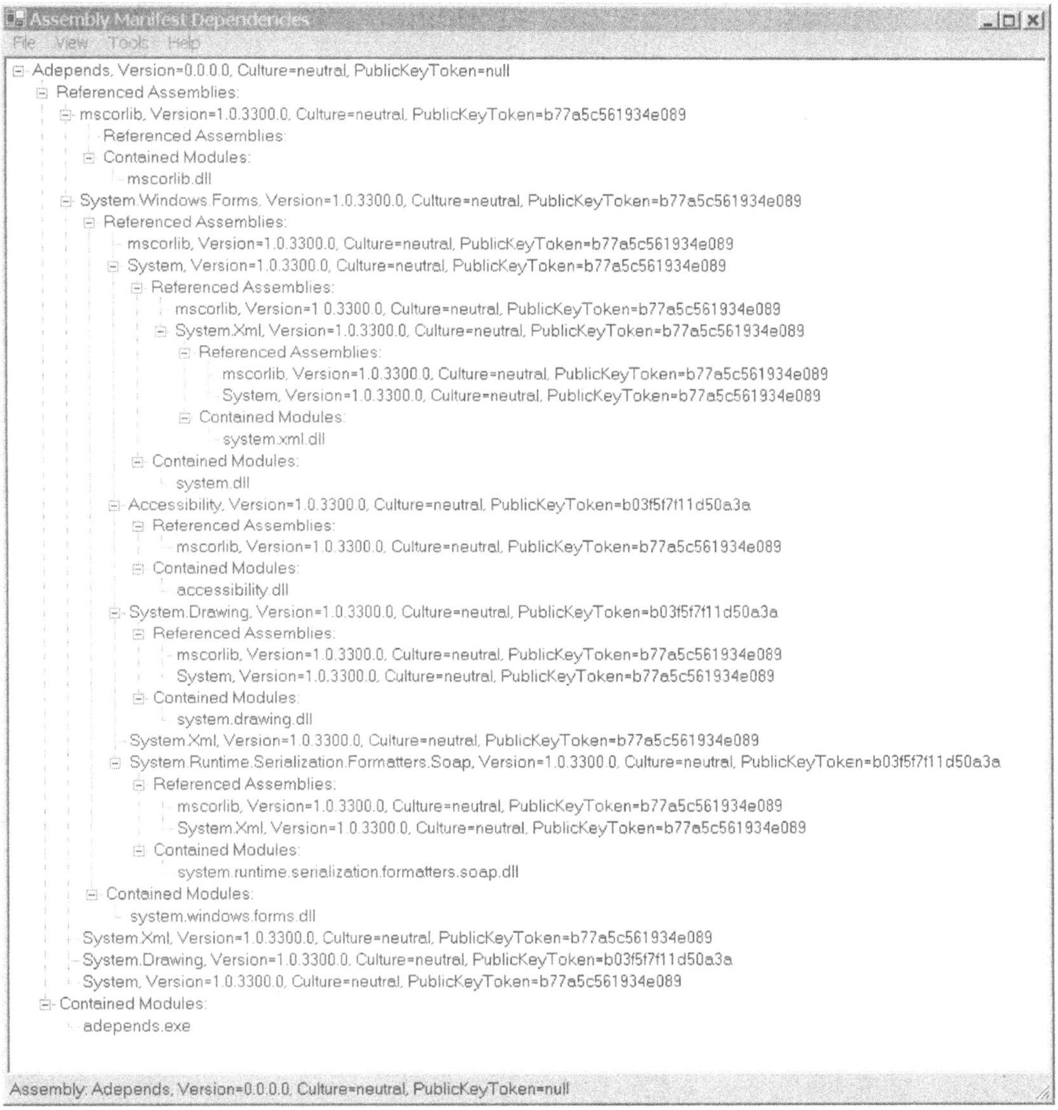

Figure 5-4. ADepends's view of itself

PermView: Viewing Assembly Permissions

PermView is a .NET utility that is a good companion to the **ADepends** program described in the previous section. Given an assembly, **PermView** tells you the minimal, optional, and refused permissions requested by the assembly, and it can optionally tell you about the assembly's declarative security.

Well, that's what the documentation says, but what does it actually mean and why is it important? To answer this, I need to take a little side tour into permissions and security. The concept here is that you can (and you often should) tell your assembly to request whatever permissions it needs from the CLR when it starts to execute. To request permissions for your assembly, you first add attributes to your code. The VB .NET language compiler then stores the requested permissions in the program when it's compiled.

When your assembly is loaded by the CLR, these permissions are checked against the security policy rules, and any permission that is not granted is flagged with a security exception. This exception usually doesn't give much helpful information; rather, it says something generic like "System.Security.Policy.PolicyException: Failed to acquire required permissions". This is where **PermView** is invaluable: Developers and system administrators can use it to check exactly what permissions an assembly is requesting. Once a developer or system administrator knows these permissions, he or she can then examine and change the relevant security policy file to grant the necessary permissions to the assembly.

There are three types of permissions that you can request for your assemblies:

1. *RequestMinimum:* The minimum permissions that your assembly needs in order to execute successfully. This might include, for instance, a request for permission to perform file input/output.

2. *RequestOptional:* The permissions that your assembly would like to have but are not essential for successful execution. This could, for instance, be a request for permission to write to a specific log file in a specific folder.

3. *RequestRefused:* The permissions that your assembly specifically does not want, usually to avoid their misuse by code that calls your assembly. This might be declining permission for any action that involves a write to the registry.

Explicitly requesting these permissions means that an administrator can see your assembly's permission requirements and adjust the assembly's security policy accordingly. It also means that your code is more likely to run properly; if the correct permissions are not specified, your code must deal with every possible permission failure internally if it's to execute without causing an exception.

One interesting "gotcha" is that once you've started adding permission requests, you need to specify *all* the permissions needed by your assembly. This is because once an assembly has requested a permission, the CLR denies all other permissions that haven't been specifically requested, even if the relevant security policy grants those other permissions. **PermView** can be useful for spotting this type of situation, which can cause an application to cease working completely for no obvious reason.

PermView Within Visual Studio

The easiest way to invoke **PermView** on a regular basis is to create a new item on the Tools menu. You can do this by going to Tools ➤ External Tools and completing the External Tools dialog box with the following entries:

Title: Permissions (or whatever title you want)

Command: C:\Program Files\Microsoft.Net\FrameworkSDK\bin\permview.exe

Arguments: $(TargetPath)

Initial directory: $(TargetDir)

You should also check the *Use Output window* option, as this creates a custom pane in the Output window where **PermView** can display its information. You should now have a new item on the Tools menu. Selecting this new menu item invokes **PermView** on the current assembly, allowing you to view the permissions requested for the assembly.

PermView from the Command Line

Invoking **PermView** from the command line is just as easy as invoking it from within Visual Studio. When it's used in this manner, **PermView** displays its findings directly to the console window. The following command line shows the permissions granted to the assembly MyAssembly.exe:

```
PERMVIEW MyAssembly.exe
```

Investigating Permissions

Rather than go into ponderous detail that you can easily find in the documentation, I present in this section some examples of attributing an assembly to request specific permissions and what those permission requests look like when you examine them using **PermView**.

Example 1. Assembly Must Execute with Full Trust

```
Imports System.Security.Permissions
<Assembly: PermissionSetAttribute(SecurityAction.RequestMinimum,
Name:="FullTrust")>
```

Running **PermView** produces the following permission sets:

```
Microsoft (R) .NET Framework Permission Request Viewer.  Version 1.0.3705.0
Copyright (C) Microsoft Corporation 1998-2001. All rights reserved.
```
minimal permission set:
```
<PermissionSet class="System.Security.PermissionSet"
               version="1"
               Unrestricted="true"/>
```
optional permission set:
```
  Not specified
```
refused permission set:
```
  Not specified
```

Example 2. Assembly Must Execute with Internet Trust

```
<Assembly: PermissionSetAttribute(SecurityAction.RequestMinimum,
Name:="Internet")>
```

Running **PermView** produces the following:

```
minimal permission set:
<PermissionSet class="System.Security.PermissionSet"
               version="1">
   <Ipermission
class="System.Security.Permissions.FileDialogPermission, mscorlib,
Version=1.0.3300.0, Culture=neutral,
PublicKeyToken=b77a5c561934e089"
               version="1"
               Access="Open"/>
   <IPermission
class="System.Security.Permissions.IsolatedStorageFilePermission,
mscorlib, Version=1.0.3300.0, Culture=neutral,
PublicKeyToken=b77a5c561934e089"
               version="1"
               Allowed="DomainIsolationByUser"
               UserQuota="10240"/>
   <IPermission
class="System.Security.Permissions.SecurityPermission, mscorlib,
```

```
Version=1.0.3300.0, Culture=neutral,
PublicKeyToken=b77a5c561934e089"
                version="1"
                Flags="Execution"/>
   <IPermission class="System.Security.Permissions.UIPermission,
mscorlib, Version=1.0.3300.0, Culture=neutral,
PublicKeyToken=b77a5c561934e089"
                version="1"
                Window="SafeTopLevelWindows"
                Clipboard="OwnClipboard"/>
   <IPermission class="System.Drawing.Printing.PrintingPermission,
System.Drawing, Version=1.0.3300.0, Culture=neutral,
PublicKeyToken=b03f5f7f11d50a3a"
                version="1"
                Level="SafePrinting"/>
</PermissionSet>
```

Example 3. Assembly Must Have Full Rights to a Specific File and Folder

```
<Assembly: FileIOPermissionAttribute(SecurityAction.RequestMinimum,
_ All:="C:\log\logfile.txt")>
```

Running **PermView** produces the following:

```
minimal permission set:
<PermissionSet class="System.Security.PermissionSet"
                version="1">
   <IPermission
class="System.Security.Permissions.FileIOPermission, mscorlib,
Version=1.0.3300.0, Culture=neutral,
PublicKeyToken=b77a5c561934e089"
                version="1"
                Read="C:\log\logfile.txt"
                Write="C:\log\logfile.txt"
                Append="C:\log\logfile.txt"
                PathDiscovery="C:\log\logfile.txt"/>
</PermissionSet>
```

Example 4. Assembly Must Be Allowed to Read Anything in a Specific Folder

```
<Assembly: FileIOPermissionAttribute(SecurityAction.RequestMinimum,
Read:="C:\temp")>
```

Running **PermView** produces the following:

```
minimal permission set:
<PermissionSet class="System.Security.PermissionSet"
                version="1">
    <IPermission
class="System.Security.Permissions.FileIOPermission, mscorlib,
Version=1.0.3300.0, Culture=neutral,
PublicKeyToken=b77a5c561934e089"
                version="1"
                Read="C:\temp"/>
</PermissionSet>
```

Example 5. Assembly Must Be Able to Read Part of the Registry

```
<Assembly:
RegistryPermissionAttribute(SecurityAction.RequestMinimum, _
Read:="HKEY_LOCAL_MACHINE\HARDWARE\DESCRIPTION\System\
CentralProcessor")>
```

Running **PermView** produces the following:

```
minimal permission set:
<PermissionSet class="System.Security.PermissionSet"
                version="1">
    <IPermission
class="System.Security.Permissions.RegistryPermission, mscorlib,
Version=1.0.3300.0, Culture=neutral,
PublicKeyToken=b77a5c561934e089"
                version="1"
Read="HKEY_LOCAL_MACHINE\HARDWARE\DESCRIPTION\System\CentralProcessor"/>
</PermissionSet>
```

Example 6. Assembly Must Be Able to Use the Clipboard

```
<Assembly: UIPermissionAttribute(SecurityAction.RequestMinimum, _
Clipboard:=UIPermissionClipboard.OwnClipboard)>
```

Running **PermView** produces the following:

```
minimal permission set:
<PermissionSet class="System.Security.PermissionSet"
                version="1">
    <IPermission class="System.Security.Permissions.UIPermission,
```

```
mscorlib, Version=1.0.3300.0, Culture=neutral,
PublicKeyToken=b77a5c561934e089"
                version="1"
                Clipboard="OwnClipboard"/>
</PermissionSet>
```

Example 7. Assembly Must Have Access to System Dialog Boxes

```
<Assembly: UIPermissionAttribute(SecurityAction.RequestMinimum, _
Window:=UIPermissionWindow.SafeTopLevelWindows)>
```

Running **PermView** produces the following:

```
minimal permission set:
<PermissionSet class="System.Security.PermissionSet"
                version="1">
   <IPermission class="System.Security.Permissions.UIPermission,
mscorlib, Version=1.0.3300.0, Culture=neutral,
PublicKeyToken=b77a5c561934e089"
                version="1"
                Window="SafeTopLevelWindows"/>
</PermissionSet>
```

Example 8. Assembly Must Be Able to Use Assertions

```
<Assembly: SecurityPermissionAttribute(SecurityAction.RequestMinimum, _
Assertion:=True)>
```

Running **PermView** produces the following:

```
minimal permission set:
minimal permission set:
<PermissionSet class="System.Security.PermissionSet"
                version="1">
   <IPermission
class="System.Security.Permissions.SecurityPermission, mscorlib,
Version=1.0.3300.0, Culture=neutral,
PublicKeyToken=b77a5c561934e089"
                version="1"
                Flags="Assertion"/>
</PermissionSet>
```

Summary

In this chapter, you saw some of the debugging tools that come with Visual Studio and the .NET Framework. First under the microscope were **Cordbg** and **Dbgclr**, two debuggers that supplement the Visual Studio debugger and can replace it in certain situations. You also investigated **Ildasm**, the CIL disassembler that allows you to peek inside your code to see what's really happening. Then you saw how the Performance Monitor utility can help you to investigate the internal performance of your application. Finally, you explored **ADepends** and **PermView**, two utilities that show you assembly dependencies and assembly permission requests.

In the complex world of .NET, you should try to add these and other weapons to your debugging arsenal. Some of the new bugs can seem quite intractable in such a new and novel environment, so the more angles of attack you have, the quicker you're likely to resolve your application's problems.

INTERLUDE

MY TOP 5 BUGS

Top 10 lists seem to be all the rage nowadays, so I thought I'd make my own contribution. Unfortunately, I've led a relatively clean life and couldn't find ten bugs that were worth discussing. Instead, here's a list of the five most memorable bugs that I've encountered in my 23 years of commercial programming.

Number 5: The Bold Performer

I was asked to investigate a performance problem where a trading application written in VB.Classic was taking more than 2 minutes to start. This slow startup time was really annoying the traders using the application, to the point where they were threatening dire retribution if the problem wasn't fixed. So I decided to explore the issue by using a third-party profiler to look in detail at the startup performance.

After constructing call graphs and mapping the most expensive procedures, I found a single statement that was occupying no less than 50% of the startup time! The two grid controls that formed the core of the application's GUI were referenced by code that marked every other grid column in bold. There was one statement inside a loop that changed the font to bold, and this statement was the culprit. Although the line of code only took milliseconds to run, it was executed over 50,000 times. The original developer had used small volumes of data and hadn't bothered to check whether the routine was being called redundantly. Over time, as the volume of data grew, the startup times became slower and slower.

After changing the code so that the grid columns were set to bold only once, the application's startup time dropped by nearly a minute and the day was saved. The moral here is that it's very easy to spend a lot of time tuning the wrong part of your program. It's better to get significant portions of your application to work correctly and then use a good profiler to look at where the real speed bumps are hiding. Finally, when your whole application is up and running correctly, use the profiler again to discover any remaining performance issues caused by your system integration.

Number 4: The Twilight Zone

This bug lived in the same trading application mentioned in the preceding section. While testing some new functionality that I had recently added, I happened to notice that the code to display the results of a certain type of trade would never work properly. After looking at the source control system, it was obvious that this bug had existed for at least a year, and I was amazed that none of the traders had ever spotted it. After puzzling for a while and checking with a colleague, I fixed the bug and went on testing my new functionality.

About 3 minutes later, my phone rang. On the other end of the line was an irate trader who complained that one of his trades wasn't showing correctly. Upon further investigation, I realized that the trader had been hit with the exact same bug I had noticed in the code 3 minutes earlier. This bug had been lying around for a year, just waiting for a developer to come along and spot it so that it could strike for real.

This is a good example of a type of bug known as a *Schroedinbug,* which I discuss in Chapter 7's Interlude section. While most of us have heard about these peculiar entities, it is an eerie feeling when you actually encounter one in the wild.

Number 3: The Crawling Horror

While working for a software house, I was given the task of making a minor amendment to a deal-entry application. I innocently opened the source code to find an extraordinary mess that defied description. The code contained everything from hard-coded value changes (If PageLine = 17 and VarValue = 23.7 Then VarValue = 16.1) to variable gotos (Goto Line(VarX+VarY-5)). After a couple of hours' investigation, I counted something like 30 bugs. After a couple of *days*, the bug count was over 200. It was like walking into an insane asylum. The original code author was long gone, and I was left with a true crawling horror.

This was perhaps my moment of conversion, when I started to devote some significant hours to the pursuit of software quality. It even led, indirectly, to the writing of this book. There's nothing like a few scarring experiences to teach you about software development.

Number 2: Hide the Furniture

Possibly the most bizarre "bug" that I have ever encountered happened in the mid-1980s. One of my company's inventory programs, running on a Nixdorf 8870 minicomputer, always crashed when used by a certain administrator. When it was used by anybody else, the program ran without a murmur, but it seemed to have a distinct aversion to this specific woman.

I first thought that she was performing some arcane program operation that wasn't done by the other staff. After quizzing her for a while, I still couldn't understand what was going wrong. I tried several other hunches, but nothing would explain why the program was crashing. I even wondered whether her clothes were generating some static electricity that was upsetting the computer!

In the end, I actually went to the woman's office to do some serious debugging. From the moment that she arrived in the room I watched her like a hawk, expecting her to do something that would lead to the problem. What she actually did was fairly mundane. Because the normal chair in the room didn't ergonomically suit her back, she went to the office next door to retrieve a chair that she liked better. Then she sat down, and about a minute later the program crashed.

In a flash of inspiration, I took the chair apart. After locating a magnet, I tested the inside of the chair. Sure enough, the core of the chair had somehow become magnetized, and this was what was causing the computer to react violently to this woman's presence. Problem solved.

I still maintain that this was my finest debugging hour—everything since has been downhill.

Number 1: The Bug from Hell

The occasion was the rollout of a new version of my group's in-house trading application to all of the commodity traders, and the time was 6:00 P.M. on a Friday. The estimate for three of us to complete the rollout was 2–3 hours, although the traders wouldn't be back until 9:00 A.M. the following day. We'd already performed a test rollout to a couple of production PCs, and everything had worked perfectly. Full of optimism, we set to work.

At about 8:00 P.M., we realized that we had a problem. On just three of the ten PCs, our application refused to start properly, producing a strange error that suggested a registry problem. By midnight, after increasingly frustrated efforts to locate the problem, we were reduced to adding copious trace statements and then recompiling the application in order to find the exact line where the error was occurring. This line turned out to be a Dim statement, a nonexecutable line that would never normally give an error.

By 3:00 A.M., after numerous experiments and diagnostic attempts, we were still baffled. As far as we could tell, the problem was some sort of registry issue that occurred because the Windows user profile was corrupted—re-creating the user profile from scratch cured the problem. Unfortunately, it appeared that running certain other programs would then corrupt the profile again, and our program would stop working. Why this problem happened on some PCs but not others was also a mystery. The installation scripting process for that particular company was a real witch's brew.

By 6:00 A.M., 12 hours after we had started, we still hadn't found a satisfactory solution or workaround, and desperation was starting to set in.

By 9:00 A.M., as the traders came in to work, we decided that they could cope with the seven PCs that were working, and we would fix the other three PCs on the following Monday. Exhausted and frustrated at being beaten, we retired to our respective homes to lick our wounds.

Several *months* later, we still weren't able to diagnose the exact problem, even with the help of other teams. In fact, the bug was never found. It finally disappeared when we moved from Windows NT to Windows 2000 as the base operating system, but this still remains the most exasperating bug that I've ever encountered.

CHAPTER 6

Tracing and Instrumentation

TRACING AND INSTRUMENTATION refers to the process of adding code to your application in order to locate and diagnose errors, identify application status, and measure performance. Instrumentation is about adding the tracing code, and tracing is about directing and otherwise controlling the information generated by the tracing code. Needless to say, there's a third step: analyzing the generated information.

In a way, this process is similar to the use of black boxes in commercial and many private aircraft. Black boxes consist of a Flight Data Recorder (FDR) and a Cockpit Voice Recorder (CVR) that together record a large amount of information about the state of an aircraft and the behavior of its flight crew. Since their implementation, they have been invaluable in identifying and diagnosing nearly all of the problems that have caused airplane incidents and crashes.

You can think of adding tracing code as the equivalent of creating an FDR for your application. This is important because monitoring, supporting, and maintaining a software system, especially a distributed application, usually takes far more time than its original development. Typically, 80% of the effort put into an application goes into support after the application has gone into production. Developers often ignore this support burden because much of it is mostly invisible to them, but in the distributed and more complex world of .NET, these support costs need to be actively contained. It's no good building your company's best decision-support application (or trading application, or whatever) if it proves impossible to keep the system running in a cost-effective way. This problem becomes even worse if you build a system that your customers then come to depend on—at that point, you're unlikely to have the luxury of reengineering your code to reduce its support burden.

This chapter looks at useful types of diagnostic information, who is likely to use this information, how to use the diagnostic tools available in .NET, and how to control the data that is generated. It deals in detail with the following subjects:

- Types of diagnostic information that are useful to record

- Tracing in VB .NET, including recording, listening, and configuration

- Tracing with ASP.NET

- Using custom performance counters with Performance Monitor

Tracing in ASP.NET applications is covered in Chapter 9, which covers the debugging of ASP.NET applications.

Useful Diagnostic Information

Before you look at how to use the tracing tools provided by .NET, you need to understand who will be using the information provided by the tracing code and how they will use that information. The four most common stakeholders are the application's end users, the application's support team, the application's testing team, and the application's development team.

Application End Users

An application's end users have to know information that could adversely affect their use of the application. These people need status information from an application that helps them to

- Identify application status and failures, especially during lengthy operations

- Identify application mistakes that might affect business processes

- Work around certain application problems

Application Support Team

Some applications have the luxury of a dedicated support team, whereas others have to make do with the support available from the general help desk. However support is handled, a first-level support team has to respond directly to end users when they're having trouble using an application. This team needs status and debugging information from an application that helps them to

- Identify the application's status and behaviors

- Diagnose application errors and identify the causes

- Fix or work around the straightforward problems

- Pass diagnostic information to developers for problems that can't be solved

- Assist end users with performing certain application tasks

- Improve an application's availability to its end users

Application Development Team

An application development team has to identify the causes of application errors, fix an application when it goes wrong, and generally maintain and enhance the application's code. This team needs debugging, status, and metrics information from an application that helps them to

- Diagnose application errors and identify the causes

- Identify and understand end user/tester actions causing application problems

- Identify application performance bottlenecks and reliability "hot spots"

- Improve an application's reliability and availability

- Provide further tracing code to isolate and identify tenacious problems

Diagnostic Categories

As you can see from the preceding sections' requirements lists, the four groups of people need similar information. The main difference is often the level of detail each group needs. If the required information is categorized, there are four main types of diagnostic data:

1. *Failure data:* Exceptions, errors, warnings, crashes, and assertion failures

2. *Timing data:* Performance, communications, queries, and lengthy operations

3. *Statistical data:* Traffic volumes and usage patterns

4. *Debugging data:* User actions, program state, and program data

It is the job of a developer to include tracing code to emit all of this data, and it is quite an art to identify exactly which information will be useful for solving a wide variety of potential problems. At the very least, I suggest that your tracing code be capable of recording each of the following situations:

- Every program crash and the call stack that led to the crash

- Every exception and the call stack that led to the exception

- Every assertion failure (I discuss assertions in the next section)

- Every "Page not found" (404) error

- Every component or page time-out

- Timing data for every lengthy software operation

- Timing data for every business-critical software operation

- Timing data for every database query

- Timing data for any "real-time" communication with another application

- Status data recording the results of application health checks

- Status data reporting any communication problems between components

- Records of all messages involving communication between components

- Traffic volumes, especially any large increases in traffic volume

- Usage patterns, especially any significant changes in usage

Note that having tracing code that records this information doesn't mean that all of the tracing code needs to be activated all of the time. As you'll see later in the section titled "Step 5: Trace Control at Runtime," it's possible to use an application's configuration file at runtime to control which information is actually emitted at a fine level.

Of course, you also need to record information that pinpoints the exact location and type of problem. This might include some sort of standard header incorporating the following data:

- Component name and path

- Machine name, IP, and maybe its geographic location if applicable

- Type of environment (e.g., dev, integration test, user test, live, or contingency)

- Whether support is required and the support group to be contacted

The bottom line is that all of this diagnostic information helps you to improve your application's availability through better and faster understanding of problems. In the case of a large distributed application where problems can be especially hard to locate and diagnose, this information can make the difference between your application being viable and not viable.

Design Recommendations

No matter what tracing tools you use, there are some design decisions that you need to make. Here are a few rules of thumb that have proven to be useful for many applications, even those built before .NET arrived:

- *Centralize tracing code:* Create reusable tracing classes or components that standardize logging information and provide tracing facilities without bothering developers with unnecessary details.

- *Centralize diagnostic information:* Place all diagnostic information in one central location (such as a database) to allow easier monitoring and statistical analysis.

- *Minimize performance degradation:* Use trace control mechanisms to ensure that you don't emit diagnostic information unless it's needed and to postpone the gathering of expensive diagnostic information until it's really necessary.

- *Analyze failures and keep metrics:* To improve the service offered to an application's end users, you should study its failures and then provide the support team with the root cause of each problem and a list of possible solutions. Providing metrics in the form of charts can also help the support people to identify reliability and availability trends.

VB .NET Tracing

Having hopefully persuaded you that instrumentation and tracing is critically important when building any nontrivial application, I'll now show you how to add the most common type of tracing to your VB .NET software. You need to deal with five basic elements:

1. Add tracing code to your application with the **Trace** class.

2. Activate or deactivate tracing code at compile time with the **TRACE** flag.

3. Specify the destination of tracing information with the **TraceListener** class.

4. Specify the level of tracing at runtime with the **TraceSwitch** class.

5. Control and override tracing behavior at runtime with the application's configuration file.

An important point to make here is that everything I'm about to discuss deals with tracing in non-ASP.NET applications. ASP.NET tracing is done differently, and I cover it in Chapter 9, which deals with debugging ASP.NET applications.

Step 1: Trace Creation

The **System.Diagnostics.Trace** class is the cornerstone of instrumentation and allows you to write tracing code that sends diagnostic information to all of the current trace listeners. It has several methods for this purpose. I describe these methods in the sections that follow.

The Write and WriteLine Methods

The **Write** method is used to produce diagnostic information without a linefeed, so that further information can then be appended to the same line. The **Write-Line** method is used to produce diagnostic information with a linefeed. Both of these methods are overloaded so that you can supply optional parameters. See Listing 6-1 for some examples of using this method.

Listing 6-1. Using Trace.WriteLine

```
'This overload takes just a string
'and will produce the trace message Some diagnostic information
Trace.WriteLine("Some diagnostic information")

'This overload takes two strings, a diagnostic message and a user-defined
category
'and will produce the trace message Warning: A was supposed to equal B
Trace.WriteLine("A was supposed to equal B", "Warning")

'This overload takes an object and passes its .ToString value
'and will produce a trace message with the value of MyObject.ToString
Trace.WriteLine(MyObject)

'This overload takes an object and a user-defined category
'and will produce the trace message Information: MyObject.ToString
Trace.WriteLine(MyObject, "Information")
```

The interesting idea here is to find a good use for the user-defined category. One good use is shown in the preceding examples: a message level. In this scheme, you specify different levels of importance so that people looking at the tracing output can easily categorize the information into routine messages, warnings, and errors, or indeed whatever other scheme you devise. Another possibility is to specify the class name as the category, so that you can easily tell which class produced each trace message.

The WriteIf and WriteLineIf Methods

These two **Trace** class methods are almost identical to their **WriteLine** and **Write** siblings, but each also takes a boolean expression that has to evaluate to **true** for the trace information to be emitted. You would write something like the code shown in Listing 6-2.

Listing 6-2. Using Trace.WriteLineIf

```
Trace.WriteLineIf(IsTracingActive, GetStack() & GetDatetime() _
        & "Some diagnostic info")
```

The only caveat with these conditional methods is performance. Even if the boolean expression evaluates to **false**, the whole statement will be processed—there is no short-circuit. From the point of view of performance, it is better to write the code shown in Listing 6-3.

Listing 6-3. Trace.WriteLineIf Performance Constraint

```
If IsTracingActive = True Then
    Trace.WriteLine(GetStack() & GetDatetime() & "Some diagnostic info")
End If
```

The Assert and Fail Methods

These two **Trace** class methods implement *assertions*, which are safety checks within your code designed to catch conditions that theoretically shouldn't happen. Assertions are very useful because they can detect many bugs automatically, especially those bugs that result from invalid assumptions. The use of assertions is only bounded by your own imagination, but typically an assertion might be used to

- Detect an illegal condition that should never occur (e.g., checking that a configuration file setting has a legal value).

- Check that a component is operating properly (e.g., that a class has its internal flags in a mutually consistent state).

- Check that procedure parameters supplied by your own code (as opposed to the code of another developer) are really valid.

- Document an assumption that you make during coding (e.g., that another developer's component always gives an answer within a certain range).

The **Assert** method therefore tests an expression that you define, which should normally evaluate to **true**. If instead the condition evaluates to **false**, the assertion has failed and the **Assert** method automatically displays one or more messages that should contain your explanation of how and why the condition failed. See Listing 6-4 for some examples of using **Trace.Assert**.

Listing 6-4. Using Trace.Assert

```
Dim VbClassic As Int16, VbNet As Int16
'Does TRUE have the same value when using
'VB.Classic functions and VB .NET functions?
VbClassic = CInt(True)
VbNet = Convert.ToInt16(True)

'This overload just shows the call stack leading to the assertion failure
Trace.Assert(VbClassic = VbNet)
```

```
'This overload adds an brief explanation of the assertion failure
Trace.Assert (VbClassic = VbNet, "Assertion failed: _
                          VbClassic(True) <> VbNet(True)")


'This overload adds a more detailed explanation of the assertion failure
Trace.Assert (VbClassic = VbNet, "Assertion failed: _
                          VbClassic(True) <> VbNet(True)", _
                          "CInt(True)=" & VbClassic.ToString & _
                          " : Convert.ToInt16(True)=" & VbNet.ToString)
```

The **Fail** method is simply an assertion that always fails, and it's typically used to signal that the software doesn't understand what it's trying to process. For example, a **Select** statement that runs out of options should use **Trace.Fail** to show that the **Else** clause has been reached. The **Fail** method is also overloaded, so you can supply just a single message or, as shown in the code in Listing 6-5, a summary message together with a more detailed message.

Listing 6-5. Using Trace.Fail

```
Select Case TestNum
    Case 1
        'Valid value - something happens here
    Case 2
        'Valid value - something happens here
    Case 3
        'Valid value - something happens here
    Case Else
        Trace.Fail("TestNum=" & TestNum.ToString, _
                              "TestNumber must be between 1 and 3")
End Select
```

One major advantage of using assertions is that the complete call stack is added automatically to the generated message. This even includes the line number of the assertion if your application is running as a debug build. Listing 6-6 shows the detailed assertion message produced by the code shown in Listing 6-4 executing as a result of a command button click.

Listing 6-6. Example of an Assertion Message

```
---- DEBUG ASSERTION FAILED ----
---- Assert Short Message ----
Assertion failed: VbClassic(True) <> VbNet(True)
---- Assert Long Message ----
CInt(True) = -1 : Convert.ToInt16(True) = 1
```

```
     at TraceDebug.btnTrueIsFalse_Click(Object sender, EventArgs e)
   C:\Visual Studio Projects\TraceAndDebug\TraceDebug.vb(117)
     at Control.OnClick(EventArgs e)
     at Button.OnClick(EventArgs e)
     at Button.OnMouseUp(MouseEventArgs mevent)
     at Control.WmMouseUp(Message& m, MouseButtons button, Int32 clicks)
     at Control.WndProc(Message& m)
     at ButtonBase.WndProc(Message& m)
     at Button.WndProc(Message& m)
     at ControlNativeWindow.OnMessage(Message& m)
     at ControlNativeWindow.WndProc(Message& m)
     at NativeWindow.Callback(IntPtr hWnd, Int32 msg, IntPtr wparam, IntPtr
lparam)
     at UnsafeNativeMethods.DispatchMessageW(MSG& msg)
     at ComponentManager.System.Windows.Forms.UnsafeNativeMethods+
   IMsoComponentManager.FPushMessageLoop(Int32 dwComponentID,
   Int32 reason, Int32 pvLoopData)
     at ThreadContext.RunMessageLoop(Int32 reason, ApplicationContext context)
     at Application.Run(Form mainForm)
     at TraceDebug.Main()  C:\Visual Studio
Projects\TraceAndDebug\TraceDebug.vb(19)
```

Using Assertions

An assertion really has two uses. During development and unit testing, an assertion failure is shown directly to the developer so that the problem can be investigated and fixed. Therefore, the default output of an assertion failure is to display the call stack and any programmer-defined messages to the developer using a message box. The developer can then choose to stop program execution immediately by clicking Abort, drop into the debugger at the point of assertion failure by clicking Retry, or ignore the failure and continue program execution by clicking Ignore.

During application integration testing and when in production, there is no point in displaying assertion failures to the end user—these messages would just be confusing. Instead, the application can be told to redirect assertion failures to a log file. I discuss this later when I cover investigating the use of application configuration files.

An important point to remember is that assertions should not take the place of defensive programming. Assertions are intended to detect "impossible" conditions, and they can therefore be sprinkled liberally through your code in an effort to find as many problems and mistaken assumptions as possible. However, adding defensive code to cater to each and every possible assertion failure is counterproductive. Assertions should never normally fail, and adding large amounts of defensive code just makes your application more complex and introduces a strong probability of extra bugs. You should have defensive code for critical areas of your application, but try to use each assertion as a warning beacon, not as a support fixture for some defensive programming. If you are actually seeing regular assertion failures, the solution is to eliminate them by fixing the code rather than trying to defend the code.

Try to document your assertions thoroughly, as it can be very exasperating to hit an assertion failure in somebody else's code and have no idea what that assertion is trying to do. A comment explaining why the assertion check exists can help to stop rogue developers from simply ripping out your carefully constructed code.

Step 2: Trace Activation

Once you've added tracing code to your application with the **Trace** class, you need a way of activating and deactivating it. At compile time, this can be controlled with a conditional compilation flag called **TRACE**. When this flag is set to **true**, any **Trace** class method is compiled as normal; when it is set to **false**, any **Trace** class method is removed from your application. You can set this flag in one of three ways:

1. *From the command line:* Use */d:TRACE=True* or */d:TRACE=False* when compiling your application from the command line.

2. *In Visual Studio:* In the Project properties ➤ Configuration properties ➤ Build window, select or deselect the "Define TRACE constant" check box when compiling your application from VS .NET.

3. *In code:* Within your code, define the **TRACE** constant using the syntax #Const TRACE = True or #Const TRACE = False.

By default, the **TRACE** flag is set to **true** in all debug and release builds. Somebody made an assumption that you will normally want tracing code to be permanently enabled. This is a sensible assumption because control of the resulting diagnostic information can be done using trace switches, an option that has its own dedicated section later in this chapter (see "Step 4: Trace Control at Compilation Time").

You can also remove any diagnostic checks that you don't require when tracing is deactivated—this can be useful for improving performance. To do this, you should use the **#If...#End If** directive with the **TRACE** constant, as shown in

Listing 6-7. If tracing is not active, none of the diagnostic code will be compiled into your program.

Listing 6-7. Determining If Tracing Is Active

```
#If TRACE Then
    'Some expensive diagnostic code goes here
#End If
```

Step 3: Trace Listening

Once you've instrumented your code so that it's producing tracing information, the next step is to direct that information to the required destinations. You do this with one or more trace listeners.

The TraceListener Class

The **System.Diagnostics.TraceListener** class is the abstract base class that you need to implement in order to create your own custom trace listeners. The job of a trace listener is to write the information emitted by the **Trace** class (using **Write**, **WriteLine**, and so on) to a specific destination, such as the console, a log file, or a database.

The .NET Framework provides some predefined listeners that handle the most common destinations for diagnostic information. The first is the **Default-TraceListener**, which writes to the **OutputDebugString** Win32 API, whereupon the VS .NET debugger redirects the information to the Output window. Other predefined listeners include the **TextWriterTraceListener**, which writes to a log file or other output stream such as the console, and the **EventLogTraceListener**, which writes to any of the Windows event logs. Adding an instance of one of these listeners to the **Trace.Listeners** collection directs tracing information to the specified destination. The following sections look at using these predefined event listeners and also cover how to define and use a custom event listener.

Using the DefaultTraceListener

When you start an application with tracing, the **DefaultTraceListener** is automatically instantiated and added to the **Trace.Listeners** collection. As a result, by default all information produced by the **Trace** class is written to the attached debugger, which in the case of VS .NET shows the information in the Output window. Normally, you don't need to write any code to support this functionality, but

Listing 6-8 shows you how to remove the default trace listener, perhaps for performance reasons.

Listing 6-8. Removing the Default Trace Listener

```
Option Strict On

Class Test
    Public Shared Sub Main()

        'Remove the default trace listener from the listeners collection
        'This method takes either a string containing the listener name
        'or the listener object
        Trace.Listeners.Remove("DefaultTraceListener")

    End Sub
End Class
```

Using the TextWriterTraceListener

One of the most common requirements is to log diagnostic information in a text file. The **System.Diagnostics.TextWriterTraceListener** class has been created specifically for this purpose. To be more precise, this class can direct tracing information to any type of **Stream** or **Writer**, which gives you considerable flexibility in arranging your output. You may, for instance, want a trace listener that writes trace information to the system console. Listing 6-9 shows how you could accomplish this.

Listing 6-9. Sending Trace Information to the System Console

```
Option Strict On

Class Test
    Public Shared Sub Main()

        'Create a trace listener that writes trace information to the console
        Dim objTraceToConsole As New TextWriterTraceListener(System.Console.Out)

        'Add the new trace listener to the collection of listeners
        Trace.Listeners.Add(objTraceToConsole)

        'Write trace information to all listeners, including the console
        Trace.WriteLine("This trace information is for all listeners")
```

```
            'Write trace information to just the console listener
        objTraceToConsole.WriteLine _
            ("This trace information is just for the console listener")

        'Pause application to see console output
        Console.ReadLine()

        'Finish and clean up our console listener
        objTraceToConsole.Flush()
        objTraceToConsole.Close()
        objTraceToConsole.Dispose()

    End Sub
End Class
```

Notice that you can send trace information to just one specific trace listener if you wish. Although this might be useful when you want to send each category (information, error, and warning) of trace information to a different listener, it subverts the flexibility of tracing where you can add trace listeners at runtime using a configuration file and expect to see the tracing output. I go into more detail about this in the section titled "Step 5: Trace Control at Runtime."

Listing 6-9 also shows the code that you need to run when you're finished with a particular trace listener. The **Flush** method ensures that all the information is actually written to the console, and the **Close** and **Dispose** methods make sure that all of the resources associated with the trace listener are released in a timely manner.

Of course, you might not want to send diagnostics to the console in this manner because the information won't be recorded permanently, but it could be useful when you want an end user to view and report a specific problem.

You might also want to send the diagnostic information to a text file, especially where the tracing database is not available. Listing 6-10 shows an example of doing this.

Listing 6-10. Sending Trace Information to a Text File

```
Option Strict On

Class Test
    Public Shared Sub Main()

        'Create a trace listener that writes trace information to a text file
        Dim objTextFile As Stream = "TraceListener.txt"
        Dim objTraceToText As New TextWriterTraceListener(objTextFile)
```

```
            'Add the new trace listener to the collection of listeners
            Trace.Listeners.Add(objTraceToText)

            'Write trace information to all listeners, including the text file
            Trace.WriteLine("This trace information is for all listeners")

            'Finish and clean up our console listener
            objTraceToText.Flush()
            objTraceToText.Close()
            objTraceToText.Dispose()

      End Sub
End Class
```

Notice the necessity in both listings to flush and close the trace listener after you've finished with it. Although the CLR promises to perform garbage collection on an object at some point after it goes out of scope, this cleanup can be delayed for a long time. Any resources used by the object won't be released until the garbage collection has taken place, which would be bad news if some other part of the code wanted to make use of the same resources before the cleanup occurred.

Using the EventLogTraceListener

The **System.Diagnostics.EventLogTraceListener** class allows you to direct tracing information to any of the Windows event logs. This can be very useful, especially for middle-tier application servers where administrators often expressly monitor these logs. It can also be useful for remote diagnostics because you can easily view another machine's Windows event log using your machine's event viewer if you have the right permissions.

Listing 6-11 shows you how to create a trace listener that writes tracing information to the Application event log, specifying the program and trace listener names as the event source. You can also write to a custom event log for your application by specifying the name of your application's custom log in the **EventLog.Log** property.

Listing 6-11. Sending Trace Information to the Application Event Log

```
Option Strict On

Class Test
    Public Shared Sub Main()
```

```
            'Create an event log trace listener, give it a name, and configure it
            Dim objTraceToAppLog As New EventLogTraceListener("LogTraceListener")
            With objTraceToAppLog
                'Write to the Application event log
               .EventLog.Log = "Application"
                'Specify source of tracing information
               .EventLog.Source = "AppName." & .Name
            End With

            'Add the new trace listener to the collection of listeners
            Trace.Listeners.Add(objTraceToAppLog)

            'Write trace information to all listeners,
            'including the Application event log
            Trace.WriteLine("This trace information is for all listeners")

            'Finish and clean up our console listener
            With objTraceToAppLog
                .Flush()
                .Close()
                .Dispose()
            End With

    End Sub
End Class
```

It's important to remember that the Windows event log has limited storage available. If you wish to write to the event log, it's better to do this away from the main code path—in other words, only when an error has occurred. If you insist on writing routine information, anybody monitoring the event log is likely to be drowned in diagnostic information, and the event log may also run out of space rather quickly.

Creating a Custom Trace Listener

You can also create a custom trace listener when you want to send diagnostics to a nonstandard destination or augment the tracing information in some manner. Listing 6-12 shows a custom trace listener derived from the **TextWriterTraceListener** class. This custom trace listener writes timing information to an XML trace file to record specific performance information produced by your application.

Listing 6-12. Custom Trace Listener for Recording Performance Data

```vb
Option Strict On
Imports System.Diagnostics
Imports System.Threading
Imports System.Text
Imports System.IO
Imports System

Public Class TimerTraceListener : Inherits TextWriterTraceListener
    Private msbBuffer As New StringBuilder()
    'All of our constructors are here
    Public Sub New(ByVal Stream As Stream)
        MyBase.New(Stream)
        EmitHeader()
    End Sub

    Public Sub New(ByVal Stream As Stream, ByVal Name As String)
        MyBase.New(Stream, Name)
        EmitHeader()
    End Sub

    Public Sub New(ByVal Writer As TextWriter)
        MyBase.New(Writer)
        EmitHeader()
    End Sub

    Public Sub New(ByVal Writer As TextWriter, ByVal Name As String)
        MyBase.New(Writer, Name)
        EmitHeader()
    End Sub

    Protected Sub EmitHeader()
        'Start tracing performance data
        MyBase.WriteLine("<trace>")
    End Sub

    Public Overloads Overrides Sub Write(ByVal Message As String)
        If msbBuffer Is Nothing Then
            msbBuffer = New StringBuilder()
        End If
        msbBuffer.Append(Message)
    End Sub
```

```vb
Public Overloads Overrides Sub WriteLine(ByVal Message As String)
    If Not (msbBuffer Is Nothing) Then
        Message = msbBuffer.ToString & Message
        msbBuffer = Nothing
    End If
    EmitMessage(Message)
End Sub


Protected Sub EmitMessage(ByVal Message As String)
    'Write performance data
    Dim objNow As DateTime = New System.DateTime().Now
    Dim objCalledFrom As New StackFrame(4)

    MyBase.WriteLine("<entry>")
    'Timing data
    With objNow
        MyBase.WriteLine(CreateTag("time", .ToLongTimeString() & "." _
& .Millisecond.ToString))
        MyBase.WriteLine(CreateTag("message", Message))
    End With
    'Caller data
    With objCalledFrom.GetMethod
        MyBase.WriteLine(CreateTag("method", .DeclaringType.FullName & "." _
& .Name))
    End With
    'Thread data
    MyBase.WriteLine(CreateTag("thread", Thread.CurrentThread.Name))
    'Finish log entry
    MyBase.WriteLine("</entry>")

End Sub


Protected Function CreateTag(ByVal TagName As String, _
ByVal TagContents As String) As String
    'Return an XML tag
    Return "<" & TagName & ">" & TagContents & "</" & TagName & ">"
End Function


Public Overrides Sub Flush()
    'Flush any remaining information to file
    If Not (msbBuffer Is Nothing) Then
        EmitMessage(msbBuffer.ToString)
        msbBuffer = Nothing
```

```
        End If
        'Don't forget to chain to MyBase
        MyBase.Flush()
    End Sub


    Public Overrides Sub Close()
        'Finish tracing performance data
        MyBase.WriteLine("</trace>")
        Me.Flush()
        'Don't forget to chain to MyBase
        MyBase.Close()
    End Sub

End Class
```

Using this trace listener is simplicity itself. See the code in Listing 6-13 for an example that writes the trace information to a file called Performance.xml. Notice that as it stands, this listener will hear all trace information emitted from anywhere in your application. You might want to restrict the listener to recording only performance data—for instance, listening only to procedure entries and exits. To do this, you could establish some special prefix to the trace message, and then this listener can be told to ignore any trace message without this prefix. Alternatively, you can use the custom trace listener directly without adding it to the collection of trace listeners.

Listing 6-13. Using the Custom Trace Listener

```
Imports System.IO
'Activate the custom trace listener and its output file stream
Dim objPerformOutput As Stream = File.Create("Performance.xml")
Dim objPerformRecorder As New TimerTraceListener(objPerformOutput)
Trace.Listeners.Add(objPerformRecorder)
'Add this statement at the start of every monitored procedure
Trace.WriteLine("Entering procedure")
'Add this statement at the end of every monitored procedure
Trace.WriteLine("Leaving procedure")
'Add these statements when closing the custom trace listener
objPerformRecorder.Flush()
objPerformRecorder.Close()
```

To see some example performance diagnostics produced by this custom trace listener, look at the XML in Listing 6-14. This listing shows just two trace entries, the first written upon entering a procedure and the second produced when exiting the same procedure.

Listing 6-14. The XML Produced by the Custom Trace Listener

```
<trace>
    <entry>
        <time>17:06:01.861</time>
        <message>Entering procedure</message>
        <method>ConsoleAndText.Module1.Main</method>
        <thread></thread>
    </entry>
    <entry>
        <time>17:06:01.907</time>
        <message>Leaving procedure</message>
        <method>ConsoleAndText.Module1.Main</method>
        <thread></thread>
    </entry>
</trace>
```

Step 4: Trace Control at Compilation Time

Once your application is producing and recording tracing information, the next step is to control the tracing process and the amount of diagnostic information produced. This is necessary because if you emit and record all of your diagnostic information all of the time, you'll find that your application is degraded in performance and your support team will suffocate under a huge pile of mostly useless information. Trying to find the significant application issues in a giant haystack of tracing information is almost impossible, especially if your application is large and/or distributed.

You've already seen that you can control the production of all tracing information at build time with the **TRACE** conditional compilation flag. This is, however, a single on/off decision; either you see all of the tracing information or you see none of it. To control the tracing process at a more granular level, you need to use one or more trace switches.

There are two predefined trace switch classes, both of which are in the **System.Diagnostics** namespace. The first is the **TraceSwitch** class, which gives you up to five trace levels to control the production of trace information. The second is the **BooleanSwitch** class, which gives you just two trace settings (on and off). The major benefit these two switch classes give you is the ability to specify several different tracing levels at runtime without recompiling your application. You can also define a custom trace switch if you want to add to, or extend, the standard trace switch functionality.

Using the BooleanSwitch Class

The **BooleanSwitch** class has an **Enabled** boolean property that can be set either in code, from a registry or other setting, or by using an application configuration file. Setting it to 1 or above returns **true**; setting it to 0 or not setting it returns **false**. The code in Listing 6-15 shows a boolean switch being created and set to show all trace messages. Then it shows you how to test the property before writing a trace message.

Listing 6-15. Using the BooleanSwitch Class

```
'Create switch for controlling tracing in hypothetical component and set
'the boolean for this switch - setting could come from registry or config file
Private bswTraceOutput As New BooleanSwitch("MyAppTracing", "Test boolean
switch")
bswTraceOutput.Enabled = True

Public Sub Test
    'Show whether the BooleanSwitch is enabled or disabled
    If bswTraceOutput.Enabled Then
        Trace.WriteLine(bswTraceOutput.DisplayName & " is enabled")
    Else
        Trace.WriteLine(bswTraceOutput.DisplayName & " is disabled")
    End If
End Sub
```

Using the TraceSwitch Class

Whereas the **BooleanSwitch** is either on or off, the **TraceSwitch** class is more flexible and supports five possible switches, as listed in the **TraceLevel** enumeration. Table 6-1 shows the supported values.

Table 6-1. TraceLevel Enumeration Values

LEVEL	VALUE
Off	0
Error	1
Warning	2
Info	3
Verbose	4

You can set the level of a trace switch either in code, from a registry or other setting, or by using an application configuration file. Notice that the higher levels assume the lower levels, so a setting of **Warning** would also show **Error** trace messages, and **Verbose** would show all trace messages. The code in Listing 6-16 shows a trace switch being created and set to show all trace information with a level of **Warning** or higher. Then it shows you two different ways of testing the trace switch's level before writing a trace message.

Listing 6-16. Creating and Using the TraceSwitch Class

```
'Create switch for controlling tracing in hypothetical component and set
'trace level for this switch - setting could come from registry or config file
Private tswTraceControl As New TraceSwitch("SwitchTrace", "Test trace switch")
tswTraceControl.Level = TraceLevel.Warning


Public Sub Test
    'Either check the TraceError, TraceWarning, TraceInfo
    'or TraceVerbose properties
    If tswTraceControl.TraceError Then
        Trace.WriteLine("Trace only shows if traceswitch is set to show errors")
    End If
    'Or check the Level property against the TraceLevel enumeration
    If tswTraceControl.Level = TraceLevel.Warning Then
        Trace.WriteLine _
            ("Trace shows if traceswitch is set to show warnings or errors")
    End If
End Sub
```

Creating a Custom Trace Switch

You can create a custom trace switch by inheriting the **TraceSwitch** class. For instance, you might want to create custom tracing levels, maybe one for performance data, one for error information, and so on.

To demonstrate the creation of a custom trace switch, I've created one that adds extra information to any trace message and removes the task of checking the trace switch's trace level before writing the message. Before you look at the code for this trace switch, look at Listing 6-17 to see how you would use this switch.

Listing 6-17. Using the Custom Trace Switch

```
Private AppTrace As New TraceSwitchCustom("AppTrace", "A custom trace switch")

  Public Sub Test()
    'Show a trace information message
    AppTrace.MessageInfo("Trace information message", _
 "This is a verbose version of the trace information")
    'Show a trace warning message
    AppTrace.MessageWarning("Trace warning message", _
        "This is a verbose version of the trace warning")
    'Show a trace error message
    AppTrace.MessageError("Trace error message", _
    "This is a verbose version of the trace error")
End Sub
```

As you can see, this class is designed to avoid having the developer mess around with either trace levels or code dealing with extra trace diagnostics. The code in Listing 6-18 shows how such a trace switch class might be implemented. All trace messages are funneled through to the **ControlTraceOutput** procedure, where extra trace diagnostics such as the trace originating procedure and the date and time of the trace message are added.

Listing 6-18. Creating the Custom Trace Switch

```
Public Class TraceSwitchCustom : Inherits TraceSwitch

    Sub New(ByVal DisplayName As String, ByVal Description As String)
        'Chain call to base class, then show that tracing has started
        MyBase.New(DisplayName, Description)
        ControlTraceOutput(TraceLevel.Info, Me.DisplayName & _
 " trace listener created - trace level is " & Me.Level.ToString, "", 1)
    End Sub

    Protected Overrides Sub OnSwitchSettingChanged()
        'Show that switch setting has changed
        If Me.TraceInfo Then
            ControlTraceOutput(TraceLevel.Info, Me.DisplayName & _
 " trace level is now " & Me.Level.ToString, "", 1)
        End If
    End Sub
```

```vb
Public Sub MessageError(ByVal Message As String, _
                                        ByVal VerboseMessage As String)
    'Show trace error message if errors are switched on
    If Me.TraceError Then
        ControlTraceOutput(TraceLevel.Error, Message, VerboseMessage, 2)
    End If
End Sub


Public Sub MessageWarning(ByVal Message As String, _
    ByVal VerboseMessage As String)
    'Show trace warning message if warnings are switched on
    If Me.TraceWarning Then
        ControlTraceOutput(TraceLevel.Warning, Message, VerboseMessage, 2)
    End If
End Sub


Public Sub MessageInfo(ByVal Message As String, ByVal VerboseMessage As _
String)
        'Show trace information message if information messages are switched on
        If Me.TraceInfo Then
            ControlTraceOutput(TraceLevel.Info, Message, VerboseMessage, 2)
        End If
    End Sub


    Private Sub ControlTraceOutput(ByVal MessageLevel As TraceLevel, _
ByVal Message As String, _
ByVal VerboseMessage As String, _
ByVal StackDepth As Int16)
            'Validate parameters supplied by caller
            If Message Is Nothing Then Message = ""
            If VerboseMessage Is Nothing Then VerboseMessage = ""

            'Add system date/time to the trace message
            Dim strDateTime As String = New System.DateTime().Now.ToString
            'Add originating module/procedure name to the trace message
            '(catch any stackframe error, probably a permission problem)
            Dim strTraceSource As String
            Try
                Dim objStackFrame As New System.Diagnostics.StackFrame(StackDepth)
                strTraceSource = objStackFrame.GetMethod.DeclaringType.FullName & _
"." & objStackFrame.GetMethod.Name
            Catch
                strTraceSource = _
```

```
            "unknown procedure (stackframe call failed - check permissions)"
        Finally
            Trace.WriteLine _
           (MessageLevel.ToString & " message at " & strDateTime & _
            " from " & strTraceSource, Me.DisplayName)
        End Try


        'Write augmented trace message
        Trace.Indent()
        Trace.WriteLine(Message)
        'Emit verbose trace message if allowed and supplied
        If Me.TraceVerbose And VerboseMessage.Length > 0 Then
            Trace.Indent()
            Trace.WriteLine(VerboseMessage)
            Trace.Unindent()
        End If
        'Finish message
        Trace.Unindent()
        Trace.Flush()


    End Sub


End Class
```

Step 5: Trace Control at Runtime

Once your application is in testing or in production, the next step is to have runtime control over the tracing process and the amount of diagnostic information produced. This is necessary because you usually don't need to produce copious amounts of tracing information unless your testers or your end users are actually seeing a problem. During normal everyday use, you probably want to switch off most of the instrumentation to improve performance and to avoid generating useless information.

Though you can recompile your application to change its tracing behavior, it's much easier to do this with an application configuration file. A configuration file allows you to specify runtime decisions about adding and removing trace listeners, changing the level of trace switches, turning boolean switches on and off, and finally redirecting assertion failures to log files rather than message boxes. Together, these capabilities allow you to increase or decrease the amount of tracing information produced by your application, without actually having to recompile the application.

An application configuration file always resides in the same folder as its application, and it has to be named in the format *MyApp*.exe.config, where *MyApp* is replaced by the name of the executable. This text file must be in XML. The following sections discuss the XML formats used to control various aspects of application tracing.

Adding and Removing Trace Listeners

The application configuration file allows you to add and remove trace listeners at runtime. This is important because it affects the performance of your application. You probably want to have all of the trace listeners removed during normal operation in a live environment. Once a problem appears, you can change the configuration file to reinstate one or more of the listeners. The XML in Listing 6-19 shows how to add a **TextWriter** trace listener and remove the default trace listener using your application's configuration file.

Listing 6-19. XML to Add a Trace Listener at Runtime

```
<configuration>
    <system.diagnostics>
        <trace autoflush="true">
            <listeners>
                <add name="MyListener"
                        type="System.Diagnostics.TextWriterTraceListener"
                        initializeData="C:\MyListener.log"/>
                <remove name="Default"/>
            </listeners>
        </trace>
    </system.diagnostics>
</configuration>
```

After you've played around with this for a while, you may notice a couple of peculiarities. The first oddity is that the documentation is wrong about the format of the *type* element. If you specify the assembly name **System** after the trace listener as the documentation shows, you'll encounter an error. It seems as though this functionality was changed after the second beta, but the documentation wasn't updated. If you do want to specify the assembly, you have to identify it completely, with something like **System**, **Version**=*1.0.3300.0*, **Culture**=*neutral*, **PublicKeyToken**=*B77A5C561934e089*. The second oddity is that the autoflush doesn't always seem to work. Although the log file is always created, forcing the trace information to be written to the log file sometimes requires a **Trace.Flush** and a **Trace.Close** before you close your application.

Trace Switch Activation

The application configuration file also allows you to change the sensitivity level of your trace switches without recompiling your software. For instance, during development and unit testing, you might want to show all trace messages, whether they're informational messages, warnings, or errors. Once the application has reached system testing, you might want to show just trace warnings and errors. Finally, when your application reaches production, you could show just trace errors. Listing 6-20 shows the XML needed to set a database trace switch to show only trace errors and a component trace switch to show all errors. The numbers refer to the levels discussed earlier in the section on trace switches.

Listing 6-20. XML for Changing the Sensitivity of Two Trace Switches

```
<configuration>
    <system.diagnostics>
        <switches>
            <add name="DatabaseSwitch" value="1"/>
            <add name="ComponentSwitch" value="4"/>
        </switches>
    </system.diagnostics>
</configuration>
```

It's important to realize that, unlike the XML shown in Listing 6-19, this doesn't actually create the trace switches—it just sets the level of trace switches already defined in your code.

Boolean Switch Activation

The boolean switch activation operates in just the same way as the trace switch activation just discussed, but of course you only have two levels with which to play. The XML in Listing 6-21 shows how to disable a boolean switch using the application configuration file.

Listing 6-21. XML to Deactivate a Boolean Switch at Runtime

```
<configuration>
    <system.diagnostics>
        <switches>
            <add name="BoolSwitch" value="0"/>
        </switches>
    </system.diagnostics>
</configuration>
```

Assertion Redirection

As discussed earlier in this chapter, assertions are used to warn the developer and support teams about runtime behavior that should never happen and assumptions that are being violated. These assertions are excellent for catching many bugs automatically and for verifying developer assumptions. Whenever an assertion fails, a message box explaining the failure is shown to the developer.

The question is, what should happen with assertions when the application is promoted into production? First, if you want to keep all of the assertion checks, there's no benefit in showing each assertion failure to the end user via a message box. This is likely to prove confusing to most users and add absolutely nothing to their use of your software. Second, you might want to turn off assertions completely because all of those checks can create a serious drag on application performance. The thinking behind this is that if all of the assumptions and other checks were validated during development and testing, there's no need to waste time on them in production.

If you want to keep your assertion checks in production, you should add the XML in Listing 6-22 to the production version of your application's configuration file to redirect all assertion failures to the specified log file. This will prevent your end users from being assaulted with unfriendly message boxes.

Listing 6-22. XML to Redirect Assertion Failure Messages at Runtime

```
<configuration>
    <system.diagnostics>
        <assert assertuienabled="false" logfilename="c:\log.txt"/>
    </system.diagnostics>
</configuration>
```

If you want to turn off the assertion checks entirely once your application reaches production, you should use **Debug.Assert** (from the **Debug** class) rather than **Trace.Assert**. The two methods produce identical results, but all **Debug** class methods are automatically dropped during compilation of a release build. Please see the section titled "Using the Debug Class" later in this chapter for more details.

Tracing Summary

After such an intensive examination of VB .NET tracing and instrumentation, the following list presents a quick recap of what you've just learned about working with application tracing diagnostics:

- *Categorize your diagnostic information:* Decide what tracing information is required and divide the output into error messages, warning messages, informational messages, and extra detail (verbose) messages. These categories match the predefined tracing levels that have already been discussed.

- *Add tracing code:* Use the **Trace** class to add the required tracing code to your application.

- *Add trace listeners:* Use predefined or custom **TraceListener** classes to define the trace message destination(s).

- *Add trace switches:* Use the **TraceSwitch** and **BooleanSwitch** classes to specify when and which tracing information is shown.

- *Use runtime tracing control:* Use your application's configuration file to control trace listeners, trace switches, and assertions at runtime.

I've spent a lot of time discussing the **Trace** class and its companions, but it also has an important counterpart in the **Debug** class.

Using the Debug Class

As well as the **Trace** class, the Framework gives you the **Debug** class. The two classes are identical in their methods and properties, so why do both need to exist? The answer lies in the flexibility that they give you to control your application's tracing behavior. Because a different conditional compilation flag controls the **Debug** class, you can use the **Debug** class for tracing during development and unit testing, and you can use the **Trace** class for tracing during system testing and production. This is all done automatically when you create the normal debug and release builds, without your ever having to change your tracing code. Any tracing code using the **Debug** class simply disappears from any release build.

This inclusion or exclusion of tracing code is controlled with a conditional compilation flag called **DEBUG**. When this flag is set to **true**, any **Debug** class method is compiled as normal; when it is set to **false**, any **Debug** class method is removed from your application. Just like the **Trace** class, this flag can be set in one of three ways:

1. *From the command line:* Use */d:DEBUG=True* or */d:DEBUG=False* when compiling your application from the command line.

2. *In Visual Studio:* In the Project properties ➤ Configuration properties ➤ Build window, select or deselect the "Define DEBUG constant" check box when compiling your application from VS .NET.

3. *In code:* Within your code, define the **TRACE** constant using the syntax #Const DEBUG = True or #Const DEBUG = False.

By default, the **DEBUG** flag is set to **true** in all debug builds and **false** in all release builds. This is sensible because you normally don't want debug code to operate after release—that's what the **Trace** class is for.

You can also remove any diagnostic checks that you don't require when debug is deactivated; this can be useful for improving performance. To do this, you should use the **#If...#End If** directive with the **TRACE** constant, as shown in Listing 6-23. If debug is not active, none of the diagnostic code will be compiled into your program.

Listing 6-23. Determining If Debug Is Active

```
#If DEBUG Then
    'Some expensive diagnostic code goes here
#End If
```

Some developers like to separate their use of the **Debug** and **Trace** classes. In other words, they try not to use the same method in both classes within the same application. If, for instance, they use **Debug.Assert**, they won't use **Trace.Assert**. I can see the point behind this—it avoids having to think about which class to use for any specific method. However, I prefer to divide my usage of the two classes simply based on whether I want a trace message reported in production. If I want a message reported only during development and unit testing, I use the **Debug** class; otherwise, I use the **Trace** class.

Using Custom Performance Counters

In Chapter 5, you saw how to use the Performance Monitor utility and the built-in .NET performance counters to monitor various performance aspects of your application. Now you're going to expand on this by looking at building your own customized performance counters to measure parts of your application that Windows normally knows nothing about. In order to do this successfully, you need to learn some terminology and how the performance objects relate to each other.

A *performance counter* is what Windows uses to collect performance data on various system and application resources. For example, a performance counter might monitor a physical object such as the CPU or memory, a system object such as a process or thread, or an application object such as a page request or user. In Visual Studio and .NET in general, these monitored objects are known as *categories*. To confuse matters even further, categories can be divided into sub-categories, referred to in the documentation as *instances*.

This is perhaps easier to understand with an example. Open the Visual Studio Server Explorer window, and under Servers on your local machine, select Performance Counters. Surprisingly enough, this gives you a list of performance counters, including the Elapsed Time counter when you expand the Process node. After you select the Elapsed Time performance counter, you're presented with a list of instances including Idle (the elapsed time spent in the Idle process) and System (the elapsed time spent in the System process). Although the Server Explorer doesn't show it, these two instances are part of the Process category. So the relationship between performance counters, categories, and instances looks like Table 6-2.

Table 6-2. The Relationship Between Counters, Categories, and Instances

CATEGORY: PROCESS	
Instance: Idle	*Instance: System*
Counter: Elapsed Time	Counter: Elapsed Time

Once you've got your head around the terminology and relationships, the next step is to understand the different types of custom performance counters available to you, and how to create and manipulate these counters both at design time and within your code. To do this, I'm going to measure various aspects of two different sorting algorithms.

Creating Custom Performance Counters

The first task is to create several performance counters and add them to a new custom category. This new category is going to deal with performance data relating to the performance of various sorting algorithms. Each of the sorting algorithms will correspond to an instance of the new category. Table 6-3 shows the relationships of the performance objects that will form the basis of this example. The first performance counter is the number of items in a list that will be sorted. The second counter is the maximum value allowed for each item in the list. The final counter measures how many steps each of the sorting algorithms takes when sorting the list under different starting conditions as measured by the first two counters.

Table 6-3. Sorting Category and Related Counters and Instances

CATEGORY: SORTING	
Instance: QuickSort	*Instance: MagicSort*
Counter: Number of items	Counter: Number of items
Counter: Maximum item value	Counter: Maximum item value
Counter: Number of sort steps	Counter: Number of sort steps

Although the program will only investigate the performance of the two sorting algorithms mentioned in Table 6-3, each of the many other sorting algorithms available would constitute another instance of the Sorting category. The idea for each sort algorithm is to measure the effect that changing the first two counters has on the third counter. Listing 6-24 shows how to create the three performance counters and the performance category that contains them. Notice that this is a once-only task; once you create the performance category and its counters, these are persistent across sessions (unless they're deleted). Therefore, you should always check that the category doesn't already exist before you create it.

Listing 6-24. Creating the Performance Category and Counters

```
Imports System.Diagnostics
If PerformanceCounterCategory.Exists("Sorting") = False Then
    'Create the three performance counters
    Dim cntrNumberOfItems As New CounterCreationData("NumberOfItems", _
"Tracks the number of items to be sorted", _
PerformanceCounterType.NumberOfItems32)
    Dim cntrMaxItemValue As New CounterCreationData("MaxItemValue", _
"Tracks the maximum value in items to be sorted", _
```

```
PerformanceCounterType.NumberOfItems32)
     Dim cntrNumberOfSortSteps As New CounterCreationData("NumberOfSortSteps", _
"Tracks the number of steps needed to sort a list", _
PerformanceCounterType.NumberOfItems32)
        'Set up performance counter collection
        Dim SortingCounters As New CounterCreationDataCollection()
        With SortingCounters
            .Add(cntrNumberOfItems)
            .Add(cntrMaxItemValue)
            .Add(cntrNumberOfSortSteps)
        End With
        'Create the performance category and pass the collection to it.
        PerformanceCounterCategory.Create("Sorting", _
"This category deals with sorting algorithm performance", SortingCounters)
End If
```

In addition to using code to create performance objects, you can create performance objects at design time by using Visual Studio's Server Explorer. Just
select Performance Counters under Servers on your local machine and add the
required counters and categories.

Manipulating Performance Counter Instances

Once you've created your counters and categories, you obviously need to be able
to update them from within your program. In this specific example, I want to create an instance of each performance counter before starting a sort and then
update the **NumberOfSortSteps** counter during the sort. Listing 6-25 shows the
creation and initialization of the performance counter components that manipulate each of the performance counter instances during a **MagicSort**. The
PerformanceCounter component is, in my humble opinion, badly misnamed.
It's not a performance counter at all—it's a component with which you can
manipulate a performance counter. This subtle distinction is rather annoying
and a potential source of confusion.

But moving on to Listing 6-25, you can see that setting an instance name
on a **PerformanceCounter** component creates a new instance, in this case for
a **MagicSort**. If the code was doing a **QuickSort** instead, that's how the instance
would be named. Then the performance counter instance represented by each
PerformanceCounter component (I told you it was confusing) is initialized to its
starting value.

Listing 6-25. Initialization of Each Performance Counter Instance

```
Dim NumItems As New PerformanceCounter("Sorting", "NumberOfItems", False)
'Upper bound of list to be sorted
NumItems.InstanceName = "MagicSort"
NumItems.RawValue = ListToSort.GetUpperBound(0)
'Maximum data value in list to be sorted
Dim MaxValue As New PerformanceCounter("Sorting", "MaxItemValue", False)
MaxValue.InstanceName = "MagicSort"
MaxValue.RawValue = MaxValueInList
'The number of steps that the sorting algorithm will take
'This will be incremented by each step of the sort
Dim SortSteps As New PerformanceCounter("Sorting", "NumberOfSortSteps", False)
SortSteps.InstanceName = "MagicSort"
SortSteps.RawValue = 0
```

Running the program starts several **MagicSorts** followed by several **Quick-Sorts**, each with a different set of starting conditions. If you start the Performance Monitor and then monitor these performance counters as described in Chapter 5, you can see the effects that the different starting conditions have on the efficiency of the two sorting algorithms. Notice how the much-lauded **QuickSort** is usually unable to match the **MagicSort** unless the starting conditions are rather extreme.

If you want to extend this program, you could consider adding a procedure to perform each of the other sorting algorithms and then creating performance counter instances to monitor each of these algorithms as well. You might also wish to perform some more sophisticated performance measurements. The **PerformanceCounterType** enumeration that you specify during the creation of a performance counter contains some very useful types of measurement that you can use to do quite complex monitoring of your applications.

Summary

I've covered a rather wide area in this chapter. You first came to grips with why instrumentation and monitoring are useful in developing and supporting your applications. Then I listed some of the types of diagnostic data that are useful when you're monitoring an application, especially in a production environment. Next, you saw how to implement tracing in VB .NET using the **Trace**, **TraceListener**, **TraceSwitch**, and **Debug** classes, including the use of assertions to check your assumptions. Finally, you saw how you can use custom performance counters to show what's happening within the depths of your application.

INTERLUDE

THE $500 MILLION EXCEPTION

On June 4, 1996, the maiden flight of the European Space Agency's Ariane 5 launcher ended after 40 seconds with the rocket veering off its flight path, breaking up, and exploding. The total (uninsured) cost of the crash was reported to be in the region of $500 million!

The detailed report that ensued from the accident noted that the failure of the flight was caused by the complete loss of guidance and altitude information approximately 37 seconds after the start of the main engine ignition sequence. This loss of information was in turn caused by specification and design errors in the software of the inertial reference system. The report concluded that the problem was a technical one, and not one caused by incompetence or managerial negligence.

The actual coding problem at the source of the accident was an unhandled exception in an Ada program that caused the inertial reference system to shut down. In an attempt to convert a 64-bit floating-point value into a 16-bit signed integer value, the floating-point number had a value that was greater than could be represented by the integer. In the Ada software, this resulted in an Operand exception. When the inertial reference system failed, it transmitted diagnostic data to the launcher's main computer, where it was interpreted as flight data and used for flight control calculations. This in turn caused a rapid change in altitude, which caused the launcher to disintegrate due to aerodynamic forces.

Although similar conversion instructions in the vicinity had been protected with error handling, this specific instruction had not been protected, with the idea of enhancing performance. The reasoning was that the potential result was physically limited, a theory that was true with the Ariane 4 launcher but proved false with the much higher acceleration and horizontal velocity of the Ariane 5 rocket.

VB .NET, of course, has similar functionality. The equivalent of an Ada Operand exception in .NET is a **System.OverflowException**, and any unhandled exception will cause the VB .NET program in which it occurs to shut down.

The error was really a reuse error, in that the software module for the Ariane 5 launcher was reused from 10-year-old software used for Ariane 4. The original specification did actually imply that the result should always fit into a 16-bit integer without explicitly stating it, but this implied requirement was nowhere to be found in the code.

I'm not sure what the moral of this story is. Peter van der Linden, the C language guru, suggests that developers of mission-critical software such as that used on aircraft and on space missions should have the privilege of accompanying the software on its first operational flight, thus having a major incentive to debug the program properly when things go wrong. Obviously, writing "safeware" is very difficult. Some people have suggested that the use of assertions might have picked up the problem at the core of the Ariane crash during the testing phase. Others point to the fact that using assertions in real-time systems can hide timing problems such as race conditions and deadlocks, which might then occur when the assertions are removed during the release build.

Debugging Applications

"When you do not know what you are doing, do it neatly."
—Anonymous

Windows Forms Debugging

Now that you've gained a good understanding of the Visual Studio .NET debugger's capabilities, in this chapter I'll look in more detail at how to debug Windows Forms applications, including class libraries and Windows control libraries (known in the COM world as *dynamic link libraries* [DLLs] and *Windows controls*, respectively). During this chapter you're going to use the Visual Studio debugger and its facilities in earnest. If you haven't already read my discussions on this debugger and its facilities in Chapters 3 and 4, now would be an excellent time to go back and do this.

This chapter first looks at debugging a relatively simple real-life Windows Forms application—in fact, it uses the sorting application originally mentioned at the end of Chapter 4 in the context of code optimization. Later I show you how to handle some tricky debugging situations associated with Windows Forms applications. Finally, you'll learn how to debug Windows Forms controls, Visual Studio add-ins, and Windows control designers.

Debugging a Windows Forms Application

The first application to be debugged is a Windows Forms program that compares the performance of various sorting algorithms. The application is a Visual Studio solution containing two VB .NET projects; you can find this solution in the DebugDemo folder. The first project in the solution, **DebugDemoForm**, is a form that acts as the user interface for the application, and the other project, **DebugDemoLogic**, is a class library containing each of the sorting algorithms being tested. Though it would be simpler to add the sorting algorithm class to the main application, separation of the user interface and the business logic into two components is good development practice and also makes it easier to show you some subtleties in the debugging process.

Figure 7-1 shows the user interface for the sort testing application. The text boxes on the left side of the window allow you to specify the length and values of the array to be sorted, and the radio buttons on the right side allow you to choose the sort algorithm to be tested. The label placed in the lower right corner of the window shows the time that the chosen algorithm took to sort the chosen array.

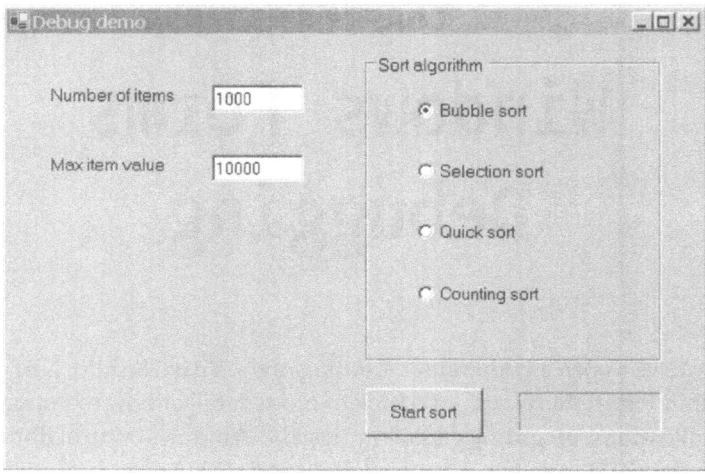

Figure 7-1. User interface for the sort testing application

Building the Application

Having set all of the appropriate debugging options as discussed in Chapter 4, you now need to build the application before you can debug it. From the Build ➢ Configuration Manager menu item, check that the active solution configuration is set to Debug and that each project's Configuration setting also shows Debug. This tells the compiler that you want to create a debug build of the application.

For the purposes of this chapter, you should also ensure that the Build check box is selected for each of the projects. If you're working with an application where you know that some of the solution's projects won't change while you're testing or debugging, then you can deselect the Build option for projects that you don't want to build every time. This can save you a considerable amount of build time when you have a solution with multiple projects.

Now you can build the application by choosing the Build ➢ Build Solution menu item. For this application, the build process creates an .exe file for the user interface and a .dll file for the class library. In addition, it creates a .pdb file containing debug symbols for each of these two components. The Output window should show that both of the components have been built successfully. If there had been any compilation errors or warnings, these would appear in the Task List window.

Breaking Into the Application

After completing the debugging preparations, you can finally begin the debugging investigation. Start the sorting program by pressing F5, which is the standard shortcut key for starting a program with debugging enabled. If the Debug and Debug Location toolbars aren't visible, you should right-click in the toolbar area and select these two toolbars from the drop-down menu.

To break into a program automatically, you can add a breakpoint in the program's Source window and then perform a program action that causes this breakpoint to be hit. This program containing the breakpoint will then become the active debug process. For the purposes of this debugging session, you should add a breakpoint on line 178 in the DemoForm.vb source code by clicking this line in the far-left shaded area of the Source window. The result should be an active breakpoint glyph: a black circle representing an active breakpoint.

Now you can right-click the black circle representing the breakpoint and select Breakpoint Properties from the resulting menu. The resulting dialog window, as shown in Figure 7-2, shows that a file breakpoint has been set at the first character of line 178 in the DemoForm.vb source file. The reason that this dialog window allows a character setting other than 1 is that you might have multiple statements on a single line and want to set the breakpoint on one of the later statements. You can also see that this is a simple breakpoint. To set an advanced breakpoint, you would use either of the two buttons shown in the dialog window to add a breakpoint condition or a hit count, as I discussed in Chapter 3.

If you now click the program's Start sort button, the application drops into the debugger at the breakpoint that you added on line 178. Looking at the Debug Location toolbar, you can see that it's no longer grayed-out—the Program drop-down shows the name of the executable and its process ID, the Thread drop-down shows the ID of the program's main thread, and the Stack Frame drop-down shows the current call stack. The executable's process ID is the same as the PID shown in the Processes tab of Task Manager.

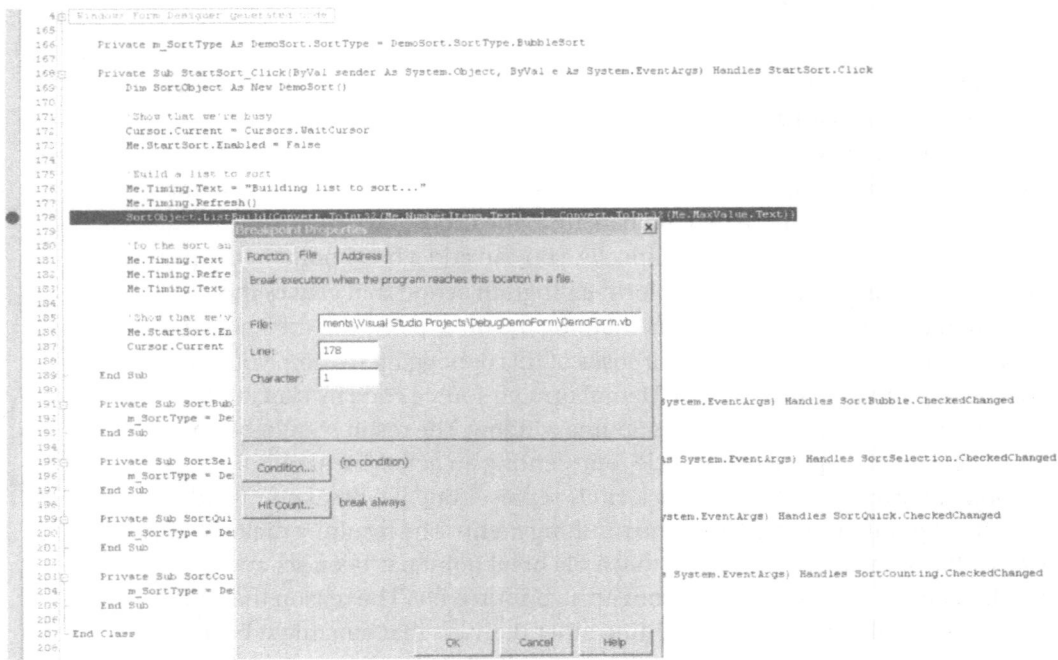

Figure 7-2. Dialog window showing simple breakpoint properties

Hitting Breakpoints

If you ever have any problems with breakpoints not being hit, the first step you should take is to check the Modules window. You can find this on the Debug ➤ Windows menu. This window shows you every module loaded by your program. The two modules of interest now are DebugDemoForm.exe and DebugDemoLogic.dll. The Information column in the Modules window shows you whether or not debug symbols were loaded for each module. These debug symbols are contained within the .pdb file generated by the build process for each module, as explained in Chapter 3. Unless these symbol files are loaded, the debugger is unable to work back from the processor-native code being executed to the associated source code, which means that your breakpoints won't be hit and you won't be able to debug the application.

Another common reason for breakpoints not being hit is when you start an application from within Visual Studio by using Ctrl-F5 rather than F5. Ctrl-F5 is the menu shortcut that tells Visual Studio to start your application without attaching a debugger, so breakpoints will simply be ignored.

A third reason for missing breakpoints is when multiple copies of your solution's projects exist on disk, and Visual Studio is loading a version without a compatible debug symbol file. You can spot this situation by checking the load path of each of your solution's modules in the Modules window. If this happens, you need to stop the program and then tell Visual Studio to load and execute the correct version of the errant module. The best way of doing this is to rename or delete any stray versions that are causing Visual Studio to become confused.

A fourth reason for missing breakpoints is when you launch your application in a **Release** configuration rather than a **Debug** configuration. You can tell which configuration is being used by checking the Configuration drop-down on the Standard toolbar. The default release configuration doesn't allow debugging.

A final reason for breakpoints not being hit is when the debug symbol file doesn't match the code actually executing. In this case, the debugger either will be unable to load the debug symbols or will load them but be unable to construct a path back from the native code to your source code. This is one reason why it's very important to keep a matching .pdb file for every production assembly that you build.

Examining Program State

Once the sorting application has stopped at the breakpoint on line 178, you can use the mouse to "hover" over variables and functions to see both values and definitions. For instance, if you hover with the mouse over the function in line 183 called **DoSort**, you can see that this function is called with an enumeration called **m_SortType** and returns a variable of type **Double**. Then if you look in the same way at the actual argument to the function, the ToolTip will show that **m_SortType = BubbleSort**. It's useful to note that these ToolTips also work at design time, when you're writing your code—you're able to see the definition of every constant, variable, and function.

Like most of the debugging windows, the Me window can be found hanging off the Debug menu. This window provides you with a very quick way of seeing the values belonging to whichever object is currently in scope—in this case, the form called **DemoForm**. Figure 7-3 shows this window, with one of the form's text box controls expanded for easier viewing. As you can see, the property evaluations are disabled within the Me window because of my earlier recommendation to turn off property evaluation in the debugging windows.

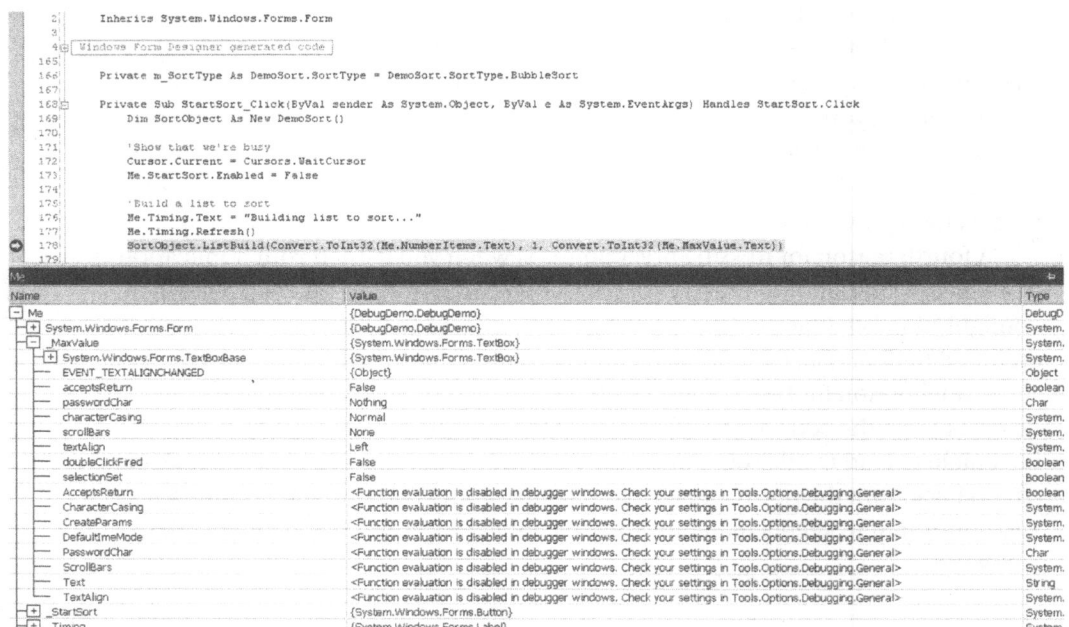

Figure 7-3. *Using the Me window to examine the current object*

The Breakpoints window allows you to examine and manipulate all of the breakpoints in your solution. One neat facility available from this window is the ability to disable one or more breakpoints. This means that you can ignore breakpoints that don't apply to your current debugging scenario, but you can still have them available when your scenario changes. Combine that with the fact that all breakpoints are stored in a solution's .suo file so that you can unload and reload solutions without losing the breakpoints and you have a major advance over debugging within the VB.Classic environment.

Now bring up the first Watch window and double-click the **SortObject** variable on line 178. You can drag this variable onto the Watch window and see its associated values. Keep this window open because you'll be using it again very shortly.

Stepping into the **DoSort** procedure using the Debug ➤ Step Into menu item provides an opportunity to investigate another debugging window. If you stop on line 51 of the DemoSort.vb file and display the Call Stack window, you can see the current call stack. This lists all of the procedure calls that are currently active, starting at the top with the current procedure. The lines shown in gray are the ones for which debug symbols are not available. Now drag the **ArrayItem** variable from line 51 onto the same Watch window that's displaying the **SortObject** variable. Notice that only one of these variables is in scope, so only one value is being shown.

The Call Stack window allows you to switch the current program context, otherwise known as the *stack frame*. If you right-click the second line in the Call Stack window, the one that represents the procedure that invoked the current procedure, you can choose the Switch To Frame menu item. Now you can see that the **SortObject** variable shown in the Watch window is back in scope, and the **ArrayItem** variable is not. The ability to perform this type of "backward" debugging can make a major contribution to the swift location of bugs.

Another good use of the Call Stack window is to display the call stack after a bug has been found. This makes it easier to discover methods that are being invoked at the wrong time or from the wrong place.

Now you can use the Debug ➢ Step Out menu item to return to line 178 of the DemoSort.vb file. Disable the breakpoint on line 178 by removing the check mark on the left side of the Breakpoints window and then press F5 to continue executing the program. It's time to go bug hunting.

Finding the Bug

For demonstration purposes, I've added a subtle bug to the procedure that performs the selection sort. After each array sorting, a procedure called **SortCheck** is called that verifies that the array has really been sorted correctly. If you test the "Selection sort" option while setting the "Max item value" to 100, you can see that the **SortCheck** routine uses an assertion to report that the array hasn't been sorted correctly. The task now is to find where the bug is happening and ultimately how to fix it. To do this, you need to look at the selection sort procedure to find out how it's supposed to work and then run one or more tests to establish where and how the bug is occurring.

A quick look at the **SortSelection** procedure shows you that the code runs through the unsorted array multiple times, and on each occasion it finds the lowest (by value) unsorted item and swaps that with the lowest (by index) unsorted item. Because the selection sort works item by item upward through the array, it should never move a sorted item to a position where it has a larger value than the unsorted item directly above it. This can therefore be the condition for the advanced breakpoint, which will be placed at the point in the sorting process where each unsorted item is about to be swapped into its correct sorted position.

Run the sorting application and set the number of array items to 10 and the range of array item values to 100. These low numbers should give a manageable array size and make it easier for you to inspect the array values.

Now right-click the gray band to the left of line 167 and add a file breakpoint. In the breakpoint condition, add **BestValue>=ListBeingSorted(LoopOuter+1)** as the breakpoint condition, and then set the breakpoint condition to be "is true". This test is designed to trigger the breakpoint only when the selection sort sets the **BestValue** variable to a wrong value (i.e., a value that is larger than the value of the unsorted item directly above it).

Next, launch Watch window 1, clear any variables currently shown in this window, and then drag the **ListBeingSorted**, **BestValue**, and **LoopOuter** variables to this window. You can use this window to monitor the state of the array as it is sorted. Then launch Watch window 2 and drag the **ListUnsorted** variable to this window. This will show the original unsorted array for comparison with the array that is being sorted.

Now choose the "Selection sort" option and start the sort. When the conditional breakpoint is hit, your display should look something like Figure 7-4. Your numbers should be identical to those shown because the list to be sorted is always produced from the same seed. If you look closely at the array being sorted in Watch window 1, you can see that something is very wrong. The **BestValue** variable contains a value (12) that doesn't actually exist in the unsorted array. Here's the first clue to the bug—it looks as though **BestValue** is being corrupted somewhere. Notice how you were able to find preliminary information about this problem with a single breakpoint and without having to step through the code. Conditional breakpoints allow you to go straight to the heart of a problem because you can calculate expressions and conditions that express a problem precisely, and your breakpoints can be set up to trigger only when those calculated conditions are met.

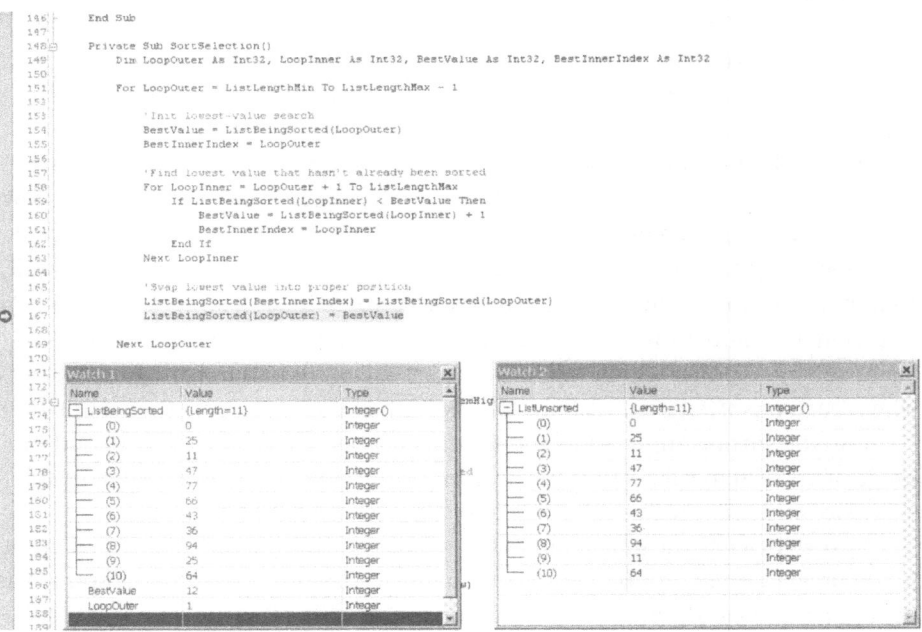

Figure 7-4. Debugging with Watch windows and a conditional breakpoint

Now that you've found a possible cause of the bug, the next step is to locate where the **BestValue** variable is being corrupted. First, you'll need to find all statements where **BestValue** is changed. Here you can employ a little trick. If you change the declaration of **BestValue** so that it's named differently (say, by adding a single letter to the end of the variable name), **BestValue** will become undefined and every place that it's mentioned in the Source window will be underlined with a colored squiggle. In this way, you can locate every instance where **BestValue** is modified. If you use this trick in the **SortSelection** procedure, you can see that this variable is modified on lines 154 and 160. So now you can add a file break-point to both of these lines, with a conditional expression of **BestValue = 12** (this being the rogue value that you found when the breakpoint on line 167 was hit). Finally, perform another selection sort using the same parameters as before. You should find that the first breakpoint to be triggered is the one on line 160—this looks like it could be the statement to blame.

A close look at the statement on line 160 shows you that while **BestValue** has a value of 12, no such value exists in the unsorted array. The closest value is 11, which appears twice in the unsorted array at positions 2 and 9. Looking at the **LoopInner** variable, you can see that it shows a value of 9. The item at position 9 in the unsorted array has a value of 11, not 12. So it looks as though this might be an off-by-one error: The statement on line 160 is adding 1 to the value of each item that it's sorting, which definitely doesn't seem to be correct. If you remove the **+ 1** from the statement on line 160 and rerun a selection sort using the same parameters, you can see that the problem appears to be fixed, in that the **SortCheck** procedure doesn't detect any further sorting problems.

Notice how with just two conditional breakpoints and no single-stepping through code, you were able to diagnose and fix a quite subtle bug. Of course, I've simplified the debugging process in this example because in the real world you need to review and test each bug fix to ensure that it hasn't caused any new bugs, and you also ought to look through the rest of your application for similar types of bugs.

Tricky Debugging Situations

There are some common debugging issues with Windows Forms that bite every-body at least once, so this section describes these situations and looks at ways to handle them.

Window Painting Code

One of the very first drawing issues you may notice is that your application's win-dow will not repaint itself while you're in the debugger. For instance, you might be adding items to a list box in a loop and have a breakpoint on the **ListBox.Items.Add** statement in the middle of the loop in order to see where a rogue item is being added to the list box. You'll find that as soon as you hit the first breakpoint iteration and start stepping, the form won't redraw itself while you're stepping. For a VB.Classic developer used to seeing a form redraw itself after every step, this behavior is a little annoying. The best way of handling this situation is to use a conditional breakpoint so that your code only stops at the exact point where you want to debug. This avoids having to use the debugger to step through the code, and therefore the window will be drawn properly right up until the point where the breakpoint (and the bug) occurs.

A related issue concerns the debugging of window repainting code (usually in the **OnPaint** event) where activation of the debugger window interferes with the window painting done by your application. For example, you might put a breakpoint on one of the first statements in a form's **OnPaint** event. As soon as that breakpoint is hit, the debugger window activates and comes to the front of the screen, thereby overlapping or covering the window that you're debugging. After you've looked around at a few variable values, you resume execution of the program, expecting to see the next breakpoint being hit. Because resuming code execution brings your application window to the front once more, Windows quite sensibly decides to send a message to your window telling it to repaint itself. This causes the original breakpoint at the beginning of the **OnPaint** event to be triggered again, and you're back where you started.

There are some effective solutions to this nasty problem. If you have two monitors on your PC, your application window can sit in one monitor and the debugger can sit in the other; in this way, you can avoid window overlap problems. Alternatively, you can use remote debugging, as described in Chapter 15. With remote debugging, your application resides on one machine and displays its window on that machine's screen, while you sit at another machine that executes the debugger. The final solution that I'm going to suggest involves a neat trick using Windows Terminal Server (WTS). Try creating a WTS session from your machine back onto your machine and starting your application in the WTS window. Then you can start the debugger as normal and attach to the WTS session. Now you won't see any interference between the application and debugger windows, even though they're running on the same monitor.

Focus Code

When you're debugging control and window focus problems, you can use the same solutions described previously for solving issues with window painting code.

Mouse Handling Code

Another tricky problem can occur when you try debugging the code in a **MouseMove** or **MouseEntry** event handler. As soon as the mouse moves, your breakpoint will be hit. This isn't very useful, because normally you want to investigate only a specific sort of mouse movement (for instance, at a particular location in a window). This is a perfect situation for using a conditional breakpoint. You really want the breakpoint to trigger only when the mouse event happens at the same time as you're pressing a certain key, so that you can control the breakpoint's behavior. You might try adding the following expression to a breakpoint, which should only trigger the breakpoint when you're holding down the Shift key:

```
(Control.ModifierKeys And Keys.Shift) = Keys.Shift
```

Unfortunately, this doesn't work because the debugger is unable to evaluate the **Keys.Shift** expression. You'll just see a message stating that the breakpoint can't be set because the "condition is invalid." Instead, you have to use the literal key representation in the breakpoint, so the following conditional expression works just fine when you hold down the Shift key:

```
(Control.ModifierKeys And 65536) = 65536
```

Debugging **MouseDown** and **MouseUp** events can also cause problems because the **MouseUp** event is never triggered if you release the mouse button while paused on a breakpoint in a **MouseDown** event handler. Everett McKay, in his excellent book *Debugging Windows Programs* (Addison-Wesley, 2000), comes up with an interesting solution to this problem. He recommends keeping the mouse button pressed down while operating the debugger with the keyboard alone. Then you can release the mouse button when the application window has regained the focus.

Keyboard Code

When you're debugging **KeyDown** and **KeyUp** event handlers, the same considerations apply as discussed previously with **MouseDown** and **MouseUp** event handlers.

Debugging Other Windows Forms Applications

There are several types of Windows Forms applications, most of which are perfectly straightforward to debug. The following section describes some aspects of the debugging process that may not be completely straightforward.

Debugging a Class Library

Although debugging class libraries is very similar to normal Windows Forms debugging, there are a few subtleties that are worth noting. In this debugging session, the class library is automatically loaded by the application, but it's common to have situations where you're debugging a solution that contains a class library but doesn't contain an application to launch it. In this case, you need to go to the project's Properties ➤ Configuration Properties ➤ Debugging page, as shown in Figure 7-5.

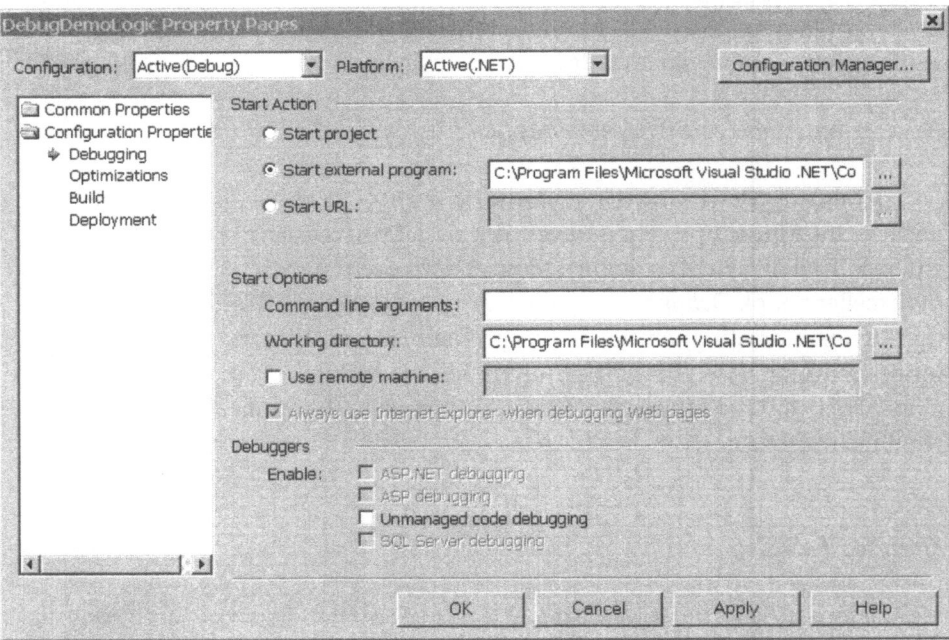

Figure 7-5. The project start options page

On this page, you have the option to start the debugging of your project by using an external program or a URL. You can specify a prebuilt component that will launch your class library by using the "Start external program" option. If your class library is invoked from a Web site, you can specify the URL by using the "Start URL" option. Finally, you should use the "Wait for an external process to connect" option when your class library is part of a Web application or a Web service—the debugger will then attach to any process that calls into your project.

Occasionally, you can find that there are multiple copies of your class library spread around your hard disk, and your solution doesn't load the one that you were expecting. If the class library was installed into the global assembly cache (GAC) so that it could be shared with other applications, this can take precedence of any local copy, which can be confusing. To verify the load path of your class library, go to the Modules window and check the Path column of the module. This will tell you which location was used to load the class library.

Multiple copies of a class library can also cause the debugger to become confused about which debug symbols to use, and it can sometimes lead to no debug symbols being loaded for the class library. This in turn means that none of your class library's breakpoints will be hit. You can use the Modules window to check whether debug symbols were loaded for the library. Look at the Information column. If it shows that no symbols were loaded for the module, you can right-click the module and select "Reload symbols" to specify where the correct debug symbol file can be found.

Sometimes your application crashes in an unknown class library or in a system DLL. If all that you know is a crash address, you can rerun your application and go to the ever-helpful Modules window. If you sort the module list using the Address column, you can find the module that instigated the crash by finding the class library whose address range contains the crash location.

A final point is that if the application that uses your class library was written using unmanaged code, you need to go to the project's Properties ➢ Configuration Properties ➢ Debugging page and select the "Unmanaged code debugging" option.

Debugging a Windows Forms Control

To debug a Windows Forms control where you have access to the source, you normally have to add that control's project to the solution that uses the control. If you don't want to import the whole control project, you can instead add just the control's source modules in which you're interested.

To illustrate this, I created a new Windows Forms control that inherits and extends the standard **TextBox** control to permit the entry of positive integers only. To try this control, load the DebugDemo solution discussed previously and go to the Tools ➢ Customize Toolbox menu item. Click the .NET Framework Components tab. Then click the Browse button and navigate to the \DebugDemoControl\bin folder. Here you can add the DebugDemoControl.dll control to the Toolbox so that you're able to start using the control. The **NumericTextBox** control should now appear in the General tab of the Toolbox.

After you bring the **DemoForm** form to the front in the IDE Source window, drag the **NumericTextBox** control from the Toolbox and drop it on the form. If you run the solution and try to type text into this customized text box, you'll find that you can only type numbers into the control—all other keys are suppressed.

Assuming that you wanted to debug this control, you don't need to add the control's entire project. Instead, go to the File ➢ Add Existing Item menu item and navigate to the \DebugDemoControl folder. Double-click the NumericTextBox.vb file, which will add the source code for the control to your solution. With the source code for the control displayed in the Source window, you can set a breakpoint for the control that will be hit as normal. When you've finished debugging the control, right-click the newly added file in Solution Explorer and select the Remove menu item. This is a quick and nonintrusive way of debugging external class libraries and controls that are used by your solutions.

It's worthwhile to examine the source of the **NumericTextBox** custom control because it demonstrates a debugging idea that's useful to both the control authors and the users of their controls. If you look at the control's source code shown in Listing 7-1, you can see that it defines and raises control debug events. These events supply debugging information to a user of a control when that user has no access to the control's source code. If the developer changes the control's **DebugMode** property to **true**, the control raises a debug event every time it does something that might be of interest in debugging. The control's user can trap these events to get a better understanding of the control's behavior and to gather debugging information that can be communicated to the control's author.

Listing 7-1. Implementing the Numeric TextBox Control

```
Option Strict On
Imports System.Windows.Forms

Public Class NumericTextBox : Inherits TextBox

    Private m_DebugMode As Boolean = False

    'This public property allows the control's user
    'to see debug events raised by the control
    Public Property DebugMode() As Boolean
        Get
            DebugMode = m_DebugMode
        End Get
        Set(ByVal Value As Boolean)
            m_DebugMode = Value
        End Set
    End Property
```

```
      Private Sub NumericTextBox_KeyPress(ByVal sender As Object, _
            ByVal e As System.Windows.Forms.KeyPressEventArgs) _
                                    Handles MyBase.KeyPress
        'Suppress any non-numeric keys
        If e.KeyChar < "0"c Or e.KeyChar > "9"c Then
            e.Handled = True
            ShowDebugMessage("Suppressed character: " & e.KeyChar.ToString)
        End If
      End Sub


      Private Sub ShowDebugMessage(ByVal DebugComment As String)
        'Raise debug event if user wants to see debug events
        If m_DebugMode = True Then
          Dim CallingMethod As New System.Diagnostics.StackFrame(1)
          RaiseEvent DebugMessage(CallingMethod.GetMethod.Name, _
                                  DebugComment)
        End If
      End Sub


      Public Event DebugMessage(ByVal DebugMethod As String, _
                                ByVal DebugComment As String)


End Class
```

As you can see, the control's **DebugMode** property is set to **false** by default, but it can be set to **true** if the control's user wants to see the debug events. The **KeyPress** event supplies a debugging comment, in this case a remark showing the non-numeric character that was suppressed. The **ShowDebugMessage** procedure decides whether to raise the debug event depending on the setting of the **DebugMode** property and also adds the name of the procedure that produced the debug comment. Finally, it raises the **DebugMessage** event to the control's container.

Now you can look at these control debug events from the viewpoint of the control's user. Listing 7-2 shows some code that might be written in the control's container, in this case a standard Windows form.

Listing 7-2. Controlling and Viewing Control Debug Events

```
Option Strict On
Public Class ControlContainer : Inherits System.Windows.Forms.Form


      Private Sub ControlContainer (ByVal sender As System.Object, _
                                    ByVal e As System.EventArgs) _
                                    Handles MyBase.Load
```

```
         'Switch on control debugging
         CustomControl.DebugMode = True
     End Sub


     Private Sub ShowDebugMessage(ByVal DebugMethod As String, _
                              ByVal DebugComment As String) _
                              Handles CustomControl.DebugMessage
         'Show the debug message
         MsgBox(DebugComment, _
             MsgBoxStyle.OKOnly Or MsgBoxStyle.Information, _
             DebugMethod)
     End Sub

End Class
```

In the **Form_Load** event, the control's **DebugMode** property is set to **true** so that the control's debug events can be monitored. Then, in this example, every debug message raised by the control is displayed in a message box. In reality, all of this debugging information would more likely be written to a trace listener, a log file, or some other form of logging. This is a valuable debugging aid because it enables the control's user to monitor and understand the control's behavior and, if necessary, report any problems to the control's author with some evidence to confirm the problem report.

Debugging a Visual Studio Add-In

Debugging a Visual Studio add-in is slightly different from debugging most other application types. To show this, I created an add-in called **DebugAddIn**, represented by the solution that you can find in the \DebugAddIn folder. This simple add-in merely pops up a message box, but it's functional enough to demonstrate add-in debugging.

Once you've loaded the solution into Visual Studio, put a breakpoint on line 67, where the message box is displayed. Then check the **DebugAddIn** project's Properties ➤ Configuration Properties ➤ Debugging property page, where you can see that the wizard that created this add-in specified that the project should be started using the external program devenv.exe, which is the Visual Studio executable.

So when you press F5 to start executing the add-in, you'll find that a new instance of Visual Studio will start. If you go to the Tools menu of this new instance, you can see that the add-in shows itself with a cheery little emoticon. When you actually run the add-in, the breakpoint that you created on line 67 in the first Visual Studio instance will be hit. What's happening is that the debugger in the first instance of Visual Studio has started and then attached itself to the second Visual Studio instance.

You can now debug as normal, but when you've finished debugging you should always close the add-in and the second Visual Studio instance before closing the first instance.

Debugging a Control Designer

Debugging a control designer is very similar to debugging a Visual Studio add-in. You add your control onto a form and then load your control designer solution into a second instance of Visual Studio. In this second instance, go to the Debug ➤ Processes menu item and attach the debugger to the first instance of Visual Studio. This will show as a process in the Processes window called devenv.exe. Then just add breakpoints to your designer code and start manipulating the control in the first instance of Visual Studio. Your breakpoints will then be hit normally.

Summary

This chapter followed on from the introduction to the Visual Studio debugger in Chapters 3 and 4 by looking in some detail at the debugging of a Windows Forms application. After you looked at some tricky debugging situations associated with Windows Forms, you discovered how to debug a class library, a Windows Form control, and a Visual Studio add-in.

Debugging Windows Forms applications is usually very straightforward. As long as you have matching executables and debug symbol files, and you watch the Modules window to check that the debug symbols are being loaded, you should have no problem with hitting breakpoints and stepping from form to class library to control library and back again. As long as you're careful about debugging windows drawing, mouse move, and control focus events, you'll find that facilities such as advanced breakpoints give you superior functionality to the VB.Classic debugger.

INTERLUDE

THE BUG DICTIONARY

There has long been an unofficial bug taxonomy, or classification. Nearly all bugs fall into one of the following categories:

- *Bohrbug:* A bug that is repeatable; one that shows itself reliably under a possibly unknown but well-defined set of conditions.

- *Compoundbug:* A bug not found during testing because it is hiding behind another bug. It is quite common for a bug fix to reveal several more bugs hiding behind the original defect. Often, the new bugs appear to be completely unrelated to the original error, although later investigation will usually reveal the subtle links that tie the bugs together. Compoundbugs are one of the main reasons why even correct bug fixes can adversely affect the stability of a program.

- *Heisenbug:* A bug that disappears or alters its behavior when you try to probe or isolate it. This is not unusual, because using a debugger can alter the environmental conditions of a program enough for it to no longer fail. This is particularly common with timing bugs and race conditions found in multithreaded programming.

- *Mandelbug:* A bug whose underlying cause is so complex or obscure that its behavior appears to be chaotic or nondeterministic.

- *Schroedinbug:* This is the strange one—it's a bug that doesn't manifest itself until someone reading the source or using the program in an unusual way notices that it never should have worked, whereupon the program promptly stops working for everybody until the bug is fixed. This sounds impossible, but I can testify to finding several Schroedinbugs during the last two decades.

To add to the bug dictionary, there are many semi-humorous definitions floating around in cyberspace that somebody ought to collect together for the creation of a *Devil's Dictionary of Debugging.* Here are some examples:

- *Dug:* A documentation bug.

- *Fug:* A bug that causes you to give up ("Fug it!").

- *Glug:* A bug that drives you to drink.

- *Hug:* A deadly embrace bug (also known as a "deadlock").

- *Jug:* A bug that can get you jailed (such as penetrating security).

- *Lug:* A big, lovable bug (e.g., Unix).

- *Mug:* A bug that makes you feel stupid when you discover its cause.

- *Pug:* A bug that makes you want to climb into a boxing ring with its author.

- *Plug:* A bug that keeps a system going.

- *Rug:* A bug that knocks a system flat.

- *Slug:* A bug that slows everything down, leaves a trail of slime, and eats up your lettuce.

- *Smug:* A bug that you can't find.

- *Snug:* A bug that you put in to ensure job security.

- *Tug:* A bug that you can't forget, no matter how long ago it was.

- *RIP:* An acronym for "rest in peace," meaning a bug that completely kills an application.

- *TCB:* An acronym for "trouble came back." Usually associated with a developer who claims that a bug went away by itself. A bug that goes away by itself nearly always comes back by itself.

- *Twiddle:* A small and insignificant change to a program. Usually fixes one bug and generates several new ones.

- *Crawling horror:* A program so infested by bugs that it starts to resemble one of H. R. Giger's more imaginative creations.

- *Nailing the corpse in an upright position:* The VB.Classic practice of sprinkling plentiful **On Error Resume Next** statements throughout the code to stop a program from aborting. In VB .NET, the same effect can be attained by judicious use of **Try...Catch** constructs.

CHAPTER 8

Web Services Debugging

WEB SERVICES ARE ONE of the most hyped parts of the whole .NET extravaganza. The idea is that Web services can form a component technology for the intranet and the Internet, just as COM offers a component technology for the desktop. Up until now, the Internet has been dominated by e-mail and Web browsers, both used extensively by people, whereas the vision of Web services is that applications can communicate with each other over the Internet as easily as people.

The first part of this chapter covers how to set up a Web service and its clients for debugging. Web services offer a rather different debugging experience from desktop applications. When debugging Web services, you have to deal with potential complications caused by elements such as firewalls, security, Internet Information Server (IIS), ASP.NET, HTTP, and the Simple Object Access Protocol (SOAP). When everything works smoothly, you can step seamlessly from a client application into a Web service and back again. However, when debugging doesn't work so well, you usually need some understanding of the underlying technologies to identify exactly where the debugging process is failing. This chapter aims to give you a good introduction to these underlying technologies.

The second part of this chapter looks at various "how-to" scenarios. It starts by debugging a very simple Web service when using Internet Explorer as a client. Then it examines debugging a Windows Forms application invoking the same Web service, continuing with an introduction to debugging issues raised by proxy components and SOAP. In the final "how-to" section, you'll see how to debug a remote Web service and a Web service that's already been deployed into production.

The final part of the chapter examines exception handling and SOAP message logging. First I discuss ways in which a Web service client can deal with exceptions thrown by a Web service and how a Web service should deal with unhandled exceptions. Then you'll learn how to intercept and log raw SOAP messages at both the Web service and client ends of the message flow.

Debugging the ASP.NET Worker Process

The aspnet_wp.exe executable (or w3wp.exe on .NET Server) implements the HTTP runtime, which controls all of the components that make up a Web service. This executable runs an ASP.NET worker process controlled by IIS. On a single-processor system, IIS 5.0 runs all Web applications, including Web services, within this single process.

The most important point to remember is that IIS 5.0 currently has the limitation that only one debugger can be attached to this ASP.NET worker process at any one time. Even though internally the worker process isolates your Web application from other applications by using application domains, it's not possible for more than one developer at a time to debug Web services (or other Web applications) on the same machine. The Microsoft development model seems to encourage each developer to test and debug her Web service on her local machine before moving the service to a proper Web server in a production environment. If you want multiple developers to debug their Web applications on a single machine using IIS 5.0, you're unfortunately out of luck.

This restriction goes away on IIS 6.0, because each **AppDomain** (logical process) can run in its own application pool if you so desire. Because each application pool is in turn running its own w3wp.exe process, multiple developers can debug on a single IIS 6.0 Web server.

Debugging Preparation

By default, a Web service runs under the standard ASPNET user account. This is really a security feature, in that this account is given limited permissions by default and so can do only a limited amount of damage if hijacked. The important issue from a debugging point of view is that a developer can only debug a process running under another user account (such as ASPNET) if that developer belongs to the Administrators group on the machine where the process is running. In other words, if you want to debug a Web service, it's not sufficient to just be in the Users and Debugger Users groups, as discussed at the beginning of Chapter 4.

To add user accounts to and remove user accounts from groups when using Windows 2000, go to the Control Panel and choose Administrative Tools ➤ Computer Management ➤ System Tools ➤ Local Users and Groups ➤ Groups. Windows XP and .NET Server also allow maintenance of users and groups from the Control Panel.

If you really don't want, or aren't allowed, to add the developer doing the debugging to the Administrators group, there's a workaround. You can tell the ASP.NET worker process to run under a specific developer's account by adding some entries to the .NET machine configuration file, machine.config.

Security issues are involved with this approach, but full details on how to do it are in Chapter 9 if you need to adopt this procedure.

The **TimeServer** Web service serves as the demonstration application for this chapter. The **TimeServer** Visual Studio solution contains two projects. The first project is the **TimeServer** Web service, and the second project is a Windows Forms application called **TimeServerClient**.

After you load this solution into Visual Studio, you should check that the Web service project is configured for ASP.NET debugging. Right-click the **TimeServer** project in Solution Explorer, go to the Properties ➤ Configuration Properties ➤ Debugging property page, and make sure that the ASP.NET debugging option is selected.

On the same property page, you can specify how a Web service should be started for a debug or test session. This is controlled by the Start Action setting, which has four options:

- *Start project:* This option allows the Web service project to be started directly and accessed through its built-in test Web page. The default Web browser will be launched and point at the test page. This is the best option to use when you're doing unit testing of a Web service's methods, because it allows you to perform testing and debugging without having to write a custom client for the Web service.

- *Start external program:* Select this option if you want to test a Web service using another program as its client. When you choose this option, the Visual Studio debugger attaches to the Web service, but not to the external program that you're using to invoke the Web service.

- *Start URL:* You should choose this option only if you want to debug and test a Web service by invoking it from a specific Web page.

- *Wait for an external process to connect:* This option is similar to the "Start external program" option discussed previously, but the Visual Studio debugger attaches itself to both the Web service and the process that invokes the Web service. This option is most useful when you're testing and debugging the Web service and its client application together.

For the first demonstration, you should ensure that the Start Action setting is set to the first option (Start project) and that the start page is set to TimeService.asmx.

On the Properties ➤ Configuration Properties ➤ Build property page of the **TimeServer** and **TimeServerClient** projects, ensure that the "Generate debugging information" option is selected. This ensures that debug symbols will be generated for all precompiled components in the Web service and its client.

Next, use Solution Explorer to go to the solution's Properties ➤ Common Properties ➤ Startup Project property page and check that the Single Startup Project option is selected. The Multiple Startup Projects option on the same page should be used when the Web service to be debugged and its client exist in the same solution, as I demonstrate in the section "Debugging Using a SOAP Client" later in this chapter.

For the next preparation task, go to the Solution Explorer window and open the file named Web.config in the **TimeServer** project. This XML configuration file includes settings that control Web service behavior. Listing 8-1 shows the **debug** setting, though you will be looking at other Web.config settings when you examine Web service error handling later in this chapter.

Listing 8-1. The Debug Setting in TimeServer's Web.config

```
<system.web>
    <compilation defaultLanguage="vb" debug="true" />
</system.web>
```

Setting this **debug** XML attribute to **true** tells Visual Studio to generate debug symbols for any dynamically generated page and insert them into the page. It also allows the Visual Studio debugger to attach to the Web service. The major reason to be wary about this setting is that enabling debugging will make the Web service run much slower than normal, so it's advisable to make sure that this attribute is set to **false** when you release a Web service into a production environment.

ASP.NET automatically detects any changes to Web.config, so you don't need to reboot or restart the server for changes to take effect. But be aware that these attribute names are case sensitive, so using **Debug** rather than **debug** won't work!

Still in Visual Studio, select Debug ➤ Exceptions ➤ Common Language Runtime Exceptions ➤ System. Make sure that the "When the exception is thrown" option is set to "Continue" and the "If the exception is not handled" option is set to "Break into the debugger". (For a much more detailed explanation of these options, please see Chapter 13.) These settings ensure that when I start to demonstrate Web service exceptions later in this chapter, the Visual Studio debugger won't interrupt the flow of control unless it has no choice.

Debugging Using a Web Browser

Later in this chapter you'll look at debugging the **TimeServer** Web service while it's being called from the **TimeServerClient** application, but initially I want to look at calling the Web service from a Web browser. To do this, make sure that the Start Action setting is configured to the Start project option as discussed previously, and that the start page defined by this setting is TimeService.asmx. To check that everything compiles okay, you can now build the solution either by selecting Build ➢ Build Solution or by pressing Ctrl+Shift+B (the default keyboard shortcut).

Assuming that the Web service compiled successfully, add a breakpoint on line 48 of the source code displayed in TimeService.asmx.vb. Listing 8-2 shows the code that makes up the **CurrentTime** Web method, and adding a breakpoint to line 48 (shown in bold in Listing 8-2) will enable the debugger to break into the **CurrentTime** method as soon as it's called.

Listing 8-2. The TimeService Class

```
Option Strict On
Imports System.Web.Services

<Web.Services.WebService(Namespace:="http://debugvb.net/TimeServer/TimeService")> _
Public Class TimeService : Inherits System.Web.Services.WebService

#Region " Web Services Designer Generated Code "
    'Wizard-generated code omitted for brevity
#End Region

    <WebMethod()> _
    Public Function CurrentTime() As String
        Return System.DateTime.Now.ToLongTimeString
    End Function

End Class
```

Before you start the service, if you're using Internet Explorer as your default Web browser, you should switch off its default "friendly" HTTP error handling. If you select Tools ➢ Internet Options, and then go to the Browsing section of the Advanced tab, you'll see the option "Show friendly HTTP error messages". For the purposes of this demonstration, you can deselect this option. The difference between selecting and deselecting this option is the effect that a Web service exception has on the browser. If you opt for friendly HTTP error handling, the result of a Web service exception is the standard browser "Page cannot be displayed" message. If you turn off this option, the browser displays the actual exception message. I presume that "friendly" in this context means friendly to non-technical users.

Now start the **TimeServer** solution from Visual Studio by pressing F5. Visual Studio should open your default Web browser (Internet Explorer 6 in my case) and display the three public methods of the **TimeService** class: **CurrentTime**, **ThrowExceptionRaw**, and **ThrowExceptionCustom**. This page is provided by Visual Studio as a convenient way to test a Web service without having to write a custom client.

Click the **CurrentTime** method displayed in the browser and you'll see a new Web page that describes how this Web service method can be called using either a SOAP request or a raw HTTP POST and what the Web method will return as a response. Figure 8-1 shows the test page for the **CurrentTime** Web method.

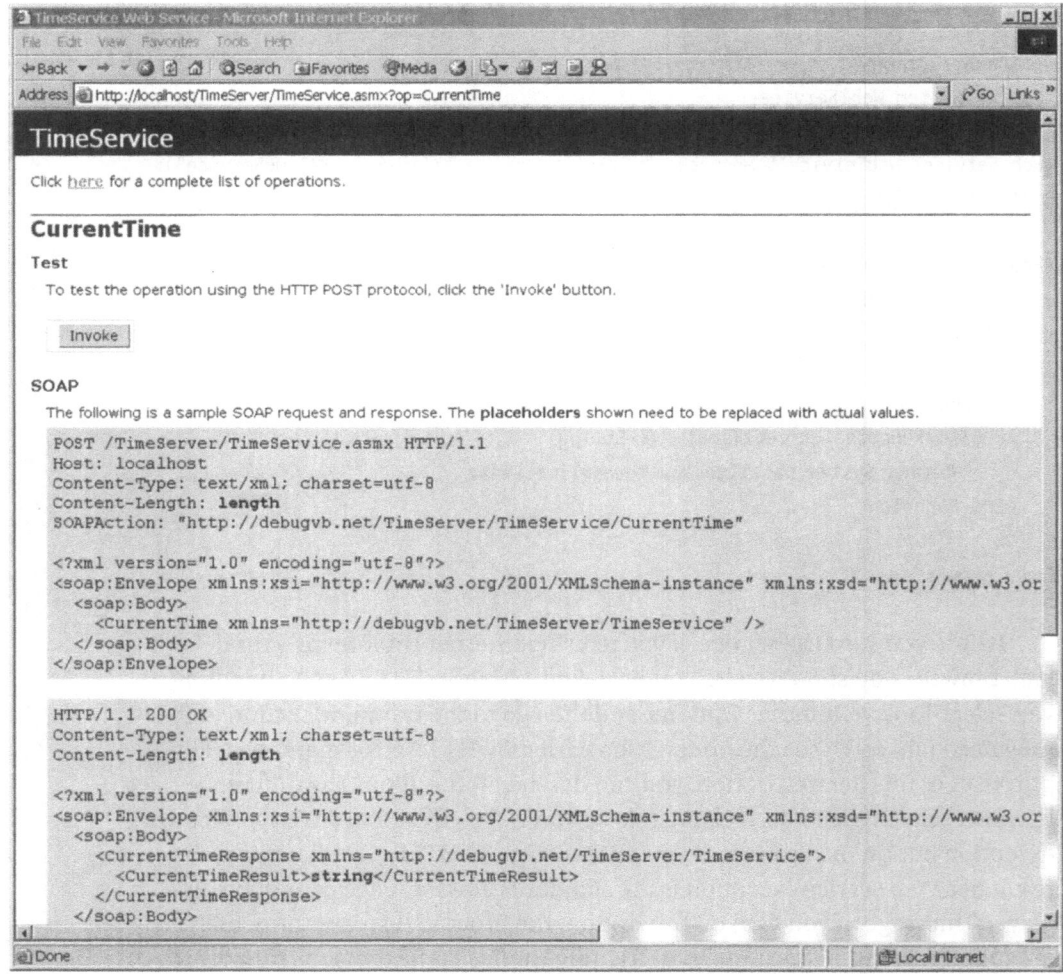

Figure 8-1. Test Web page for the CurrentTime Web method

Most of the time, Web service clients use SOAP requests and responses, but a Web browser client uses a plain HTTP POST transmission. SOAP is the more common protocol because it provides true cross-platform support, more flexible data types (including Datasets), and support for SOAP headers and extensions that allow you to add features such as tracing and security. Most of the examples in this chapter use SOAP messages, because SOAP is the default in .NET.

If you switch back to Visual Studio and go to the Debug menu to select the Processes menu item, you can see what the Visual Studio debugger has done after you pressed F5. The Processes dialog window shows that the debugger has attached itself to the aspnet_wp.exe process, which is the ASP.NET worker process that I discussed at the beginning of this chapter. It's also attached itself to your Web browser process—in my case iexplore.exe, because I'm using Internet Explorer. Figure 8-2 shows how this looks in Visual Studio.

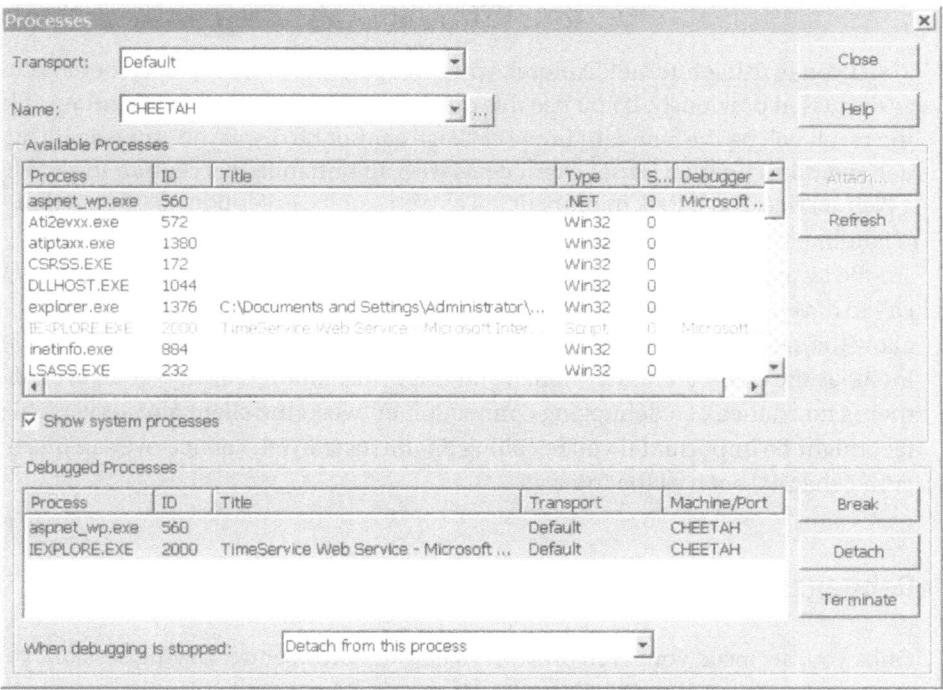

Figure 8-2. Processes debugged by Visual Studio during a standard browser test

Going back to the Web browser test page, at long last you can click the Invoke button on the Web page that tests the **CurrentTime** Web method. The breakpoint that you placed inside the Web method will be triggered, and you can step through the Web service just like any other type of .NET application. When you step out of the **CurrentTime** Web method, your Web browser will show the XML document returned by the method. This should come as no surprise, because

Web services are designed to communicate between components by using XML. Note that if you had used a SOAP client, the message returned would have been in SOAP format.

If you close the instance of your Web browser that shows the returned XML, you can click Back from the **CurrentTime** test page to go to the original Web service test page. Now click the link to the **ThrowExceptionRaw** method and you'll see a Web page that you can use to test that method. Once again, click the Invoke button. This time, your Web browser should show the text of the exception that this method throws, as shown in Listing 8-3.

Listing 8-3. Exception Produced by the ThrowExceptionRaw Web Method

```
System.NullReferenceException:Object reference not set to an instance of an
object.
   at TimeServer.TimeService.ThrowExceptionRaw() in
   c:\inetpub\wwwroot\TimeServer\TimeService.asmx.vb:line 55
```

If you're using Internet Explorer, you can opt for friendly HTTP error handling as discussed previously. If you use this option with the **ThrowExceptionRaw** link, the result will be the standard browser "Page cannot be displayed" message. This demonstrates how a browser client deals with an unhandled exception thrown by a Web service. You'll look in more detail at Web service exceptions in the section "Handling Web Service Failure" later in this chapter.

Be aware that when you use Visual Studio to debug a client making an HTTP call to a Web service, an additional header is included in the POST request to allow the server and client to synchronize and do step-in debugging. This header includes the client computer name, and this information is always sent, even if there's no chance of a debugging connection between the client and server. This fact might be important if you're calling an untrusted Web service over an unsecured channel such as the Internet.

Debugging Using a SOAP Client

Once you've closed your Web browser to end the browser debugging session, you can use the **TimeServerClient** application in the **TimeServer** solution to investigate debugging a Web service with a SOAP-based client. To do this, you should start by using Visual Studio's Solution Explorer to go to the solution's Properties ➤ Common Properties ➤ Startup Project property page and select the Multiple Startup Projects option. Make sure on this property page that the start actions of the **TimeServer** and **TimeServerClient** projects are both set to Start. This means that you're going to start the debugging session with the client application and the Web service will be started when first invoked by the client.

On the **TimeServer** project's Properties ➤ Configuration Properties ➤ Debugging property page, change the Start Action option to "Wait for an external process to connect," as discussed previously in the "Debugging Preparation" section. This specifies that the Web service will be started and debugged as soon as it's called by the client application. As before, on the same page check that the ASP.NET debugging option is selected.

Before you start the application, you should add a breakpoint on line 118 of the **ClientForm.vb** class. This is the line of code in the client application that invokes the **CurrentTime** Web service method when the GetTime command button is clicked. While you're in this method, take a quick look at the code in the form's **Load** event. After creating the Web service proxy, it sets the proxy timeout to –1. This line of code prevents any Web method call from ever timing out. Without this, if you spend any significant time debugging a Web service call, you will see a time-out error that throws you back into the proxy method and you'll be unable to continue debugging. When you release your Web service client into production, you should ensure that this line of code is removed.

```
'Create web service instance (via proxy) and
'ensure timeout never happens during debugging
m_TimeTest = New localhost.TimeService
#If DEBUG Then
    m_TimeTest.Timeout = -1
#End If
```

Now start the **TimeServer** solution from Visual Studio by pressing F5. This should launch the client's user interface that allows you to call into the Web service. Figure 8-3 shows this interface.

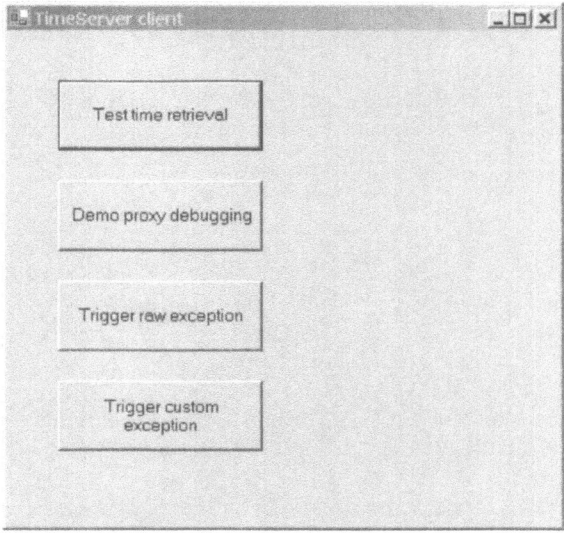

Figure 8-3. User interface for testing the TimeServer Web service methods

The first command button, Test time retrieval, calls the Web method **CurrentTime**, which returns exactly that. The second command button, Demo proxy debugging, calls **ThrowExceptionRaw** and will come in handy later for demonstrating proxy debugging. The third command button, Trigger raw exception, also calls **ThrowExceptionRaw**, but this time to demonstrate how a Web service translates a specific exception into a rather meaningless generic exception. The final command button, Trigger custom exception, calls the Web method **ThrowExceptionCustom** and demonstrates how a useful exception can be produced from within a Web service.

Clicking the Test time retrieval command button should trigger the breakpoint that you've just set. From here, you can step into the Web service and then back to the client form before the result returned by the Web service method is printed on the label to the right of the command button. While you're stepping through the Web service you have access to all of the normal debugging windows and other facilities.

You may notice that the first time a method is called on a Web service during a debugging session, the response is rather slow. Unfortunately, there's rather a lot of machinery sitting between (and inside) the client and the Web service, and this machinery needs to be cranked up for debugging. Further calls are executed much faster than the first call. If you set the **debug** attribute in Web.config to **false** and start the solution without debugging (by pressing Ctrl+F5 rather than F5, if you use the standard keystrokes), everything will run considerably faster.

Some of the machinery that is being concealed from you to facilitate the process of calling a Web service is actually useful to know from a debugging point of view. Figure 8-4 shows the normal interactions between a Web service and a typical SOAP client. Even a brief examination of this diagram shows you that there's more going on here than the debugger is showing you by default.

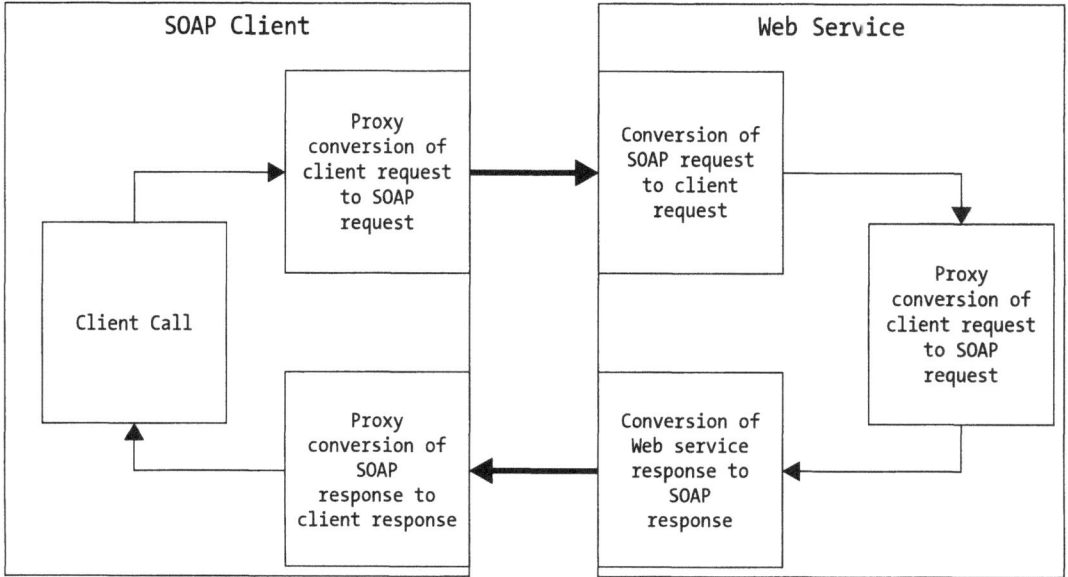

Figure 8-4. Interactions between a Web service and a SOAP client

Leaving some of the exact message serialization details for later, this is what happens when a Web service interacts with a client of that Web service using SOAP:

1. The client makes a call to a proxy class method.

2. The proxy method translates the call into a SOAP request message.

3. The SOAP request is sent over the network to the Web server.

4. The SOAP request is translated back into a .NET call.

5. The Web method receives the client's call.

6. The Web method processes the call and returns a result.

7. The .NET result is translated into a SOAP response message.

8. The SOAP response is sent over the network to the client proxy.

9. The SOAP response is translated into .NET result by the proxy method.

10. The client receives the .NET result from the proxy method.

The next section shows you more about what's under the hood by looking at how to debug the client proxy class that sits between the client and the Web service and is responsible for processing the SOAP request and response messages on the client side. Knowledge of this proxy class can be useful for debugging many Web service issues.

Debugging the Client Proxy

To debug the client proxy class that sits between the client and the Web service, you need to modify the proxy class so that you can step into it with the debugger. Visual Studio creates this proxy class automatically for you when you add a Web reference to a Web service. If you take the option to Show All Files in the Solution Explorer window, you can find the proxy class shown in the **TimeServer** project under the localhost ➤ Reference.map ➤ Reference.vb node. If you double-click the class to open it, you should see a class attribute called **System.Diagnostics.DebuggerStepthroughAttribute** at the top of the class. This attribute tells the debugger to ignore this class when stepping through the client code. The benefit of hiding the proxy code in this way is that developers aren't confused by having to step through code that they didn't write. The drawback is that it can be very useful to see and debug this proxy code in the event of Web service problems.

If you remove this attribute from the class, you'll find that you can step into and through the proxy code without a problem. To test this, remove the attribute, recompile the solution, and start it by pressing F5. Now click the Demo proxy debugging button, and the debugger should display a message about the unhandled **SoapException** thrown by the Web service. If you click the Break button, you can see that the debugger has stopped on the client proxy call to the Web service rather than on the client call. The method where the debugger breaks into the proxy class code is called **ThrowExceptionRaw**, just like its Web service counterpart. This proxy method is the one that the client is actually calling when it looks as though it's calling directly into the Web service method. If you step from the client into the Web service without removing this attribute, the debugger never steps into this proxy method, even though it's being executed.

You do need to bear in mind that whenever you need to update the Web reference because the Web service has changed, this attribute will be automatically regenerated and you'll need to remove it again if you want to continue debugging the proxy class.

NOTE *You should stop the solution and add **Debugger-StepthroughAttribute** back at the beginning of the proxy class before continuing with the chapter.*

Debugging a Remote Web Service

Debugging a Web service on a remote machine works in almost the same way as debugging a local Web service, but there are some initial steps that you must take in order to make everything work properly.

First make sure that the Visual Studio remote debugging components have been installed on the machine hosting the Web server. Chapter 15 discusses remote debugging setup in some detail. To grant access to the user who is performing the debugging, you must add that user in the Debugger Users group on the remote machine. Finally, as discussed in the "Debugging Preparation" section at the beginning of this chapter, you also need to add the same user account to the Administrators group on the remote machine. This is because, by default, the ASP.NET worker process runs as a SYSTEM process, and you're not allowed to debug a process running under another account unless you're an administrator.

After this, you should be able to debug the remote Web service almost as though you're debugging a local Web service. There are, however, a few differences, such as not being able to invoke Web service methods from the test Web page.

Debugging a Deployed Web Service

To debug a deployed Web service that's already running, you need to attach to the aspnet_wp.exe process manually. To do this in Visual Studio, show the Processes window by selecting Debug ➤ Processes. Make sure the "Show system processes" option is selected, choose the aspnet_wp.exe process in the top window as the process to debug, and click the Attach button. Select which types of code you want to debug, and make sure that you've chosen the correct action to take when you've finished debugging. You can choose either to detach from the process being debugged or to terminate the process. Because terminating the ASP.NET worker process will terminate all ASP.NET applications running on that Web server, you should normally choose the former option.

Assuming that you have the Web service project loaded in Visual Studio, you should now be able to debug normally. Bear in mind that when the debugger is in break mode while attached to the aspnet_wp.exe process, all ASP.NET applications will be frozen and none of them will respond to Web page or other requests.

Handling Web Service Failure

Like any other component, a Web service should throw an unhandled exception to its client when it's unable to deal with the exception internally. However, two factors complicate this process. The first factor is that the client of the Web service might well be external to the organization running the service—for instance, a client somewhere on the Internet. It's often not a good idea to throw detailed individual exceptions in these situations, because they can contain information that could be very useful to hackers trying to understand or break the Web service. The second factor is that when a SOAP client accesses a Web service, .NET will always translate any unhandled exception thrown by the Web service into a generic **SoapException**, thereby losing some of the information in the original exception. This can make debugging more difficult from the client point of view, so you need to consider how to make your Web service exceptions both easier to debug for authorized developers and harder to understand for unauthorized hackers.

Understanding Web Service Exception Flow

If you click the Trigger raw exception button, you can see how the exception that's deliberately thrown by the Web service is perceived by the client application.

The resulting message box is shown in Figure 8-5. It shows quite clearly that the exception thrown by the Web service isn't the same as the one received by the client. Whereas the **ThrowExceptionRaw** Web method throws a **NullReferenceException**, the client in this case actually receives a **SoapException**. The **SoapException** message does show the text of the original exception, but that text is mixed with the standard "Server was unable to process request" exception message that you saw earlier in the Web browser. To try to extract the original exception details would be rather messy. The **SoapFault** field is correct, showing that the error occurred on the server, but the Web service URL is shown as blank.

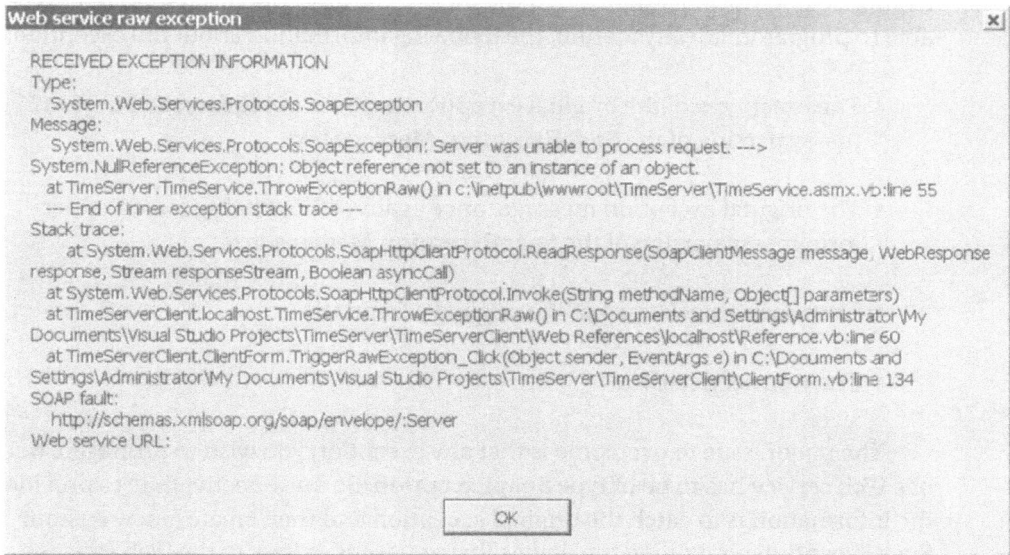

Figure 8-5. A Web service exception as it appears on the client

The most interesting information is in the first line of the stack trace—the exception was thrown by the **SoapHttpClientProtocol.ReadResponse** method. The client—or to be more precise, the client proxy—uses this method to read the SOAP response message sent by the Web service method.

The sequence of events is that after the Web service throws an unhandled exception, the HTTP Web service handler catches the exception and converts it into a SOAP response message. When the client proxy receives the SOAP response containing the exception information, it in turn converts that SOAP response into a **SoapException**. Finally, the client receives this **SoapException**. This mandatory process means that there's no way of throwing an exception from a Web service to its clients without having that exception converted into a generic **SoapException**. The message box in Figure 8-5 shows that this generic exception contains very little useful information. So the challenge is to devise a scheme that allows you to pass much more detailed and useful exception information from the Web service to its client.

Improving Web Service Exceptions

Obviously, the information shown in Figure 8-5 is not adequate for easy understanding of what went wrong inside the Web service. It would be much better if you could provide a custom exception with exactly the information that you need to know, whatever that might be. At the most basic level, you probably want to be able to programmatically identify the following information about the exception:

- The exact type of the original exception, without being forced to perform messy parsing of the **SoapException.Message** text

- The original exception message, once again without being forced to perform messy parsing of the **SoapException.Message** text

- The precise stack trace of the original exception

- The Web service URL

The major issue to overcome is that any exception you wish to propagate out of a Web service has to be of type **SoapException**. So one effective way to provide the information is to catch the original exception and then create a new custom **SoapException** containing the details that you want to pass to the Web service client. Listing 8-4 shows the Web method **ThrowExceptionCustom**, which deliberately triggers an exception and then calls into another method to create a custom exception before throwing that back to the Web service client. This custom **SoapException**, therefore, replaces the generic **SoapException** that would otherwise be produced automatically by the Web service.

Listing 8-4. The ThrowExceptionCustom Web Method Throws a Custom Exception

```
<WebMethod()> _
Public Sub ThrowExceptionCustom()
    Try
        'This code will throw an exception
        Dim Test As Object
        Test.ToString()
    Catch Exc As Exception
        'Substitute custom exception
        Throw CustomException(Exc)
    Finally
        'Do cleanup here
    End Try
End Sub
```

The real work is, of course, done within the private **CustomException** method, as shown in Listing 8-5. This function analyzes the original exception in order to build and return a custom **SoapException** containing the information that I mentioned previously as being the minimum required.

Listing 8-5. Creating a Custom SoapException with Required Information

```
Private Function CustomException(ByVal Exc As Exception) As SoapException
    Dim doc As New System.Xml.XmlDocument

    'Create detail node
    Dim DetailNode As System.Xml.XmlNode = _
                doc.CreateNode(XmlNodeType.Element, _
                            SoapException.DetailElementName.Name, _
                            SoapException.DetailElementName.Namespace)

    'Add original exception type
    Dim ExcType As System.Xml.XmlNode = _
                doc.CreateNode(XmlNodeType.Element, _
                            "ExceptionType", _
                            SoapException.DetailElementName.Namespace)
    ExcType.InnerText = Exc.GetType.ToString

    'Add original exception message
    Dim ExcMessage As System.Xml.XmlNode = _
                doc.CreateNode(XmlNodeType.Element, _
                            "ExceptionMessage", _
                            SoapException.DetailElementName.Namespace)
    ExcMessage.InnerText = Exc.Message

    'Add original exception stack trace
    Dim ExcStackTrace As System.Xml.XmlNode = _
                doc.CreateNode(XmlNodeType.Element, _
                            "ExceptionTrace", _
                            SoapException.DetailElementName.Namespace)
    ExcStackTrace.InnerText = Exc.StackTrace

    'Append the extra details to main detail node
    DetailNode.AppendChild(ExcType)
    DetailNode.AppendChild(ExcMessage)
    DetailNode.AppendChild(ExcStackTrace)

    'Build and return new custom SoapException
    Return New SoapException("", SoapException.ServerFaultCode, _
                            Context.Request.Url.AbsoluteUri, DetailNode)
End Function
```

The key to understanding the code in Listing 8-5 is that every **SoapException** can have a **Detail** XML node. By convention, this node contains application-specific error information. The **CustomException** method builds the **Detail** node and adds three child nodes, each containing an important piece of information from the original exception. The three items of information specified here are the original exception type, the original exception message, and the original exception stack trace. Once these child nodes have been created, they're added to the **Detail** node, and then the custom **SoapException** is built. The constructor that I'm using to create the new exception contains four arguments:

- *Message:* This is left blank, because the Web service will populate it automatically before the exception reaches the client. You aren't really interested in this message because it doesn't provide useful information in an easily accessible way.

- *Code:* This contains one of four predefined SOAP codes. Here it's being populated with the **ServerFaultCode**, signifying that the problem lies with the code inside the Web service.

- *Actor:* By convention, this argument contains the URL of the Web service that caused the error.

- *Detail:* This node contains the application-specific information that I'm interested in, namely the details that I grabbed from the original exception.

The code on the client side that catches the exception and displays it is shown in Listing 8-6. As you can see, it extracts the custom information that I specified by referring to each of the **Detail** child nodes by name. It also extracts the raw SOAP message for comparison and then displays the extracted information in a message box.

Listing 8-6. Displaying the Custom Exception in the Client Application

```
Private Sub TriggerCustomException_Click(ByVal sender As System.Object, _
                    ByVal e As System.EventArgs) _
                    Handles TriggerCustomException.Click
    Dim ExceptionMessage As String, Sep As String = Space$(4)

    'Trigger custom exception and show it
    Try
        m_TimeTest.ThrowExceptionCustom()

    Catch SoapExc As System.Web.Services.Protocols.SoapException
```

```
With SoapExc
    ExceptionMessage = "ORIGINAL EXCEPTION INFORMATION"
    ExceptionMessage += Environment.NewLine
    ExceptionMessage += "Type: " & Environment.NewLine
    ExceptionMessage += Sep & .Detail("ExceptionType").InnerText
    ExceptionMessage += Environment.NewLine
    ExceptionMessage += "Message: " & Environment.NewLine
    ExceptionMessage += Sep & .Detail("ExceptionMessage").InnerText
    ExceptionMessage += Environment.NewLine
    ExceptionMessage += "Stack trace: " & Environment.NewLine
    ExceptionMessage += Sep & .Detail("ExceptionTrace").InnerText
    ExceptionMessage += Environment.NewLine
    ExceptionMessage += "SOAP fault: " & Environment.NewLine
    ExceptionMessage += Sep & .Code.ToString
    ExceptionMessage += Environment.NewLine
    ExceptionMessage += "Web service URL: " & Environment.NewLine
    ExceptionMessage += Sep & .Actor.ToString
    ExceptionMessage += Environment.NewLine
    ExceptionMessage += "Raw SOAP message: " & Environment.NewLine
    ExceptionMessage += Sep & .Message
End With

MessageBox.Show(ExceptionMessage, _
                            "Web service custom exception", _
                            MessageBoxButtons.OK)

    End Try

End Sub
```

After all of this work, Figure 8-6 shows the message box as it displays the custom information that I added inside the Web service. If you contrast this information with that shown in Figure 8-5, you can see that a major improvement has taken place. Instead of having to parse the generic **SoapException.Message** in a messy way, all of the information is now readily available in individual child nodes.

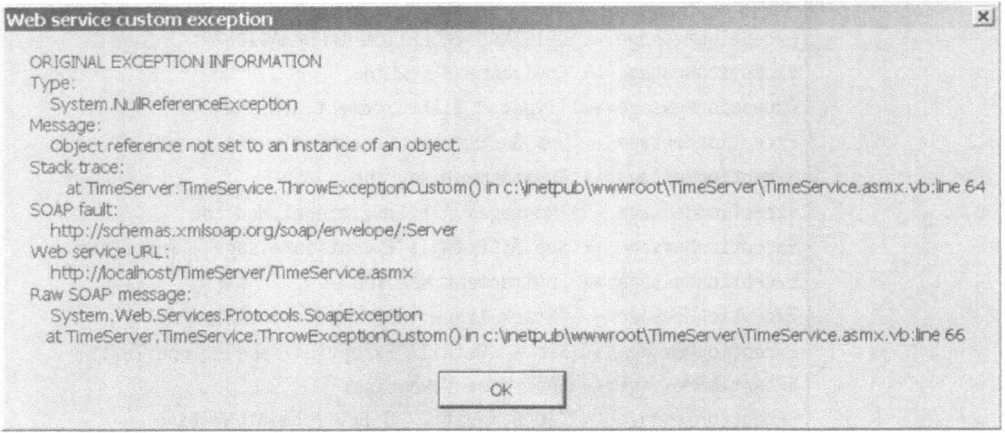

Figure 8-6. A Web service custom exception as it appears on the client

Of course, you can adapt this code to add as many items of information as you wish to transfer, simply by creating an extra child node for each item.

Hiding Exception Details

If your Web service is running on the Internet, and is therefore subject to all of the security risks that come with that very public environment, you probably don't want to provide these detailed exception messages. They give away too much information to any hacker who's looking to probe or attack your Web service. It's far better in these circumstances to emit a bland, generic error message in the event of Web service failure. Listing 8-7 modifies the **CustomException** method shown previously in Listing 8-5 to check whether the client is on the same machine as the Web service. If not, it populates the exception **Detail** node with exception information that gives absolutely nothing away.

Listing 8-7. Hiding Exception Details for Nonlocal Users

```
Private Function CustomException(ByVal Exc As Exception) As SoapException
    Dim doc As New System.Xml.XmlDocument

    'Create detail node
    Dim DetailNode As System.Xml.XmlNode = _
                doc.CreateNode(XmlNodeType.Element, _
                            SoapException.DetailElementName.Name, _
                            SoapException.DetailElementName.Namespace)
```

```vbnet
'Add original exception type
Dim ExcType As System.Xml.XmlNode = _
            doc.CreateNode(XmlNodeType.Element, _
                    "ExceptionType", _
                    SoapException.DetailElementName.Namespace)
If Context.Request.UserHostAddress = "127.0.0.1" Then
    ExcType.InnerText = Exc.GetType.ToString
Else
    ExcType.InnerText = "SoapException"
End If


'Add original exception message
Dim ExcMessage As System.Xml.XmlNode = _
            doc.CreateNode(XmlNodeType.Element, _
                    "ExceptionMessage", _
                    SoapException.DetailElementName.Namespace)
If Context.Request.UserHostAddress = "127.0.0.1" Then
    ExcMessage.InnerText = Exc.Message
Else
    ExcMessage.InnerText = "Error - no details available"
End If


'Add original exception stack trace
Dim ExcStackTrace As System.Xml.XmlNode = _
            doc.CreateNode(XmlNodeType.Element, _
                    "ExceptionTrace", _
                    SoapException.DetailElementName.Namespace)
If Context.Request.UserHostAddress = "127.0.0.1" Then
    ExcStackTrace.InnerText = Exc.StackTrace
Else
    ExcStackTrace.InnerText = "No stack trace available"
End If


'Append the extra details to main detail node
DetailNode.AppendChild(ExcType)
DetailNode.AppendChild(ExcMessage)
DetailNode.AppendChild(ExcStackTrace)


'Build and return new custom SoapException
Return New SoapException("", SoapException.ServerFaultCode, _
                    Context.Request.Url.AbsoluteUri, DetailNode)
End Function
```

Figure 8-7 shows the resulting message box displayed for a remote client. The custom information has been suppressed, and the Web service client is left with little information useful for hacking the Web service.

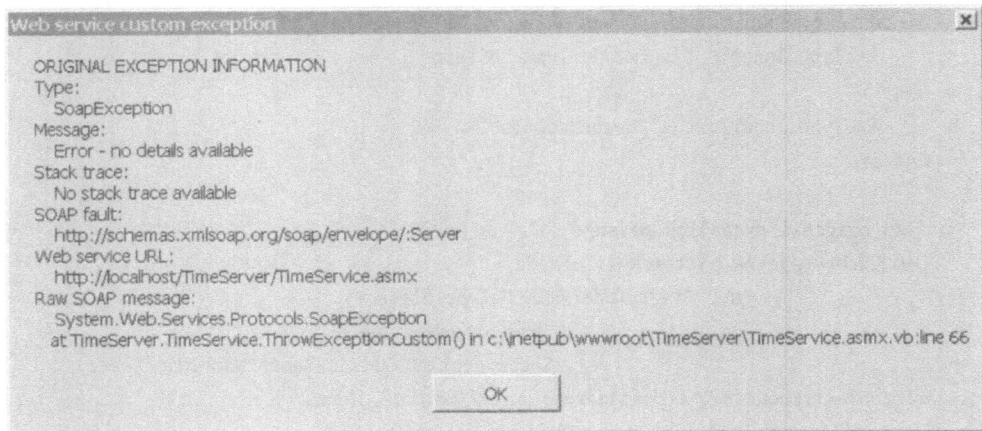

Figure 8-7. A Web service exception as it appears on a nonlocal client

The one remaining piece of giveaway information is the raw message that the HTTP handler adds to the custom SOAP exception. This contains information about the exception's stack trace that is better to suppress. The key to removing this last clue lies in the **CustomErrors** section of Web.config. This setting has three values:

- *On:* Display "friendly" (i.e., nondetailed) error information for all clients.

- *Off:* Display detailed error information for all clients.

- *RemoteOnly:* Display detailed error information for local clients and non-detailed error information for remote clients.

The best setting for most environments is **RemoteOnly**, which is also the default setting, as shown in Listing 8-8.

Listing 8-8. CustomErrors Setting in TimeServer's Web.config

```
<system.web>
    <customErrors mode="RemoteOnly" />
</system.web>
```

This setting will remove the stack trace from the SOAP message for any non-local client. Note that you may need to reboot Visual Studio for this setting to take effect during Web service development.

Trapping Unhandled Exceptions

You can normally catch unhandled exceptions in ASP.NET applications by adding code to the **Application_Error** event in the global.asax file. Unfortunately, this doesn't work for unhandled exceptions within a Web service. This is because the HTTP handler for XML Web services catches any unhandled exception and turns it into a SOAP fault before the **Application_Error** event is called. This SOAP fault then becomes a **SoapException** or a **SoapHeaderException**, depending on whether or not the exception was thrown while processing a SOAP header.

Using any of the other unhandled exception filters described in Chapter 13 also doesn't work for the same reason. So either you have to add exception handling to every single Web method or you create a SOAP extension, as described in the next few sections, that's bound to every Web method. The SOAP extension route is attractive because you don't have to add error handling to every Web method and you can write custom exception information directly into the SOAP response stream. The problem with this approach is that you no longer have access to the original exception or its context, which makes it rather difficult to create a custom exception with meaningful information. For this reason, adding error handling to every Web method is the recommended solution.

Tracking SOAP Messages

Once you start developing Web services and have overcome the initial knowledge hurdles, it's easy to become seduced by the ease with which it all works. Most of the details are hidden from you, which is great until something stops working. So now that you've seen the basic information transfer mechanism used by Web services (see Figure 8-4), it's time to dig into some of the messy details behind this mechanism. To really debug interactions between a Web service and its clients, you need to be able to see the underlying SOAP messages that implement Web service requests and responses. This is especially true when you have to understand whether a communication problem is caused by a wrongly formatted SOAP message or by incorrect application information passed to or from the Web service.

Building the SoapMonitor SOAP Extension

To see the underlying SOAP stream from within a Web service, you need to write a custom SOAP extension. *SOAP extensions* allow you to intercept the process shown in Figure 8-4, so that you can process the SOAP message before it's sent and after it's received. Listing 8-9 shows a minimum custom SOAP extension called **SoapMonitor** that will later be developed to form a SOAP message logger.

Listing 8-9. The Bare-bones SoapMonitor Custom SOAP Extension

```
Option Strict On
Imports System.Web.Services.Protocols

Public Class SoapMonitor : Inherits SoapExtension

    Public Overloads Overrides Function GetInitializer _
                        (ByVal serviceType As System.Type) As Object
    End Function

    Public Overloads Overrides Function GetInitializer _
                        (ByVal methodInfo As LogicalMethodInfo, _
                         ByVal attribute As SoapExtensionAttribute) _
                        As Object
    End Function

    Public Overrides Sub Initialize(ByVal initializer As Object)
    End Sub

    Public Overrides Sub ProcessMessage(ByVal Message As SoapMessage)
        'Major SOAP message processing will go here
    End Sub

End Class
```

The overloaded **GetInitializer** and **Initialize** methods have to be overridden but can be left blank for this purpose. The major work will need to be done in the **ProcessMessage** method, where you have access to the SOAP message. This method is actually called four times during processing of a SOAP request and response. You can tell which stage is happening by looking at the **Stage** member of the **Message** argument. The message stage has the following four possible values at the Web service end of the message transfer:

- *BeforeDeserialize:* At this point, you have access to the SOAP request before it's been translated into a .NET call. This is where you want access to the SOAP request message.

- *AfterDeserialize:* At this stage, the SOAP request has been read and translated, but it's now empty.

- *BeforeSerialize:* At this stage, the SOAP response hasn't yet been created, so it isn't accessible at all.

- *AfterSerialize:* Now the SOAP response has been created, but unfortunately it can't be read, although it can be written. This is where you want access to the SOAP response message.

So the **ProcessMessage** method allows you to read the SOAP request directly, but not the SOAP response. To do this, you need to override the **ChainStream** method, so that you can have direct access to the memory buffer containing the SOAP message. You need to be careful here because when you access the memory buffer directly in this way, you have to retrieve and pass on the memory stream. Listing 8-10 shows a typical pattern that you can use to set up safe access to the SOAP stream.

Listing 8-10. Setting Up Access to the SOAP Stream Memory Buffer

```
Option Strict On
Imports System.Web.Services.Protocols

Public Class SoapMonitor : Inherits SoapExtension
    Private OldStream As Stream
    Private NewStream As Stream

    Public Overrides Function ChainStream(ByVal stream As System.IO.Stream) _
                                                    As System.IO.Stream

        OldStream = stream
        NewStream = New MemoryStream
        Return NewStream
    End Function

End Class
```

The code inside the **ChainStream** method saves a reference (in class member variables) to both the stream coming into the method and the stream being returned by the method. Now you're ready to create the logic within the

ProcessMessage method for logging the SOAP request and response messages. Listing 8-11 shows all of the **SoapMonitor** code you have seen so far and adds the **ProcessMessage** logic to save the SOAP request and response at the **BeforeDeserialize** and **AfterSerialize** stages, respectively.

Listing 8-11. Complete SoapMonitor Custom SOAP Extension

```
Option Strict On
Imports System.Web.Services.Protocols
Imports System.IO

Public Class SoapMonitor : Inherits SoapExtension
    Private OldStream As Stream
    Private NewStream As Stream

    Public Overloads Overrides Function GetInitializer _
                        (ByVal serviceType As System.Type) As Object
    End Function

    Public Overloads Overrides Function GetInitializer _
                        (ByVal methodInfo As LogicalMethodInfo, _
                         ByVal attribute As SoapExtensionAttribute) _
                        As Object
    End Function

    Public Overrides Sub Initialize(ByVal initializer As Object)
    End Sub

    Public Overrides Sub ProcessMessage(ByVal Message As SoapMessage)
        Dim Logfile As New FileStream("C:\test\test.log", _

FileMode.Append, _

FileAccess.Write)
        Dim LogfileWriter As New StreamWriter(Logfile)

        Select Case Message.Stage

            Case SoapMessageStage.BeforeDeserialize
                'Write header details
                With LogfileWriter
                    .WriteLine("**************************************************")
                    .WriteLine("Web service: " & Message.Url)
```

```
                .WriteLine("Web method: " & Message.Action)
                .WriteLine("Called at " & DateTime.Now)
                .Write("Message stage: SOAP REQUEST")
                .WriteLine(" (" & Message.Stage.ToString & ")")
                .WriteLine()
                .Flush()
        End With
        'Write incoming SOAP request message
        CopyStream(OldStream, NewStream)
        NewStream.Position = 0
        CopyStream(NewStream, Logfile)
        NewStream.Position = 0
        'Blank separating line
        LogfileWriter.WriteLine()

    Case SoapMessageStage.AfterSerialize
        'Write header details
        With LogfileWriter
            .WriteLine("*************************************************")
            .WriteLine("Web service: " & Message.Url)
            .WriteLine("Web method: " & Message.Action)
            .WriteLine("Called at " & DateTime.Now)
            .Write("Message stage: SOAP RESPONSE")
            .WriteLine(" (" & Message.Stage.ToString & ")")
            .Write("Exception thrown? ")
            If Message.Exception Is Nothing Then
                    .WriteLine("No")
            Else
                    .WriteLine("Yes")
            End If
            .WriteLine()
            .Flush()
        End With
        'Write outgoing SOAP response message
        NewStream.Position = 0
        CopyStream(NewStream, Logfile)
        NewStream.Position = 0
        CopyStream(NewStream, OldStream)
        'Blank separating line
        LogfileWriter.WriteLine()

End Select
```

```vb
            Logfile.Flush()
            Logfile.Close()

        End Sub

        Public Overrides Function ChainStream(ByVal stream As System.IO.Stream) _
                                                        As System.IO.Stream
            OldStream = stream
            NewStream = New MemoryStream
            Return NewStream
        End Function

        Private Sub CopyStream(ByVal FromStream As Stream, ByVal ToStream As Stream)
            Dim FromReader As TextReader = New StreamReader(FromStream)
            Dim ToWriter As TextWriter = New StreamWriter(ToStream)

            ToWriter.WriteLine(FromReader.ReadToEnd)
            ToWriter.Flush()

        End Sub

End Class
```

This SOAP extension writes the SOAP request and response messages to a hard-coded log file (in this case, C:\test\test.log). It also logs the Web method that was called, the date and time of the call, and whether the Web service threw an exception in response to the client call. Later you'll see an example of a log file produced by this code, but I still need to demonstrate how to hook up this SOAP extension to one or more Web methods so that it's invoked automatically when the Web method is called.

Building the SoapMonitor Attribute

In order to bind a custom SOAP extension to a Web method, you need to build a corresponding custom SOAP extension attribute. To do this, you inherit from the **SoapExtensionAttribute** type. This allows you to identify your SOAP extension. Listing 8-12 shows how to create the **SoapMonitorAttribute** custom attribute that you can use for binding the **SoapMonitor** extension. This custom attribute overrides the **ExtensionType** property to return the type of the **SoapMonitor** extension and it also overrides the **Priority** property to define the SOAP extension's priority relative to other extensions. The lines highlighted in bold are the ones that you'll need to modify when creating your own **SoapExtensionAttribute**.

Listing 8-12. The SoapMonitorAttribute Custom SOAP Attribute

```
Option Strict On
Imports System.Web.Services.Protocols


Public Class SoapMonitorAttribute : Inherits SoapExtensionAttribute
    'Add this custom attribute to any web method where you want
    'to monitor the SOAP request and response messages

    Public Overrides ReadOnly Property ExtensionType() As System.Type
        Get
            Return GetType(SoapMonitor)
        End Get
    End Property

    Public Overrides Property Priority() As Integer
        Get
            Return 0
        End Get
        Set(ByVal Value As Integer)
        End Set
    End Property

End Class
```

Having created the **SoapMonitorAttribute** attribute, Listing 8-13 shows you how to bind a custom attribute's extension to a Web method, in this case the **ThrowExceptionCustom** method. The line highlighted in bold applies the attribute to the method. Notice how you can omit the final part of the attribute's name (Attribute) when you specify it.

Listing 8-13. Binding the SoapMonitor Extension to a Web Method

```
<WebMethod(), SoapMonitor()> _
Public Sub ThrowExceptionCustom()
    'This method throws a customized exception
    Try
        Dim Test As Object
        Test.ToString()
    Catch Exc As Exception
        Throw CustomException(Exc)
    End Try

End Sub
```

At this point, any SOAP call to the **ThrowExceptionCustom** Web method will result in the **SoapMonitor.ProcessMessage** method being called four times, once for each stage of the SOAP message serialization process.

Putting It All Together

This is the log file produced when the **ThrowExceptionCustom** Web method is given the **SoapMonitorAttribute** attribute and then called by a SOAP client:

```
**************************************************
Web service: http://localhost/TimeServer/TimeService.asmx
Web method: http://debugvb.net/TimeServer/TimeService/ThrowExceptionCustom
Called at 09/11/2002 16:24:31
Message stage: SOAP REQUEST (BeforeDeserialize)

<?xml version="1.0" encoding="utf-8"?>
<soap:Envelope xmlns:soap=http://schemas.xmlsoap.org/soap/envelope/
 xmlns:xsi="http://www.w3.org/2001/XMLSchema-instance"
xmlns:xsd="http://www.w3.org/2001/XMLSchema">
  <soap:Body>
    <ThrowExceptionCustom xmlns="http://debugvb.net/TimeServer/TimeService" />
  </soap:Body>
</soap:Envelope>


**************************************************
Web service: http://localhost/TimeServer/TimeService.asmx
Web method: http://debugvb.net/TimeServer/TimeService/ThrowExceptionCustom
Called at 09/11/2002 16:24:31
Message stage: SOAP RESPONSE (AfterSerialize)
Exception thrown? Yes

<?xml version="1.0" encoding="utf-8"?>
<soap:Envelope xmlns:soap="http://schemas.xmlsoap.org/soap/envelope/"
xmlns:xsi="http://www.w3.org/2001/XMLSchema-instance"
xmlns:xsd="http://www.w3.org/2001/XMLSchema">
  <soap:Body>
    <soap:Fault>
      <faultcode>soap:Server</faultcode>
      <faultstring>System.Web.Services.Protocols.SoapException
   at TimeServer.TimeService.ThrowExceptionCustom() in
```

```
 c:\inetpub\wwwroot\TimeServer\TimeService.asmx.vb:line
66</faultstring>
       <faultactor>http://localhost/TimeServer/TimeService.asmx</faultactor>
       <detail>
         <ExceptionType>System.NullReferenceException</ExceptionType>
         <ExceptionMessage>Object reference not set to an instance of an object.
         </ExceptionMessage>
         <ExceptionTrace>   at TimeServer.TimeService.ThrowExceptionCustom()
 in c:\inetpub\wwwroot\TimeServer\TimeService.asmx.vb:line
64</ExceptionTrace>
       </detail>
     </soap:Fault>
   </soap:Body>
</soap:Envelope>
```

Armed with this kind of low-level information, it's much easier to determine whether a Web service communication problem is an application error or a SOAP formatting issue. Among other things, you can use this SOAP extension to log every exception that occurs within your Web service.

Bear in mind that there is a performance penalty to be paid when you use SOAP extensions and attributes to do SOAP logging in this manner. You have to make a tradeoff here, so you might want to log messages only when your Web service is in its beta phase, and perhaps log only exceptions when you go into production.

SOAP Logging at the Client

What happens when you need to read the SOAP messages going back and forth between your client and a third-party Web service, where you don't have access to the source code of the Web service? In this case, there's no way of adding your custom **SoapMonitor** extension at the Web service end. Instead, you can create a very similar custom SOAP extension at the client end and then attach this extension to the proxy class methods that you want to monitor or debug.

The client **SoapMonitor** extension will be almost identical to the one created at the Web service end. The only change comes in the client extension's **ProcessMessage** method, as shown in Listing 8-14. If you compare this with the equivalent Web service **ProcessMessage** shown in Listing 8-11, the differences between the two listings are highlighted in bold.

Listing 8-14. The ProcessMessage Method on a Client-Based SOAP Extension

```
Public Overrides Sub ProcessMessage(ByVal Message As SoapMessage)
    Dim Logfile As New FileStream("C:\test\test.log", _

FileMode.Append, _

FileAccess.Write)
    Dim LogfileWriter As New StreamWriter(Logfile)

    Select Case Message.Stage

        Case SoapMessageStage.AfterSerialize
            'Write header details
            With LogfileWriter
                .WriteLine("***********************************************")
                .WriteLine("Web service: " & Message.Url)
                .WriteLine("Web method: " & Message.Action)
                .WriteLine("Called at " & DateTime.Now)
                .Write("Message stage: SOAP REQUEST")
                .WriteLine(" (" & Message.Stage.ToString & ")")
                .WriteLine()
                .Flush()
            End With
            'Write incoming SOAP request message
            CopyStream(OldStream, NewStream)
            NewStream.Position = 0
            CopyStream(NewStream, Logfile)
            NewStream.Position = 0
            'Blank separating line
            LogfileWriter.WriteLine()

        Case SoapMessageStage.BeforeDeserialize
            'Write header details
            With LogfileWriter
                .WriteLine("***********************************************")
                .WriteLine("Web service: " & Message.Url)
                .WriteLine("Web method: " & Message.Action)
                .WriteLine("Called at " & DateTime.Now)
                .Write("Message stage: SOAP RESPONSE")
                .WriteLine(" (" & Message.Stage.ToString & ")")
                .Write("Exception thrown? ")
                If Message.Exception Is Nothing Then
```

```
                        .WriteLine("No")
            Else
                        .WriteLine("Yes")
            End If
            .WriteLine()
            .Flush()
        End With
        'Write outgoing SOAP response message
        NewStream.Position = 0
        CopyStream(NewStream, Logfile)
        NewStream.Position = 0
        CopyStream(NewStream, OldStream)
        'Blank separating line
        LogfileWriter.WriteLine()

    End Select

    Logfile.Flush()
    Logfile.Close()

End Sub
```

On the server-based **ProcessMessage**, the **BeforeDeserialize** message stage was used to read the SOAP request and the **AfterSerialize** stage to read the SOAP response. At the client end, these stages are, of course, swapped around because the client initiates the whole response/request cycle. So the message stages at the client end look like this:

- *BeforeSerialize:* Before the .NET call has been translated into a SOAP request

- *AfterSerialize:* After the SOAP request has been created and is about to be passed over the network to the Web service

- *BeforeDeserialize:* After the SOAP response has been received, but before it's been translated back into a .NET result

- *AfterDeserialize:* After the SOAP response has been translated back into a .NET result

Finally, you need to bind the SOAP extension to one or more client proxy methods. Listing 8-15 shows the **SoapMonitor** extension bound to the **Current-Time** proxy method.

Listing 8-15. Binding the SoapMonitor Extension to a Web Method

```
<System.Web.Services.Protocols.SoapDocumentMethodAttribute _
        ("http://debugvb.net/TimeServer/TimeService/CurrentTime", _
        RequestNamespace:="http://debugvb.net/TimeServer/TimeService", _
        ResponseNamespace:="http://debugvb.net/TimeServer/TimeService", _
        Use:=System.Web.Services.Description.SoapBindingUse.Literal, _
        ParameterStyle:=System.Web.Services.Protocols.SoapParameterStyle.Wrapped), _
        SoapMonitor()> _
Public Function CurrentTime() As String
    Dim results() As Object = Me.Invoke("CurrentTime", New Object(-1) {})
    Return CType(results(0),String)
End Function
```

As I stated before, you need to be aware that updating the Web service reference automatically regenerates the client proxy class, so you'll need to reattribute the appropriate proxy methods when this happens.

Tracing and Instrumentation

Tracing and instrumentation in a Web service is handled exactly like it is in a non-ASP.NET application. Please refer to Chapter 6 for a comprehensive treatment of this subject.

Summary

This chapter started by looking in some detail at how to prepare for debugging a Web service and its clients. Once you see some of the vigorous "under-the-surface" activity that happens in order to support the seamless interaction between a Web service and its clients, you have a much better idea of where to start when you try to set up Web services debugging properly.

The chapter continued by looking at debugging a Web service when called by a Web browser and by a Windows Forms application. The HTTP and SOAP communication protocols are different, and this can be confusing. You saw that the actual debugging of a Web service is exactly the same as for any non-Web VB .NET application.

Next, the chapter covered dealing with unhandled exceptions thrown by a Web service. You need to understand this process if you want to deliver useful error messages to developers while delivering only generic error messages to potential hackers.

Finally, the chapter explored how to intercept the SOAP stream in order to log the SOAP messages that pass back and forth between a Web service and its SOAP clients. Access to this low-level debugging information is essential for analyzing Web service communication issues.

INTERLUDE

RECONSTRUCTING FAILURE

Discovering exactly what happened before and during an accident or disaster can be crucial in establishing fault or preventing a similar incident from occurring again. Enter a company based in Menlo Park, California, called Failure Analysis Associates (FAA). FAA has more than 400 employees, including heavy-duty Ph.D. scientists and engineers, devoted to reconstructing, analyzing, and understanding catastrophic system and materials failures. FAA has analyzed incidents ranging from the Oklahoma City bombing to James Dean's fatal car accident.

The company's databases include over 350 million accident and incident records, including a copy of every U.S. death certificate filed since 1975. Their Arizona-based desert test facility has a 1,200-foot crash rail for propelling vehicles into other solid objects, a 90-foot drop tower, and a full-fledged ballistics range. In short, these people are serious about figuring out what went wrong.

One of their more lighthearted analyses was commissioned by a TV show that wanted to know if James Dean's fatal accident was indeed caused by the film star's reckless speeding, as popular folklore records. FAA used computers to reconstruct the event and analyze which of the two drivers was at fault and how fast the two cars were going when they collided.

FAA started their analysis by collecting as much information as they could. The data included the original California Highway Patrol report, statements from two witnesses, and photos of the accident scene. Then they created a computer model of the cars, the road, and the surrounding terrain. Because the original cars weren't available, FAA went out and bought two duplicate cars, as similar as they could get to the original vehicles. These cars were digitized and added to the computer simulation. As much information as possible was added, including the weight of each of the cars, their respective tire widths and crush stiffness, the road surfaces at the time, the apparent point of contact, and the finishing positions of the vehicles after the accident.

Many different combinations of speeds and angles were tried out in the computer simulation in an attempt to simulate the actual car damage and positions as accurately as possible. After extensive analysis, a 45-second computer animation was produced, showing the accident from several different points of view. The results were somewhat surprising.

With the best possible duplication of actual events, Dean's car (a Porsche Spyder) was found to have been traveling at 57 mph while the other car (a Ford) was traveling at 55 mph. Far from Dean acting recklessly, the accident appears to have been caused by the driver of the Ford turning left directly in front of Dean's oncoming car, probably making a fatal misjudgment of its speed.

In the future, as civilization becomes increasingly dependent on computer technology for controlling facilities as diverse as banking, nuclear power stations, medical tools, and weapons systems, it's likely that FAA and similar companies will be spending much of their time reconstructing and analyzing software failures and bugs.

CHAPTER 9

ASP.NET Debugging

ASP.NET IS PERHAPS THE FLAGSHIP of the .NET development product range. Microsoft has thrown away the old ASP model of developing Web applications using a combination of script and COM components. ASP.NET replaces the old model with a new "code-behind" model that combines fully compiled business logic running on the server with built-in or custom graphical controls running in the client Web browser. Another major feature of ASP.NET is XCOPY deployment of applications in many scenarios, which is a huge improvement over the ASP deployment story.

The new development model offered by ASP.NET very much resembles (perhaps deliberately) the Windows Forms event-driven model of coding. ASP.Classic developers are facing a bigger paradigm shift than their VB colleagues because of this shift from procedural code to event-driven code, and the resulting separation of presentation code from business code. Their VB.Classic colleagues don't escape completely unscathed, however, as the ASP.NET similarity to the Windows Forms event-driven development model tends to hide differences that can cause bugs for the unwary.

This chapter investigates the debugging of ASP.NET applications, with the exception of XML Web services because these are discussed in Chapter 8. You'll focus on the debugging of ASP.NET programs running under Internet Information Server (IIS) 5.x and 6.0, and you'll also investigate ASP.NET tracing and error handling.

IIS Debugging Considerations

This section covers IIS information about which you should be aware when you're debugging ASP.NET applications that run under version 5.x and version 6.0 of IIS. This includes how IIS detects and deals with problems in ASP.NET applications and any debugging restrictions imposed by the different IIS 5.x and IIS 6.0 architectures.

When you run your ASP.NET application on an IIS 5.x Web server, the aspnet_wp.exe executable implements the HTTP runtime, which controls most of the elements that make up your application. This executable runs an ASP.NET worker process controlled by IIS. On a single-processor system, IIS 5.x runs all Web applications, including Web services, within this single process.

When you run your ASP.NET application on an IIS 6.0 Web server, the w3wp.exe executable implements the HTTP runtime. Just as with IIS 5.*x*, this executable runs an ASP.NET worker process controlled by IIS, but you can configure IIS 6.0 to run multiple ASP.NET worker processes.

Simultaneous Debugging with IIS 5.x

IIS 5.*x* currently has the limitation that only one debugger can be attached to an ASP.NET worker process at any one time. Even though internally the worker process isolates your Web application from other applications by using application domains, it's not possible for more than one developer at a time to debug ASP.NET applications (or other Web applications) on the same machine. The Microsoft development model seems to encourage each developer to test and debug her Web application on her local machine, before moving the application to a proper Web server in a production environment. If you want multiple developers to debug their Web applications on a single machine using IIS 5.*x*, you're unfortunately out of luck.

If your ASP.NET application is running on a multiprocessor machine, you'll see one ASP.NET worker process for each processor on the machine, an architecture sometimes referred to as a *Web garden.* You might think that having multiple ASP.NET worker processes means that multiple developers can do ASP.NET debugging simultaneously. Unfortunately, this doesn't work because there are no guarantees about which worker process will handle any particular HTTP request. Even if you manage to attach to the correct process for your application's first HTTP request, the remaining requests will potentially be processed by one of the ASP.NET worker processes to which you're not attached.

Simultaneous Debugging with IIS 6.0

A major difference between IIS 5.*x* and IIS 6.0 is that with the latter you can enable *worker process isolation mode.* This has the effect of grouping all configured Web applications into application pools, with each application pool run by a separate w3wp.exe process. You can further specify that each **AppDomain** (logical process) is executed in its own application pool. Because each application pool is in turn running its own w3wp.exe process, multiple developers can debug on a single IIS 6.0 Web server because each developer can attach his debugger to the w3wp.exe process running his own application. This removes the multideveloper debugging issue discussed in the previous section.

Process Recycling with IIS 5.x

Another issue with debugging ASP.NET applications running on IIS 5.*x* is the way in which the built-in health monitoring works. IIS 5.*x* health monitoring occurs when the <processModel **enable**=/> setting in machine.config is set to **true**. All ASP.NET worker processes are then monitored for specific health criteria. For instance, when the size of any one process reaches a certain percentage of the total memory available to the system (by default, 60% of the system's physical memory), the worker process is then recycled. This recycling involves suspending all requests to that process, routing requests to a new worker process, and then stopping and restarting the original process.

Although this health monitoring is very useful from a production support point of view, the problem is that the worker process can be recycled even though you've already attached a debugger to the process to investigate the problem. To avoid this annoying behavior, you can use the Windows registry to control whether process recycling happens when a debugger is attached to a process. Under HKLM\Software\Microsoft\ASP.NET, you should create two registry settings, namely **UnderDebugger** and **DebugOnHighMem**. These registry settings should both be created as DWORD values. Setting the **UnderDebugger** registry option to the hex value of 1 disables the process recycling mechanism. Setting the **DebugOnHighMem** registry option to the hex value of 1 is the equivalent of setting a breakpoint that triggers (by invoking the Win32 **DebugBreak** API) when the memory monitoring mechanism detects that the memory limit has been exceeded.

Both of these registry settings are officially undocumented, so they may change or even disappear altogether when a new version of ASP.NET arrives. Even for the current version of ASP.NET, I recommend that you create and use these registry settings only during a specific debugging session.

An ASP.NET worker process can, of course, be recycled for reasons other than consuming too much memory. For instance, you may see an ASP.NET process deadlock when two threads are each trying to gain access to a resource locked by the other thread. In this case, ASP.NET health monitoring will detect the deadlock and automatically recycle the process as soon as the time mentioned in the <processModel **responseDeadlockInterval**=/> machine.config setting has elapsed. If you want to attach to the process and debug a deadlock before the process has been recycled, you need either to install version 1.1 of the .NET Framework or install the hot fix discussed in Microsoft Knowledge Base article Q325947. Then you can add the registry DWORD settings **UnderDebugger** (as just discussed) and **DebugDeadlock,** both under HKLM\Software\Microsoft\ ASP.NET. Setting the latter key to the hex value of 1 triggers a break into the ASP.NET worker process (aspnet_wp.exe) when a deadlock is detected, whereas using a hex value of 2 breaks into both aspnet_wp.exe and Inetinfo.exe. This allows you to debug ASP.NET process deadlock problems without interference from process recycling. Although these registry settings are documented and shouldn't disappear arbitrarily, you should probably remove them when you aren't debugging ASP.NET applications.

Process Recycling with IIS 6.0

IIS 6.0 uses the Web Administration Service (WAS) to recycle any ASP.NET worker process that fails to meet specified health criteria or fails to respond to pings. Just like with IIS 5.*x*, this recycling can complicate debugging by removing a process before you get a change to attach a debugger. However, IIS 6.0 improves upon IIS 5.*x*'s undocumented facility for controlling this recycling.

You can configure WAS to "orphan" a process that has failed health monitoring. The worker process to be orphaned is removed from its application pool but kept running so that you can initiate a debugging investigation. Then a new worker process is started to handle the application's requests. To arrange for defective ASP.NET processes to be orphaned in this way, run the following command from the \Inetpub\Adminscripts folder, replacing <apppoolname> with the name of the relevant application pool:

```
cscript adsutil.vbs set w3svc/apppools/<apppoolname>/orphanworkerprocess 1
```

To apply this setting for all application pools, you can instead issue the following command:

```
cscript adsutil.vbs set w3svc/apppools/orphanworkerprocess 1
```

These commands allow you to debug an ASP.NET application running on IIS 6.0 even after it's failed a health monitor check and therefore been removed from service.

URLScan, IIS, and the DEBUG Verb

URLScan is an ISAPI filter supplied by Microsoft that works in conjunction with the IIS Lockdown tool to help IIS administrators secure their Web servers by restricting the HTTP requests that the servers will process. URLScan screens all incoming requests to the server and filters them based on rules defined by the IIS administrator. If the URLScan filter has been installed on your ASP.NET Web server, you'll need to configure it to allow debugging.

To do this, find the file URLScan.ini and add the keyword **DEBUG** (this is case sensitive) into the [AllowVerbs] section while making sure that the same keyword isn't in the [DenyVerbs] section. You should also ensure that the [AllowVerbs] section is enabled by adding the setting **UseAllowVerbs = 1**.

In some circumstances, especially on a production Web server, you might find that IIS itself doesn't permit the **DEBUG** verb for ASP.NET applications. To check this, run the IIS Manager utility and find your application's folder under \Inetpub\wwroot. Right-click the folder and select the Properties menu item. In the resulting Properties dialog window, go to the Directory tab and click the Configuration button. In the Application Configuration dialog window, go to the Mappings tab, as shown in Figure 9-1.

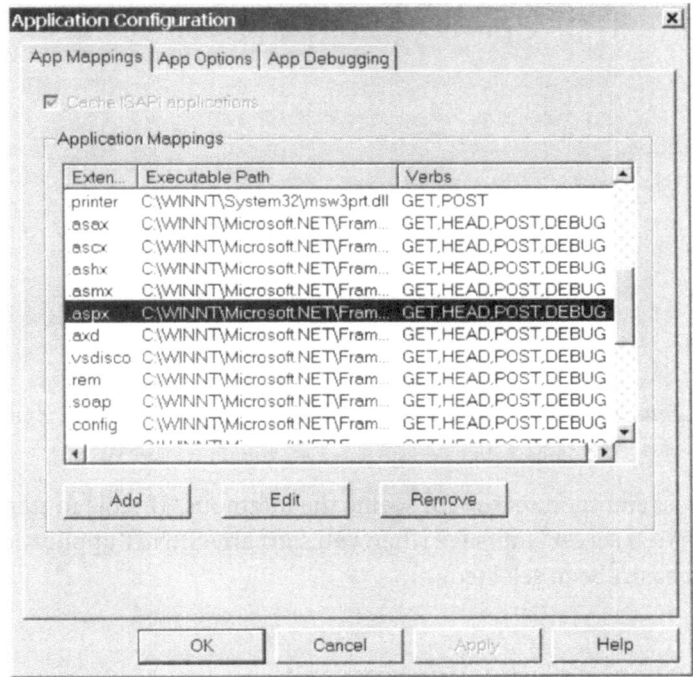

Figure 9-1. Enabling DEBUG within IIS for .aspx files

Edit the .aspx extension and make sure that **DEBUG** is in the list of allowed verbs.

IIS Authentication

You should make sure that your ASP.NET application's IIS authentication is set up in a way that permits debugging. To do this, run the IIS Manager utility and find your application's folder under \Inetpub\wwroot. Right-click the folder and select the Properties menu item. In the resulting Properties dialog window, go to the Directory Security tab and click the Edit button in the "Anonymous access and authentication control" section. In the Authentication Methods dialog window, ensure that the "Integrated Windows authentication" option is selected, as shown in Figure 9-2.

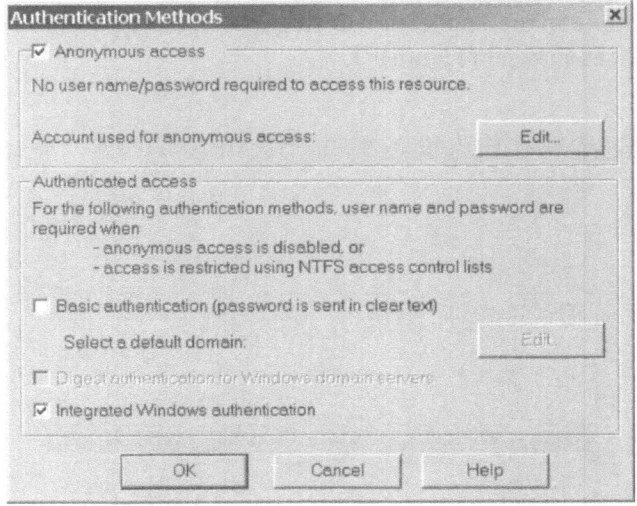

Figure 9-2. Enabling IIS debug authentication

The most common reason for seeing the infamous "Unable to start debugging on the Web server" message when you start an ASP.NET application is that this option hasn't been selected.

Multithreading Considerations

Because the ASP.NET worker process is multithreaded and processes requests asynchronously, you need to be sure that all of your ASP.NET components are either thread-safe or never called on multiple threads simultaneously. Although ASP.NET ensures that Web Forms themselves are never re-entrant, you must add your own threading synchronization anywhere that you define a **Shared** method or property and anywhere that you use .NET Framework classes that are not thread-safe. For example, none of the .NET collection classes is thread-safe, and neither is the intrinsic **Application** object. Finally, be careful if you use any single-threaded apartment COM components (such as those written in VB.Classic) in your ASP.NET applications.

To find out more about the potential problems when designing and writing multithreaded applications, please see Chapter 14.

Production Debugging

When you attach a debugger to the ASP.NET worker process, all threads in that process are frozen, which means that no HTTP requests will be serviced. This has obvious implications if you're trying to debug a production Web server, so it's normally best to withdraw the server from production before debugging it.

Debugging Preparation

ASP.NET applications offer a rather different debugging experience from desktop applications. When debugging ASP.NET, you have to deal with potential complications caused by elements such as firewalls, security, folder permissions, account permissions, and IIS itself. When everything works smoothly, you can step seamlessly from a Web page to a code-behind assembly to a class library and then back again. However, when debugging fails for some reason, you usually need some understanding of the underlying technologies to identify exactly where the debugging process is failing. This section discusses how to set up ASP.NET debugging and how to overcome some of the issues that you're likely to encounter.

User Account Permissions

By default, an ASP.NET application runs under the ASPNET Windows account. This is a security feature because the ASPNET account is given limited permissions by default and so can do only a limited amount of damage if hijacked. The important issue from a debugging point of view is that a developer can only debug a process running under another Windows account (such as ASPNET) if that developer belongs to the Administrators group on the machine where the process is running. In other words, if you want to debug an ASP.NET application, it's not sufficient for you to be in just the Users and Debugger Users groups, as discussed at the start of Chapter 4.

To add and remove user accounts to and from groups when using Windows 2000, go to the Control Panel and choose Administrative Tools ➢ Computer Management ➢ System Tools ➢ Local Users and Groups ➢ Groups. Windows XP and Windows Server 2003 also allow maintenance of users and groups from the Control Panel.

If you really don't want, or aren't allowed, to add your developer's user account to the Administrators group, there are a couple of possible workarounds. One (rather insecure) approach is to tell the ASP.NET worker process to run under your developer account by adding some entries to the .NET machine configuration file, machine.config. To do this, go to the <processModel> section of machine.config and modify the **username** and **password** settings (marked in bold in the following code) to match your Windows domain, account name, and password:

```
<processModel enable="true" timeout="Infinite" idleTimeout="Infinite"
shutdownTimeout="0:00:05" requestLimit="Infinite" requestQueueLimit="5000"
restartQueueLimit="10" memoryLimit="60" webGarden="false" cpuMask="0xffffffff"
userName="YourDomain\YourAccountName" password="YourPassword"
logLevel="Errors" clientConnectedCheck="0:00:05"
comAuthenticationLevel="Connect" comImpersonationLevel="Impersonate"
responseDeadlockInterval="00:03:00" maxWorkerThreads="20"
maxIoThreads="20"/>
```

After you make this change and save the machine.config file, you must reset IIS by using the **iisreset** command from the Visual Studio .NET command prompt. You should also give your user account full permissions to the Temporary ASP.NET Files folder, which sits under C:\WINNT\Microsoft.NET\Framework\version\. To do this, right-click the folder in Windows Explorer and select the Properties item from the context menu. In the resulting dialog window, choose the Security tab and click the Advanced button, as shown in Figure 9-3.

In the Access Control Settings for Temporary ASP.NET Files dialog window, click the Add button and add your user account. Finally, in the Permission Entry for Temporary ASP.NET Files dialog window, give your user account full permissions. After doing all of this, you should be able to debug ASP.NET applications without being an administrator, although you still need to be a member of the Debugger Users group.

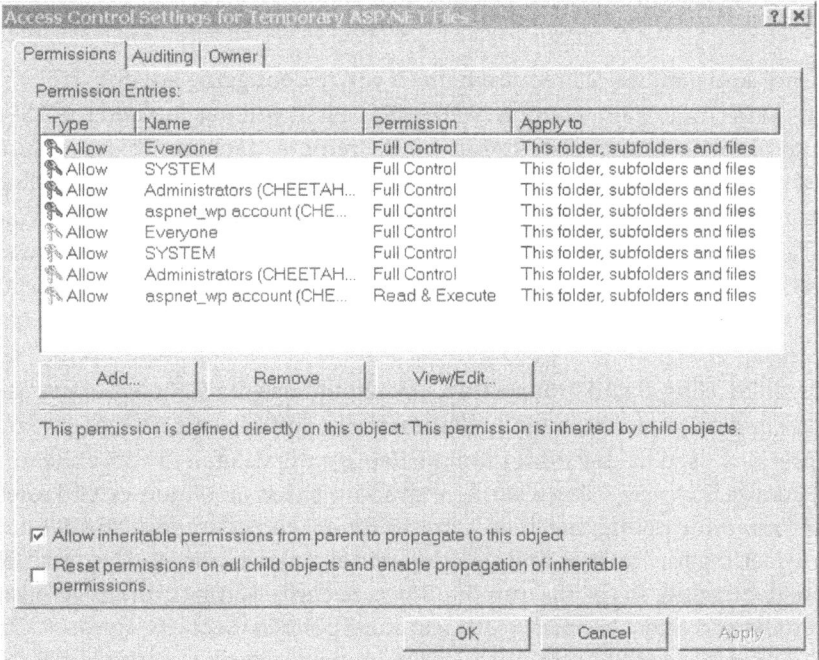

Figure 9-3. Setting ASP.NET temporary folder permissions

It's important to realize that there are security issues involved with this approach. For example, your own user account may have permissions that you wouldn't normally want to give to ASP.NET applications, but now any ASP.NET executable that runs will inherit your user account's permissions. Also, this approach means that your password is stored in clear text in machine.config. An alternative method for enabling ASP.NET debugging that doesn't have the same security issues is to create a new "weak" user account (for instance, ASPUSER) with the same permissions as the standard ASPNET account, and then configure the <processModel> section as previously to use ASPUSER for running the ASP.NET worker process. Then you can add ASPUSER to the Users and Debugger Users groups and use it to do your ASP.NET debugging. This means that the ASP.NET worker process is now running under the same account that you're using to do the debugging, so there's no requirement to add ASPUSER to the Administrators group.

Remote Server Debugging

There are some additional requirements if you're debugging an ASP.NET application that's running on a remote Web server. First, you need to add the ASPNET account to the Debugger Users group on the remote machine. This is required even if the user account you're using for debugging is in the Administrators group on the remote machine. Second, the local workstation must be running Windows NT 4.0, Windows 2000, Windows XP (any edition except Home), or Windows 2003. The remote machine must be running Windows 2000, Windows XP (any edition except Home), or Windows 2003. Finally, both machines should be in the same domain.

If you're using a workgroup setup, you should use the same Windows user account and password on both machines. If you don't do this, DCOM (the transport protocol used by default for remote debugging) will fail to authenticate your user account. If you're using a workgroup setup based on Windows XP Professional for remote debugging, there's an additional consideration. The default security setting for "sharing and security model for local accounts" doesn't allow remote debugging. To fix this, run the "Local Security Settings" utility in Administrator tools and select "Security settings\Local policies\Security options". Change the "Network access: Sharing and Security model for local accounts" from "Guest only – local users authenticate as Guest" to "Classic – local users authenticate as themselves". Then reboot the machine for the new setting to take effect. You need to do this on both the local workstation and the remote machine.

This does pose a security risk, because now any connection from one machine to the other could be authenticated as your local user account rather than as a guest, so I advise changing this setting back to its default value after you've completed the remote debugging session.

For more information on remote debugging, please see Chapter 15.

Internet Explorer Configuration

If you're using Internet Explorer to run your ASP.NET applications, there are a couple of options that you can deselect to make your debugging life easier. If you select Tools ➤ Internet Options and then go to the Advanced tab's Browsing section, you'll see the two options "Disable script debugging" and "Show friendly HTTP error messages," as shown in Figure 9-4.

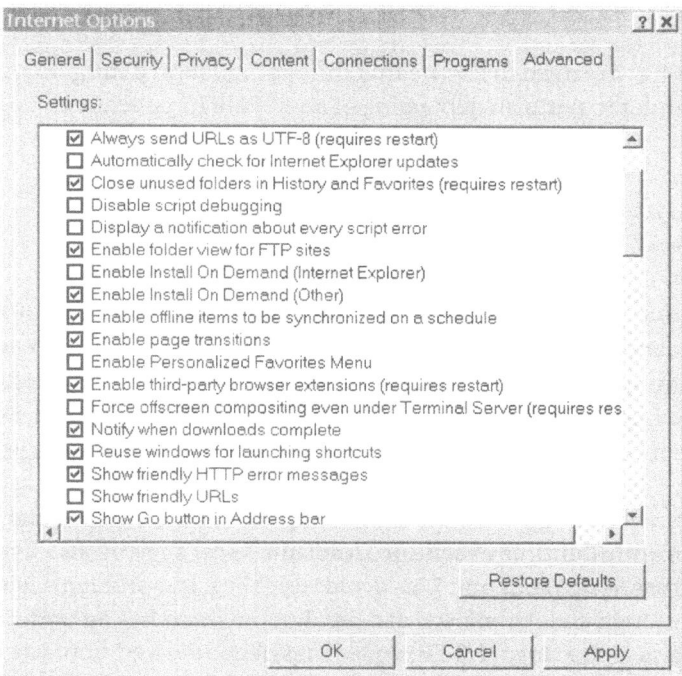

Figure 9-4. Internet Explorer's advanced options page

During ASP.NET debugging sessions, you should normally deselect both of these options. The first option setting is self-explanatory, but the second option setting deserves an explanation. The difference between selecting and deselecting this option is the effect that an ASP.NET application exception has on the browser. If you opt for friendly HTTP error handling, the result of an exception is the standard noninformative browser message "Page cannot be displayed". If you turn off this option, the browser displays the actual exception message. I presume that "friendly" in this context means friendly to the application's end users.

Application Configuration

Every ASP.NET application contains an XML configuration file named Web.config. This configuration file includes several settings that control application behavior.

Setting Debug in Web.config

In Web.config, you need to ensure that the <compilation **debug=/>** option is set to **true** in order to perform debugging of an ASP.NET application.

```
<system.web>
    <compilation defaultLanguage="vb" debug="true" />
</system.web>
```

Changing this setting to **true** tells Visual Studio to generate debug symbols for any dynamically generated page. It also allows the Visual Studio debugger to attach to the application. The major reason to be wary about this setting is that enabling debugging will make your ASP.NET application run much slower than normal, so it's advisable to make sure that this option is set to **false** before you release your application into a production environment.

Be aware that when <compilation **debug=/>** has the value of **true**, ASP.NET ignores the <httpRuntime **executionTimeOut**=/> setting and also ignores any calls to **Server.ScriptTimeout**. This avoids any time-out problems when you're stepping through code or paused at a breakpoint, but it has an undesirable side effect. If no response to an HTTP request has been received from your ASP.NET application for a period longer than that specified in the <processModel **responseDeadlockInterval**=/> configuration setting, the ASP.NET worker process is recycled and your debugging will be interrupted. To avoid this time-out issue when you're debugging, you should change the <processModel **responseDeadlockInterval**=/> configuration setting to the value of **Infinite** for the duration of a debugging session.

ASP.NET automatically detects any changes to Web.config, so you don't need to reboot or restart the server for changes to take effect. But be aware that these attribute names are case sensitive, so using **Debug** rather than **debug** won't work!

Setting CustomErrors in Web.config

Another important Web.config setting is the <customErrors **mode=/>** setting. This setting controls how errors that are unhandled at the page level are displayed to the users of your application and looks like this:

```
<system.web>
    <customErrors mode="RemoteOnly" />
</system.web>
```

There are three possible settings for this option:

- If **mode=Off**, all clients, whether remote or local, receive a detailed ASP.NET error page that "explains" the unhandled error.

- If **mode=On**, local clients see any custom error page that you've defined, whereas remote clients receive the detailed ASP.NET error page.

- If **mode=RemoteOnly**, local clients see the detailed ASP.NET error page, whereas remote clients see any custom error page that you've defined.

Normally you're likely to be developing your ASP.NET application locally. In this case, the setting you should use depends on whether you're testing your error handling. If you want to see the real exceptions, you should set **mode=RemoteOnly**. If you want to test your custom error pages, you should set **mode=On**.

If you're developing your ASP.NET application on a remote server, you need to reverse these settings. So to see the real exceptions, you should set **mode=On**, and if you want to test your error handling, you should set **mode=RemoteOnly**.

For a production server, you should always use the **mode=RemoteOnly** setting. This ensures that hackers don't see any detailed information that might be of use to them in the event of an unhandled error. Instead, the only information displayed will be one of the custom error pages that you've defined. Another reason for not displaying the detailed ASP.NET error page is that it's rarely of any use to end users, and it's quite likely to overwhelm the end users with useless information. Once again, defining and using a custom error page lets you communicate better with your end users by suggesting a workaround or allowing them to try something different.

ASP.NET automatically detects any changes to Web.config, so you don't need to reboot or restart the server for changes to take effect. But be aware that these attribute names are case sensitive, so using **on** rather than **On** won't work!

Configuring Project Debugging

You should also check that your ASP.NET application is configured for debugging within Visual Studio. Right-click your ASP.NET project in Solution Explorer and go to the Properties ➤ Configuration Properties ➤ Debugging property page and make sure that the "ASP.NET debugging" option is selected, as shown in Figure 9-5.

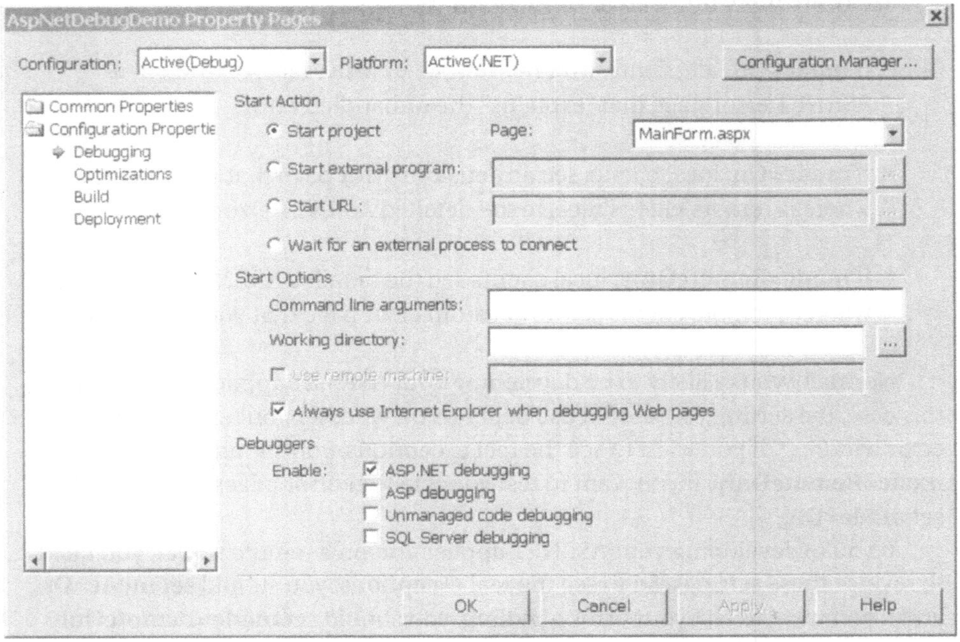

Figure 9-5. An ASP.NET project's Debugging property page

On the Properties ➢ Configuration Properties ➢ Build property page of your project, ensure that the "Generate debugging information" option is selected. This ensures that debug symbols will be generated for the project. On the same property page, you can specify how your ASP.NET application should be started for a debug or test session. This is controlled by the Start Action setting, which has four options:

- *Start project:* This option allows you to start your ASP.NET project directly at the specified Web page. The default Web browser is launched and displays this Web page. This is usually the best option to use when you're testing and debugging a straightforward project.

- *Start external program:* Select this option if you want to test a component of your ASP.NET application using a program external to your Visual Studio solution as its client. When you choose this option, the Visual Studio debugger attaches to the ASP.NET application, but not to the external program.

- *Start URL:* This has the same effect as the "Start external program" option just discussed, but it uses an external Web page as the client rather than an external program.

- *Wait for an external process to connect:* This option is really for testing a Web service rather than a standard ASP.NET application. It's similar to the "Start external program" option discussed previously, but the Visual Studio debugger attaches itself to both your ASP.NET component and the process that uses the component.

During everyday debugging, the "Start project" setting is the most likely way that you'll test and debug your application.

Debugging the AspNetDebugDemo Application

This section demonstrates how to perform ASP.NET debugging and error handling with the help of the **AspNetDebugDemo** application. Figure 9-6 shows the application's main user interface Web page. After you load the application into Visual Studio, open the source file MainForm.aspx to view the application's main page and then use the code view to see the source code behind this page.

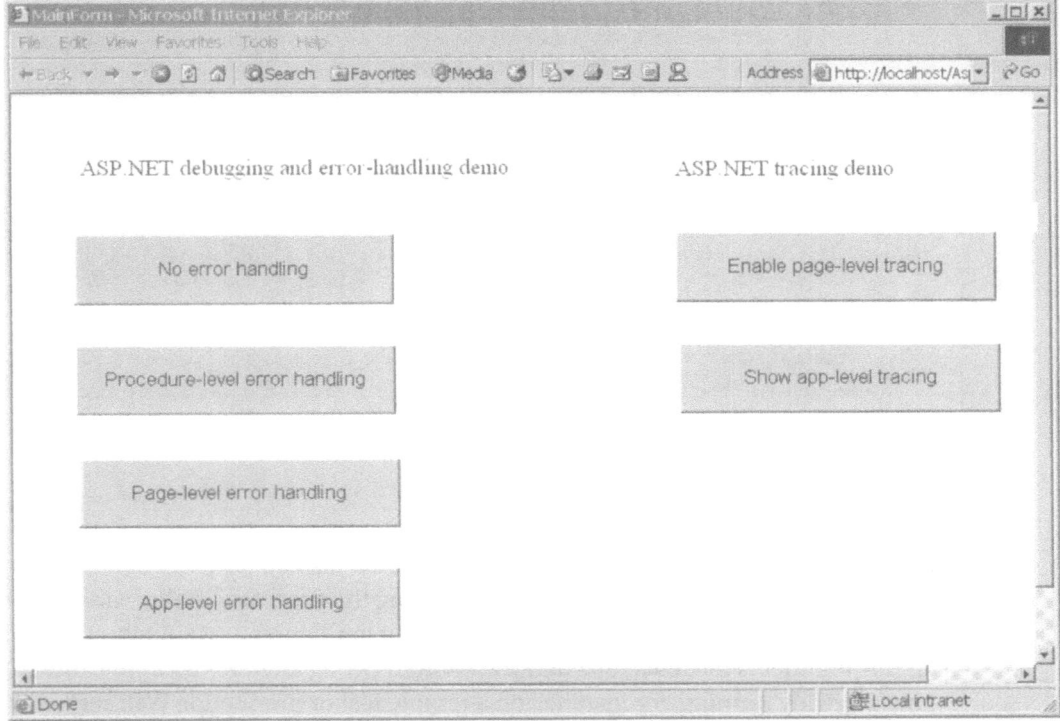

Figure 9-6. The AspNetDebugDemo front page

If you run the **AspNetDebugDemo** application within Visual Studio with debugging (by pressing F5), you can see that your default browser displays the application's main page. If you switch back to Visual Studio, go to the Debug menu, and select the Processes menu item, you can see what the Visual Studio debugger does after you press F5. The Processes dialog window (see Figure 9-7) demonstrates that the debugger has attached itself to the aspnet_wp.exe process, which is the ASP.NET worker process that I discussed earlier in this chapter. It's also attached itself to your Web browser's process—in my case iexplore.exe, because I'm using Internet Explorer.

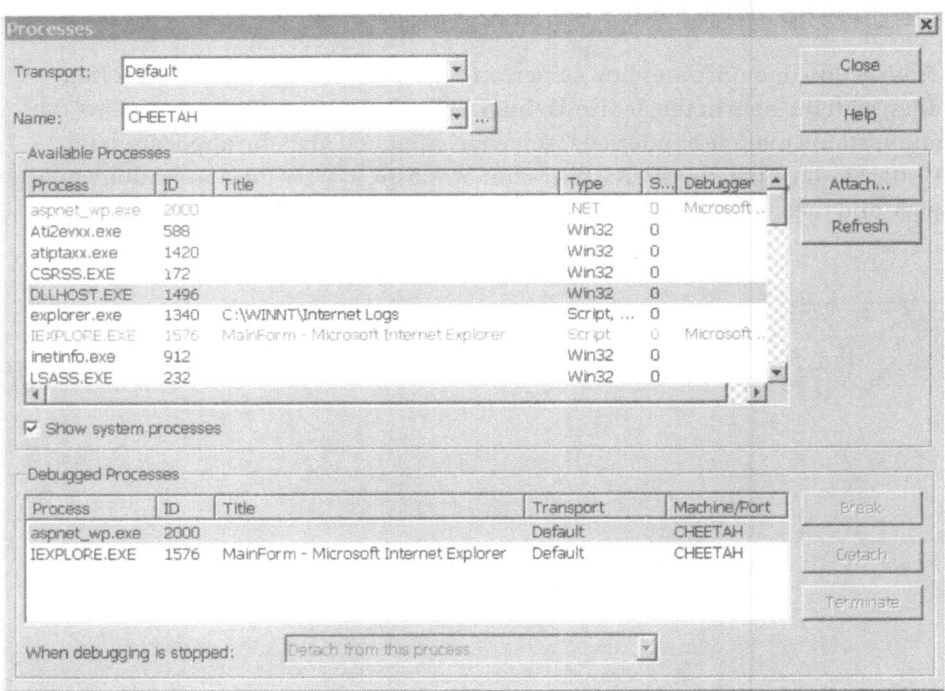

Figure 9-7. ASP.NET process debugging with Visual Studio

Although this process attachment happens automatically when you start your ASP.NET application with debugging, you can also do ASP.NET debugging by attaching to these two processes manually using the Processes dialog window, as discussed in the "Attaching to a Process" section in Chapter 3. Manually attaching in this manner is most useful when you want to debug an ASP.NET application that's already running, for instance on a remote test or production Web server.

One error that you may see when you start an ASP.NET application with debugging is the message "Error while trying to run project: Unable to start debugging on the web server". This error is commonly caused by a defective Web.config file—for example, when one of the XML elements is written using the wrong case. To test whether the Web.config file is indeed the source of the problem, try starting your application without debugging (using Ctrl+F5). If the Web.config file is at fault, you'll see a page describing which setting ASP.NET believes is incorrect.

ASP.NET Error Handling

The buttons on the main page demonstrate how you can perform error handling at various levels of your application. When an error occurs, you can handle it using one or more of the following methods:

- Don't handle the error at all—let it bubble up through your application's call stack until it becomes a completely unhandled error.

- Use **Try...Catch...Finally** to catch and deal with an error in a procedure within the call stack, as described in Chapter 13.

- Use page-level error handling to catch any error within a specific page that isn't caught at the procedure level.

- Use application-level error handling to catch any error within your application that isn't caught at the procedure level or the page level.

Of course, you can and should use a mixture of these error-handling methods if you want to catch and handle all errors properly. The next four sections of this chapter look at ASP.NET debugging and error-handling with the help of the **AspNetDebugDemo** application.

No Error Handling

The top button on the main page of the **AspNetDebugDemo** application demonstrates what happens when you don't handle exceptions that occur within your ASP.NET application. To demonstrate this, you first need to switch off page-level and application-level error handling within the program. To switch off page-level error handling, make sure that the **MainForm.ErrorPage** property is blank in the form's Properties window. To switch off application-level error handling, you should ensure that the **customErrors** setting in Web.config is set to **RemoteOnly**, as discussed in the previous section "Setting CustomErrors in Web.config."

Having switched off page-level and application-level error handling, you can restart the application and add a breakpoint to the **btnNoLevel_Click** procedure on line 42, the line marked in bold in Listing 9-1.

Listing 9-1. Triggering an Unhandled Exception

```
Private Sub btnNoLevel_Click(ByVal sender As System.Object, _
                    ByVal e As System.EventArgs) Handles btnNoLevel.Click
    'Doesn't catch or deal with error at all
    'Displays error using ASP.NET default error page
    Dim Test As Object
    Test.ToString()
End Sub
```

Then launch the application with debugging (by using F5) and click the No Error Handling button. The breakpoint should be hit and you can step through the code shown in Listing 9-1. This code triggers an unhandled exception. Because the exception isn't handled within the application, the ASP.NET worker process displays the error page shown in Figure 9-8. This page shows a description of the error, the source code that triggered it, and the error's stack trace.

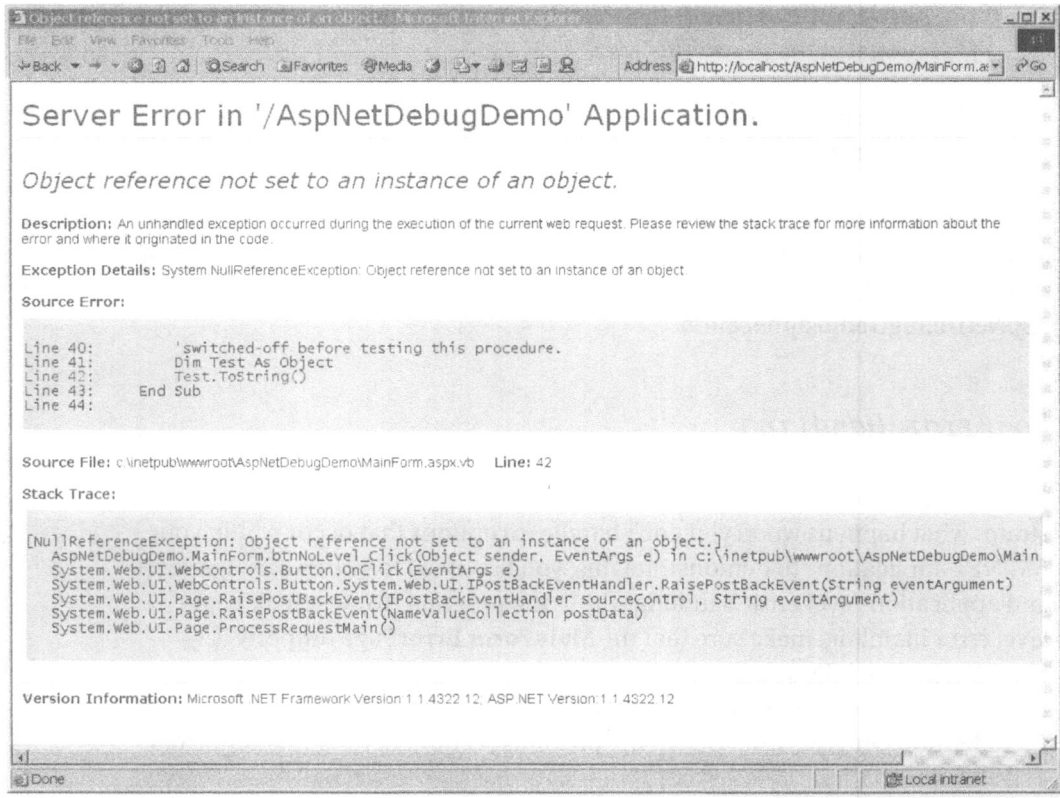

Figure 9-8. The default ASP.NET error page

As you can see, there's a fair amount of detail shown on this page. This is ideal when you're testing and debugging your application, but you probably wouldn't want to have your end users seeing this page, let alone any hackers who might be interested in doing some digging. So ideally, you want to have some error handling in place to prevent this page from appearing.

Procedure-Level Error Handling

To demonstrate procedure-level error handling, add a breakpoint on line 49, the line marked in bold in Listing 9-2. This code triggers an exception that is caught and displayed using the **Try...Catch...Finally** construct.

Listing 9-2. Triggering and Catching an Exception Within a Procedure

```
Private Sub btnProcLevel_Click(ByVal sender As System.Object, _
             ByVal e As System.EventArgs) Handles btnProcLevel.Click
    'Catches error at procedure-level
    'Deals with error in Catch clause
    'Displays error in Catch clause
    Try
        Dim Test As Object
        Test.ToString()
    Catch ex As Exception
        Me.lblException.Text = ex.Message
    Finally
        Server.ClearError()
    End Try
End Sub
```

Then click your browser's Back button to return to the application's main page, and this time click the button marked "Procedure-level error handling". When the exception is triggered as shown in Listing 9-2, the exception is caught and the exception message is displayed next to the button.

For exceptions that you can anticipate, handling them at the procedure level like this is usually the best way of dealing with them. If you want to see more information about how **Try...Catch...Finally** works, it's discussed in detail in Chapter 13.

Page-Level Error Handling

The button marked "Page-level error handling" demonstrates how you can catch an error at the page level if it's not dealt with at the procedure level, how you can clean up after a page-level error by adding code to the **Page_Error** event of a Web Form, and how you can then display a custom error page using the **ErrorPage** property of a Web Form.

To demonstrate page-level error handling, you first need to configure the application to use this level of error handling. First, change the **customErrors** setting in Web.config to **On** as discussed in the section "Setting CustomErrors in Web.config." Next, enable the **Page_Error** event handler for MainForm.aspx by removing the comment symbol from line 77 in this procedure. Finally, add a breakpoint to line 63 in the **btnPageLevel_Click** procedure, as marked in bold in Listing 9-3, and restart the application.

Listing 9-3. Triggering a Page-Level Exception

```
Private Sub btnPageLevel_Click(ByVal sender As System.Object, _
            ByVal e As System.EventArgs) Handles btnPageLevel.Click
    'Catches error at page level
    'Deals with error in Me.Page_Error event
    'Displays error using Me.ErrorPage property
    Me.ErrorPage = "CustomErrorPage.aspx"
    Dim Test As Object
    Test.ToString()
End Sub
```

Now click the button marked "Page-level error handling". This executes the code shown in Listing 9-3, which first sets the **ErrorPage** property of the main page and then triggers an exception. Because this exception isn't handled within the procedure, it bubbles up to the Web page's **Page_Error** event, the code for which is shown in Listing 9-4. The demonstration code simply writes the exception message to any attached trace listeners, but you could place any cleanup or logging code that you wish in this procedure. Note that the **Server.ClearError** statement is commented-out in this code—if you don't want to display a custom page, you can use this statement to suppress the exception and then redirect your user back to one of your application's pages after you've logged and dealt with the error.

Listing 9-4. Dealing with a Page-Level Error Using the Page_Error Event

```
Private Sub Page_Error(ByVal sender As System.Object, _
            ByVal e As System.EventArgs) Handles MyBase.Error
    Trace.Write(Server.GetLastError.Message)
    'Server.ClearError
End Sub
```

After the code in this procedure has been executed, the exception is redirected for display to the page specified in the **ErrorPage** property, in this case the **CustomErrorPage** page. This page is shown in Figure 9-9. It does very little except allow you to return to the page that produced the exception, but you can modify your custom error pages to be as flashy as you want.

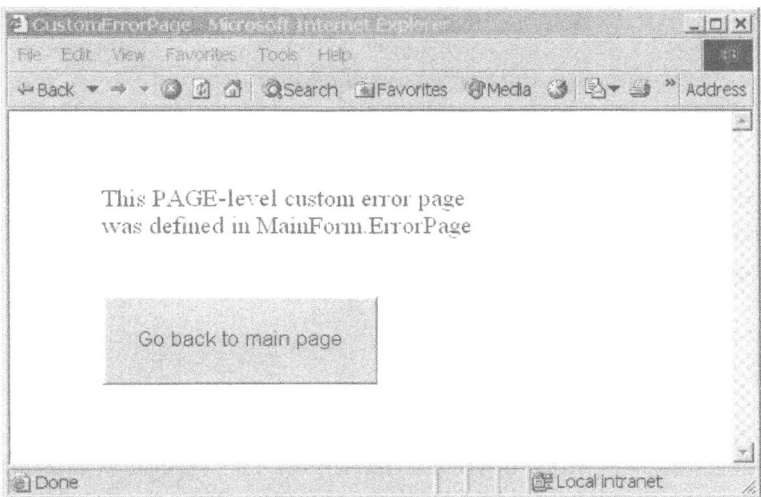

Figure 9-9. The page-level custom error page

Application-Level Error Handling

The button marked "App-level error handling" demonstrates how you can catch an error at the application level if it's not dealt with at the procedure or page level. It shows how you can clean up after an application-level error by adding code to the **Application_Error** event in Global.asax and how you can then display a custom error page using the **Redirect** facility in Web.config.

To demonstrate application-level error handling, you first need to configure the application to use this level of error handling. Then change the **customErrors** setting in Web.config to **On** as discussed in the section "Setting CustomErrors in Web.config," and add a **defaultRedirect** attribute to the **customErrors** setting, as shown in Listing 9-5. A line with this setting and attribute already exists in the **AspNetDebugDemo** application, but you should check that the line isn't commented-out. This attribute redirects any application-level exception to the specified custom error page, in a similar fashion to the way that the **ErrorPage** property of a Web Form contains a custom error page for redirecting page-level exceptions.

Listing 9-5. Using Web.config to Redirect an Exception to a Custom Page

```
<customErrors mode="On" defaultRedirect = "DefaultErrorPage.aspx" />
```

Finally, add a breakpoint to line 73 in MainForm.aspx.vb as marked in bold in Listing 9-6 and another breakpoint to line 49 in Global.asax.vb as marked in bold in Listing 9-7. Now you can restart the application with debugging (using F5).

Listing 9-6. Triggering an Application-Level Exception

```
Private Sub btnAppLevel_Click(ByVal sender As System.Object, _
            ByVal e As System.EventArgs) Handles btnAppLevel.Click
    'Error will be caught at application level
    'Deals with error in Global.asax.Application_Error event
    'Displays error using redirect in Web.config
    Dim Test As Object
    Test.ToString()
End Sub
```

Click the button marked "App-level error handling" to execute the code shown in Listing 9-6, which triggers an exception. This exception isn't handled within the procedure, but it's handled at the page level because there's code present in the **MainForm.Page_Error** event handler. Because the code in the **Page_Error** procedure doesn't call **Server.ClearError**, the exception continues to bubble up until it reaches the **Application_Error** event in Global.asax, the code for which is shown in Listing 9-7. This demonstration code simply writes the exception message to any attached trace listeners, but you could place any cleanup or logging code that you wish in this procedure.

Listing 9-7. Dealing with an Application-Level Error Using an Application_Error Event

```
Sub Application_Error(ByVal sender As System.Object, _
                                    ByVal e As System.EventArgs)
    Context.Trace.Write(Server.GetLastError.InnerException.Message)
End Sub
```

Notice the requirement to look at the **InnerException** property of **Server.GetLastError**, rather than the page-level technique of looking at **GetLastError** directly. This is necessary because by the time an unhandled exception reaches the application level, it will be an **HttpUnhandledException** type. To retrieve the original exception, you need to use the **InnerException** property.

After the code in this procedure has been executed, the exception is redirected for display to the page specified in the **defaultRedirect** attribute of the **customErrors** setting, in this case the **DefaultErrorPage** page shown in Figure 9-10. This page does very little except allow you to return to the page that produced the exception, but you can modify your custom error pages to be as glitzy as you wish.

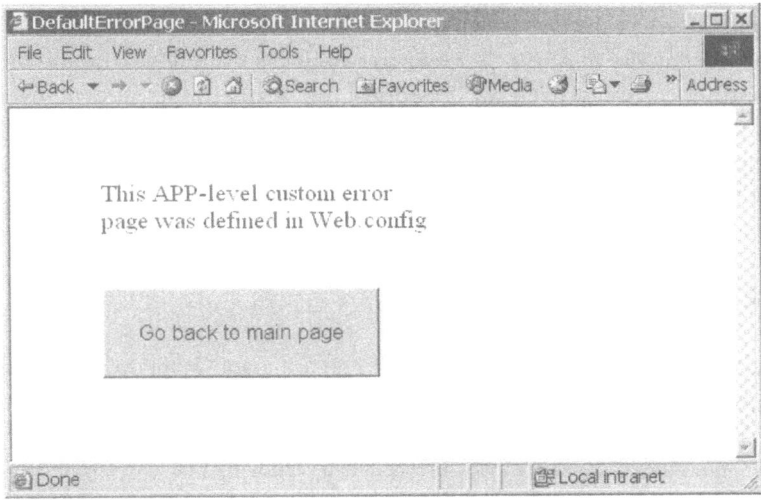

Figure 9-10. The application-level custom error page

In addition to having a default error page for application-level unhandled exceptions, you can use the **customErrors** setting in Web.config to add a specific page redirection for each type of error. This is shown in Listing 9-8.

Listing 9-8. Using Web.config to Redirect Various Exception Types

```
<customErrors mode="On" defaultRedirect = "DefaultErrorPage.aspx" >
    <error statusCode="403" redirect = "/AccessForbidden.aspx" />
    <error statusCode="404" redirect = "/MissingPage.aspx" />
    <error statusCode="500" redirect = "/Support.aspx" />
</customErrors>
```

This ability to combine procedural, page-level, and application-level ASP.NET error handling gives you a lot of flexibility in the way that you log, recover from, and display your application's exceptions.

Using ASP.NET Tracing

Chapter 6 discussed in detail how to use tracing in your VB .NET applications to locate and diagnose problems, record application status, and find performance bottlenecks. ASP.NET offers a similar tracing facility that records the main page and code events, gives you programmatic access to this information, and lets you add your own custom trace information. Good tracing information allows you to record and understand your application's behavior and can significantly improve your application's maintenance costs.

The trace facility in ASP.NET works at two levels. Page-level tracing records trace information about each HTTP request and displays that information after the page's rendered HTML. Application-level tracing records trace information for multiple pages and allows you to access this information through a special Uniform Resource Identifier (URI) called trace.axd.

Page-Level Tracing

Page-level tracing is disabled by default. To enable page-level tracing at design time, you set a Web Form's **Trace** property to **true**, which adds the **trace** attribute to the **@ Page** directive in the .aspx file. Listing 9-9 shows what the **@ Page** directive looks like when the **Trace** property is set to **true**. You can also use the Web Form's **TraceMode** property to ask for the trace information to be sorted either by time or by category.

Listing 9-9. Enabling Page-Level Tracing at Design Time

```
<%@ Page Language="vb"..........trace="True" %>
```

You can also control page-level tracing at runtime by changing the Web Form's **Trace.IsEnabled** property to **true** or **false**. This obviously only works on a request-by-request basis, as the property state won't be maintained between HTTP requests. The code that sits behind the "Enable page-level tracing" button of the **AspNetDebugDemo** application is shown in Listing 9-10. This code enables page-level tracing for the current request, asks for the trace information to be sorted by time, and then writes a custom trace message and a custom trace warning. The difference between these two trace types is that a trace message is displayed in black and a trace warning is displayed in red.

Listing 9-10. Enabling Page-Level Tracing at Runtime

```
Private Sub btnPageTracingOn_Click(ByVal sender As System.Object, _
                ByVal e As System.EventArgs) Handles btnPageTracingOn.Click
    With Me.Trace
        .IsEnabled = True
        .TraceMode = TraceMode.SortByTime
        .Write("Information", "This is some custom trace information")
        .Warn("Warning", "This is a custom trace warning")
    End With
End Sub
```

When you switch on page-level tracing, the trace information is displayed in the Web page along with your controls and any other elements on the Web page. Figure 9-11 shows the **AspNetDebugDemo** application's main page when page-level tracing is enabled by clicking the button marked "Enable page-level tracing". Notice that the information shown in the Trace Information section includes the custom trace message and warning discussed earlier. It's also worth noting that this trace information is on a per-request basis and isn't stored anywhere unless application-level tracing is switched on.

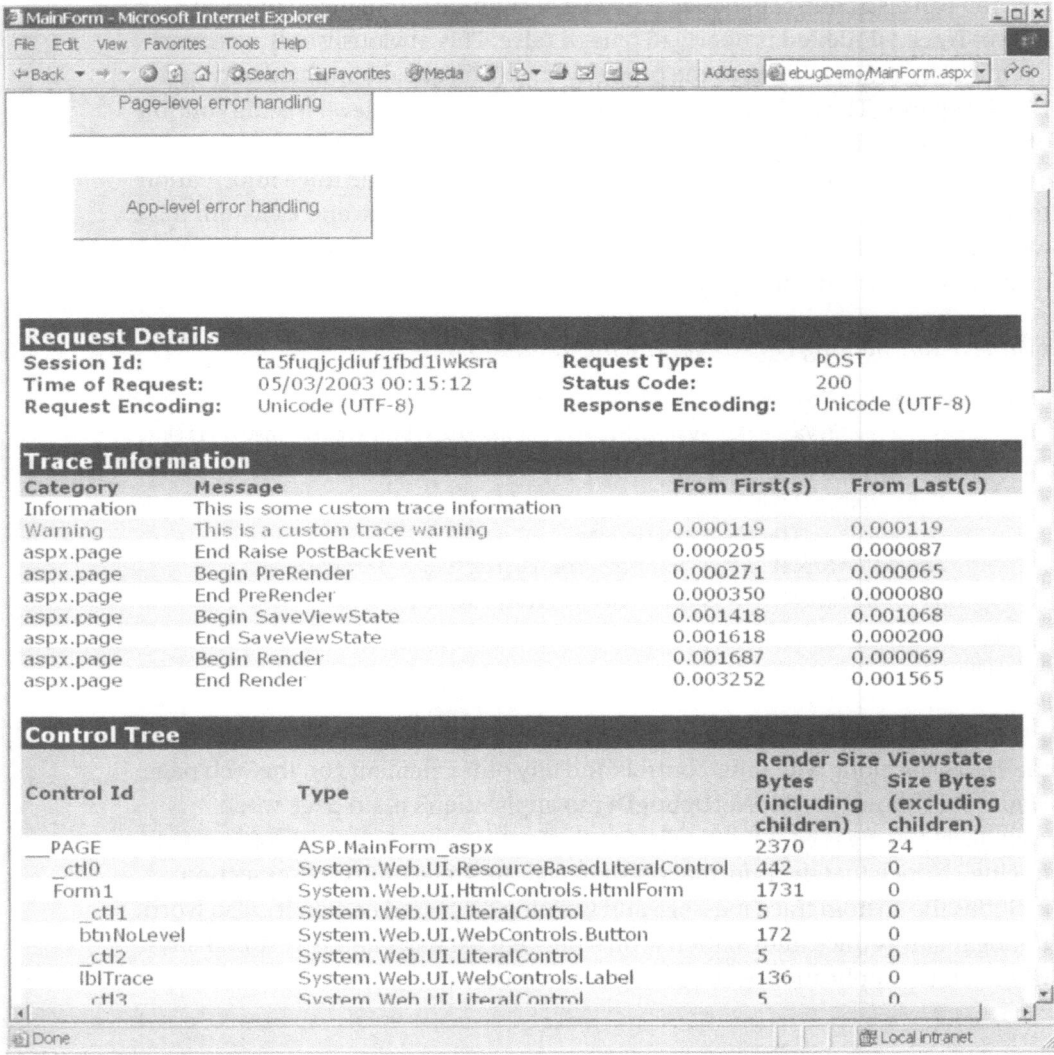

Figure 9-11. Showing page-level trace information

As you can see, there's a lot of tracing information available to you. The following list describes the information displayed within each of the page-level trace sections.

- *Request Details:* Contains information about the HTTP request, including data from the HTTP request header.

- *Trace Information:* Contains information about page events, including timing statistics so that you can do performance evaluation. You can use **Trace.Write** and **Trace.Warn** to add your own custom trace information to this section.

- *Control Tree:* Includes information about the controls on the Web page, describing their type, render size, and view state size.

- *Cookies Collection:* Describes the name, value, and size of every cookie passed in the HTTP response.

- *Headers Collection:* Includes information about every header specified in the HTTP response.

- *Form Collection:* Describes the name and value of every nonblank control in the Web Form that generated the request.

- *Server Variables:* This section is self-explanatory—it relates the name and value of each of the server variables.

Page-level tracing will slow down your application, but you can disable it by setting each Web Form's **Trace** property to **false**. Leaving tracing code within your application doesn't matter because the JIT compiler won't compile the tracing code when the Web Form's **Trace** property is set to **false**.

Application-Level Tracing

Page-level tracing is very useful during development and testing to help you understand the behavior of individual Web pages within your application. However, the output from page-level tracing is transient and not stored anywhere. If you want to understand more about your application as a whole, or if you want to record your application's behavior when in production or its behavior during different execution runs for comparison purposes, then you need to use application-level tracing.

Application-level tracing involves tracing information being recorded for every page within an application. ASP.NET contains a built-in trace viewer for each application's trace information, which is invoked used a special page called trace.axd, off the application root. This level of tracing is disabled by default, but you can enable it by setting the **enabled** attribute of the **<trace>** section in Web.config. Listing 9-11 shows a typical **<trace>** section.

Listing 9-11. Enabling Application-Level Tracing

```
<trace enabled="true"
          requestLimit="10" pageOutput="false"
          traceMode="SortByTime" localOnly="true"
/>
```

The following list presents the meaning of each of the attributes in the **<trace>** section:

- *enabled:* If this attribute is set to **true**, application-level tracing is enabled. If it's set to **false**, application-level tracing is disabled.

- *requestLimit:* Specifies the number of trace requests that are stored on the Web server.

- *pageOutput:* If this attribute set to **true**, trace information is displayed on individual pages and on the trace.axd page. If it's set to **false**, trace information is still displayed on the trace.axd page, but the **Trace** property of each page determines whether the trace information is shown on that page.

- *traceMode:* Just as with page-level tracing, this attribute controls whether displayed trace information is sorted by time or sorted by category.

- *localOnly:* If this attribute is set to **true**, you can view the trace.axd page only in a browser running on the same Web server as the application. If it's set to **false**, remote browsers can also view the trace.axd page.

To view application-level trace information in the **AspNetDebugDemo** application, you should run the solution in Visual Studio without debugging (using Ctrl+F5). Clicking several of the buttons that demonstrate error handling will generate some application activity and trace information. You can view this information using the trace viewer, which you access by clicking the button marked "Show app-level tracing". The code behind this button is shown in Listing 9-12.

Listing 9-12. Loading the Trace Viewer Page

```
Private Sub btnAppTracingShow_Click(ByVal sender As System.Object, _
                ByVal e As System.EventArgs) Handles btnAppTracingShow.Click
    Response.Redirect("trace.axd")
End Sub
```

The trace viewer page for the **AspNetDebugDemo** application is shown in Figure 9-12. This page shows which application pages have been requested, including the time of the request, and gives you access to the detailed trace for each of the page requests.

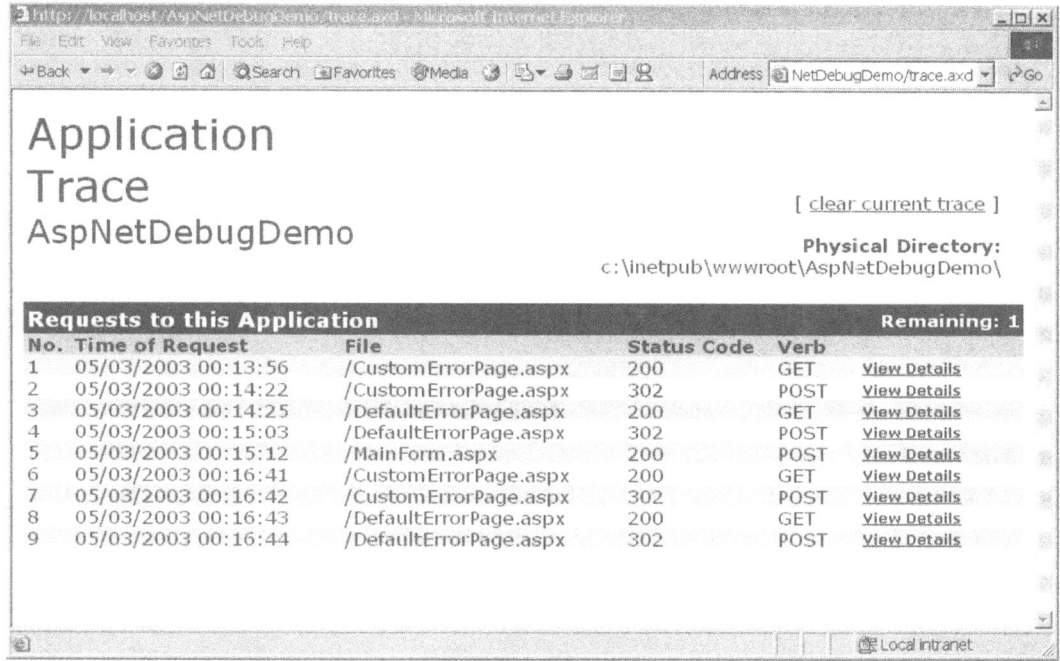

Figure 9-12. Showing application-level trace information using trace.axd

Figure 9-13 shows the detailed trace for a page request, which you can access by clicking one of the View Details links shown in Figure 9-12. This page looks similar to the page-level trace information that you saw earlier, but of course without the page controls or any other page elements. Just as with page-level tracing, this page shows any custom trace information that has been generated.

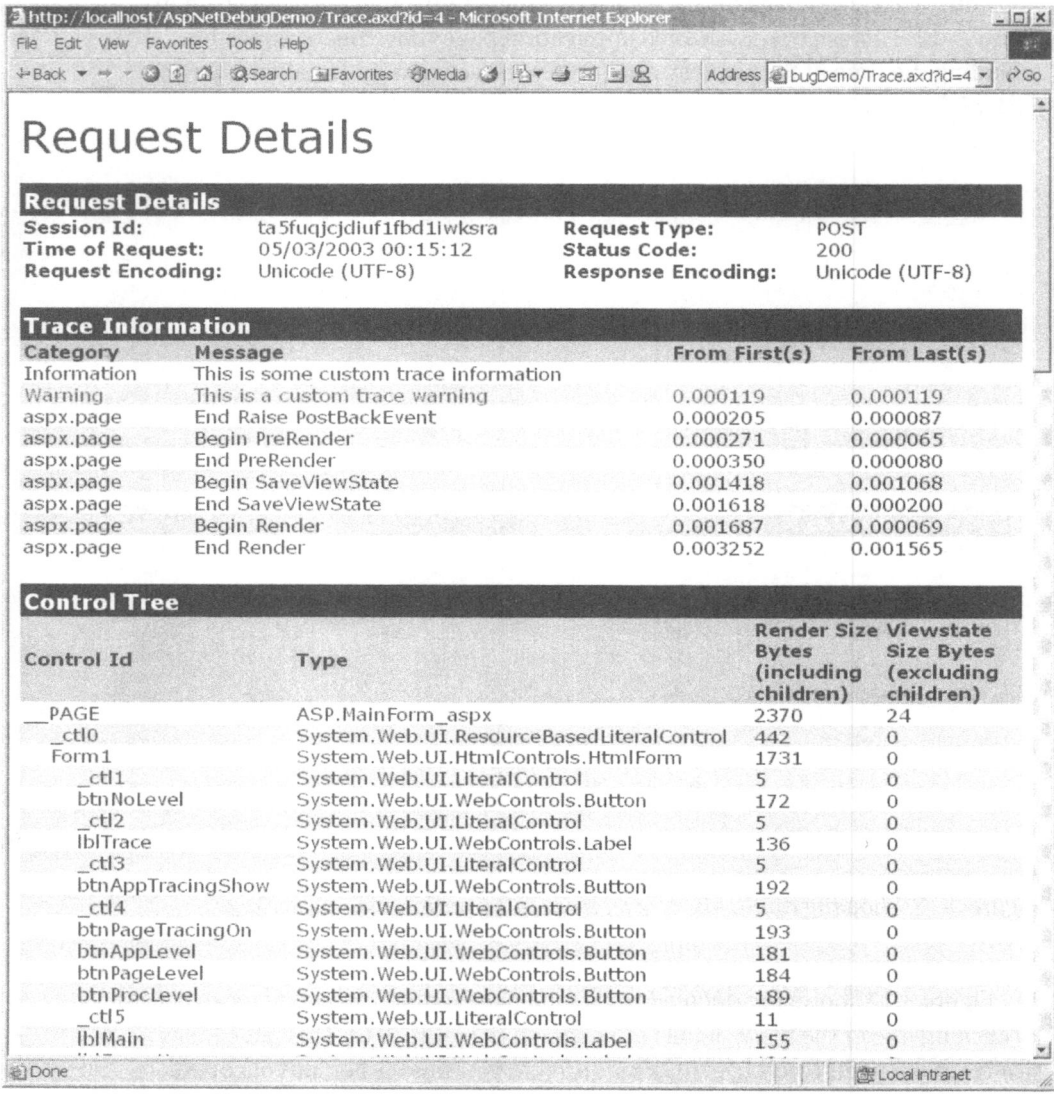

Figure 9-13. Showing the detailed trace of a page request

Application-level tracing is most useful for recording and understanding your ASP.NET application's behavior as a whole, whereas page-level tracing is more useful for testing and debugging individual Web pages. In both cases, ASP.NET provides you with the easy-to-use tools that you need to debug your Web applications.

Summary

This chapter looked first at how to configure IIS, your Web server, and your ASP.NET application to enable debugging. This can be tricky because there are so many different configuration options and because each operating system and IIS version has its own peculiar requirements.

The chapter continued by showing you how to step through and debug an application that demonstrated different ASP.NET error handling and tracing techniques. After looking at handling errors within ASP.NET procedures, you saw how to deal with errors at the page and application levels. Combining these error-handling techniques enables you to create a complete ASP.NET error-handling framework.

The final part of this chapter showed you how to implement page-level and application-level tracing to help you record and understand your application's behavior. This completely new tracing facility provided by ASP.NET is a huge improvement over the crude **Response.Write** statements that you had to use when debugging ASP.Classic applications.

INTERLUDE

GORILLA TESTING

Nowadays there are many sophisticated testing tools, ranging from unit testing frameworks such as NUnit through to profiling tools such as Compuware's Dev-Partner Studio. With the help of these tools and useful techniques such as code inspection, it's possible to be confident that you've found most of the bugs hiding within your application. But one technique that seems to have fallen out of favor among mainstream developers is the idea of random testing.

Although the concept of random testing might conjure up images of a late-night debugging session where you do a passable imitation of an angry gorilla by haphazardly pressing as many keys as possible on your keyboard in order to upset your program, there are better ways of doing it. One random testing tool is called fuzz, a program written by Justin Forrester and Barton Miller in the computer sciences department at the University of Wisconsin. This interesting tool can be used to generate and send a stream of random valid and invalid Win32 messages or random valid mouse/keyboard events to a Windows application. The idea is to test the stability of your application when it's subjected to a large amount of random input. If, as a result of the random input, your application crashes or hangs in some way, it's considered to have failed the test.

The first technique of sending a stream of random mouse and keyboard events to your application simulates the behavior of a very erratic end user who just keeps banging away at your software in a haphazard and tireless fashion. The other technique of sending a stream of random Win32 messages simulates what might happen when your application receives one or more dodgy messages from the Windows kernel, or when it's subject to an attack by a malicious program. In either case, you want your application to resist the onslaught or at least fail in a graceful manner by saving the end user's work before crashing.

The authors of this clever tool tested many Windows and Unix programs, including some of Microsoft's most popular applications. The results make sobering reading. Using Windows 2000, 64.3% of the applications tested with random valid mouse and keyboard events failed with either a crash (42.9%) or a hang (21.4%). Some of the programs that failed this test included Access 2000, Netscape 4.7, Paint Shop Pro 5.03, PowerPoint 2000, and Word 2000. When the same applications were tested using random valid and invalid **PostMessage** calls, a total of 71.4% of them failed. Using random valid and invalid **SendMessage** calls was even worse—85.7% of the applications failed by crashing or hanging!

If you want to download this freeware tool and try it against your .NET applications, you can find fuzz and a short paper discussing it at `http://www.cs.wisc.edu/~bart/fuzz/fuzz-nt.html`.

CHAPTER 10

Windows Services Debugging

CREATING A WINDOWS SERVICE with VB.Classic is always a messy and error-prone activity. You can use the **srvany** utility or the **ntsvc.ocx** control, but both of these methods have problems and debugging the resulting issues is difficult and frustrating (see Microsoft Knowledge Base article Q175948 for some warnings about the problems). This restriction on VB.Classic's capability to create reliable Windows services is a shame because these programs can be invaluable for creating long-running processes that can function without an interactive user. I've used Windows services to act as permanently available middle-tier application components, as load-balancing database gateways, as application sentinels to monitor various components, and as programs that allow remote control (over an intranet) of other services on a machine.

With VB .NET, you finally have the tools to create reliable Windows services. With this freedom come some responsibilities, as these services typically require multithreading skills and knowledge of a slightly unusual flow of control. This chapter examines how to debug Windows services, including both in-place and IDE debugging, debugging of the **OnStart** method, and debugging installation issues.

Debugging the ServiceAdmin Service

The **ServiceAdmin** Windows service is a real-life program written to solve a specific problem. It's very common in distributed applications to place middle-tier components on one or more application server machines, and frequently those middle-tier components are Windows services. When your application misbehaves, possibly because of a middle-tier component problem, it can be very tiresome to have to trudge around each of the application servers looking for the errant service. Even if you have a server administrator to do the serious legwork for you, you still have to give him or her precise instructions about which services to investigate and what to do in the event of finding a problem. Often you need to have a form signed in triplicate by three pointy-haired bosses just to restart a production service.

ServiceAdmin is a Windows service that you can run on each of your application servers. It presents a Web page that allows you to see the status of designated Windows services on that server. You can monitor each server just by typing its IP address and a port number into a Web browser. You could even enhance **ServiceAdmin** to allow you to pause, stop, start, or restart the services that you're monitoring. The idea is to save you from having to walk around investigating each of your servers in person, and to give you control over your middle-tier Windows services without having to trouble your server administrators. In essence, **ServiceAdmin** is a remote service administrator program acting as a miniature Web server.

Debugging Preparation

Running and debugging a Windows service by pressing F5 within the IDE is problematic because a service normally has to be installed before it can run. Later in this chapter, in the section entitled "Debugging a Service Without Installing It," I describe a technique for doing exactly that by writing code that simulates a service start when using the **Debug** configuration. For the moment, I'll talk about debugging a service after it's been released and installed.

First, load and build the **ServiceAdmin** solution, taking care to ensure that you build using the **Release** configuration (not the **Debug** configuration). Once you've loaded and built the **ServiceAdmin** solution, you need to install it as a service on your machine. You can do this using the installutil.exe utility. Go to the .NET command line and navigate to the folder containing the **ServiceAdmin** executable. Then type the command line **installutil /Logfile=install.txt ServiceAdmin.exe**. The installer utility will install this service under the LocalSystem account, which doesn't require you to provide an account password. If, alternatively, you want to install your service under a user account, you should be careful to specify the full machine name before the account name when prompted by the installer. This is because the installer seems to be rather finicky about the exact format of the account name that it accepts. On my machine, **Cheetah\MarkPearce** works fine because my machine is called Cheetah.

Once the installation routine has run, you can check that the service installed properly by using the Services applet in the Control Panel to check its status. If the service didn't install for some reason, you should check the installation log file (in this case, install.txt) to see why the installation failed. The most common reasons for failure are using an incorrect machine name, account name, or account password, but this can be difficult to diagnose because some of the failure messages are rather cryptic. In addition, if you're running a local firewall, you may be prompted by the firewall to give **ServiceAdmin** permission to listen on port 5005.

Once you've successfully installed **ServiceAdmin**, you can start the service from the aforementioned Services applet. At this point, the service spawns a main thread that listens on the designated port for client requests. Each client request starts a new thread that responds to the request and then sends a fresh Web page to the client showing the status of the services after the request has been performed.

Figure 10-1 shows the Web page produced by **ServiceAdmin** when I type the URL `http://localhost:5005/status.html` into my Web browser. Note that the `//localhost` address means that I'm talking to **ServiceAdmin** running on my local machine. If you wanted to communicate with **ServiceAdmin** running on a remote machine, you would replace **localhost** with the remote machine's IP address, which you can find by running ipconfig.exe from the command line of the remote machine. The number 5005 is the port on which **ServiceAdmin** is listening for client requests. Currently this port number is hard-coded, but in the real world it should really be specified using **ServiceAdmin**'s configuration file.

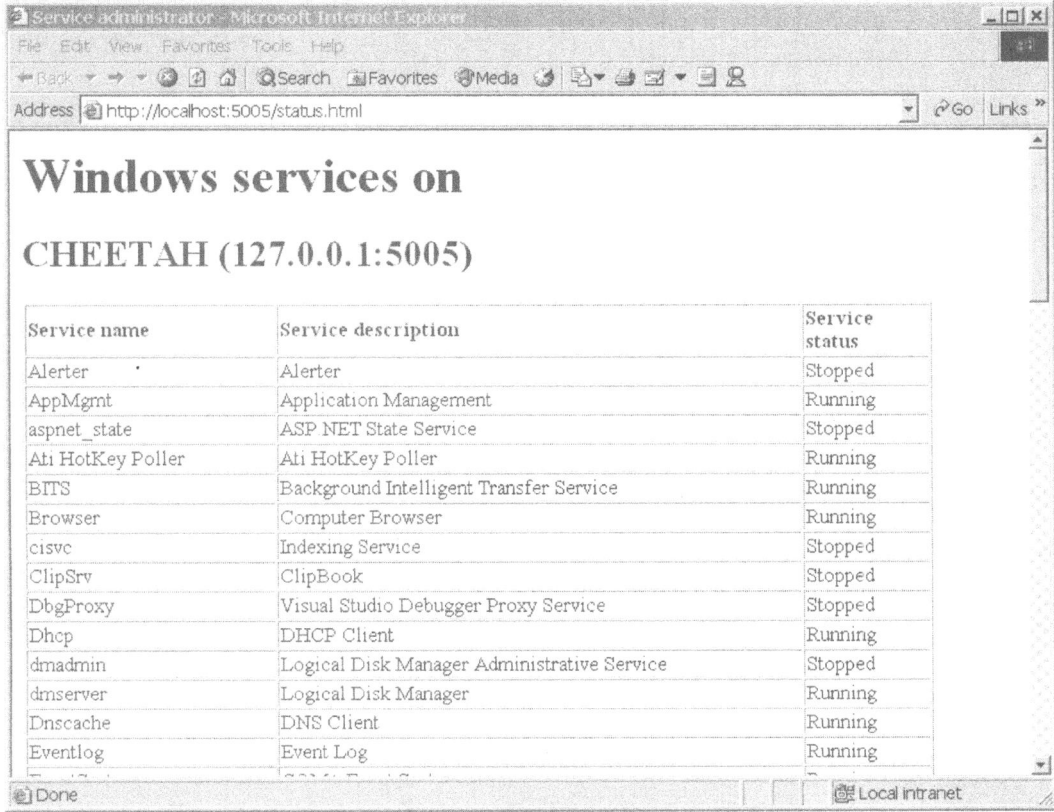

Figure 10-1. The ServiceAdmin Web interface for remote control of services

Debugging with Process Attach

Once the service is up and running, you can attach the Visual Studio debugger to the service process. To do this, load the **ServiceAdmin** solution into Visual Studio and add a breakpoint to line 42 of the **ServiceListener.vb** class in the **ServiceAdmin** project. Line 42 is the line that accepts a new client request, namely

```
ThisClient = New Client(MyTcpListener.AcceptSocket())
```

From the Debug menu, select the Processes menu item to launch the Processes dialog window. In this dialog window, make sure that Show system processes is selected, because the service is running under the LocalSystem account. In the Available Processes subwindow, double-click the **ServiceAdmin** process. If you can't find the process in the subwindow, check that the service is actually started. Figure 10-2 shows the service process highlighted.

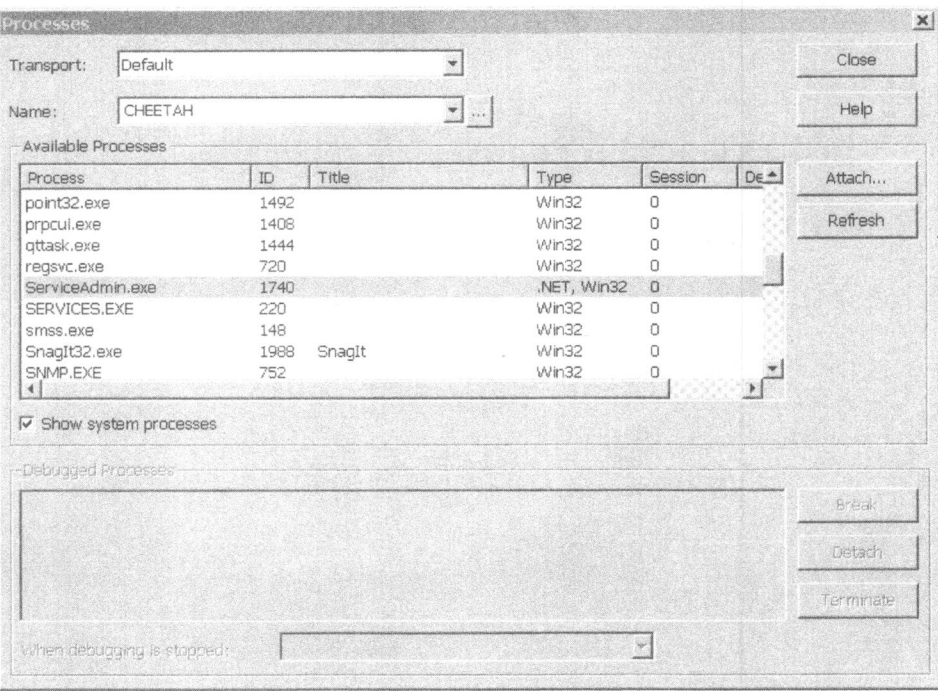

Figure 10-2. Attaching to the ServiceAdmin process for debugging

Attaching from Visual Studio

Once you've double-clicked the service process, Visual Studio presents you with the Attach to Process dialog window, which asks you which types of program you wish to debug. You should select the Common Language Runtime option and deselect all the others. If you also select the Native option, you'll find later that you may not be able to detach the debugger from the process. Unless you're using the Visual Studio Debugger Proxy service as described in Chapter 3, debugging native code means that you'll only be able to stop debugging by terminating the process. This is because the native debugger isn't designed to detach from a process.

Once the debugger has successfully attached to the **ServiceAdmin** process, you can close the Processes dialog window. Your breakpoint should be hit whenever the service receives a client request from a Web browser, so fire up your favorite browser and enter the URL `http://localhost:5005/status.html`. When you do this, you should find that your breakpoint is triggered immediately. At this point, you can single-step through the code and debug the Windows service just like any other application type. After you've finished investigating the code with the debugger, just press F5 and **ServiceAdmin**'s Web page showing the status of various Windows services should appear in your browser. If the browser experiences a time-out because you're investigating the code, you may need to refresh the page request by pressing F5 in the browser.

When you've finished debugging the service, simply go to the Processes window again, click the **ServiceAdmin** process in the Debugged Processes subwindow, and then click the Detach button. This causes the Visual Studio debugger to detach from the service process.

Ensuring the Correct Debug Settings

If you debug your service in this way, you have to make sure you have matching debug symbols for your executable and preferably that code optimization is switched off. This is described in detail in Chapters 3 and 4, and building your solution in the default debug configuration does all of this automatically. But what happens if you're trying to debug a release build of your Windows service?

First, you should always generate debug symbols, even for release builds. This means changing the release configuration for your project to generate debugging symbols by default. To do this, go to the **ServiceAdmin** project's Configuration Properties ➤ Build property page, set the build configuration to Release, and make sure the Generate debugging information option is checked. Saving the solution will ensure that debugging symbols are always generated, even for a release build. You can also turn off JIT code optimization for a release build, though some developers think this is going a bit far because it can affect the speed of your program in some circumstances. If you want to do this, turn off the Enable optimizations option on your project's Configuration Properties ➤ Optimization property page. There is, however, an alternative that gives you the best of both worlds: code optimization when running normally, but no code optimization while doing debugging. I described this technique in Chapter 4, but I'll repeat the description here to save you from having to refer back to that chapter.

If you place a configuration file (called *MyApp*.ini, where *MyApp* is the name of your executable) in the same folder as your .exe, it allows you to configure debug tracking and code optimization on a run-by-run basis. This is possible because the actual JIT compilation takes place at runtime rather than at compile time. The lines in the configuration file that control these settings are as follows (where 1 equals **true** and 0 equals **false**):

```
[.NET Framework Debugging Control]
GenerateTrackingInfo=1
AllowOptimize=0
```

This allows you to override the settings that you specified when you originally built your service, and it's ideal for investigating those troublesome production problems that you're unable to find or duplicate during development and unit testing. As long as you make sure that the correct debug symbol (.pdb) file is available, you'll be able to step through source code and do full debugging without recompiling your Windows service.

Debugging a Service Without Installing It

The Visual Studio documentation insists that you install your service before you can debug it. During development of a Windows service, it can be a real pain to have to uninstall the previous version of the service and then reinstall a new version every time you want to test a change to your code. Fortunately, you can set up your code so that when using the **Debug** configuration it operates as a standard executable, and when using the **Release** configuration it reverts back to being a service.

To do this, you need to emulate what the Service Control Manager (SCM) does when it starts your service—in other words, invoke your service's **OnStart** method. Listing 10-1 shows the code required for the **ServiceAdmin** service. The source lines marked in bold are the ones that you need to add to the standard code generated by the service wizard. These lines instantiate your service class and call its **OnStart** method. From there, the service can run quite happily within the IDE.

Listing 10-1. Running a Windows Service As a Standard .exe

```
      ' The main entry point for the service process
      <MTAThread()> _
      Shared Sub Main()
#If Debug Then
          Dim DebugService As New ServiceAdmin()
          DebugService.OnStart(Nothing)
#Else
          Dim ServicesToRun() As System.ServiceProcess.ServiceBase
          ServicesToRun = New ServiceBase () {New ServiceAdmin}
          ServiceBase.Run(ServicesToRun)
#End If
      End Sub
```

This approach also allows you to debug your **Main** procedure and the code in your **OnStart** method. This is otherwise rather tricky because these two procedures have already been executed (during service startup) before you get a chance to attach to the service process for debugging. If, additionally, you want to debug other service commands such as **Stop** or **Pause**, you can invoke the appropriate method from the Immediate window.

Debugging the OnStart Method

Sometimes the previous technique isn't applicable because you just have to debug your Windows service after it's been installed. This usually occurs when you have to solve specific security or other problems that don't show themselves when the service is running within the IDE.

The main problem with debugging the **OnStart** method is that you can't attach to your service process until after the service has been started, but at this point the **OnStart** method has already been executed. One trick is to sleep the service thread for 25 seconds at the very start of the **Main** procedure. This hopefully gives you enough time to rummage through the Processes window, find your process, and then attach the debugger to it. Unfortunately, even if you do manage this feat of speed, the SCM calls a time-out if your service doesn't start after 30 seconds and the service start is aborted. This leaves you just a few seconds for debugging!

If you really need the whole 30 seconds for debugging, or you don't care whether the service start is aborted as long as you can start debugging, there's a way to do this. The key is to have two services within your service application. This is allowed because multiple services can share the same process. You start a "dummy" service to launch the service process, and then attach to this process.

Add a breakpoint to your real service and use the SCM to start that service, and immediately your breakpoint should be hit. After debugging and before you do any proper release, you should, of course, remove the second service (and also its installer) from your Visual Studio solution.

Adding the dummy service to your application is easy. Just add a new service class and copy your real service class code into the new class so that you have a duplicate service. The only thing that you need to change in this dummy service is the service name. Then add an installer for your new dummy service by right-clicking its designer page and selecting Add installer from the drop-down menu. Make sure that the installer's service name matches your dummy service name. Finally, tell the application to start both services. In the **ServiceAdmin** application, the line of code in the **Main** procedure that starts the service is

```
ServicesToRun = New ServiceBase() {New ServiceAdmin()}
```

After you add the new dummy service, the revised code that starts both services is

```
ServicesToRun = New ServiceBase() {New ServiceAdmin(), New DummyService()}
```

That's all there is to it. Installing the application will install both your real service and the dummy service. Using the SCM to start the dummy service launches your application's process so that you can attach the debugger to it. From there you can start, stop, and otherwise debug your real service at your leisure. Just remember to remove the dummy service before you do any production release.

Debugging Installation Issues

You can also debug your service installation code. To demonstrate one way of doing this, I've added some custom code to the **ProjectInstaller.vb** class that updates **ServiceAdmin**'s description as shown in the Description column of the Services applet. Thanks to what looks like a bug in the Framework class library, there's no way of specifying your service's description. If you try using the **ServiceProcessDescription** attribute, it just overwrites what's displayed in the Name column. To overcome this, the code in Listing 10-2 overrides the project installer's **Install** virtual method, performs the actual installation, and then opens the appropriate registry key and hacks the service description manually. Although this code isn't very elegant, it does the job and serves as a way of looking at the debugging of installation code.

Listing 10-2. Updating ServiceAdmin's Description During Installation

```
Imports Microsoft.Win32

<RunInstaller(True)> Public Class ProjectInstaller
    Inherits System.Configuration.Install.Installer

    'Wizard-generated installer code omitted for the sake of brevity

    Public Overrides Sub Install(ByVal stateSaver As Collections.IDictionary)

        'First do the install
        MyBase.Install(stateSaver)

        'System.Diagnostics.Debugger.Launch()
        'Navigate to the correct registry key
        Dim SystemKey As RegistryKey = Registry.LocalMachine.OpenSubKey("System")
        Dim ControlSetKey As RegistryKey = _
                    SystemKey.OpenSubKey("CurrentControlSet")
        Dim ServicesKey As RegistryKey = ControlSetKey.OpenSubKey("Services")
        Dim ServiceKey As RegistryKey = _
                    ServicesKey.OpenSubKey(Me.ServiceInstaller1.ServiceName, True)

        'Now we can set the service description
        ServiceKey.SetValue("Description", "Allows remote service administration")

        'Cleanup
        ServiceKey.Close()
        ServicesKey.Close()
        ControlSetKey.Close()
        SystemKey.Close()

    End Sub

End Class
```

Before you run installutil.exe, open the **ServiceAdmin** solution and remove the comment mark from the following line of code after the call to **MyBase.Install(stateSaver)** shown in Listing 10-2:

```
'System.Diagnostics.Debugger.Launch()
```

When you actually install the service, this line of code launches the CLR's JIT debug dialog window. From this dialog window, select to debug using the instance of Visual Studio that contains the **ServiceAdmin** solution. From the next dialog window, choose to debug only .NET code by deselecting the native code option. At this point, the debugger will break on the source line that launched the debugger. Now you can single-step through the installation code.

Be Careful

Because Windows service applications are usually up and running all of the time while their host machine is active, you need to be especially careful about managing resources such as memory, database connections, disk files, and unmanaged objects. If an application runs 24/7, even a small resource management issue is likely to grow into a nasty problem quite quickly. Similarly, multithreading situations are very common when developing Windows services, and these situations also need to be handled with care. For some detailed information about multithreading and resource management, please see Chapter 14.

Summary

This chapter showed you some of the ways that you can debug a Windows service. After a short discussion on debugging preparation, it covered attaching to a service process using Visual Studio, debugging a service without installing it, and debugging a service's **OnStart** method. Finally, you learned how to debug code that runs when your service is installed.

INTERLUDE

The following story was related to me by a friend who used to work as a development engineer in the aircraft industry. It's a classic tale of what can happen if somebody decides that he or she knows best and can ignore the warnings given by colleagues.

"Many years ago I was a development engineer in the aircraft industry working for a company specializing in aircraft electrical components and systems. We had the contract for the entire electrical system for one of the UK's V-bombers. The prototype of one of these aircraft crashed following some high-speed, high-altitude (20,000 meters—yes, meters!) trials.

"One of the devices I helped develop was an actuator reversing switch, which among other things controlled the pitch of the horizontal tail surfaces. The entire surface moved, not just the elevators, and when the aircraft remains were recovered it was found that the tail plane was locked in the high-speed, high-altitude position. Further, the reversing switch had locked out, which it was designed to do in the event of the contacts welding together. Indeed, one set of contacts was welded and the other contact pair had interrupted the current. This prevented fire but left the aircraft impossible to handle at low altitude.

"The switch unit had passed all its development tests, including extensive tests at simulated high altitude (low pressure and low temperature) and the type had its Air Registration Certificate. The question was why had it locked out, an event that could from the tests only happen if the contacts were opened slowly leading to severe arcing. The next question was why had the contacts opened slowly?

"This is when the unpredictable occurred. In carrying out the development trials, I had insisted that the bearings in the mechanism were lubricated with a special low-temperature constant (with temperature) viscosity oil called 'UNIVIS P38'. To ensure that the viscous friction was reduced to the absolute minimum I also had the bearing, which consisted of a stainless steel shaft running in a sintered bronze tube, modified so that the bearing clearance was increased from 10 microns to 60 microns. The shaft was also modified to look like a bobbin with bearing surfaces at each end rather than continuous.

"The net effect of these modifications was to reduce the friction torque by a factor of between 500 and 1,000, enough to ensure snappy action even at the highest altitudes. The downside was that the mechanism was slightly 'sloppy,' but again extensive tests demonstrated that there was no deterioration in wear rate due to vibration or repeated operation. The trial units lasted in excess of 10,000 operations, equivalent to substantially more than the aircraft lifetime.

"So what went wrong? In transferring the design, tooling, and so on to the production team, one of the production engineers, unknown to the development team, decided that the tolerances and clearances needed to be tightened up! He did not want to be responsible for sloppy mechanisms leaving the factory. So, ignoring the warning note on the part and the assembly drawings that the clearance of 60 microns was correct, he modified the shafts to reduce the clearance back to 10 microns without consulting the development team and ignored the large letters on all the company's drawings that insisted, in large letters:

IF IN DOUBT ASK

His actions caused the total loss of one prototype machine costing in today's money £10^N ($\$15^N$), where N is around 9. But luckily, the members of the crew were saved by their Martin Baker ejection seats.

"The lesson to be learned from this case and thousands of others like it is that individual engineers have a duty to pay great attention to detail and to communicate continuously about what they are doing and explain their decisions and actions. Even then the only certainty is that the unforeseen will happen."

VB.Classic Debugging

I**T'S CLEAR THAT IN SPITE OF** the arrival of .NET, VB.Classic applications are still going to be around for a long time. Moving a company's business applications from VB.Classic to VB .NET is simply not a cost-effective proposition in most cases, not to mention the problem with re-skilling whole IT departments. Fortunately, Microsoft realizes that it isn't feasible to ask companies to abandon or migrate all of their legacy code, so they've provided a COM Interoperability (usually shortened to "Interop") layer to allow cooperation between the managed and unmanaged worlds. This chapter discusses the debugging of the COM Interop layer between VB .NET and VB.Classic.

This chapter first provides an overview of the very different ways in which COM and .NET view the world. It then looks at debugging Interop with a COM component written in VB 6.0 and called by a VB .NET application. Next is an investigation of debugging Interop with a VB .NET component called by a VB 6.0 application. Finally, you'll look at some of the finer details of debugging COM Interop applications.

VB.Classic Versions

You can use either VB 5.0 or VB 6.0 projects with VB .NET, but I recommend using VB 6.0 exclusively if possible. One problem is that the debug symbol files produced by VB 5.0 can cause difficulties when you try to view VB 5.0 variables from within the Visual Studio debugger. Another problem with the same debug symbol files affects the VB 5.0 source code mapping. This results in the Visual Studio IDE showing the wrong VB 5.0 source lines being executed. In fact, this can also be a problem with VB 6.0 unless Service Pack 3 (SP3) or higher has been applied. The final problem that I've encountered with both VB 5.0 and VB 6.0 (without SP3 or higher applied) is that VB.Classic components are prone to crashing during shutdown.

I recommend using VB 6.0 with the latest service pack applied, SP5 at the time of writing. With this combination, I haven't experienced any debugger-related problems.

If you're using Windows NT 4.0 as your operating system, you'll need to install NT 4.0 SP4 or higher. You won't be able to debug VB 6.0 components from VB .NET without this.

Managed vs. Unmanaged

Before you delve deeply into COM Interop, it's a good idea to understand the completely different views that managed and unmanaged code have of the world. When you have a good understanding of these two views and where they agree and disagree, it's much easier to debug the inevitable problems that COM Interop throws up.

The following list presents the major differences between these two architectures:

- *Coding model:* The managed world uses an object-based view of code, whereas the COM world thinks of code in terms of interfaces. This means that Interop has to generate an interface to expose managed code to the unmanaged world, unless the managed code already provides such an interface.

- *Error handling:* The usual COM practice is to return an HRESULT to signify whether a method has succeeded or failed. VB 6.0 developers get a break here because they're already used to the practice of raising errors using the **Err** object. COM Interop maps VB 6.0 errors to .NET exceptions, and it maps .NET exceptions to VB 6.0 errors.

- *Identities:* COM uses globally unique identifiers (GUIDs) to identify unmanaged types and interfaces, whereas .NET uses strong names, which uniquely identify assemblies and managed types. COM Interop can generate GUIDs for .NET assemblies and strong names for COM components.

- *Type compatibility:* Although some managed and unmanaged types are compatible, others are not. Fortunately there are .NET attributes that can solve most type compatibility problems.

- *Type definitions:* A COM type library is optional and only contains public types, whereas .NET metadata is mandatory and describes both public and private types. COM Interop is quite successful at converting between type libraries and metadata.

- *Versioning:* VB 6.0 allows you to extend interfaces without breaking binary compatibility, but COM interfaces are generally considered to be immutable. However, .NET interfaces can evolve while keeping the same name. When you step into the unmanaged world, you need to be careful about versioning issues, which are sometimes known as *DLL Hell*.

In this chapter I point out some of the issues raised by these two very different views of the world and discuss how you avoid or work around them.

VB .NET Application Using a VB 6.0 Component

The first example application (InteropDebug.sln and ComPrintUtils.vbp) consists of a VB .NET Windows Form project calling a VB 6.0 component to perform a specific printing task. Rather than invent a COM component for demonstration purposes, I decided to use a real-life component that has proved to be useful in the past and would be a little tricky to port over to VB .NET because of its extensive use of Win32 API calls.

Figure 11-1 shows the very simple user interface for this application. The single button shown on the .NET Windows Form calls a public method, **PrintPictureToFitPage**, in the VB 6.0 dynamic link library (DLL). This method takes a window handle as a parameter and then calls several private methods to print a sized and rotated graphic of the specified window.

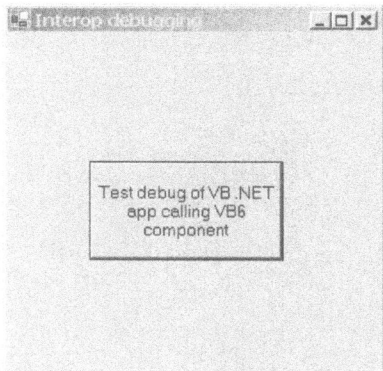

Figure 11-1. Simple VB .NET user interface for testing a VB 6.0 component

The VB 6.0 component was originally written to handle the well-known problems with VB.Classic's **PrintForm** method, which only prints the client area of a form, refuses to print any form graphics, and doesn't make sensible decisions about sizing or rotating form graphics. The component was later expanded to print any specified window, the currently active window, or the desktop itself.

VB.Classic Preparation

First you should build the **ComPrintUtils** component, which is a VB 6.0 ActiveX DLL. When you first load the ComPrintUtils.vbp project, you'll see a message warning you that the binary compatibility component doesn't exist. This warning appears because you haven't created the component yet. Go to the File ➤ Make ComPrintUtils.dll menu option. Click the Options button on the Make Project dialog window, and go to the Compile tab, as shown in Figure 11-2. You must choose the Compile to Native Code option because the Visual Studio debugger doesn't understand p-code. You should also select the No Optimization and Create Symbolic Debug Info compilation options. The former option allows the debugger to map the executing program back to the source code accurately, just as the same option works when compiling a VB .NET application. The latter option ensures that the VB 6.0 compiler produces a debug symbol file, without which the binary-to-source code mapping can't occur.

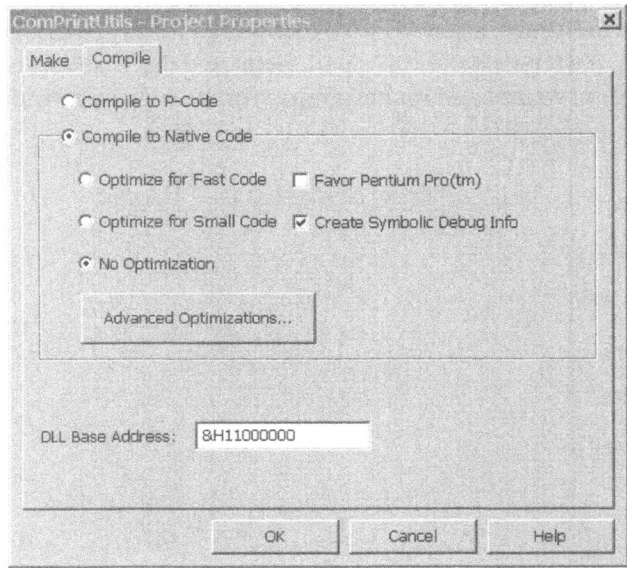

Figure 11-2. Compiling a VB 6.0 component for use from VB .NET

Compiling the VB 6.0 component automatically registers it as far as COM is concerned, thus enabling VB .NET to see the component and its public interfaces. If your own COM component is for some reason not registered on the machine on which you wish to use it, then you should register it using regsvr32.exe from the command line.

Once you've created the VB 6.0 component, you should copy the binary to a project subfolder and then set the project's binary compatibility option to point at this binary-compatible version. You can do this using the Component tab on the dialog window you access by selecting the Project ➤ ComPrintUtils properties menu item. Doing this ensures that all of the COM registry entries stay the same when you change and recompile the component.

VB .NET Preparation

The first major gotcha awaiting you is the fact that you need to install VC7++ before you can use the native debugger required for VB.Classic debugging. This is an unfortunate requirement because the VC7++ package that comes with Visual Studio is rather large, but I've been unable to find any way around this.

Now you can load the **InteropDebug** solution. To use the VB 6.0 component that you've just built in this solution, go to the Project ➤ Add Reference menu option and click the COM tab. Find the **ComPrintUtils** component in the top window of the tab, double-click it to add the component to the solution, and then click the OK button. To confirm that the COM component has been added to the solution, go to the Solution Explorer window and look for the References item underneath the **InteropDebug** project. Underneath the References item should be a reference to the **ComPrintUtils** component, as shown in Figure 11-3. There should also be a reference to **stdole**, the COM automation library required for using any COM component.

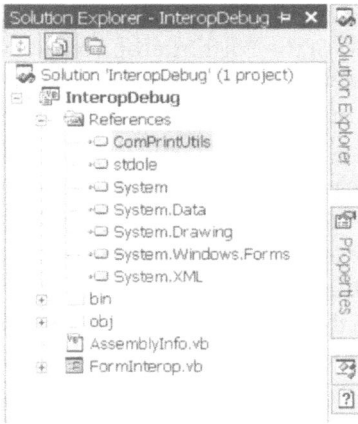

Figure 11-3. VB .NET project with reference to VB 6.0 project

Visual Studio has created a .NET Interop assembly called **Interop.ComPrintUtils.dll** in the \bin and \obj subfolders of the .NET solution. The CLR will make this component accessible to any .NET application by creating a Runtime Callable Wrapper (RCW). The RCW fools the .NET application into thinking that it's calling a .NET component rather than a COM component.

If you change any code within a VB 6.0 component, you should remove its reference from the VB .NET application (by right-clicking the reference and choosing Remove) before you add the reference again. This is the best way to ensure that the VB .NET application always refers to the correct version of the VB 6.0 component. If you don't do this, you might end up with mismatched source, binary, and debug symbols for the VB 6.0 component. This is because simply recompiling the VB 6.0 component won't cause a new Interop assembly to be created or allow the .NET application to recognize that the VB 6.0 source code has changed.

The final debugging preparation step is to switch on unmanaged debugging for the VB .NET project by right-clicking the project in the Solution Explorer window and going to the Configuration Properties ➢ Debugging window. There you should select the check box marked Unmanaged code debugging. If you forget to select this setting, you can tear out your hair for hours wondering why your VB 6.0 breakpoints aren't being hit.

Debugging the First COM Interop Application

Set a breakpoint on line 62 of the FormInterop.vb code window, where the call is made to **DebugTest.PrintPictureToFitPage**, and press F5 to start the application running. When you click the single command button provided, you should land on the breakpoint that you've just set. If you then press F8 to step into the VB 6.0 component, a new source code window should open showing the VB 6.0 code, and the debugger should step into the VB 6.0 **CaptureForm** function. Once again, it's imperative that you've enabled unmanaged debugging in your VB .NET project—without this, the debugger will simply step over any call to a VB 6.0 method. At this point, you can use the Visual Studio debugger to step back and forth quite freely between the managed and unmanaged worlds.

When Visual Studio knows where the VB 6.0 source code and debug symbols reside, it opens the source code window automatically as just discussed. More commonly, however, you need to inform the debugger exactly where the VB 6.0 source code and debug symbols can be found. For VB 6.0 source code, go to the solution's Properties ➢ Common Properties ➢ Debug Source Files dialog page as shown in Figure 11-4. Here you can specify the path (or paths) that contains the source code files. In a similar fashion, you can use the solution's Properties ➢ Common Properties ➢ Debug Symbol Files dialog page to specify the path that contains the VB 6.0 debug symbol files. Like VB .NET debug symbol files, these have a .pdb suffix.

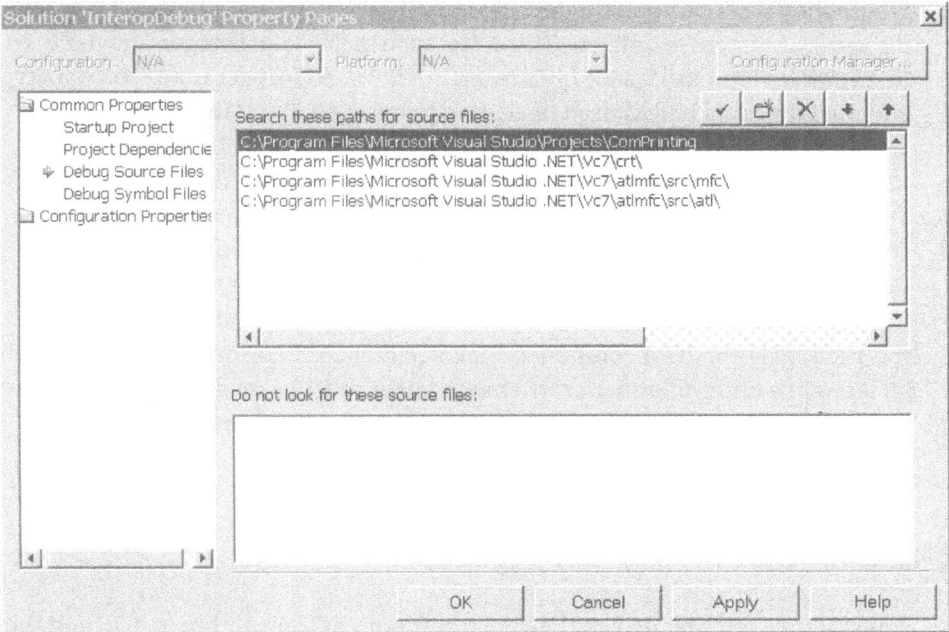

Figure 11-4. Specifying the location of VB 6.0 source code files

You may notice that debugging of unmanaged code is very slow, sometimes taking 2 or 3 seconds to step from one line to another, and also that this performance problem can appear when debugging managed code if unmanaged debugging has been selected. Unfortunately, this is currently an unavoidable overhead when you do unmanaged debugging, so you'll have to live with it until Microsoft addresses the performance issue in a new release of the .NET Framework. C# has the same performance issue when working with unmanaged code.

Debugging Tips

It's worth taking a minute at this stage to compare the different ways that VB 6.0 and VB .NET view the public methods of a VB 6.0 component. If within the VB 6.0 IDE you examine the Declarations drop-down in the top right corner of the Source window, you can see the six methods declared by the VB 6.0 component. In the Visual Studio IDE, right-click **ComPrintUtils** on line 61 of the FormInterop.vb code window and choose the Go To Definition menu option. This should show the Object Browser window where you can see that the same six methods form the **ComPrinting** class and the **_ComPrinting** public interface. If you look closely at the method definitions, you can see one interesting point.

Where the VB 6.0 component declares a method argument as **Long**, VB .NET sees the same argument as **Integer**. This is because in .NET, an **Integer** is actually an **Int32**, which represents a 32-bit integer. In VB 6.0, an **Integer** is a 16-bit data type and the **Long** data type is used instead to represent a 32-bit integer.

Another point to note is the call to **InteropServices.Marshal.ReleaseComObject()** in the VB .NET code. This method call takes place after the application has finished using the VB 6.0 component, but before the COM object variable is set to **Nothing**. The method decrements the RCW's COM reference count and is used for explicit control of the lifetime of a COM object used from managed code. You should always call this method if the COM component holds references to resources that need to be released in a timely manner or when references must be released in a specific order. In the absence of this call, you can find yourself debugging strange and intermittent resource errors, which is really no fun at all.

Using the VB 6.0 Debugger

You might be tempted to run the VB 6.0 component from within its IDE and then jump into the VB 6.0 IDE from the Visual Studio IDE, in a similar manner to the traditional VB 6.0 approach of running two IDE sessions side by side and transferring smoothly between the two IDEs. However, running the Visual Studio and VB 6.0 IDEs side by side doesn't work. It might appear to work for a short time, but as soon as control transfers back from the VB 6.0 IDE to the Visual Studio IDE (and sometimes before), you'll see a major error and the whole house of cards will come tumbling down. Therefore, you need to compile the VB 6.0 component before you can debug it from Visual Studio. This is similar to the VB 6.0 approach of using a project group containing multiple projects within a single IDE session, with the VB .NET solution being the equivalent of the VB 6.0 project group.

So what happens if you really do need to debug the VB 6.0 component from within the VB 6.0 IDE, perhaps to take advantage of VB 6.0's capability to edit code during a debugging session? I've found a way to do this, but it only works until the first time that control is returned to the .NET application. After the first call into VB 6.0 and transfer back to VB .NET, the CLR triggers an exception, and you won't be able to continue debugging. If you can live with this restriction, you can try the following method.

First, build InteropDebug.sln as discussed previously. Then switch to the VB 6.0 IDE and go to the Project ➤ ComPrintUtils properties menu option. In the resulting Project Properties dialog window, choose the Debugging tab and select the Start program option. The program that you need to launch the VB 6.0 component is, of course, the InteropDebug.exe application, so browse to the \InteropDebug\bin folder and double-click the executable.

Now place a breakpoint on the first statement of the VB 6.0 method that will be the first to be called, in this case the **CaptureForm** function in the **ComPrinting** class module. Finally, press F5 in the VB 6.0 IDE to start the debugging session. The VB .NET Windows Form should appear, and you can click the single command button. Now your VB 6.0 breakpoint should be hit. From here you can step through the code in your VB 6.0 component, at least until control returns back to VB .NET application. At this point you should see the standard Windows Forms dialog window warning you about an unhandled exception. Click the Continue button to just ignore the exception. The VB .NET application is now likely to be unstable, so you should close it at the first opportunity.

As I stated previously, this isn't an ideal way to debug VB 6.0 COM Interop, but it does at least allow you to use the VB 6.0 IDE when you really need to do so.

VB 6.0 Application Using a VB .NET Component

The second example application (InteropDemo.sln with InteropDebug.vbp) consists of a VB 6.0 Windows Form project calling a VB .NET component to add two numbers together. This time I'm back to using an artificial component rather than a real-life one. The idea is that you can readily use and debug your .NET components from your VB 6.0 applications.

Figure 11-5 shows the very simple user interface for this application. The single button shown on the VB 6.0 Windows Form calls a public method, **AddTwoNumbers**, in the VB .NET DLL. This method takes two numbers and simply adds them together.

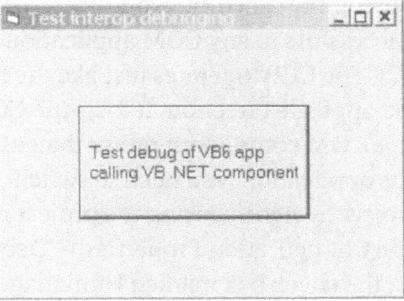

Figure 11-5. Simple VB 6.0 user interface for testing a VB .NET component

Listing 11-1 shows the VB .NET class that forms the component that will be called by the VB 6.0 application.

Listing 11-1. VB .NET Component Code for Use by a COM Client

```
Option Strict On
Imports System.Runtime.InteropServices

<ClassInterface(ClassInterfaceType.AutoDual)> _
Public Class MathClass

    Public Sub New()
    End Sub


    Public Function AddTwoNumbers(ByVal FirstNumber As Double, _
                          ByVal SecondNumber As Double) As Double
        'Return the result to COM client
        Return FirstNumber + SecondNumber
    End Function

End Class
```

VB .NET Preparation

First you need to build the VB .NET component, which is the **InteropDemo** class library project in InteropDemo.sln. To allow a COM application to use this component, go to the project's Properties ➢ Configuration Properties ➢ Build property page and select the Register for COM Interop check box.

When you mark the project for COM Interop in this fashion, Visual Studio creates a .NET Interop assembly called **Interop.InteropDemo.dll**. The CLR will make this component accessible to any COM application by creating a COM Callable Wrapper (CCW). The CCW operates just like the RCW that I discussed previously, except in the opposite direction. It fools the COM application into thinking that it's calling a COM component rather than a .NET component.

As with the previous application, you need to switch on unmanaged debugging for the VB .NET project by right-clicking the project in the Solution Explorer window and going to the Configuration Properties ➢ Debugging property page. There you should select the check box marked Unmanaged code debugging. If you forget to do this, your VB 6.0 breakpoints won't be recognized.

Compiling the **InteropDemo** solution automatically registers it as far as COM is concerned, thus enabling VB 6.0 to see the component and its public interfaces. If you have a .NET assembly that isn't registered on the machine on which you wish to use it, you can register it using regasm.exe from the command line. You can consider regasm.exe as the .NET equivalent of regsvr32.exe for COM registration.

VB.Classic Preparation

Now you can prepare the **InteropDebug** VB 6.0 application for debugging. Once you've loaded the InteropDebug.vbp project, you need to add a reference to the .NET component that you've just built. To do this, go to the Project ➤ References menu option and select **InteropDemo** from the list of available references.

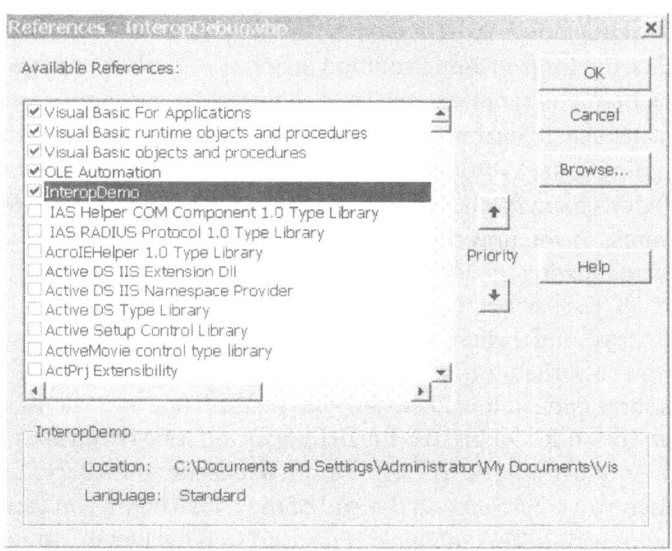

Figure 11-6. Adding a VB .NET component reference to the VB 6.0 application.

After you add the .NET assembly reference, save the VB 6.0 application and then compile it by going to the File ➤ Make InteropDebug.exe menu option. Click the Options button on the Make Project dialog window, and go to the Compile tab, as shown earlier in Figure 11-2. You must choose the Compile to Native Code option because the Visual Studio debugger doesn't understand p-code. You should also select the No Optimization and Create Symbolic Debug Info compilation options. The former option allows the debugger to map the executing program back to the source code accurately, just as the same option works when compiling a VB .NET application. The latter option ensures that the VB 6.0 compiler produces a debug symbol file, without which the binary-to-source code mapping can't occur.

Debugging the Second COM Interop Application

Because you're debugging this application completely within Visual Studio, you need a way of starting the VB 6.0 part of the application from Visual Studio. To do this, use Solution Explorer to go to the Configuration Properties ➤ Debugging property page of the **InteropDemo** project and change the Start Action to be Start external program. Then navigate to the InteropDebug.exe VB 6.0 program, as this will launch the whole application. On the same property page, ensure that unmanaged debugging is switched on.

Next, click the **InteropDemo** solution in Solution Explorer and go to the File ➤ Add Existing Item menu option. Navigate to the folder containing the VB 6.0 application and select FormInterop.frm. This is the VB 6.0 user interface form that you're going to step through in debug mode. You should see in Solution Explorer that this form has been added to the solution in its own category titled "Solution Items." If you now double-click this form in Solution Explorer, a Source window opens showing the VB 6.0 code that makes up the form. Add a breakpoint to line 28 (the start of the **DebugTest_Click** method) in the FormInterop.frm source window, and finally press F5 to start the application.

When you click the button on the VB 6.0 form, the debugger will break into the VB 6.0 source code at line 28, where you placed your breakpoint. Now single-step through the code. On line 32, the debugger will jump from the unmanaged VB 6.0 world to the managed VB .NET world, to execute the VB .NET class constructor. When you single-step to the end of the constructor, you can see something interesting. The debugger refuses to step back to the unmanaged world, unless you place another breakpoint in the VB 6.0 code. So the debugger doesn't reach line 32 in the VB 6.0 code, but instead stops single-stepping completely and runs the program until the result of the method call is displayed on the command button. At the time of this writing, this is a known COM Interop debugging problem with stepping into VB .NET class constructors, although it may have been fixed by the time that you read this. The only workaround I've found is to add breakpoints in the VB 6.0 and/or VB .NET code at the places where I want the debugger to stop the program flow. You should be aware that a .NET class must have a public default constructor if you want to use it from VB 6.0, but you shouldn't step into this constructor while debugging.

Now that I've shown you this issue, you should remove the breakpoint on line 28 of the VB 6.0 code and instead add a new breakpoint at line 32. By not telling the debugger to step into the VB .NET class constructor, you should find that stepping between managed and unmanaged code is much more stable. Press F5 to start the application again and click the button. The debugger now stops on line 32 and you can step into the VB .NET method and then back into the VB 6.0 code after the method call has completed. If you continue to single-step after **End Sub** on line 36 of the VB 6.0 code, you may find that the debugger steps into assembly code in the Disassembly window. This is because there are no more lines of source code for the debugger to step through, so it presents the VB 6.0 assembly code instead. Just press F5 to tell the debugger to stop single-stepping and the result of the method call is displayed on the command button.

As you can see from the two examples just presented, it's very easy to debug your COM Interop projects just like your pure VB .NET projects. As long as you keep in mind the minor caveats that I've mentioned, you can almost ignore the type of code that's being debugged. The rest of this chapter covers situations where COM Interop problems are somewhat more complex.

Overcoming COM Versioning Problems

Most VB 6.0 developers are only too familiar with COM interface and binary compatibility issues when maintaining VB 6.0 classes. Commonly known as DLL Hell, these problems arise because developers need to change or extend COM interfaces after they've been distributed and are already in use by client applications. In the .NET world, there are mechanisms to allow you to alter component interfaces at will without dire consequences, but when you have COM Interop projects, you're back to dealing with interface versioning issues again. More specifically, when you expose a VB .NET class to a VB 6.0 application, you need to understand how to keep the client and server synchronized.

If you look at the **MathClass** class in the **InteropDemo** VB .NET project, you can see that the class is marked with the attribute **<ClassInterface(ClassInterfaceType.AutoDual)>**. If you try removing this attribute, rebuilding the VB .NET solution, and then rereferencing the VB .NET component in its VB 6.0 host application, you'll see that the VB 6.0 IntelliSense no longer shows the VB .NET method or its parameters. In addition, the VB 6.0 object browser will no longer show the VB .NET method. The code will carry on working as before, but developer productivity in COM Interop situations is likely to plummet without the help of the VB 6.0 object browser and IntelliSense. So why doesn't the VB .NET compiler include this seemingly essential attribute by default?

If you recall from my earlier discussion of the differences between the managed and unmanaged worlds, COM only works with interfaces, whereas .NET has an object-based view of the world. By default, the VB .NET compiler adds a **ClassInterface** attribute with a type of **AutoDispatch** to any VB .NET class marked for COM Interop. This automatically generates a dispatch-only class interface for COM clients to consume. This type of class interface omits the interface description from the resulting type library. This means that Visual Studio (or **Regasm**) doesn't publish any type information for the exposed methods. Listing 11-2 shows the type library that the **OleView** utility shows is produced by Visual Studio (or **Regasm**) for the **MathClass** class with a **ClassInterface** attribute of **AutoDispatch**. As you can see, it shows no information about the class method and its parameters.

Listing 11-2. Type Library Information with a ClassInterface Attribute of AutoDispatch

```
[
    uuid(E3F24144-AD11-3282-8347-B1AF8D277B1B),
    hidden,
    dual,
    custom(0F21F359-AB84-41E8-9A78-36D110E6D2F9, InteropDemo.MathClass)
]
dispinterface _MathClass {
    properties:
    methods:
};
```

The benefit of this approach is that it doesn't break late-bound VB 6.0 (or other COM) clients when you modify the VB .NET component, because information about the component is retrieved dynamically at runtime rather than at compile time.

The drawback of using a **ClassInterface** of **AutoDispatch** is that VB clients of the component can only do late binding to the .NET class, as there's no interface description in the type library. Hence, the VB 6.0 object browser and IntelliSense are blind to the class methods. Although this approach gives you some flexibility in modifying your .NET classes, it means that you'll encounter the standard problems with late binding: no compile-time checking and slower performance. The lack of compile-time checks means that you won't see any problems involved with calls into the VB .NET component until the method calls actually execute, which means a significant likelihood of runtime bugs in your code.

Overriding the COM Interop default by setting the **ClassInterface** attribute explicitly to **AutoDual**, as I did in the second example application, gives you back the benefits of early binding. You can see the methods and method arguments in the VB 6.0 object browser and IntelliSense, and the compiler can check your method calls before your code starts to run. Listing 11-3 shows the **OleView** listing of the type library produced by Visual Studio (or **Regasm**) for the **MathClass** class, which has a **ClassInterface** attribute of **AutoDual**. As you can see, it shows full information about the class method and its parameters.

Listing 11-3. Type Library Information with a ClassInterface Attribute of AutoDual

```
[
    uuid(04EFAF41-9530-3EA1-BFAE-7B2655428B28),
    hidden,
    dual,
    nonextensible,
    custom(0F21F359-AB84-41E8-9A78-36D110E6D2F9, InteropDemo.MathClass)
]
```

```
dispinterface _MathClass {
    properties:
    methods:
        [id(00000000), propget,
          custom(54FC8F55-38DE-4703-9C4E-250351302B1C, 1)]
        BSTR ToString();
        [id(0x60020001)]
        VARIANT_BOOL Equals([in] VARIANT obj);
        [id(0x60020002)]
        long GetHashCode();
        [id(0x60020003)]
        _Type* GetType();
        [id(0x60020004)]
        double AddTwoNumbers(
                        [in] double FirstNumber,
                        [in] double SecondNumber);
};
```

Unfortunately, this early binding convenience comes at the cost of breaking the interface between the VB 6.0 application and the VB .NET component every time that you change your VB .NET component, regardless of whether you change the actual interface. For instance, adding a new method to the class interface causes the type library to be regenerated with the methods potentially in a different order and using completely different dispatch IDs. This breaks both early-bound and late-bound COM clients, and it means that any change to the VB .NET component requires a recompilation of every VB 6.0 client of that component.

The recommended way of allowing early binding in this situation while still being able to handle versioning issues is to set the **ClassInterface** attribute explicitly to **None**, and factor the public interface methods into a completely separate interface that is then implemented by the .NET component. Listing 11-4 shows how you could do this for the **MathClass** class. Compare this with Listing 11-1 to see the changes.

Listing 11-4. VB .NET Can Combine COM Early Binding with Good COM Versioning

```
Option Strict On
Imports System.Runtime.InteropServices


Public Interface IMathClass
    Function AddTwoNumbers(ByVal FirstNumber As Double, _
                            ByVal SecondNumber As Double) As Double
End Interface
```

```
<ClassInterface(ClassInterfaceType.None)> _
Public Class MathClass : Implements IMathClass

    Public Sub New()
    End Sub

    Public Function AddTwoNumbers(ByVal FirstNumber As Double, _
                            ByVal SecondNumber As Double) As Double _
                            Implements IMathClass.AddTwoNumbers
        'Return the result to VB6
        Return FirstNumber + SecondNumber
    End Function

End Class
```

The separation of the interface from its implementation means that Visual Studio or **Regasm** will generate a dispatch-only interface for the **IMathClass** interface and not generate any COM interface for the implementation class. Now you're free to change the code within the implementing class without breaking the interface. Although this is slightly more work, it allows COM early binding together with flexibility to change the .NET component without breaking the interface. This is likely to mean fewer bugs, more stable code, and better developer productivity. Listing 11-5 shows the type library produced for the source code shown in Listing 11-4. Notice that **IMathClass** is now the default interface for the .NET component.

Listing 11-5. Type Library Information with a Separately-Implemented Interface

```
[
  odl,
  uuid(F7826BDD-938F-3BD5-9D4F-7C8D95DE5C4C),
  version(1.0),
  dual,
  oleautomation,
  custom(0F21F359-AB84-41E8-9A78-36D110E6D2F9, InteropDemo.IMathClass)

]
interface IMathClass : IDispatch {
    [id(0x60020000)]
    HRESULT AddTwoNumbers(
                    [in] double FirstNumber,
                    [in] double SecondNumber,
                    [out, retval] double* pRetVal);
};
```

So as a final reminder of how to handle COM versioning when writing COM Interop applications, this list summarizes the advantages and disadvantages of each way of generating a .NET class interface:

- **ClassInterfaceType.AutoDispatch** is the default. It's friendly about COM versioning, but at the cost of allowing only late-bound COM clients and potential bugs that won't be found until runtime.

- **ClassInterfaceType.AutoDual** allows early-bound COM clients and compile-time checking, but completely ignores COM versioning, meaning that you have to recompile your COM clients every time the VB .NET component is changed.

- **ClassInterfaceType.None** together with a separation of the class interface from its implementation gives you the best of both worlds: early binding and compile-time checking together with the flexibility to change the VB .NET component.

Summary

This chapter first looked at some of the differences between the managed and unmanaged worlds that can help you to understand some of the COM Interop problems that can arise. Then it examined the debugging of COM Interop between a VB 6.0 component and its host VB .NET application followed by a VB .NET component hosted by a VB 6.0 application. Finally, you learned how to reduce problems caused by COM versioning problems when using VB .NET components from VB 6.0 applications.

INTERLUDE

THE LAST BUG

Nearly every developer is obsessive about fixing bugs that have been found in his or her program. There's even a famous aphorism that says no program is ever actually finished, the developer just stops working on it. Sometime in the late 1960s or early 1970s, an aspiring poet decided to commemorate this obsession in entertaining verse. There are various versions of this poem floating about on the Internet, so I've tried to compile the most complete version.

The Last Bug

"But you're out of your mind,"
They said with a shrug
"The customer is happy,
What's one little bug?"

But he was determined
As others went home
He spread out the program
Deserted, alone

The cleaning men came
The room became cluttered
With memory dumps
"I'm close now," he muttered

Chain-smoking, cold coffee,
With logic, deduction,
"I've got it!" he cried
"Just change this instruction!"

Then change two, then change more
As day followed night
There was a solution
He would get it right

It still wasn't perfect
As year followed year
And strangers would comment
"Is that guy still here?"

He died at the console
Of hunger and thirst
Next day he was buried
Face down, nine edge first

His wife, through her tears
Accepted his fate
"He's not really gone,
He's just working late."

And the last bug in sight
An ant passing by
Saluted his tombstone
And whispered "Nice try!"

SQL Server Debugging

WHEN I FIRST CAME face-to-face with a real relational database engine (Sybase) in the early 1990s, I couldn't see what all the fuss was about. I was accustomed to FoxPro and its built-in database, and a relational database driven from a Unix command line didn't have many attractions. It took a while for me to realize just how powerful this new paradigm was.

Today, SQL Server, Sybase, Oracle, and other relational databases have proved their worth beyond doubt. I simply can't imagine building an enterprise-level application without Structured Query Language (SQL), stored procedures, triggers, constraints, and all of the other database development aids. There are even claims that the next version of SQL Server will allow stored procedures to be written using any .NET language and then executed within the CLR.

As an increasing amount of business and data transformation logic comes to live in stored procedures, and these stored procedures become more complex and have multiple execution paths, it's important to be able to trace exactly what's happening in the depths of your SQL code. Although it's taken a while for the debugging tools to catch up with the development tools, Visual Studio .NET finally brings a grown-up debugger to SQL Server development.

Debugging Requirements

Because SQL Server debugging is quite pedantic in its requirements, you should perhaps read this section rather carefully. Here are the basic version and compatibility requirements:

- The database must be SQL Server 6.5 (Service Pack 3 [SP3] or later), SQL Server 7.0, or SQL Server 2000.

- The database server must be running Windows NT 4.0 or later.

- The application that you're debugging must be using the managed data adapter for SQL Server.

- You must be using OLE DB, ODBC, or DB-LIB as the database connection protocol.

- The desktop edition of SQL Server 2000 can be debugged using the Professional version (or higher) of Visual Studio .NET.

- The full edition of SQL Server needs the Enterprise Developer or Enterprise Architect version of Visual Studio.

- If you can't see stored procedures in Visual Studio's Server Explorer window, it's likely that you're trying to debug the full edition of SQL Server with only the Professional version of Visual Studio—this won't work.

- Although Query Analyzer 2000 has a new built-in debugging feature, which incidentally works when used with either SQL Server 7.0 or SQL Server 2000, Query Analyzer 7.0 doesn't have this feature.

One important point to consider is that it isn't advisable to debug a production database server. Single-stepping through a stored procedure can cause the debugger to lock system resources that are needed by other SQL Server processes, which could cause nasty production problems.

Debugging Installation

Before you can debug SQL Server, you must install the SQL Server debugging components. You can do this either during SQL Server installation or at a later time by using your SQL Server installation media. The debugging components aren't installed by default, but the option to install them is very prominent, as you can see in Figure 12-1.

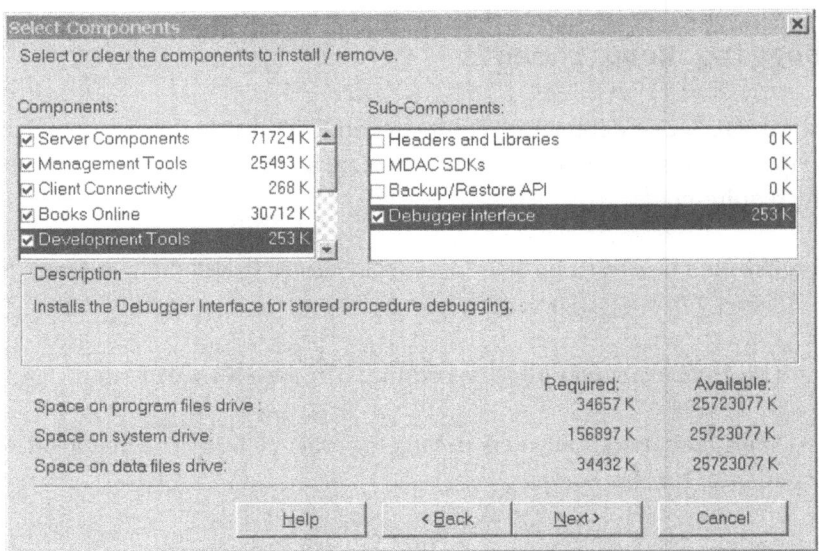

Figure 12-1. Option to install SQL Server debugging components

If you're having trouble setting up the SQL debugging components, you should check for the existence of the following files:

- Sqlle.dll and sqldbreg2.exe must exist on your debugging workstation. The former library is the SQL language engine for the debugger.

- Sqldbg.dll must exist on both the database server and the debugging workstation. This library is the SQL debugging proxy.

- Mssdi98.dll must exist in the \binn subfolder of every SQL Server instance on the database server.

If you're running the full version of SQL Server, Visual Studio installs a version of mssdi98.dll in the appropriate location, correctly overwriting the version that SQL Server installs by default. If you're using the desktop edition of SQL Server 2000 together with the Professional version of Visual Studio, the Professional edition of Visual Studio doesn't install mssdi98.dll in the correct folder. Instead, you need to copy the library manually to the \binn folder of every SQL Server instance on the database server. In addition, if Visual Studio isn't installed on the same machine as the desktop edition of SQL Server, you should copy sqldbg.dll to the following folder on the SQL Server machine:

```
\Program Files\Common Files\Microsoft Shared\SQL Debugging
```

Once you've copied this library to the correct location, you need to register it with the following command at the command line:

```
regsvr32.exe sqldbg.dll
```

Permissions and sp_sdidebug

Any SQL Server user account involved during SQL debugging must have "execute" rights on an extended stored procedure called **sp_sdidebug**, a right that only the system administrator account (sa) has by default. This extended stored procedure seems to be an application programming interface (API) to the previously mentioned mssdi98.dll, though I can't find any publicly available documentation for it. The *sdi* in the stored procedure's name stands for *SQL debugging interface*.

Whether the SQL Server account belongs to a developer who is debugging via Visual Studio's Server Explorer window or using Query Analyzer, or the account is the one specified in the SQL Server connection string used by an application, you need to establish that this account is permitted to execute **sp_sdidebug**. To check this, use the account to log onto the SQL Server and then type the following SQL command using Query Analyzer or any other tool of your choice:

```
EXEC master..sp_sdidebug
```

You'll see either a result stating that the command completed successfully or an execute permission error. If you see the latter result, you should also check that the account has permission to the *master* database itself. It's not unknown for a DBA to give permission to the stored procedure, but not to the *master* database. The quickest way to grant execution rights for a SQL Server account to **sp_sdidebug** is to enter the following SQL using a tool such as Query Analyzer:

```
GRANT EXECUTE
ON sp_sdidebug
TO SpecificAccountName
```

Another permission issue with **sp_sdidebug** can occur with SQL Server running under Windows NT 4.0. Some NT 4.0 configurations have the SQL Server service set to run using the *System* account, which doesn't have permission to execute the **sp_sdidebug** stored procedure. To make this work, you can change the user that runs the SQL Server service. You can do this by going to the service configuration screen, clicking the Start button, and selecting Settings ➢ Control Panel ➢ Services ➢ MSSQLServer ➢ Properties. Then go to the Startup section and change the Logon account from System to a specified user account that you know is allowed to execute the aforementioned stored procedure. Once again, this workaround is only necessary if you have SQL Server running under Windows NT 4.0.

Finally, if you've installed SQL Server SP3, then you'll encounter a new security switch that was added as a part of SP3. This switch only affects SQL debugging from a client application, not SQL debugging directly from Visual Studio. To gain permission for SQL debugging with SP3, you have to execute the following additional command:

```
EXEC master..sp_sdidebug 'legacy_on'
```

Unfortunately, this setting isn't persistent, so you'll need to re-execute the command if you reboot your SQL Server.

Remote Debugging Permissions

Remote SQL Server debugging is done using Distributed Component Object Model (DCOM), and this can be tricky to configure properly. First, you need to install the full remote debugging components on the remote machine using the Visual Studio CD. You may also need to repeat this process every time the SQL

Server is upgraded with a service pack or a patch. Then you must configure DCOM on the SQL Server machine to allow a remote user to attach the debugger to a process on the SQL Server machine. To do this, you should follow the instructions in the SDK documentation, as the procedure is different for each operating system. You can find this documentation at `ms-help://MS.VSCC/MS.MSDNVS/vsdebug/html/vxtskconfiguringdcomforsqldebugging.htm`. For more information about installing and using remote debugging, please see Chapter 15.

Direct Debugging with Visual Studio

This section looks at debugging a stored procedure directly from Visual Studio, using either Server Explorer or the Source window. Server Explorer presents the same sort of SQL Server views as Enterprise Manager, but it has the benefit of being integrated into Visual Studio. To debug a stored procedure from Server Explorer, you first need to navigate to that stored procedure. Click the Server node in the Server Explorer window and follow the resulting tree down through the SQL Servers node to the server and database that you require. Finally, click the Stored Procedures node and choose the stored procedure that you wish to debug. Figure 12-2 shows how this looks within Visual Studio.

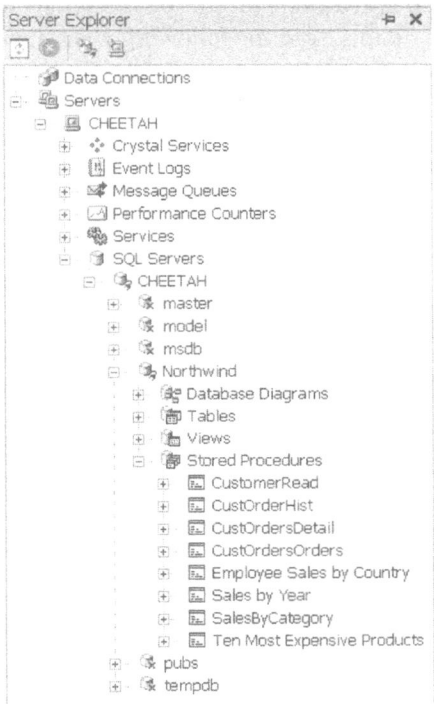

Figure 12-2. Using Server Explorer to work with SQL Server

For the purposes of this demonstration, choose the Northwind database on your favorite development server. This database ships with almost every SQL Server installation, so you should find it available. The stored procedure in this database that you're going to debug is called **SalesByCategory**. Right-click this stored procedure and choose Step Into Stored Procedure from the context menu. Because the **SalesByCategory** stored procedure has two parameters, you're now presented with a dialog window asking you to enter these parameters. Because you don't know any good values to enter at this stage, click the Cancel button. Although the stored procedure isn't executed after you click Cancel, the text of the stored procedure is presented in a new tab of the Source window.

You can also see that the Visual Studio IDE has now been given a new menu entitled Database. This menu contains options that allow you to create a new database entity such as a stored procedure or table. But the most interesting menu option is the one entitled Run Selection. The Visual Studio IDE normally allows you to execute only a complete stored procedure, but this option allows you to write an ad hoc script, place the script in any window that displays a stored procedure, select the script by highlighting it, and then execute it. This innocuous menu option is very useful for testing ad hoc scripts or checking part of a stored procedure.

Coming back to the **SalesByCategory** stored procedure, you can see that the **CategoryName** parameter will be compared to a column of the same name in the Categories table. So to find a value for this parameter, you need to see the contents of this table. To do this, type the following query just below the stored procedure text:

```
SELECT  *
FROM  Categories
```

Highlight the query by selecting it and then choose the Run Selection menu option from the Database menu. The result is a list showing all the rows in the Categories table displayed in the Database Output pane of Visual Studio's Output window.

As a sidebar, there are two other ways to look for suitable values from the Categories table. One method is to right-click the table in Server Explorer and choose the Retrieve Data from Table menu option. This displays every row from the table in a new tab of the Source window. The messier option, which is most useful if you need to create more complex ad hoc SQL queries, is to right-click in the Source window tab displaying the stored procedure and choose Insert SQL from the context menu. This adds yet another Source window tab that shows the Query Builder utility, which is similar to the Query Builder built into Microsoft Access. Close the resulting Add Table dialog window and also close the top two window panes of the Query Builder tab by right-clicking in them and choosing the Hide Pane menu option. These panes allow you to build SQL queries graphically and you don't need them for this simple query. Now you can enter the same query that I mentioned previously and execute the query by clicking the toolbar button marked with an exclamation mark. This displays all the rows in the Categories table in the results pane of the Query Builder tab.

Whichever way you choose to show the contents of the Categories table, now you can pick a value from the CategoryName column to be used as a parameter to the **SalesByCategory** stored procedure. Select the value Beverages from the query results CategoryName column by double-clicking the value and pressing Ctrl-C (to copy it to the clipboard). Go back to Server Explorer, choose the Step Into Stored Procedure option again, and this time press Ctrl-V to paste the just-copied value as the **CategoryName** parameter of the stored procedure. Finally, click the OK button, and the debugger will step to the first statement of the stored procedure.

If you hover the mouse over the **@OrdYear** and **@CategoryName** variables, you can see that it reports their values. Switch to the Database Output pane of Visual Studio's Output window, and you can see that it reports the name and parameters of the stored procedure being executed. However, if you highlight the expression **@OrdYear != '1997'** on line 4 and do a **QuickWatch** command, you can see that the debugger is unable to evaluate this SQL expression. Although the debugger can report on the value of most variables, it's not able to evaluate SQL expressions. One of the side effects of this is that conditional expression breakpoints aren't available when debugging SQL. Figure 12-3 shows the stored procedure being debugged.

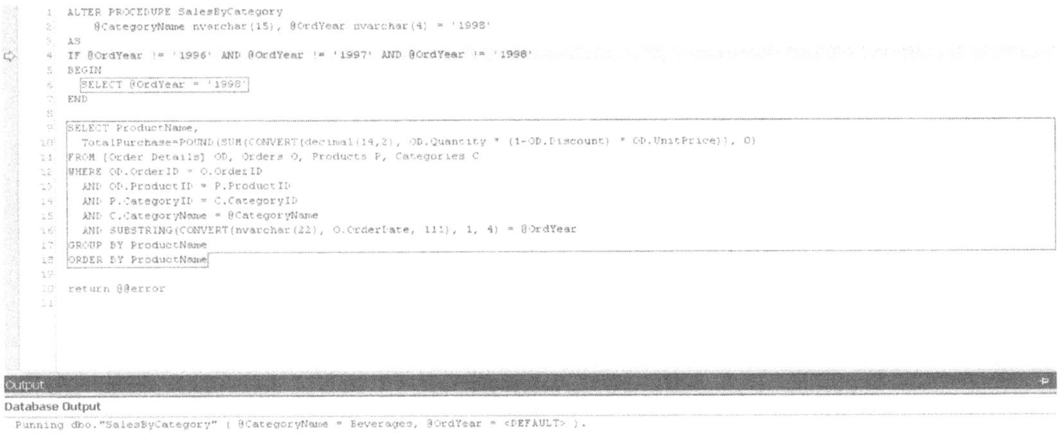

```
1   ALTER PROCEDURE SalesByCategory
2       @CategoryName nvarchar(15), @OrdYear nvarchar(4) = '1998'
3   AS
4   IF @OrdYear != '1996' AND @OrdYear != '1997' AND @OrdYear != '1998'
5   BEGIN
6       SELECT @OrdYear = '1998'
7   END
8
9   SELECT ProductName,
10      TotalPurchase=ROUND(SUM(CONVERT(decimal(14,2), OD.Quantity * (1-OD.Discount) * OD.UnitPrice)), 0)
11  FROM [Order Details] OD, Orders O, Products P, Categories C
12  WHERE OD.OrderID = O.OrderID
13      AND OD.ProductID = P.ProductID
14      AND P.CategoryID = C.CategoryID
15      AND C.CategoryName = @CategoryName
16      AND SUBSTRING(CONVERT(nvarchar(22), O.OrderDate, 111), 1, 4) = @OrdYear
17  GROUP BY ProductName
18  ORDER BY ProductName
19
20  return @@error
21
```

Output

Database Output

Running dbo."SalesByCategory" (@CategoryName = Beverages, @OrdYear = <DEFAULT>).

Figure 12-3. Debugging the SalesByCategory stored procedure

Now you can step to the next statement in the stored procedure, which selects rows matching the procedure's parameter values from several tables. One important distinction to make here is the difference between a select statement that returns a result set from a stored procedure and a select statement that alters variables local to a stored procedure (i.e., those prefixed with an at [@] symbol). The distinction is that only local variables can be viewed in the debugger, not result sets. A select statement that produces a result set, such as the one in this stored procedure, doesn't return variables. The result set columns that you see are just column names acting as placeholders for the values that will be returned in the result set.

If you step through to the end of the stored procedure, you can view the result set produced by the select statement by looking in the Database Output pane of Visual Studio's Output window.

Direct Debugging with Query Analyzer

Using the Query Analyzer application that comes with SQL Server 2000, you can debug stored procedures running on either SQL Server 2000 or SQL Server 7.0. I'm not going to spend any time discussing this because it's not .NET related, but it's useful to know at least one neat debugging trick that you can perform with Query Analyzer that I haven't seen available elsewhere. The **Auto Rollback** command lets you automatically roll back all work performed by a stored procedure that you've been debugging. Apart from this, the debugger provides you with its own window that contains separate output panes for local variables (those prefixed with @), global variables (those prefixed with @@), the call stack, and the result of the query.

Application Debugging

Although debugging SQL directly using Visual Studio or Query Analyzer is very useful, the most usual scenario involves debugging an application that's already written and that makes SQL Server calls from within its code. This section investigates SQL debugging from the point of view of an application running within Visual Studio and then the same application executing outside of Visual Studio.

Application Debugging Setup

Before investigating this example, you need to run the SQL setup script that accompanies this chapter. The first part of the script defines two tables, which are declared as shown in Listing 12-1. You'll use the table DebugTest as a test bed for inserting rows using a stored procedure, and the table DebugError will record any errors that happen while the stored procedure is executing. Notice the two constraints imposed on the KeyPrimary column of the DebugTest table. You aren't allowed to enter duplicate values into this column and any value that you do enter into this column must be greater than zero.

Listing 12-1. Creating the Test Tables

```
/* Ensure we're in the right database */
USE pubs
GO
/* Build the first table */
CREATE TABLE DebugTest
(
Id int NOT NULL IDENTITY (1,1),
KeyPrimary int NOT NULL PRIMARY KEY CHECK (KeyPrimary > 0)
)
/* Build the second table */
CREATE TABLE DebugError
(
Id int NOT NULL IDENTITY (1,1),
RowsInserted int NOT NULL,
ErrorNumber int NOT NULL,
ProblemValue int NOT NULL
)
```

The second part of the setup script is shown in Listing 12-2. This is the stored procedure that's going to be called by the test application every time it adds a new row to the DebugTest table. The stored procedure attempts to create a new row in the DebugTest table containing the value passed in the **@KeyColumn** parameter, and it then records any error that occurs in the DebugError table.

Listing 12-2. Creating the Test Stored Procedure

```
/* Ensure we're in the right database */
USE pubs
GO
/* Build this stored procedure */
CREATE PROCEDURE sp_DebugExample
    @KeyColumn    int
AS
/* Insert new row using parameter value */
INSERT      DebugTest VALUES(@KeyColumn)
/* Record any row insertion error that occurs */
```

```
IF @@error <> 0
BEGIN
    INSERT    DebugError
                (RowsInserted, ErrorNumber, ProblemValue)
    VALUES    (@@rowcount, @@error, @Keycolumn)
END
GO
```

To build the tables and stored procedure for this debugging example, log into your favorite development SQL Server using a tool such as Query Analyzer, make sure that you're in the pubs database, and then run the setup script. It should report that everything completed successfully.

Application Debugging from Inside Visual Studio

Now load the VB .NET solution named **SqlDebug**. This solution contains the **SqlDebug** project that is going to call the stored procedure that you just built. The user interface for **SqlDebug** is shown in Figure 12-4. The Create connection command button makes a connection to the database, the Insert new row command button executes the stored procedure passing as a parameter the value that you specify in the text box, and the Destroy connection command button closes the database connection. The name of the database server to be used is hard-coded in the code behind the Create connection command button, so you need to alter this setting to correspond to the name of the database server that you wish to use. My database server is called Cheetah, but it's highly unlikely that yours has the same name!

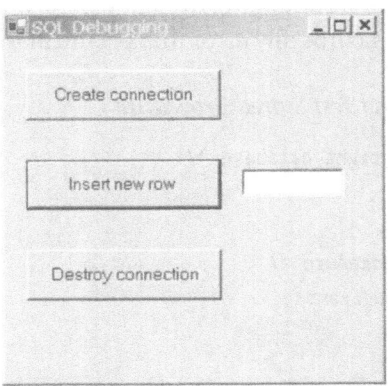

Figure 12-4. The user interface for testing SQL debugging

Before you do any SQL application debugging, you must ensure that you've told the project from which you're making the SQL Server connection that you're going to be doing SQL debugging. To do this, enable the SQL Server debugging option that you can find on the Properties ➤ Configuration Properties ➤ Debugging property page of the **SqlDebug** project. Failure to do this can result in a frustrating hour or two trying to decipher why your stored procedure breakpoints aren't being triggered. If you have another project in your Visual Studio solution from which you want to step into the project that's making the SQL Server connection, you need to enable the SQL Server debugging option for that project too. If you find that your stored procedure breakpoints aren't working during application debugging, these two option settings are the usual culprits.

Now prepare for debugging by using Server Explorer to connect to your favored database server and navigating to the **sp_DebugExample** stored procedure in the pubs database. Double-clicking the procedure opens a new tab in the Source window that displays the stored procedure's SQL code.

To start, run the application without adding any breakpoints in the stored procedure. Click the Create connection command button to make the database connection, and then specify the number **1** in the text box and click the Insert new row command button. Do this a few times, making sure that you enter a different nonzero number into the text box every time, without repeating any numbers. Then enter the following ad hoc query underneath the stored procedure:

```
SELECT  *
FROM  DebugTest
```

If you select this query and choose the Run Selection option from the Database menu, you should see a listing of the rows that you've just inserted into the DebugTest table. So far, everything looks fine, so delete the ad hoc query that you just entered.

Now enter a number into the text box that you've already used, and click the Insert new row command button again. This time you'll see an error indicating that you've violated the unique constraint on the primary key. Answer OK to this error message and then enter a new ad hoc query underneath the stored procedure:

```
SELECT  *
FROM  DebugError
```

If you execute this query as described previously, you can see that a row has been added to the DebugError table to reflect the problem that you just encountered. The only interesting fact is that the ErrorNumber column has a value of zero, which definitely doesn't look right. So now you have to debug the stored procedure to order to establish why it's not populating the ErrorNumber column with the correct value of the global variable **@@error** (2627 in this example).

Place a breakpoint at line 11 of the stored procedure. This is necessary because you can't step into a stored procedure from code; instead, you must use a breakpoint to trigger debugging. Then click the Insert new row command button again, using the same text box value as before. This time the debugger should stop on the breakpoint that you defined. Here you can check the **@@error** variable, which you can see is clearly nonzero. If you're using SQL Server 7.0 rather than SQL Server 2000, you won't be able to see the value of **@@error**, because version 7.0 unfortunately doesn't support most global variables. But as you can see from the path taken through the code, the value of **@@error** is definitely nonzero at this stage.

If you step forward one line, you can see that the value of **@@error** is now zero. What the original developer of this stored procedure overlooked is that when line 11 executes successfully the **@@error** variable is reset to zero. In fact, the only SQL statement that doesn't reset **@@error** is a declare statement. This is why the DebugError row insertion is inserting zero for the ErrorNumber column.

To fix this problem, you need to save the value of **@@error** before doing anything else. The corrected version of the **sp_DebugExample** stored procedure should look something like the code shown in Listing 12-3.

Listing 12-3. The Corrected Stored Procedure

```
/* Ensure we're in the right database */
USE pubs
GO
/* Build this stored procedure */
ALTER PROCEDURE sp_DebugExample
    @KeyColumn    int
AS
    Declare @error int,
            @rowcount int
/* Insert new row using parameter value */
INSERT    DebugTest VALUES(@KeyColumn)
/* Save global variable state so that we don't lose it */
SELECT    @error = @@error,
            @rowcount = @@rowcount
/* Record any row insertion error that occurs */
IF @error <> 0
BEGIN
    INSERT  DebugError
                (RowsInserted, ErrorNumber, ProblemValue)
    VALUES  (@rowcount, @error, @Keycolumn)
END
GO
```

After you've changed and recompiled the stored procedure, you'll need to close its Source window tab and load it again from Server Explorer if you want to continue debugging it. This time you should see that the new **@error** local variable contains the correct error number (2627) and that the ErrorNumber column is now populated correctly. As you can see, debugging a SQL stored procedure that's called from your application code is seamless, and you can step through SQL just like any other code. There are some specific debugging limitations with SQL, a list of which is presented later in this chapter.

Application Debugging from Outside Visual Studio

There are several cases where you might want to debug an application that uses SQL Server without having the application running within Visual Studio. For instance, you may be debugging a distributed application where the managed code is running on a machine different from your development machine and the SQL Server that it's using is on a separate database server. To debug this type of application, you need Visual Studio to attach to the managed process so that you can hitch a ride into SQL Server.

Restart the SqlDebug application without debugging, so that you won't hit any breakpoints. You do this by starting the application by pressing Ctrl-F5 rather than pressing just the F5 key. To prove that debugging isn't active, add a breakpoint anywhere in the **sp_DebugExample** stored procedure. Now when you use the application to connect to the database and insert a new row, you should see that the breakpoint isn't triggered.

Disconnect from the database using the Destroy connection command button. It's important that you disconnect before attaching a debugger, because you can't debug a SQL Server connection that's already active. Once the database connection has been closed, choose the Processes menu option from Visual Studio's Debug menu and locate the SqlDebug.exe process in this window. Select the process and click the Attach button. When the Attach dialog window appears, be sure to select both Common Language Runtime and Microsoft T-SQL as the program types that you want to debug. Once you've clicked the OK button, you should see SqlDebug.exe in the bottom pane of the Processes window. Now when you use the application to make the database connection and insert a new row, your breakpoint should be hit normally, showing that debugging is active. To detach from the process when you've finished debugging, click the executable in the bottom subwindow of the Processes dialog window and click the Detach button.

SQL Debugging Limitations

You've already seen a few of the limitations of SQL debugging, but here's a more comprehensive list. Most of these limitations are related to the way that SQL works and are therefore not that onerous.

- SQL supports hit count breakpoints, but not conditional expression breakpoints. This is because the debugger is unable to evaluate SQL expressions, as I discussed previously in the first debugging example.

- The Registers and Memory windows aren't supported and therefore can't be used. This is because SQL doesn't support true memory or processor registers.

- You can't use the **Set Next Statement** command to alter the current execution point or execution sequence. This is because SQL doesn't use the conventional stack frame techniques that a debugger normally exploits to perform this trick.

- You can't step into a stored procedure from managed or unmanaged code. Instead, you need to set a breakpoint within the stored procedure.

- Contrary to popular belief, you can use the **Run To Cursor** command in the Source window, but you can't use it in the Call Stack window.

- You can't use the **Break** command to halt a lengthy SQL statement while it's executing.

- The output from a SQL PRINT statement disappears into nowhere as far as the debugger is concerned. It doesn't appear in any place that you might expect if you ever used the Visual InterDev debugger, such as the Debug or Database Output panes of Visual Studio's Output window.

- Any error raised using a RAISERROR statement also disappears as far as the debugger is concerned, being nowhere to be found in the Output window.

- In SQL Server 7.0, you can't see the values of most of the global variables, for instance **@@error** or **@@rowcount**. The one global variable that you can view is **@@identity**. You can overcome this limitation easily using the storage technique recommended previously in the debugging of the **sp_DebugExample** stored procedure.

- You can't debug triggers directly. Instead, you need the stored procedure to cause the trigger to execute, whereupon you can step into the trigger.

- When SQL Server creates an execution plan for a stored procedure, it often caches variables, such as parameters to the procedure, which it doesn't believe will change over the course of the procedure. If you use the debugger to change the value of a variable that's been cached, SQL Server may well not use the new value, preferring instead to use the value from its cache. After you've changed the value of a variable with the debugger, you should check that the variable really has been set to its new value.

- If you pause on a SQL statement for a significant amount of time, you may see a time-out on the database connection. If the connection is being made using **SqlDataAdapter**, the debugger will continue despite the time-out, but debugging will end if the connection was made via **OleDbDataAdapter**. Both **SqlDataAdapter** and **OleDbDataAdapter** have a statement time-out that you can set on the **Adapter** command object. To increase the length of the time-out when using **OleDbDataAdapter**, you should change the value in the **.CommandTimeout** property of the **OleDbCommand** object.

- Debugging a stored procedure may not work more than once if connection pooling is being used, which is the default behavior. *Connection pooling* attempts to improve performance by keeping old database connections in a pool for potential reuse later. However, if a database connection is reused, SQL debugging is not re-enabled on that connection. To avoid this limitation, you can disable pooling by setting the **Pooling** switch in the database connection string to **false**.

Most of these debugging limitations aren't significant, but they're useful to know when one of them suddenly bites you. The really unfortunate limitations are the disappearing output from PRINT and RAISERROR statements, as there's no good way of seeing these values when debugging with Visual Studio.

Understanding SQL Security

For many corporations, their relational databases represent the accumulation of months and often years of hard-earned data, and these databases are usually guarded by a veritable army of highly paid database administrators (DBAs). As a SQL developer, you need to understand some SQL security issues so you don't create security bugs that can jeopardize the integrity of these databases.

As an example, what's wrong with an application that uses the following SQL connection string, taken almost directly from the .NET **SqlConnection** documentation?

```
ConnectString = "user id=sa;password=Jx$442pt;
initial catalog=pubs;data source=mySQLServer"
```

The security bug here is the use of system administrator (sa) as the SQL Server login for the application. The system administrator in this context can do almost anything that he or she wants to the database. If your end user or another developer manages to hijack your application in some way, your database could be in serious trouble. Tables could be dropped, data could be deleted or corrupted, or any other of a host of painful scenarios would be possible.

You might believe that it's not possible to hijack your application, but why take the risk? It's far more secure to either use Windows integrated security for your application's SQL Server login or set up a new user that only has the power to execute specific stored procedures. In this way, you can limit the amount of damage that can be done by a rogue developer or end user who abuses your code in order to find a way into your SQL Server.

It's also easier to hijack an application that uses SQL Server than you might think. Imagine that your program allows its end users to read a database table called AppUser, which contains a list of authorized users of your application. You give the user a text box where he or she enters an identifier for the user whose details he or she wishes to see. Then you take the ID entered by your end user, put it into a variable called **UserId**, and add it to the end of a custom query looking something like this:

```
SqlQuery = "SELECT * FROM AppUser WHERE Id = " & UserId.ToString
```

So when the end user enters something like **2** as the user ID, this query returns all the details for the application user who has the ID of 2. But instead of just entering a user ID, a malicious end user could try entering the following text:

```
2 INSERT AppUser VALUES('Mark', 'Pearce', 'SuperUser')
```

When you add this user-entered string to the end of your SQL query string and then execute the query, you'll suddenly find a new authorized application user in the AppUser table with superuser rights. This technique is called *SQL injection,* and it's a serious danger for any application that performs SQL queries with the help of text entered by the user. To avoid this type of security bug, you should always treat any user input as dangerous and validate the information before using it in a SQL query. In this case, for instance, you could validate that the text entered by your end user was numeric, which would immediately throw out any dangerous SQL injection.

Summary

This chapter started by investigating the software requirements necessary to set up SQL debugging and how to navigate the treacherous security waters that can surround your SQL debugging preparations. Then it looked at debugging a stored procedure directly from Visual Studio before examining how to debug an application that uses SQL Server. It finished with an analysis of the limitations of SQL debugging.

The ability to debug SQL means that the last major obstacle in end-to-end application debugging has been overcome. Although many developers veer away from delving into stored procedures, I would advise that you become accustomed to at least the fundamentals of SQL debugging. It makes understanding your applications much easier when you don't have to treat your database as a black box.

INTERLUDE

HOW NOT TO WRITE CODE

In my Internet travels, I came across a marvelous essay written by Roedy Green, a Canadian software developer. After finding that developers paid no attention when he talked about writing maintainable code, he decided instead to write about developing *unmaintainable* code. In a detailed and very humorous article, he shows his readers how to write code that is so difficult to understand that nobody but the author has a chance of maintaining it, thus guaranteeing employment for life.

Although the essay specifically targets Java, many of its points transfer directly to VB .NET. So with Roedy's kind permission, here are some excerpts from his article that deal with variable naming and scoping. You can find the full text of the article at **http://mindprod.com/unmain.html**. It's well worth reading the whole essay if you want to understand and avoid many common maintenance problems.

"To foil the maintenance programmer, you have to understand how he thinks. He has your giant program. He has no time to read it all, much less understand it. He wants to rapidly find the place to make his change, make it and get out and have no unexpected side effects from the change.

"He views your code through a toilet paper tube. He can only see a tiny piece of your program at a time. You want to make sure he can never get at the big picture from doing that. You want to make it as hard as possible for him to find the

355

code he is looking for. But even more important, you want to make it as awkward as possible for him to safely *ignore* anything.

"Much of the skill in writing unmaintainable code is the art of naming variables and methods. They don't matter at all to the compiler. That gives you huge latitude to use them to befuddle the maintenance programmer.

"Buy a copy of a baby-naming book and you'll never be at a loss for variable names. **Fred** is a wonderful name, and easy to type. If you're looking for easy-to-type variable names, try **adsf** or **aoeu** if you type with a DSK keyboard.

"If you call your variables a, b, c, then it will be impossible to search for instances of them using a simple text editor. Further, nobody will be able to guess what they are for. If anyone even hints at breaking the tradition honoured since FORTRAN of using **i**, **j**, and **k** for indexing variables, namely replacing them with **ii**, **jj** and **kk**, warn them about what the Spanish Inquisition did to heretics.

"If you must use descriptive variable and function names, misspell them. By misspelling in some function and variable names, and spelling it correctly in others (such as **SetPintleOpening SetPintalClosing**) we effectively negate the use of grep or IDE search techniques. It works amazingly well. Add an international flavor by spelling **tory** or **tori** in different theatres/theaters.

"In naming functions and variables, make heavy use of abstract words like *it*, *everything*, *data*, *handle*, *stuff*, *do*, *routine*, *perform* and the digits e.g. **routineX48**, **PerformDataFunction**, **DoIt**, **HandleStuff** and **do_args_method**.

"Randomly capitalize the first letter of a syllable in the middle of a word. For example: **ComputeRasterHistoGram()**.

"Extended ASCII characters are perfectly valid as variable names, including **ß**, **ð**, and **ñ** characters. They are almost impossible to type without copying/pasting in a simple text editor.

"Choose variable names that masquerade as mathematical operators, e.g.:

```
openParen = (slash + asterix) / equals
```

"Choose variable names with irrelevant emotional connotation, e.g.:

```
marypoppins = (superman + starship) / god
```

"This confuses the reader because they have difficulty disassociating the emotional connotations of the words from the logic they're trying to think about.

"Declare a global array in module **A**, and a private one of the same name in module **B**, so that it appears that it's the global array you are using in module **B**, but it isn't. Make no reference in the comments to this duplication.

"Use scoping as confusingly as possible by recycling variable names in contradictory ways. For example, suppose you have global variables **A** and **B**, and functions **foo** and **bar**. If you know that variable **A** will be regularly passed to **foo** and **B** to **bar**, make sure to define the functions as function **foo(B)** and function

bar(A) so that inside the functions **A** will always be referred to as **B** and vice versa. With more functions and globals, you can create vast confusing webs of mutually contradictory uses of the same names.

"Make sure that every method does a little bit more (or less) than its name suggests. As a simple example, a method named **isValid(x)** should as a side effect convert **x** to binary and store the result in a database.

"Use constant names like **LancelotsFavouriteColour** instead of **blue** and assign it hex value of $0204FB. The color looks identical to pure blue on the screen, and a maintenance programmer would have to work out 0204FB (or use some graphic tool) to know what it looks like. Only someone intimately familiar with *Monty Python and the Holy Grail* would know that Lancelot's favorite color was blue. If a maintenance programmer can't quote entire Monty Python movies from memory, he or she has *no* business being a programmer.

"Use very long variable names or class names that differ from each other by only one character, or only in upper/lowercase. An ideal variable name pair is **swimmer** and **swimner**. Exploit the failure of most fonts to clearly discriminate between **ilI1l** or **oO08** with identifier pairs like **parselnt** and **parseInt** or **D0Calc** and **DOCalc**. **l** is an exceptionally fine choice for a variable name since it will, to the casual glance, masquerade as the constant **1**. In many fonts **rn** looks like an **m**. So how about a variable **swirnrner**? Create variable names that differ from each other only in case e.g. **HashTable** and **Hashtable**. (Editorial note: This last trick can be done in C#, but not VB.)

"Although we have one variable named **xy_z**, there's certainly no reason not to have many other variables with similar names, such as **xy_Z**, **xy__z**, **_xy_z**, **_xyz**, **XY_Z**, **xY_z**, and **Xy_z**. Variables that resemble others except for capitalization and underlines have the advantage of confounding those who like remembering names by sound or letter-spelling, rather than by exact representations. (Editorial note: Once again, the capitalization trick can only be done with C#.)"

Part Four

Debugging Common Scenarios

"In the information-overload world we live in as software developers,
selective ignorance is the only way to survive."
—*Don Box*

Error Handling and Exception Management

Bad error handling and exception management can rapidly undermine user confidence in your software product or application, and even in your company. The average end user is becoming increasingly sophisticated in her expectations of your software. She knows that properly coded software doesn't crash and burn, lose her work, or leave her stranded facing an error message bleating feebly about "Action aborted due to file specification error." She wants a stable and polite application that doesn't blame her for every nervous breakdown suffered by the software. Most of all, she wants error handling that supplies her with the right type of information to help her complete whatever task she's trying to accomplish.

This puts a big responsibility upon us as developers to understand why and where our applications can go wrong, and to create an error-handling framework that helps our end users to accomplish their tasks and helps the support staff and maintenance developers to diagnose and find problems as quickly and easily as possible. Good exception management is important because error-handling code is a frequent cause of bugs and because bad error handling can kill your application.

The first section of this chapter suggests some ideas about what you should be trying to achieve with an error-handling scheme. The second section looks in detail at exceptions, exception management, and error handling in VB .NET, with some surprises along the way. The final section investigates unhandled exceptions and some other advanced exception management techniques.

Exceptions vs. Errors

Before I start the chapter proper, I think it's worth discussing a subtle distinction in terminology. Exceptions and errors aren't synonymous; in other words, they're different creatures. Exceptions can be used to signal errors (such as division by zero), unexpected events (for instance, the printer running out of paper), and violations of an interface's assumptions (for example, passing a parameter with a negative value when the interface expects a positive value). Although each of these three exceptions could be called an error from the point of view of the method that throws the exception, it's the developer writing the code calling the method who really knows what he or she expects and who therefore defines which of these exceptions is actually an error from the point of view of the application as a whole.

For example, a method that performs a printing task might throw an exception because the printer is out of paper, but if the code that calls that method has been programmed correctly, this would be an expected event, not an error at all. The exception would just be passed up the call stack before being transformed into a message asking the user to place some more paper in the printer.

This distinction is important because when you design a method or class, you need to decide how you're going to communicate information to the calling method and which exceptions you're going to throw. Say that you've been given the task of designing and implementing a class that validates a user login to an application. In the method that validates the user login, should an exception be thrown when the login fails or should the method return a value of **false** instead?

There is no correct answer to this question. Some developers maintain that a login failure is an error and therefore an exception should be thrown. Other developers reason that a login failure is an expected event and not really an error as far as the application is concerned, therefore the method should return a status variable rather than forcing the calling code to handle an exception. Although in this situation I favor returning a status variable and not throwing an exception, you and your team will have to decide for yourselves how you are going to handle these design decisions.

One point to bear in mind when making these types of decisions is that you, as a designer of a method or class, often don't know what the code that calls your method considers to be an error. If, for instance, you're developing a method that reads information from a file on disk, how should you signal that the calling method has read past the end of the file? Is reading past the end of the file an error or not? Because you don't know what the calling code is doing, you just don't know whether this is an error. In this situation, I would throw an exception because I just can't tell whether the calling code expected to read past the end of the disk file. Another developer might maintain that reading past the end of a file is always a possible occurrence as far as most calling code is concerned, and therefore he would design the method to return an EOF status flag rather than throw an exception.

Another point to bear in mind is that when you're designing methods that are going to be called by other developers, you should think carefully about how you're going to handle permission exceptions. The problem is that a detailed permission exception message might give away too much information to a malicious developer. Hackers frequently probe software in order to find out how it behaves, and you sometimes need to be careful about what information you reveal. As an example, the **System.IO.File.Exists** method in the .NET Framework suppresses any permission exception and instead returns a value of **false**. I think concealing information like this is bad and that the **File.Exists** method should instead return a generic security exception that reveals no dangerous information, but you should think carefully about how your application is going to handle these situations.

The best guidance I can give you is to consider carefully what the typical developer calling your method expects, and make the decision that's likely to cause the least confusion and the smallest surprise factor.

Requirements for Error Handling

Although what developers aim to achieve with their error handling might seem obvious, it's worthwhile to take some time to understand the subtleties of the process. There's far more to error handling than just catching every exception and displaying a message box to the user. Before you can build a general error-handling framework, you need to understand exactly what the requirements are. This section of the chapter discusses the requirements in three areas, based on the three groups of people involved in using and supporting a typical application.

End User Requirements

Remember that the end user is rarely interested in the precise details of a software problem or indeed why the problem happened. He just wants to use your software to accomplish something, and a detailed error message that's helpful to a developer is likely to be useless to the end user. This perspective is alien to most developers, which is why they should be careful about how they communicate a software malfunction to a user. Bearing this in mind, here's a list of ideas for you to think about when writing error-handling code that affects your end user:

- Stop the task that the software is trying to perform. Trying to continue with that task after an application error is more likely to destabilize your application and possibly make the problem worse.

- It's usually better for your application to give no answer than to give a potentially wrong answer. A wrong answer will mislead or confuse the user, especially when he doesn't see a direct link between the error and the answer.

- If at all possible, keep your application stable after an error. This normally means rolling everything back to a known safe state, a task that's made easier when you use the **Try...Catch...Finally** construct that I discuss later. Try to avoid closing your application, as this can be very annoying for a user. Instead, try to structure your code so that it can recover after most errors, at least long enough for the user to complete her task. Unfortunately, as you'll see later, there are a few exceptions that will kill your application completely.

- Don't lose or corrupt the end user's data. Nothing infuriates a user more effectively than losing information that he has spent some time compiling and entering into your application. Saving the user's data after an error can be tricky because the data in memory may have been corrupted by the error and you don't want to risk overwriting the valid information that's already stored. If necessary, save the data in memory to some temporary store to avoid disrupting information saved previously.

- Users don't read anything! Study after study has shown that the majority of users simply don't bother to read that carefully crafted error message that you present to explain the problem that your application encountered. Think of an end user as similar in some ways to your boss. She doesn't want to hear about a problem; she wants to see a solution or workaround.

- If you need to describe the problem to the end user, you should do so in that user's terms and language. Avoid obscure technical jargon, abbreviations, and acronyms.

- Following on from the previous point, try to suggest a solution or workaround to your end user. For example, rather than just presenting an error message saying that your application can't connect to its database, create an e-mail message that explains the problem and is already addressed to the application support group. Then give your user the ability to transmit this e-mail by simply clicking a button. He'll appreciate your helpfulness and come to think of your application as polite and helpful, even when it goes wrong.

Once you've written code to help your users recover from application errors, you should monitor your applications in production to make sure that the information provided is as useful and helpful as possible. You'll often have to add specific advice and workarounds over time to cope with the most common problems experienced by your users.

Operations Support Requirements

The next group of people that you want to help with solving your application's problems is the first-level support department. These are the people tasked with solving the users' day-to-day software problems and with passing on any problems that they can't solve to application or maintenance developers. If they're given the right application support, these people can be invaluable for dealing with most of the routine problems without troubling the developers. Here are some ideas for handling application errors in a way that helps the operational support staff:

- End users are notorious for failing to supply sufficient information about application problems. With some users, a bald statement that your application isn't working, never worked, and resembles a pile of rat droppings may be all the information that the support person receives. If your application actively records copious details about every problem or exception in a central location accessible to the support staff, you can make their job of investigation much easier.

- Think about proactively notifying the support staff when your software experiences a problem, without waiting for the user to complain. For example, sending a message via an instant messaging system is ideal for this task. Doing this provides a dual benefit. First, the allocated support person has a head start in tackling the problem and is aware of the situation even before being contacted by the user. Second, the user will be less unhappy if he knows that a support person is already aware of the problem and may even be investigating it.

- Provide the support staff with an escalation path for resolving the problem if it proves to be intractable. Typically, one or more developers own each component in a software application. The application can inform support staff about who is likely to be the expert in the context of the specific component that's experiencing the error. This can result in quicker and more effective problem resolution.

- Try to avoid flooding the support staff with the same problem many times within a short period. For instance, an application that monitors files within a network folder might find that somebody has changed some file or folder permissions in such a way that the application can no longer view the folder contents effectively. In this case, churning out an error message every time that the security exception is raised, maybe once a second or more, can become very annoying very quickly for the support staff. Either the software should recognize that the same exception is occurring ac infinitum and suppress its own error output for a while, or you could provide a way in which a support person can suppress a specific error message temporarily. Otherwise, the error message becomes like an irritating car alarm that wakes you up during the night and resolutely refuses to switch itself off.

- Providing a complete audit trail of the application's actions leading up to an error and information about its current status can be invaluable in helping a support person to isolate a problem. This could involve writing a trace log of the application's major actions and also of the user's actions before the error occurred.

To get some ideas for the sort of information that support staff find useful, please refer to the "Useful Diagnostic Information" section at the beginning of Chapter 6.

Developer Requirements

Maintenance developers don't want friendly, reassuring error messages or any soft padding that hides the raw details of a problem. They need to see clear signposts to an error, along with a mass of technical information to fall back on if the signposts don't point in the correct direction. These are some of the points you should think about when writing error handling and diagnostics code that produces information viewed by other developers:

- Try to keep your error handling and cleanup code together in a location separate from the main application logic. This separation of the application logic from the error handling and cleanup code makes it easier for a support developer to understand what happens in the event of a problem and makes it more likely that the cleanup code will always be executed consistently. The **Try...Catch...Finally** construct, which I discuss in detail later in this chapter, is ideal for maintaining this separation.

- Pay as much attention to your error-handling and cleanup code as you do to the application logic. Does your error-handling code leave your application in a valid business state? Have you tried passing bad arguments to your methods so that you can step through your exception logic? Have you stepped through all of your exception code with the debugger? Do your unit and regression tests exercise all reasonable paths, especially exception paths, in your code?

- If you're throwing an exception, add specific information to the exception to make it easier for the developer calling your code to determine the exact problem. For instance, instead of just reporting that an invalid parameter was passed, explain which parameter was involved and list the valid values for that parameter. One trick some developers use is to throw a custom exception that displays a complete description of a parameter's usage if the value of the parameter is null, thus providing built-in documentation for the programmer using the method. You may not want to go this far, but it's worth creating your own exception classes so that you can add custom information to your exceptions. Once again, I discuss this in detail later in the chapter.

- Document every exception that your component explicitly throws. If you look at the .NET Framework documentation, you can see that nearly every method's exceptions are documented in this fashion. This practice helps developers to understand your component and its methods. You should take special care to document any custom exceptions that can be thrown.

- Always provide an alternative code path or method in your component that allows a developer to check for a condition rather than rely on an exception being thrown. For instance, in a component that reads from a disk file, have a separate method that allows the developer to check whether the end of the file has been reached. This method will be in addition to any method that throws an EOF exception at the end of the file. This gives developers using your component more choices for handling certain situations. More choices are good in this context because many developers have fixed views about how components should work and fixed patterns in their use of components.

- Make sure that you perform adequate cleanup before you throw an exception. The developer receiving the exception is entitled to assume that there are no side effects when a method throws an exception.

- Don't swallow an exception unless you understand that exception in detail and have dealt with any side effects that the exception might have on the code in the call stack above your method. For example, contrary to what the documentation states, the **System.IO.File.Exists** method swallows all exceptions and always returns either **true** or **false**. This means that if your code sees this method returning **false**, you don't know whether it was because the file didn't exist or because there was some other problem, for instance a security exception. Don't follow Microsoft's example! Instead, be kind to developers calling your methods and avoid hiding what's really happening.

Once again, the "Useful Diagnostic Information" section at the beginning of Chapter 6 can give you some ideas about the sort of information that other developers need to support and work with your application.

Logging Exceptions

In a production environment, unhandled exceptions or any exceptions that reach an application's boundary should always be logged if you want to understand your application's problems. This exception information can then be viewed by operators and developers, and can be analyzed individually or as a whole in order to gain a clearer picture of your application's behavior over time.

Later in this chapter I go into detail on which exceptions should be logged and how to log them, but in this section I want to explain some of the possible locations for storing these exceptions. There are at least three possible locations where exceptions can be stored for later analysis:

- *The Windows event log:* The Windows event log is a proven, reliable place to store information, although it's not available on Windows 98. It has facilities for log file management, and .NET provides Framework classes such as **System.Diagnostics.EventLog** to make the event log easy to update and maintain. Because the operating system and the CLR also use the event log, it's easy to reconcile system and application events. The only major problem is that it can be difficult to combine the event logs from multiple machines, although Application Center Server from Microsoft has this facility.

- *A SQL Server database:* The major benefit of using a central database for logging exceptions is that you can store all of the exception information for all of your applications in a single application, and you can then analyze it using standard SQL stored procedures. The drawback is that you're introducing an extra point of failure, in that the database might not be available. To avoid losing exception information when using this technique, you need to use the Windows event log when the database isn't available, but this entails monitoring two specific locations for exception information.

- *A custom log:* This is rarely a better choice than the first two options, because you need to allow concurrent access to the log file, you must have a process that manages the log file size, and you need to develop tools to view and analyze the exception information.

Now that you have a fair taste of the requirements that any error-handling scheme has to meet, I can discuss how errors and exceptions are handled in VB .NET.

Exceptions and Exception Management

Errors and unexpected behavior in .NET applications are handled through a mechanism called *structured exception handling,* or SEH for short. This mechanism automatically collects and preserves information about errors and unexpected behavior in the form of an exception. An exception class is roughly equivalent to the **Err** class that you used in VB.Classic, although exception classes are much more flexible and powerful than the **Err** class. The following are some of the advantages that exceptions provide. I expand on several of these points in the next section.

- You can add custom information to your exceptions by inheriting from the **ApplicationException** class and adding new properties. These custom exceptions retain all of the standard exception functionality while allowing you to add new exception information that helps other developers to understand the exceptions better. You can even create a complete exception hierarchy for your assembly or component. This concept replaces, and is much superior to, the VB.Classic idea of defining and raising new error numbers to represent errors that are unique to your component.

- Custom exceptions are unique to the namespace in which they're defined, which means that you'll never have to worry about clashing with another component's custom exceptions. This was a big problem in VB.Classic, because the custom error numbers that you defined could easily be duplicated by other components. Any developer using both of your components would have no easy way of distinguishing between errors raised by the two components.

- The **Try...Catch...Finally** mechanism provided by VB .NET to implement SEH allows you to isolate your exception management code in a single location, which means you can write recovery and cleanup code separately from your business logic, and you can guarantee that it will execute when necessary.

- You can catch and deal with exceptions using sophisticated exception filtering, which allows you to deal with different exceptions at the precise level of granularity that you feel is necessary for each exception.

- Exception hierarchies allow you to catch a set of related exceptions using just a single statement.

- If an exception causes another exception to be thrown while it's being handled, the original exception is automatically appended to the new exception using the **InnerException** property. In this way, exceptions can be stacked without any loss of information. You can also use the **GetBaseException** method to traverse a list of inner exceptions and find the exception that was originally thrown.

- Every exception has a built-in **StackTrace** property, which shows the complete stack trace from the point that the exception was thrown. Gone are the old days when you had to add the call stack information as a part of the error handling in literally every VB.Classic method. Now you can easily record the call stack information at the point where you catch the exception.

The System.Exception Class

The **System.Exception** class is the base class for all CLS-compliant exceptions. Table 13-1 describes the properties of this class and also shows the equivalent VB.Classic **Err** properties.

Table 13-1. Explanation of System.Exception Properties

PROPERTY	DESCRIPTION	ERR EQUIVALENT
Message	Text explaining why the exception was thrown.	**Description**
Source	Text containing the name of the assembly that threw the exception.	**Source**
TargetSite	A **MethodBase** containing the method that threw the exception.	No equivalent
StackTrace	Text containing a list of names and signatures of the methods in the call stack leading to where the exception was thrown. Note that code optimization by the compiler may result in some methods being omitted from this string.	No equivalent
HelpLink	Text containing a URL to information about the exception that might be useful to a developer or user.	**HelpContext** and **HelpFile**
InnerException	If the current exception was caused by another exception, this is where the previous exception is stored. Otherwise this property is set to **Nothing**.	No equivalent
HResult	A protected property containing an **integer** used to store an error number raised by unmanaged code (such as VB.Classic). Any error raised from unmanaged code appears to managed code as an exception, with the error number stored here. To read this value, you should either pass the exception to the **System.Runtime.InteropServices.Marshal** shared **GetHRForException** method or catch the **ExternalException** type and use its **ErrorCode** property instead.	**Number**

System.Exception sits at the base of a large hierarchy, or tree, of exception types. The benefit of this hierarchy, apart from grouping related exceptions, is that whenever you write code to catch a specific exception, you also catch all of its derived exceptions. For instance, writing code to catch **ArithmeticException** will automatically catch **DivideByZeroException**, **NotFiniteNumberException**, and **OverflowException**. This can have both benefits and problems. One benefit is that it's often easier to write code to catch and deal with the parent exception without having to worry about every individual exception derived from the parent. Another benefit is that whenever a developer adds a new exception derived from an exception that you're already catching, your code will automatically catch this new exception. However, the major problem with this approach is that your code won't necessarily know what to do with this new exception, and as you'll see shortly, you should rarely catch exceptions that you don't know how to handle.

The two most important exceptions derived directly from **System.Exception** are **System.SystemException** and **System.ApplicationException**. **SystemException** is designed for exceptions thrown by the CLR and .NET Framework class library, so that your code can be notified about any runtime or Framework problems. On the other hand, **ApplicationException** is designed for use by .NET applications. Though this separation is useful, it isn't always valid. For example, the .NET Framework class library derives **IsolatedStorageException** directly from **Exception** rather than **SystemException**, and the .NET Framework also derives some reflection-related exceptions from **ApplicationException**. In addition, your own applications might want to use exceptions derived from

SystemException rather than **ApplicationException** in certain situations, such as using **ArgumentNullException** to signal that a null argument has been passed to a method or using **ArgumentOutOfRangeException** to signal an argument containing a bad value.

Before I go into more detail on managing exceptions, the next section is an explanation of the code that you have to write to handle exceptions.

Try...Catch...Finally

Try...Catch...Finally is the mechanism that VB .NET provides for protecting your code from exceptions. It allows you to place any code that you wish to protect from exceptions within a **Try...End Try** block, and then add a **Catch** block for each exception that you anticipate and want to handle. Each of these **Catch** blocks has an exception filter, which is an expression designed to catch a specific exception or set of exceptions. Within each **Catch** block you write code to handle that specific exception. Lastly, you use a **Finally** block to place any cleanup code, which consists of statements that must execute regardless of whether an exception was thrown.

A **Try...End Try** block might want to handle several different exceptions or indeed do no exception handling, so the number of **Catch** blocks is optional, from zero upward. Exception cleanup is also optional, so you can have either one **Finally** block or no **Finally** blocks. The only requirement is that your **Try...End Try** block must contain either one **Catch** block or one **Finally** block. This makes sense because there would be no point in protecting code that needs no exception recovery or cleanup when it fails.

Listing 13-1 shows some pseudo-code demonstrating where you should place code when writing a typical **Try...End Try** block.

Listing 13-1. Pseudo-Code for Try...Catch...Finally

Try

    'One or more statements that you wish to protect from exceptions goes here.

Catch ExcType1 As Type1Exception

    'This **Catch** block has an exception filter that catches a type 1 exception.

    'Code that recovers from this exception goes here.

    'This code will be executed automatically when a type 1 exception occurs,

    'or when any exception derived from a type 1 exception occurs.

Catch ExcType2 As Type2Exception When Expression1 is true

    'This **Catch** block has an exception filter that catches a

    'type 2 exception only when expression1 evaluates to true.

    'Code that recovers from this exception goes here, and this code will

    'be executed automatically when the exception filter conditions are met.

Catch ExcType2 As Type2Exception When Expression2 is true

    'This **Catch** block has an exception filter that catches a

    'type 2 exception only when expression2 evaluates to true.

    'Code that recovers from this exception goes here, and this code will

    'be executed automatically when the exception filter conditions are met.

Finally

    'Cleanup code that must run whether or not an exception was thrown goes here.

    'This code is guaranteed to execute, even if an exception occurs in the **Try**

    'block or a **Catch** block.

End Try

As you can see from this pseudo-code listing, the code that you write to deal with each exception is isolated in a single location and is guaranteed to execute whenever that exception (or an exception derived from it) occurs. This makes your error-handling code easier to maintain and separates it from the code dealing with the main business logic. This code partitioning has the added benefit of allowing you to partition your business thinking from your error thinking, which helps to reduce the severe mental load that inevitably comes as a part of software development.

Try...Catch...Finally Mechanics

Having seen how **Try...Catch...Finally** is designed to make the task of exception recovery and cleanup much easier, you need to see exactly how the CLR transfers control between blocks of code. When a statement in a **Try** block throws an exception, the following sequence of events happens:

1. The CLR walks sequentially down the list of **Catch** blocks within the local **Try...End Try** block, looking for a local **Catch** block with an exception filter matching the exception that was thrown.

2. If a local **Catch** block has an exception filter that matches the exact exception that was thrown, the code in that **Catch** block is executed, followed by the code in the **Finally** block. Then execution continues at the first statement following the **End Try**.

3. Alternatively, if the exception that was thrown derives from the exception specified by a local **Catch** block, the same actions happen as described in step 2. For example, an exception filter that catches **ArgumentException** will also catch exceptions derived from **ArgumentException**, such as **ArgumentNullException**, **InvalidEnumArgumentException**, **DuplicateWaitObjectException**, and **ArgumentOutOfRangeException**.

4. If no local **Catch** block matches the exception that was thrown, the CLR walks back up the call stack, method by method, looking for a **Catch** block that wants to respond to the exception. If no matching **Catch** block is found in the call stack, the exception is considered to be unhandled. (Please see the later section "Dealing with Unhandled Exceptions" for a discussion on dealing with these.)

5. Alternatively, if a matching **Catch** block is found somewhere in the call stack, the code in every **Finally** block between the throw and the catch is executed. This starts with the **Finally** belonging to the **Try** block where the exception was thrown and finishes with the **Finally** in the method below the method where the exception was caught.

6. After this cleanup has been completed for all methods below where the exception was caught, control is transferred to the **Catch** block that caught the exception, and this code is executed. Next to run is the **Finally** block of the **Try** where the exception was caught. Now that the call stack has been unwound and the error cleanup has been completed, the final step is to continue execution at the first statement following the **End Try** where the exception was caught.

7. If code within a **Catch** block causes another exception to be thrown, the original exception is automatically appended to the new exception using the **InnerException** property. In this way, exceptions can be stacked without any loss of information.

8. You should avoid placing cleanup code within a **Finally** block that might throw an exception, unless that code is within its own **Try** block. Without this added protection, the CLR behaves as though the new exception was thrown after the end after the **Finally** block and looks up the call stack for a remote **Catch** block that wants to respond to the new exception. The original exception will be lost unless the original **Catch** block saved it.

Notice that a statement that isn't placed within a local **Try...End Try** block may still be protected from an exception. This is because a **Catch** block active in the call stack above the method where the exception is thrown might catch that exception. Only if the CLR can't find any matching **Catch** block in the call stack is the exception considered to be unhandled.

Some developers question the need for a **Finally** clause, pointing out that code added after the **End Try** statement will always be executed. This is normally true, but not always. Code placed in the **Finally** section is always executed, even after an **Exit Sub**, a **Response.Redirect**, or an exception thrown within a **Catch** clause, and these are examples of situations where code placed after an **End Try** statement won't be executed.

Using Try...Catch...Finally Properly

How you handle exceptions depends to a large extent on whether you're writing application code or library code. When you're writing library classes and methods that are going to be used by other developers rather than by end users directly, you should really propagate every exception unless you're deliberately providing a better level of abstraction or hiding meaningless implementation details. On the other hand, writing business logic and application code that interacts with end users means that you should catch nearly every exception and transform it into a context-sensitive message that makes more sense to the end user and the task that he or she is attempting to perform.

Whenever you write exception recovery code, you're faced with choosing one of several options for dealing with each exception. The following sections give you some general guidance about which option is best for individual situations. Please bear in mind that these are only general guidelines—you should analyze each specific situation that arises in your own code.

Let an Exception Propagate Automatically

If you ignore an exception, it will automatically bubble up to the calling code. Before disrupting this process by catching an exception, you should be clear about exactly what you're doing. There are really only five reasons to catch an exception:

- *Execute recovery code:* You may explicitly need to recover from certain exceptions, for instance by reversing a transaction that failed before it completed. This strategy can involve swallowing the exception or rethrowing it, depending on circumstances.

- *Execute cleanup code:* You may need to clean up after certain exceptions, for instance by closing a file or database connection.

- *Add more relevant exception information:* You may need to add extra information to an exception before rethrowing it or throw a more meaningful exception.

- *Log exception information:* In some circumstances, especially for exceptions that have reached the end user without being intercepted, you might want to log the exception information for later analysis.

- *Prevent an exception from reaching the end user:* If an exception bubbles up through the call stack to reach the end user without being intercepted, you should usually intercept the exception at the user interface and translate it into a user-friendly message that is context-sensitive to the task the user is attempting to perform.

If you catch an exception, you're making an explicit statement that you expected that exception, you understand it, and you're going to deal with it. Unless you need to perform one or more of these five tasks, you should ignore the exception and let it propagate upward.

Catch and Swallow System.Exception

This strategy is the opposite of the previous one, in that **System.Exception** is the base of all CLS-compliant exceptions and catching it means catching all exceptions. If you catch and swallow **System.Exception**, you're saying that you understand and know how to deal with every type of exception. This is normally a bad practice, because there's no possible way for you to anticipate and understand every possible type of exception. You should therefore be very wary of any real-life code that uses **Try...Catch...Finally** like this:

```
Function CalcRatio(ByVal Top As Integer, ByVal Bottom As Integer) As Int32
    Try
        Return Top \ Bottom
    Catch Exc As Exception
        Return 0
    End Try
End Function
```

Although you might think that division by zero is the only exception that this method can throw, and therefore it's safe to catch **System.Exception**, you would be wrong. Passing **0** or **Nothing** for the second argument would indeed lead to a division by zero, but the CLR could also throw (for example) **StackOverflowException**. The catch in this method would then be hiding a potentially fatal exception, possibly leading to corruption of data or other bad side effects. The obvious answer in this case is to catch just **DivideByZeroException**.

Another way of looking at catching **System.Exception** is that it's the equivalent of the dodgy VB.Classic technique that involves using **On Error Resume Next** to protect VB.Classic code. This technique is sometimes called "nailing the corpse in an upright position," because it's saying that whatever happens, even if I've been shot through the heart, I should still keep running. Using this technique is like creating a "black hole" into which all errors coming from lower down in the call stack are sucked, never to emerge again.

You should especially not catch and swallow **System.Exception** in any method that's part of a class library, because this practice specifically denies any information to the developer that's calling your method. You often don't know what the calling code expects, and therefore you can't usually anticipate what a developer expects to happen when he or she calls your method.

During program development, some developers like to catch and swallow **System.Exception** in the last **Catch** block of each **Try...End Try** block in order to display any unhandled exception on the console using **Exception.ToString**. The idea is that this helps to isolate errors during development, and that these **Catch** clauses will be removed before the application is moved into acceptance testing or production. There are two problems with this approach. The first problem is that you might forget to remove some or all of these dodgy **Catch** blocks. The second problem is that you'll find it impossible to test how exceptions are handled when they propagate up the call stack of your application. If you're tempted to try this approach, you should always rethrow the exception using an empty **Throw** statement, as discussed in the next section.

The only place where it might be acceptable to catch and swallow **System.Exception** is in your application's unhandled exception handler, otherwise known as a "last chance" exception handler. This is because you want to keep your application going for long enough to allow your end user to save his or her work. However, even here there are some exceptions that are dangerous to catch. See the "Dealing with Unhandled Exceptions" and "Handling Special Exceptions" sections later in this chapter for more details.

Catch and Rethrow System.Exception

One situation where catching **System.Exception** as discussed in the previous section is not a heinous sin is when, after recovering from the exception, you always rethrow the same exception that you caught. There are some cases where you may need to recover from every possible exception so that you can restore your application to a safe state. For instance, in the following method you want to reverse the first money transfer if the second transfer doesn't happen, regardless of the reason why the second transfer doesn't occur. Notice that you can't reverse the first transfer in the **Finally** block because you only want to do the reversal when something goes wrong.

```
Sub AccountTransfer(ByVal AccountFrom As BankAccount, _
                                    ByVal AccountTo As BankAccount, _
                                    ByVal Amount As Decimal)
    'Make first transfer (deduct amount from first account)
    AccountFrom.Balance -= Amount
    Try
        'Make second transfer (add amount to second account)
        AccountTo.Balance += Amount
    Catch Exc As Exception
        'Something went wrong with second transfer, so reverse first transfer
        AccountFrom.Balance += Amount
        'Re-throw this exception, because we don't know how to handle it here
        Throw
    End Try
End Sub
```

After performing the reversal, you should always rethrow whatever exception you caught, because you can't possibly know how to deal with the generic **System.Exception**.

Note that although using **Throw** means that the original exception type is preserved, the stack trace starts from the line that you rethrow the exception, not from the line where the exception was originally thrown. So you lose some information (the line number) if the **Try** block contains multiple statements.

Catch an Exception and Throw a New Exception of the Same Type

You might wish to improve the quality of certain exception messages emitted from the code of other developers. As an example, I'm going to examine the possible exception messages that the **System.IO.File.Move** method can produce, and see where and how these messages need improvement.

Listing 13-2 shows some attempts to probe the **File.Move** method and groups the probes that produce unclear exception messages. I created a folder with the name of C:\Demo and placed in it two files, one named Source.txt and the other named Destination.txt. The latter file was set to be read-only. Then I executed the program shown in Listing 13-2 and made a note of any exception that produced unclear information. The program makes one test at a time, and each resulting exception is written to the console, together with a string describing the test.

Listing 13-2. Probing the System.IO.File.Move Method

```
Option Strict On
Imports System.IO


Module ExceptionWrapper

    Sub Main()
        Dim WrapperNo As Boolean = False, WrapperYes As Boolean = True

        'MOVE commands producing good exception information
        TestMove("C:\Demo\Source.txt", "C:\Demo\Destination.txt", WrapperNo, _
                        "Destination is read-only")
        TestMove("C:\Demo\Source.txt", "", WrapperNo, _
                        "Destination is empty")
        TestMove("C:\Demo\Source.txt", Nothing, WrapperNo, _
                        "Destination is nothing")
        TestMove("C:\Demo\Source.txt", "C:\Dem\Destination.txt", WrapperNo, _
                        "Wrong destination folder")
        TestMove("C:\Demo\SourceX.txt", "C:\Demo\Destination.txt", WrapperNo, _
                        "Source doesn't exist")


        'MOVE commands producing bad exception information
        TestMove("C:\Demo\Source.txt", "C:\Demo\*.txt", WrapperNo, _
                        "Wildcard in destination")
        TestMove("C:\Demo\Sou<rce.txt", "C:\Demo\Destination.txt", WrapperNo, _
                        "Bad character in source")
        TestMove("C:\Demo\Source.txt" & Space(300), "C:\Demo\Destination.txt", _
                        WrapperNo, "Source too long")
        TestMove("C:\Demo\Source.txt", "C:\Demo\", WrapperNo, _
                        "Destination is folder")
        TestMove("C:\Demo\Sou:rce.txt", "C:\Demo\Destination.txt", WrapperNo, _
                        "Dodgy character in source")
```

```
        End Sub

    Sub TestMove(ByVal SourceFile As String, ByVal DestinationFile As String, _
                        ByVal UseWrapper As Boolean, ByVal ProbeType As
String)

        Try
            If UseWrapper = True Then
                MoveFile(SourceFile, DestinationFile)
            Else
                File.Move(SourceFile, DestinationFile)
            End If

        Catch ShowException As Exception
            Console.WriteLine("TESTING: " & ProbeType)
            Console.WriteLine(ShowException.ToString)
            Console.WriteLine()
            Console.ReadLine()

        End Try

    End Sub

End Module
```

As you can see if you examine the exceptions produced by this program, some of the exception messages aren't clear, mainly because they omit the source and destination arguments to the **File.Move** method. If you were a developer tasked with understanding this exception log without having access to these arguments, it would be impossible to determine the exact problem given the information currently provided. For instance, how would you go about trying to decipher this exception?

System.ArgumentException: Illegal characters in path.
at System.Security.Permissions.FileIOPermission.HasIllegalCharacters(String[] str)
at System.Security.Permissions.FileIOPermission.AddPathList(FileIOPermissionA
ccess access, String[] pathList, Boolean checkForDuplicates, Boolean
needFullPath)
at System.Security.Permissions.FileIOPermission..ctor(FileIOPermissionAccess
access, String[] pathList, Boolean checkForDuplicates, Boolean needFullPath)
at System.IO.File.Move(String sourceFileName, String destFileName)
at ExceptionExperiments.Experiments.Main() in C:\Documents and Settings\Admin
istrator\My Documents\Visual Studio Projects\ExceptionExperiments\Experiments.vb
:line 13

One way to improve the quality of these exception messages is to write a wrapper method around the **File.Move** method. Within the wrapper, you decide to catch only the specific exceptions that you've determined are unclear, add your own improved exception message, and then throw an exception of the same type containing your improved exception message. You also keep the original exception as an inner exception to your new exception, in order to preserve the original exception information. This approach is a good way of improving third-party exception messages by making them more detailed and informative.

A possible wrapper for **File.Move** is shown in Listing 13-3. It catches all of the exceptions that the program shown in Listing 13-2 determined weren't very informative and adds some better diagnostic information, usually the values contained in each of the arguments. If you run the tests shown in Listing 13-2 with the **UseWrapper** argument set to **true**, the wrapper method shown in Listing 13-3 will be executed instead of using the **File.Move** method directly.

Listing 13-3. Improving the System.IO.File.Move Method

```
Sub MoveFile(ByVal SourceFile As String, ByVal DestinationFile As String)

    Try
        File.Move(SourceFile, DestinationFile)

    Catch Exc As ArgumentException _
            When Exc.Message = "Illegal characters in path."
        Dim HelpfulMessage As String = Exc.Message & vbCrLf
        HelpfulMessage += "Source = " & SourceFile & vbCrLf
        HelpfulMessage += "Destination = " & DestinationFile & vbCrLf
        Throw New ArgumentException(HelpfulMessage, Exc)

    Catch Exc As ArgumentException _
            When Exc.Message = "The path contains illegal characters."
        Dim HelpfulMessage As String = Exc.Message & vbCrLf
        HelpfulMessage += "Source = " & SourceFile & vbCrLf
        HelpfulMessage += "Destination = " & DestinationFile
        Throw New ArgumentException(HelpfulMessage, Exc)

    Catch Exc As IOException _
            When Exc.Message = _
            "Cannot create a file when that file already exists." & vbCrLf
        Dim HelpfulMessage As String = "Destination '" & DestinationFile
        HelpfulMessage += "' already exists" & vbCrLf
        Throw New IOException (HelpfulMessage, Exc)
```

```
        Catch Exc As PathTooLongException
            Dim HelpfulMessage As String = Exc.Message & vbCrLf
            HelpfulMessage += "Source (" & SourceFile.Length & ") = " _
                                        & SourceFile & vbCrLf
            HelpfulMessage += "Destination (" & DestinationFile.Length & ") = " _
                                        & DestinationFile & vbCrLf
            Throw New PathTooLongException(HelpfulMessage, Exc)

        Catch Exc As NotSupportedException
            Dim HelpfulMessage As String = "Either source or destination path"
            HelpfulMessage += " contains a colon" & vbCrLf
            HelpfulMessage += "Source = " & SourceFile & vbCrLf
            HelpfulMessage += "Destination = " & DestinationFile & vbCrLf
            Throw New NotSupportedException(HelpfulMessage, Exc)

        End Try

    End Sub
```

Notice in Listing 13-3 how the **When** clause is useful for filtering exceptions. With this clause, you can make your exception filters as powerful as you want. The only requirement is that the expression in the **When** clause must evaluate to a **boolean**—in other words, a value of **true** or **false**. A drawback of using the **When** clause in the manner shown is that it can incur a performance hit if the expression takes some time to evaluate. This is a tradeoff that you have to consider against the benefit of improved exception messages. As you can see, the previous exception has now been wrapped by a more informative exception:

```
System.ArgumentException: Illegal characters in path.
Source = C:\Demo\Source.txt
Destination = C:\Demo\*.txt
 ---> System.ArgumentException: Illegal characters in path.
   at System.Security.Permissions.FileIOPermission.HasIllegalCharacters(String[]
 str)
   at System.Security.Permissions.FileIOPermission.AddPathList(FileIOPermissionA
ccess access, String[] pathList, Boolean checkForDuplicates, Boolean needFullPat
h)
   at System.Security.Permissions.FileIOPermission..ctor(FileIOPermissionAccess
access, String[] pathList, Boolean checkForDuplicates, Boolean needFullPath)
   at System.IO.File.Move(String sourceFileName, String destFileName)
   at ExceptionExperiments.Experiments.MoveFile(String SourceFile, String Destin
ationFile) in C:\Documents and Settings\Administrator\My Documents\Visual Studio
 Projects\ExceptionExperiments\Experiments.vb:line 58
```

```
--- End of inner exception stack trace ---
   at ExceptionExperiments.Experiments.MoveFile(String SourceFile, String Destin
ationFile) in C:\Documents and Settings\Administrator\My Documents\Visual Studio
 Projects\ExceptionExperiments\Experiments.vb:line 64
   at ExceptionExperiments.Experiments.Main() in C:\Documents and Settings\Admin
istrator\My Documents\Visual Studio Projects\ExceptionExperiments\Experiments.vb
:line 13
```

Although this example shows how to improve on the exceptions produced by a Framework class by wrapping them, you can apply the same principle to exceptions produced by any third-party code.

When you use this technique, you should be aware of a nasty trap waiting for you, or at least for the callers of your code. Be careful to catch and throw only the most derived exception that you're looking to improve. For example, Listing 13-4 shows the wrong way to improve **ArgumentException**, by catching every **ArgumentException**, not just the specific exception that you want to improve. The problem is that **ArgumentException** is the base class for several other exceptions, and this code therefore makes the assumption that the caller never cares about the difference between these exceptions.

Listing 13-4. A Bad Way to "Improve" the System.IO.File.Move Method

```
Sub MoveFile(ByVal SourceFile As String, ByVal DestinationFile As String)

    Try
        File.Move(SourceFile, DestinationFile)

    Catch Exc As ArgumentException
        Dim HelpfulMessage As String = Exc.Message & vbCrLf
        HelpfulMessage += "Source = " & SourceFile & vbCrLf
        HelpfulMessage += "Destination = " & DestinationFile
        Throw New ArgumentException(HelpfulMessage, Exc)

    'Other Catch blocks go here

    End Try

End Sub
```

Catch exception filters can't process inner exceptions, so the method shown in Listing 13-4 forces any calling code to catch the outer exception before it can analyze the type of the inner exception. This is the only way to distinguish between each of the possible exceptions that can derive from **ArgumentException**, and it results in very clumsy, slow, and error-prone code.

Catch an Exception and Throw a Better Exception

Sometimes you want to hide the implementation details of a method or improve the level of abstraction of a problem so that it's more meaningful to the caller of a method. To do this, you can intercept the original exception and substitute a different exception that's better suited for explaining the problem.

Listing 13-5 shows an example where a method loads the requested user's details from a text file. The method assumes that a text file exists named with the user's ID and a suffix of ".data". When that file doesn't actually exist, it doesn't make much sense to throw a **FileNotFoundException** because the fact that each user's details are stored in a text file is an implementation detail internal to the method. So this method instead wraps the original exception in a standard **ArgumentException** with an explanatory message. As I explained in the previous section, the original exception should be kept by loading it as the **InnerException** property of your new exception. This means that a developer can still analyze the underlying problem if necessary.

Listing 13-5. Hiding an Implementation Detail with a Framework Exception

```
Function UserDetailsLoad(ByVal UserId As String) As Collection
    Dim HelpfulMessage As String
    Dim FileStream As System.IO.StreamReader

    'First try to open the user's data file
    Try
        FileStream = New System.IO.StreamReader(UserId & ".data")

    Catch Exc As System.IO.FileNotFoundException
        'The specified file didn't exist, but this exception won't mean
        'much to a caller who doesn't know how this method is implemented
        UserDetailsLoad = Nothing
        HelpfulMessage = "Details for user " & UserId & " cannot be located"
        Throw New System.ArgumentException(HelpfulMessage, Exc)

    Finally

    End Try

    'Code goes here to load and return user details

End Function
```

Although wrapping an exception to make it more meaningful is a reasonable strategy, an even better one is to wrap the original exception in one of your own custom exceptions, as explained in the next section.

Catch an Exception and Throw a Custom Exception

The problem with making an exception more meaningful by wrapping it in one of the standard Framework exceptions is that this technique often doesn't make the exception specific enough. Within an application, many different errors can result in an **ArgumentException** being thrown, so calling code still has to decipher more details about the exception in order to deal with it properly.

The best solution is to create a custom exception. This is similar to the VB.Classic approach of defining your own custom error numbers for specific situations. Custom exceptions are even better than custom error numbers because you can avoid error collisions by scoping your custom exceptions within each namespace, and you can provide whatever extended information you need by simply adding new exception properties. In addition, you can even create your own custom exception hierarchy for your component or application.

Listing 13-6 shows the same method as shown in Listing 13-5, but this time using a custom exception as the wrapper. Now there's no room for confusion in the calling code. If it catches the **UserMissingDetailsException**, there's no doubt about what has happened.

Listing 13-6. Hiding an Implementation Detail with a Custom Exception

```
Function UserDetailsLoad(ByVal UserId As String) As Collection
    Dim HelpfulMessage As String
    Dim FileStream As System.IO.StreamReader

    'First try to open the user's data file
    Try
        FileStream = New System.IO.StreamReader(UserId & ".data")

    Catch Exc As System.IO.FileNotFoundException
        'The specified file didn't exist, but this exception won't mean
        'much to a caller who doesn't know how this method is implemented
        UserDetailsLoad = Nothing
        HelpfulMessage = "Details for user " & UserId & " cannot be located"
        Throw New UserLoadException(HelpfulMessage, Exc, UserId)

    Finally
```

```
    End Try

    'Code goes here to load and return user details

End Function
```

You can build a custom exception by deriving it from **System.ApplicationException**. I discuss this in detail in the "Building Custom Exceptions" section later in this chapter.

Handling Special Exceptions

There are three exceptions that need special handling by your application. This is because these three exceptions indicate that the CLR, the garbage collector, or your process is in deep trouble, and therefore that your application is rather unlikely to be able to recover from the exception.

ExecutionEngineException is thrown by the CLR when it detects an internal problem, such as a bug or data corruption. None of your **Catch** or **Finally** blocks are executed when this exception is thrown, and your process will be killed by the CLR unless a debugger can be found to attach to the process.

OutOfMemoryException is thrown when the CLR or the garbage collector can't find any free memory. If the garbage collector throws this exception, your **Catch** and **Finally** blocks will execute, but your application is unlikely to be able to create any new objects. If instead the CLR throws this exception, all of your code will be blown out of the water, and the CLR will terminate your process.

StackOverflowException is thrown by the CLR when either a CLR thread or an application thread has consumed all of its stack space. If a CLR thread causes this exception, you can't catch it and none of your **Finally** blocks will execute. Alternatively, you can catch this exception if it's thrown by one of your own application's threads, but none of your **Finally** blocks can execute without stack space. As the **Finally** blocks don't execute, your application is left in an undefined state, so you should never swallow this exception. Just log the exception in the **Catch** block, and let the CLR terminate your process.

If you try, you'll see that your own code can also throw these exceptions, and indeed any other exceptions. This isn't as daft as it sounds. The idea is that this allows you to test your exception-handling code in as many situations as possible.

There's another exception that can sometimes require special handling, namely **ThreadAbortException**. For details on how to deal with this exception, please see Chapter 14, which covers debugging multithreading situations.

Building Custom Exceptions

There are three main situations where it's beneficial to specify your own custom exception. The first situation is when you want to signal an error or unexpected event that isn't described adequately by an existing exception. The second situation is when you're handling an exception raised by a component that you're calling, and you don't want to confuse the developer calling your component with an exception that's meaningless to that developer. The final situation is when you wish to wrap an existing exception to provide extra information.

As an example, I'm going to create the custom exception mentioned in Listing 13-6 and use this creation process to discuss how to build well-behaved custom exceptions.

Choosing an Exception Name

The first task is to find a good name for a custom exception, something that conveys why the exception was thrown. I chose the name **UserLoadException** because this is going to be a base exception from which I can later derive more custom exceptions. Notice that the convention is that all exception names should end with the word "Exception".

Choosing the Parent Exception

Having arrived at a name, the next task is to decide which exception class is a suitable parent from which my custom exception can be inherited. Microsoft recommends that you should use **System.ApplicationException** as the parent of your base exceptions to differentiate them from the Framework class library exceptions, which mostly derive from **System.SystemException**.

This, however, is definitely not a hard-and-fast rule. For instance, in the method shown in Listing 13-6, you could consider deriving your exception from **System.ArgumentException**, or even directly from **System.Exception**. Deriving your custom exception from **ArgumentException** gives the benefit that any code already catching **ArgumentException** will also catch your new exception. Unfortunately, this is a dubious benefit because it's unlikely that pre-existing code will know how to handle your new exception. Deriving directly from **Exception** means that your new exception probably won't be caught by any pre-existing code, at least not until the application's unhandled exception handler is reached.

So deriving your base custom exceptions from **ApplicationException** is perhaps the best choice in most situations. Notice that **Exception**, **ApplicationException**, and **SystemException** all provide the same functionality, so you don't need to make a choice based on functionality.

Creating Exception Constructors

Before you can use a custom exception, you obviously need to define constructors so that the exception can be created. The **System.Exception** base type
defines three public constructors, so you should do the same. The first constructor should have no arguments; it can be used to create an instance of the
exception with all properties set to default values. The second constructor should
take a single string argument called **message**, which allows an exception message
to be defined when the exception is created. The third constructor takes a string
called **message** and an instance of an **Exception**-derived type. This second argument can be used to set the inner exception of the custom exception, as shown
previously in Listing 13-6.

Notice that for these three constructors, each constructor can normally just
call its base constructor to provide its functionality. Listing 13-7 shows the custom exception that I have defined so far.

Listing 13-7. A Usable UserLoadException Custom Exception

```
Option Strict On

Public Class UserLoadException : Inherits System.ApplicationException

    'For new exception instance with default property values
    Public Sub New()
        MyBase.New()
    End Sub

    'For new exception instance with specified message
    Public Sub New(ByVal message As String)
        MyBase.New(message)
    End Sub

    'For new exception instance with specified message and inner exception
    Public Sub New(ByVal message As String, ByVal innerException As Exception)
        MyBase.New(message, innerException)
    End Sub

End Class
```

This custom exception is already perfectly usable, but there are a couple of
enhancements that can make it even more useful.

Serializing a Custom Exception

When an exception is passed across **AppDomain**s or from one machine to another, it has to be deserialized and serialized before it can be used by the calling code. You can think of this as being similar to the *Star Trek* transporter process, where serialization is the equivalent of being sent (dematerialized at the sending end), and deserialization is similar to being received (rematerialized at the receiving end). To make sure that your custom exception can be marshaled in this manner, you need to make some additions to the code.

To make your custom exception serializable, you just need to add the **Serializable** attribute to the exception class. To enable the serializer to deserialize your exception properly, you must add a new deserialization constructor similar to the one that can be found in **System.Exception**. If your custom exception can be inherited, then this constructor should be defined as **Protected**, so that it's visible from any derived exception. If instead your exception is marked as **NotInheritable**, you should define the deserialization constructor as **Private**.

So with the addition of the serialization code, the custom exception now looks like Listing 13-8.

Listing 13-8. UserLoadException Custom Exception with Serialization

```vbnet
Option Strict On
Imports System.Runtime.Serialization


<Serializable()> _
Public Class UserLoadException : Inherits System.ApplicationException

    'For new exception instance with default property values
    Public Sub New()
        MyBase.New()
    End Sub


    'For new exception instance with specified message
    Public Sub New(ByVal message As String)
        MyBase.New(message)
    End Sub


    'For new exception instance with specified message and inner exception
    Public Sub New(ByVal message As String, ByVal innerException As Exception)
        MyBase.New(message, innerException)
    End Sub
```

```
'To re-materialize exception at the receiving end
Protected Sub New(ByVal info As SerializationInfo, _
                                    ByVal context As StreamingContext)
    MyBase.New(info, context)
End Sub
```

```
End Class
```

Now this custom exception can be marshaled across **AppDomain** and machine boundaries.

Adding a Custom Exception Property

One of the benefits of custom exceptions is that you can add your own exception properties to help the consumers of your exceptions understand and handle them better. In this case, it would be beneficial to create an exception property that stores the **UserId** property, to avoid a developer having to store this somewhere or parse it out of the exception message. Listing 13-9 shows the custom exception with this additional property and now with two extra constructors so that the **UserId** property can be set when creating an instance of this exception.

Listing 13-9. UserLoadException Custom Exception with the UserId Property

```
Option Strict On
Imports System.Runtime.Serialization

<Serializable()> _
Public Class UserLoadException : Inherits System.ApplicationException

    'Internal storage of the UserId property
    Private m_UserId As String = ""

    'For new exception instance with default property values
    Public Sub New()
        MyBase.New()
    End Sub

    'For new exception instance with specified message
    Public Sub New(ByVal message As String)
        MyBase.New(message)
    End Sub
```

```
'For new exception instance with specified message and UserId
Public Sub New(ByVal message As String, ByVal UserId As String)
    MyBase.New(message)
    m_UserId = UserId
End Sub


'For new exception instance with specified message and inner exception
Public Sub New(ByVal message As String, ByVal innerException As Exception)
    MyBase.New(message, innerException)
End Sub


'For new exception instance with specified message, inner exception and
UserId
Public Sub New(ByVal message As String, ByVal innerException As Exception, _
                        ByVal UserId As String)
    MyBase.New(message, innerException)
    m_UserId = UserId
End Sub


'To re-materialize exception at the receiving end
Protected Sub New(ByVal info As SerializationInfo, _
                                ByVal context As StreamingContext)
    MyBase.New(info, context)
End Sub


'UserId property, to help exception consumers
ReadOnly Property UserId() As String
    Get
        UserId = m_UserId
    End Get
End Property

End Class
```

This custom exception is now looking fairly complete. The only remaining problem is that the new **UserId** property won't be serialized and deserialized automatically.

Serialization of Custom Exception Properties

When you add custom properties to your custom exceptions, the serializer has to be told how to serialize and deserialize these properties. The first task is to serialize (in other words, dematerialize) the new **UserId** property. You do this by overriding the **GetObjectData** method that's called by the serializer to get the exception data, as shown in this code snippet:

```
'To serialize (de-materialize) custom property at the sending end
Public Overrides Sub GetObjectData(ByVal info As SerializationInfo, _
                                        ByVal context As
StreamingContext)
    MyBase.GetObjectData(info, context)
    info.AddValue("UserId", m_UserId)
End Sub
```

The next task is to deserialize (in other words, rematerialize) the new **UserId** property at the receiving end. You do this by adding an extra line of code (shown in bold) to the previously implemented deserialization constructor, as shown in the following code snippet:

```
'To re-materialize exception and property at the receiving end
Protected Sub New(ByVal info As SerializationInfo, _
                                    ByVal context As StreamingContext)
    MyBase.New(info, context)
    m_UserId = info.GetString("UserId")
End Sub
```

The final task is to override and change the **Message** property so that it includes the value of the **UserId** property. This ensures that when a developer invokes **ToString** on the exception, he or she will see the exception message and the all-important user identifier.

```
'To add custom property to standard exception message
Public Overrides ReadOnly Property Message() As String
    Get
        Return MyBase.Message & Environment.NewLine & "User id: " &
m_UserId
    End Get
End Property
```

Finally, after all this work, Listing 13-10 now shows the complete, ready-to-use, custom exception that I've created.

Listing 13-10. UserLoadException Complete Custom Exception

```
Option Strict On
Imports System.Runtime.Serialization


<Serializable()> _
Public Class UserLoadException : Inherits System.ApplicationException

    'Internal storage of the UserId property
    Private m_UserId As String = ""

    'For new exception instance with default property values
    Public Sub New()
        MyBase.New()
    End Sub

    'For new exception instance with specified message
    Public Sub New(ByVal message As String)
        MyBase.New(message)
    End Sub

    'For new exception instance with specified message and UserId
    Public Sub New(ByVal message As String, ByVal UserId As String)
        MyBase.New(message)
        m_UserId = UserId
    End Sub

    'For new exception instance with specified message and inner exception
    Public Sub New(ByVal message As String, ByVal innerException As Exception)
        MyBase.New(message, innerException)
    End Sub

    'For new exception instance with specified message, inner exception and
UserId
    Public Sub New(ByVal message As String, ByVal innerException As Exception, _
                            ByVal UserId As String)
        MyBase.New(message, innerException)
        m_UserId = UserId
    End Sub
```

```vbnet
'To re-materialize exception and custom property at the receiving end
Protected Sub New(ByVal info As SerializationInfo, _
                                    ByVal context As StreamingContext)
    MyBase.New(info, context)
    m_UserId = info.GetString("UserId")
End Sub

'To de-materialize exception and custom property at the sending end
Public Overrides Sub GetObjectData(ByVal info As SerializationInfo, _
                                    ByVal context As
StreamingContext)
    MyBase.GetObjectData(info, context)
    info.AddValue("UserId", m_UserId)
End Sub

'To add custom property to standard exception message
Public Overrides ReadOnly Property Message() As String
    Get
        Return MyBase.Message & Environment.NewLine & "User id: " &
m_UserId
    End Get
End Property

'UserId property, to help exception consumers
ReadOnly Property UserId() As String
    Get
        UserId = m_UserId
    End Get
End Property

End Class
```

Custom Exceptions and Remoting

There's one final issue that you might have to deal with when you create custom exceptions. If you throw a custom exception across a machine or **AppDomain** (logical process) boundary, there's no guarantee that the component that receives the exception will be able to interpret it. An assembly will only know about custom exceptions that have been defined within its own **AppDomain**.

As an example, if your application is talking via remoting to a third-party application, and that application throws a custom exception, the CLR on your machine will throw a **FileNotFoundException** unless your application already knows about that custom exception. In a similar fashion, in the less likely situation of your **AppDomain** creating another **AppDomain**, any custom exception thrown by an assembly in the second **AppDomain** will cause a problem for your **AppDomain** unless the custom exception is defined in an application base common to both **AppDomain**s.

There are two possible solutions to this issue. The first solution is to create an assembly containing the exception information and place that assembly into a common application base shared by both **AppDomain**s. The second solution is to create the same assembly, sign it with a strong name and then place it in the global assembly cache (GAC). I usually prefer the first method because user-defined GAC assemblies can sometimes lead to policy configuration issues, but you should look carefully at your own application's needs before deciding which of these two methods makes the most sense in your situation.

Custom Exceptions Summary

To summarize, here's a list of the actions that you need to take when you build a custom exception:

- Find a good name that conveys why the exception was thrown and make sure that the name ends with the word "Exception".

- Ensure that you implement the three standard exception constructors.

- Ensure that you mark your exception with the **Serializable** attribute.

- Ensure that you implement the deserialization constructor.

- Add any custom exception properties that might help developers to understand and handle your exception better.

- If you add any custom properties, make sure that you implement and override **GetObjectData** to serialize your custom properties.

- If you add any custom properties, override the **Message** property so that you can add your properties to the standard exception message.

Debugging Exceptions

The Visual Studio IDE lets you specify how the debugger should treat exceptions that are thrown while you're debugging within the IDE. You can access the dialog window that controls this by selecting Debug ➢ Exceptions (see Figure 13-1).

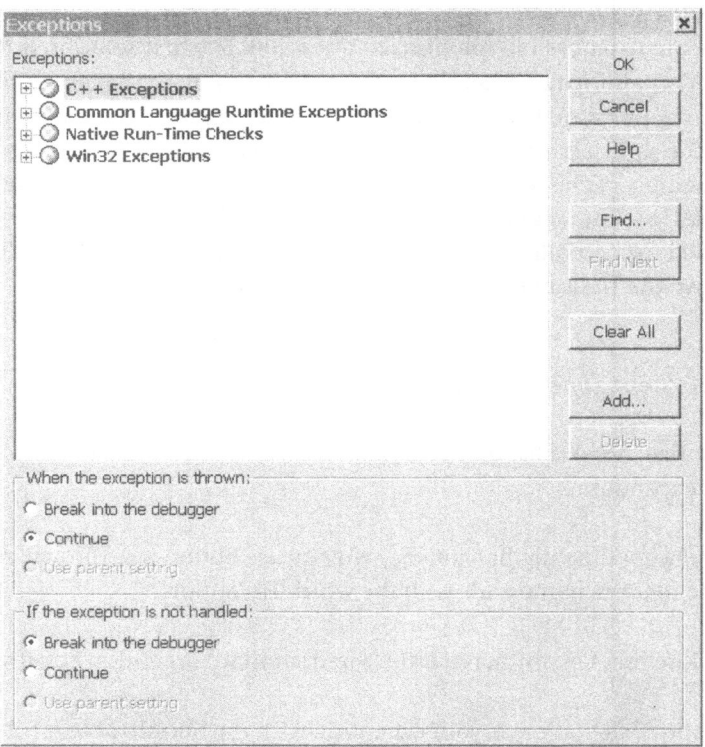

Figure 13-1. The Exceptions dialog window

Controlling Debugger Handling of Exceptions

The dialog window in Figure 13-1 shows the categories of exceptions that Visual Studio understands. If you haven't installed the C++ components of Visual Studio, you'll see only the Common Language Runtime Exceptions category. If you've installed C++, you'll see the following four exception categories:

- *C++ Exceptions:* This option helps you work with unmanaged C++ exceptions.

- *Common Language Runtime Exceptions:* This option helps you work with managed exceptions, including those thrown by VB .NET, C#, and Managed C++. Note that errors raised by VB.Classic components accessed through COM Interop are converted into CLR exceptions.

- *Native Run-Time Checks:* This option is only useful if you're writing unmanaged C++ code.

- *Win32 Exceptions:* This option is for working with exception codes thrown by unmanaged Win32 code.

I concentrate in this section on the CLR exceptions category, as these are by far the most common exceptions encountered by VB .NET developers. If you select this category, you can see that the exceptions are grouped by namespace. Selecting a namespace shows you a flat list of every exception within that namespace, as shown in Figure 13-2.

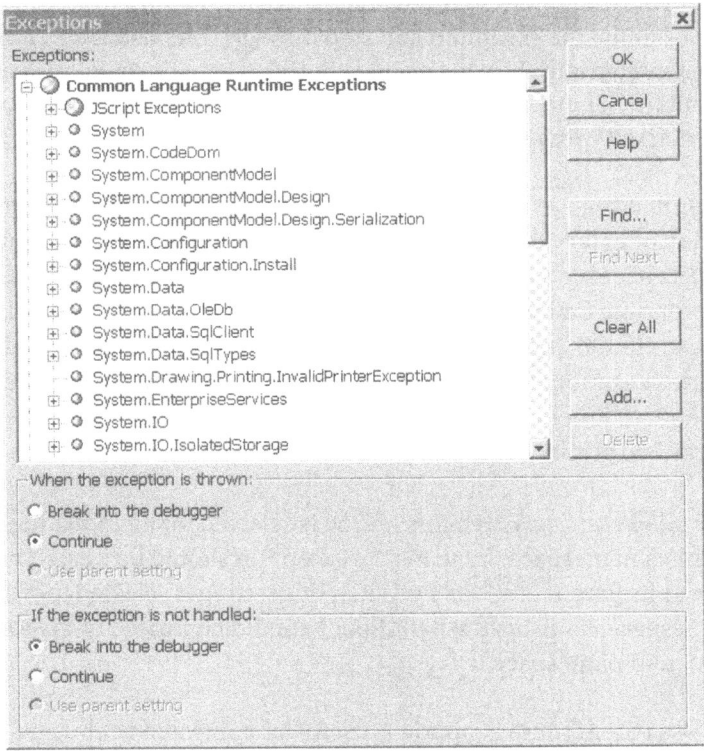

Figure 13-2. Showing CLR exceptions in the System.IO namespace

The two frames at the bottom of this dialog window allow you to control what happens when an exception is thrown and what happens when an exception is unhandled.

Debugger Treatment of First-Chance Exceptions

The first frame in Figure 13-2 contains three options for controlling what the debugger does as soon as an exception is thrown, before your application has a chance to handle it. These options apply to either an entire category of exceptions, the exceptions within a single namespace, or a single exception, depending upon which level of the exception hierarchy that you select in the Exceptions dialog window. The options for how the debugger treats an exception that's just been thrown are as follows:

- *Break into the debugger:* This setting is most useful when you're debugging your exception-handling code. The debugger breaks execution at the line where the exception occurred and hands over control to you so that you can examine the exception and step through your **Catch** and **Finally** blocks. Alternatively, you can just continue from the break and exception handling will proceed normally. Exceptions that you select to treat this way are marked with a red ball glyph showing a white X.

- *Continue:* This setting causes your component to continue normal execution after an exception, with the CLR looking locally and in the call stack for a catch exception filter that matches that exception. If the CLR finds an appropriate **Catch** block, your application continues normally. If no **Catch** block is found and therefore the exception is unhandled, the debugger will pause execution of your component and inform you about the unhandled exception. Exceptions that you select to treat this way are marked with a gray ball glyph.

- *Use parent setting:* When this setting is selected for an individual exception within a namespace, it means the exception should be treated in the same way as its parent namespace. When this setting is selected for a complete namespace, it means the namespace should be treated in the same way as its parent namespace.

The "Use parent setting" option is useful for controlling debugger behavior for a whole group of exceptions simultaneously, but it isn't as useful as it first appears. Because this dialog window groups exceptions into namespaces rather than exception inheritance hierarchies, you can't specify that the debugger should treat derived exceptions like their base exception. To take an example, most developers aren't very interested in the debugger treating all of the exceptions within the **System** namespace in the same manner. Instead, they're more likely to want the debugger to handle the derived exceptions **DivideByZeroException**, **NotFiniteNumberException**, and **OverflowException** like their common base exception **System.ArithmeticException**. Unfortunately, this option isn't available.

Debugger Treatment of Unhandled Exceptions

The second frame in Figure 13-2 contains three options for controlling how the debugger deals with an unhandled exception—one that doesn't match any **Catch** block exception filters in your application. As described previously, the options for dealing with unhandled exceptions apply to either an entire category of exceptions, the exceptions within a single namespace, or a single exception, depending upon which level of the exception hierarchy that you select in the exceptions dialog window. The options for how the debugger treats an unhandled exception are as follows:

- *Break into the debugger:* When an exception is unhandled, this setting tells the debugger to break execution at the line where the exception occurred and hand over control to you. This is the default behavior, and I recommend always using this setting.

- *Continue:* This setting causes the debugger to ignore unhandled exceptions, which means that the CLR will terminate your process when an unhandled exception occurs. This setting is useless for managed applications, but it will let your application continue executing after an exception occurs in, and stops, scripting code.

- *Use parent setting:* As before, this tells the debugger to apply the setting you've defined for the parent node to the selected child node in the Exceptions window. This setting has the same drawback mentioned previously.

Please see the "Dealing with Unhandled Exceptions" section later in this chapter for a detailed look at how you can deal with unhandled exceptions in various types of VB .NET applications.

Adding Custom Exceptions

You can add your own exceptions to this dialog window. If you select the Common Language Runtime Exceptions node and click the Add button, you can enter the fully qualified name of a custom exception. The only slight caveat is that if you have two or more custom exceptions with the same name, but in different assemblies, this dialog window gives you no way of distinguishing between these exceptions. There's no validation that a custom exception with the name that you enter actually exists in your component. You should also be aware that the exception names are case-insensitive, so you can't define two exceptions whose name differs only by case.

You can also use the Clear All button to remove all user-defined exceptions from this dialog window, although there's no way to remove individual exceptions.

Breaking into the Debugger

When a first-chance CLR exception is thrown, and you specify the "Break into the debugger" option for that exception, the debugger will break into your code at the line where the exception occurs, before any of your exception-handling code has had a chance to execute. You are then presented with the dialog window shown in Figure 13-3.

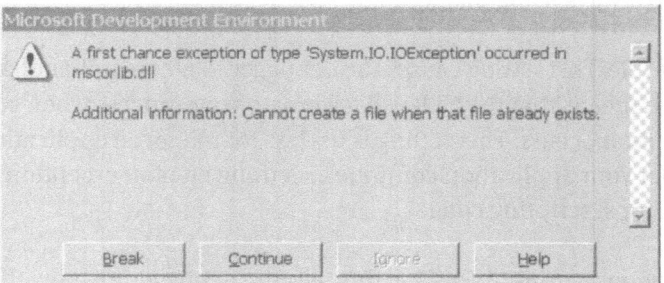

Figure 13-3. The exception thrown dialog window

Clicking the Break button puts you on the line of code that caused the exception. Unfortunately, you can't get access to the exception itself at this point. If you look in the Output window, you can see the same exception message that the dialog window showed you, and if you look in the Call Stack window, you can see the exception call stack. Getting access to the other properties of the exception is not possible, but you can step from here into your exception-handling code for further debugging.

Clicking the Continue button lets the CLR continue execution of your code, so that it can attempt to find a **Catch** block with an exception filter matching the exception that was thrown. If the CLR doesn't find a suitable exception filter, it will terminate the thread in which the exception happened. If this was the main thread of your process, the process itself will be terminated. This is because, by design, the CLR is unable to continue after an unhandled exception on the main thread of a process.

Dealing with Unhandled Exceptions

One of the great benefits of SEH is that you can choose to handle the exceptions that you understand and just ignore the ones that you don't. These latter exceptions are then automatically propagated up the call stack for some other code to handle. But what happens if the CLR can't find a **Catch** block anywhere in the call stack with an exception filter that matches a specific exception?

Such an exception is called an *unhandled exception.* The problem with such an unhandled exception is that it can cause the CLR to terminate your application's process, or at least terminate the thread in which the exception occurred. This abrupt termination is usually a bad thing, because it's not what your end users want or expect, and it can result in corrupt or lost data. The fact that an exception wasn't handled just because it wasn't expected isn't usually a good reason for terminating your application. Normally, your application should terminate and roll back the task that was being performed when the exception occurred, but leave the application still running. This allows the end user to try some other way of performing the task or to continue with some other task.

Figure 13-4 shows the dialog window that the debugger produces when you opt to break into the debugger after an unhandled exception. At this point, clicking Break will cause the debugger to drop into the source code at the line that threw the exception, and clicking Continue will cause the process to terminate unless you have an unhandled exception filter in place. This is because the CLR can't continue properly after an unhandled exception in an application's main thread.

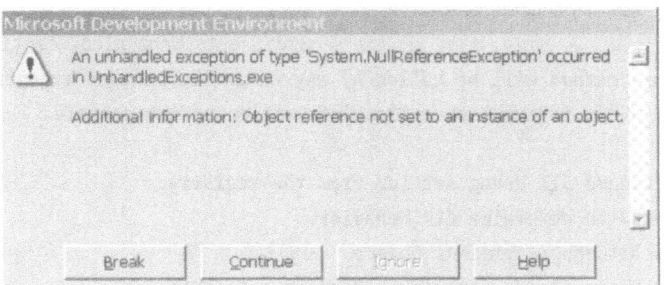

Figure 13-4. The debugger's unhandled exception dialog window

You can tell the CLR to notify you about all unhandled exceptions with just a few lines of code. Listing 13-11 shows a skeleton console application that has implemented an unhandled exception filter to catch all unhandled exceptions and report information about the exception and the CLR's intentions. The code shown constructs a delegate for **System.UnhandledExceptionEventHandler** at the start of the application, in this case at the beginning of the **Main** method. This delegate is registered with **AppDomain**'s **CurrentDomain.UnhandledException** event. Whenever a managed thread has an unhandled exception, the CLR will invoke the **UnhandledExceptionFilter** method. Note that unhandled exceptions in unmanaged threads are ignored by the CLR.

Listing 13-11. An Unhandled Exception Filter That Reports Exception Information

```
Option Strict On
Imports System
Imports Microsoft.Win32

Module Startup

    Sub Main()
        'Register my unhandled exception filter with the AppDomain.
        'This means that my UnhandledExceptionFilter method will be
        'called whenever an unhandled managed exception occurs.
        AddHandler AppDomain.CurrentDomain.UnhandledException, _
                        AddressOf UnhandledExceptionFilter

        'Here's where the normal application code should appear.
        'In this case, deliberately create an exception instead
        'so that we can test the unhandled exception filter.
        Dim objTest As Object
        objTest.ToString()

    End Sub


    Private Sub UnhandledExceptionFilter(ByVal sender As Object, _
                                    ByVal e As UnhandledExceptionEventArgs)
        'This method will be called by any unhandled managed exception.
        'It dumps relevant exception information to the console.

        'Retrieve JIT debug setting from the registry.
        'This can determine CLR behavior.
        Dim JitDebugSetting As Object
        Dim RegKey As RegistryKey = Registry.LocalMachine
```

```
        RegKey = RegKey.OpenSubKey("Software\Microsoft\.NetFramework")
        JitDebugSetting = RegKey.GetValue("DbgJitDebugLaunchSetting")


        'Debug or Release configuration?
#If Debug Then
        Console.WriteLine("DEBUG configuration")
#Else
        Console.WriteLine("RELEASE configuration")
#End If


        'Is a debugger attached to this process?
        Console.WriteLine("Debugger attached? " + Debugger.IsAttached.ToString)


        'Does this application have a user interface?
        Console.WriteLine("End-user present? " + _
                Environment.UserInteractive.ToString)


        'Is this a CLS-compliant exception?
        Console.WriteLine("CLS-compliant exception? " _
                    + ((TypeOf e.ExceptionObject Is Exception).ToString))


        'What's the CLR going to do with the process?
        If e.IsTerminating = True Then
            Console.WriteLine("CLR will terminate this process")
        Else
            Console.WriteLine("CLR won't terminate this process")
        End If


        'What's the CLR going to do about debugging?
        If Debugger.IsAttached = True Then
            Console.WriteLine("CLR didn't talk to user or spawn a debugger')
        Else


            'If process is terminating, CLR checks registry for action.
            'NB The CLR acted on this setting BEFORE this method was called!
            If e.IsTerminating = True Then
                If JitDebugSetting Is Nothing Then
                    Console.WriteLine("No JIT debug setting in registry")
                Else
                    Console.WriteLine("JIT debug setting: " + _
                        JitDebugSetting.ToString)
                    Select Case JitDebugSetting
                        Case 0
```

```
                                    Console.WriteLine("CLR asked about starting
        debugger")
                              Case 1
                                    Console.WriteLine("CLR didn't ask or start
        a debugger")
                              Case 2
                                    Console.WriteLine("CLR started debugger
        automatically")
                              Case Else
                                    Console.WriteLine("JIT debug setting is invalid!")
                        End Select
                  End If
            Else
                  Console.WriteLine("CLR didn't talk to user or spawn
        a debugger")
                  End If

            End If

            'Write exception to console
            Console.WriteLine(Environment.NewLine + "Exception text is:")
            Console.WriteLine(e.ExceptionObject.ToString)
            Console.ReadLine()

      End Sub

End Module
```

One important concept to realize is that this method is considered by the CLR to be a catch filter, so that at this point in the process none of the **Finally** blocks between the method where the exception was thrown and this method at the top of the call stack have been executed. As soon as this unhandled exception filter has finished executing, any outstanding **Finally** blocks are in turn executed, starting at the bottom of the call stack and moving upward.

The unhandled exception filter in Listing 13-11 dumps some interesting information about the exception and the local environment to the console. If you execute this code under different application types and configurations, and with different exceptions, you will see the wide variety of situations that an unhandled exception filter has to deal with. When designing a realistic unhandled exception filter, you need to bear in mind several points:

- Is this process running in **Debug** mode or **Release** mode?

- Is a debugger attached to this process?

- Does the application have a user interface?

- Is the exception CLS-compliant?

- Is the CLR going to terminate this process as a result of the exception?

- What's the CLR going to do about debugging the process?

Apart from these factors, you also need to know whether you're dealing with a Windows Forms application, as the CLR exhibits some extra behavior in this case and you might want to intercept this behavior. Before going further, I'm going to discuss each of these points. Then I can put everything together and come up with something that tackles all of the possible scenarios.

Unhandled Exception Filter Considerations

The first and most important factor to consider is whether the CLR is going to terminate the process as a result of the exception. The CLR decides this by examining the type of thread that threw the exception.

If the thread was the finalizer thread, the CLR simply swallows the exception and moves on to call the next object's **Finalize** method. For any thread started manually with **System.Threading.Thread**, the CLR swallows the exception and kills the thread. For a thread in the thread pool, once again the exception is swallowed and then the thread is returned to the pool. In each of these cases, the CLR won't kill the process.

Only when the exception occurs on the main thread of a process does the CLR elect to kill the process. To reflect what's going to happen, the **e.IsTerminating** property is set to **true** or **false**.

Obviously, this factor will play some part in determining how you deal with the unhandled exception. If the process is going to terminate, you should definitely log this fact. If the application has a user interface (see the **Environment.UserInteractive** property), you might also want to produce a dialog window to inform the user about the exception and process termination, and maybe ask whether the user wants this exception reported automatically. This dialog window could perhaps offer to restart the application automatically and reload the user's work-in-progress. On the other hand, if the application is a Windows service or an XML Web service, displaying a user dialog would be futile. Instead, you need to warn any monitoring application about what's going to happen and maybe report the process death to the Windows event log.

If the process is going to be terminated as a result of the exception, you also need to deal with how the CLR makes choices about launching a debugger. The CLR first determines if a debugger is already attached to the process—you can check this by using the **System.Debugger.IsAttached** property. If a debugger is attached, the CLR will let the process terminate without taking any further action, as soon as the unhandled exception filter has finished executing. If a debugger isn't already attached, the CLR uses the registry setting *DbgJITDebugLaunchSetting*, which exists under the HKEY_LOCAL_MACHINE section of the registry, as discussed in Chapter 3. This setting has three possible values, which have the following meanings:

- *0:* The CLR displays the dialog window shown in Figure 13-5. If the user elects to debug the process, the CLR will launch a debugger using the command line specified in the *DbgManagedDebugger* registry subkey. If instead the user chooses not to debug the process, only then is your unhandled exception filter invoked followed by termination of the process.

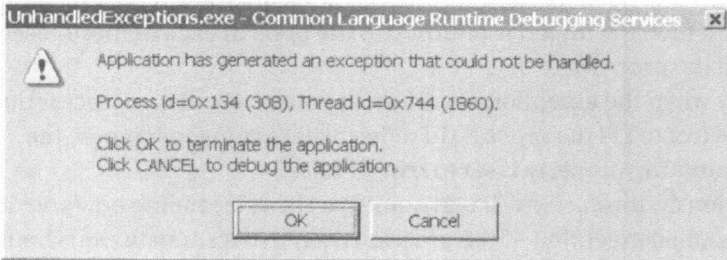

Figure 13-5. The CLR asks the user whether he or she wants to debug an unhandled exception.

- *1:* The CLR doesn't display a dialog window or launch a debugger. It just invokes your unhandled exception filter, followed by termination of the process.

- *2:* Without displaying any dialog box, the CLR launches the debugger specified in the *DbgManagedDebugger* registry subkey and attaches it to the offending process. If the launched debugger is the Visual Studio debugger, you should remember that it has its own dialog window that asks the user how he or she wants to debug the application.

It's important to realize that when the CLR is going to terminate the process, all of this happens *before* your unhandled exception filter is invoked. If you want to alter this CLR debugging behavior, your application should arrange for this registry setting to be altered appropriately. The most flexible approach for any end user's production machine is probably to set this registry value to 1, so that you can control everything from your unhandled exception filter.

Alternatively, if the CLR isn't going to terminate the process as a result of the exception, you might consider launching a debugger yourself (using **Debugger.Launch**), providing the application is running in **Debug** mode and a debugger isn't already attached.

The final factor to consider is whether the exception is CLS-compliant. In the majority of cases, this will always be true and you will have access to all of the standard exception properties. Otherwise, you only have access to the standard **Object** properties, such as **ToString**.

A Realistic Unhandled Exception Filter

Pulling together all the information discussed in the previous section, I can start to put together a realistic unhandled exception filter that can cope with each of the possible scenarios. Listing 13-12 shows the same skeleton console application, but this time with a more sensible filter.

Listing 13-12. Implementing a Realistic Unhandled Exception Filter

```
Option Strict On
Imports System
Imports Microsoft.Win32


Module Startup


    Sub Main()
        'Register my unhandled exception filter with the AppDomain.
        'This means that my UnhandledExceptionFilter method will be
        'called whenever an unhandled managed exception occurs.
        AddHandler AppDomain.CurrentDomain.UnhandledException, _
                        AddressOf UnhandledExceptionFilter


        'Here's where the normal application code should appear.
        'In this case, deliberately create an exception instead
        'so that we can test the unhandled exception filter.
        Dim objTest As Object
        objTest.ToString()
```

```vbnet
    End Sub

    Private Sub UnhandledExceptionFilter(ByVal sender As Object, _
                                    ByVal e As UnhandledExceptionEventArgs)
        'This method will be called by any unhandled managed exception
        Dim MessageFriendly As String, MessageDetail As String

        'Log detailed exception message if no debugger is attached to this
process
        If Debugger.IsAttached = False Then
            MessageDetail = "An unhandled exception occurred!"
            MessageDetail += Environment.NewLine
            MessageDetail += e.ExceptionObject.ToString
            MessageDetail += Environment.NewLine
            MessageDetail += "Application user was " + Environment.UserName
            MessageDetail += Environment.NewLine
            If e.IsTerminating = True Then
                MessageDetail += "CLR will terminate process"
                MessageDetail += " (exception was on main thread)."
            Else
                MessageDetail += "CLR won't terminate process"
                MessageDetail += " (exception was not on main thread)."
            End If
            'Write detailed message to the Windows event log
            Dim EventLogWriter As New EventLog("Application", ".", _
                            System.AppDomain.CurrentDomain.FriendlyName)
            EventLogWriter.WriteEntry(MessageDetail, EventLogEntryType.Warning)
            EventLogWriter.Close
            EventLogWriter.Dispose
        End If

#If Debug = True Then
        'Launch the debugger if DEBUG build, no debugger already attached
        'and this is an interactive process (user is present)
        If Environment.UserInteractive And (Debugger.IsAttached = False) Then
            Debugger.Launch()
        End If
#Else
        'If RELEASE build and this is an interactive process (user is present),
        'then show user either a warning or a critical message
        If Environment.UserInteractive = True Then
            MessageFriendly = "Unfortunately, this application hit an problem."
            MessageFriendly += Environment.NewLine
```

```
            If e.IsTerminating = True Then
                MessageFriendly += "You can restart app after it has closed."
                MessageFriendly += Environment.NewLine
                MessageFriendly += "Please ask support team to examine event
log."
                MsgBox(MessageFriendly, _
                            MsgBoxStyle.Critical Or MsgBoxStyle.OKOnly, _
                            "Sorry for the inconvenience")
            Else
                MessageFriendly += "Please save your work asap "
                MessageFriendly += "before restarting the application."
                MsgBox(MessageFriendly, _
                            MsgBoxStyle.Exclamation Or MsgBoxStyle.OKOnly,
                            "Sorry for the inconvenience")
            End If
        End If
#End If

    End Sub

End Module
```

Just like in Listing 13-11, the console application shown in Listing 13-12 starts by constructing a delegate for **System.UnhandledExceptionEventHandler**. Once the unhandled exception filter has been called, it records a detailed exception message in the Windows event log, providing that no debugger is attached to the process. If a debugger is attached, it assumes that no exception logging will be needed.

After this, it will launch the debugger if the application is a debug build, no debugger is already attached and, most important, this is an interactive session. There is no point in launching a debugger automatically for an XML Web service or a Windows service.

If the application is instead a release build, and also only if it's an interactive process, the method displays either a message warning to the user to save his or her work if the process isn't going to terminate or a message telling the user that the application is going to close and referring the application support team to the detailed exception message in the Windows event log.

You should experiment and change this method to suit the exact requirements of your application. Perhaps you'll want to e-mail the exception message automatically and restart the application automatically. Or maybe you don't want to inform the user at all if the exception isn't going to result in process termination. There are many possibilities here, and you should think about these in the context of your own applications.

Unhandled Exceptions in Windows Forms

A Windows Form application adds yet another quirk to the process of dealing with unhandled exceptions. If a debugger is attached, everything will behave in the manner that you've already seen. However, if a debugger isn't attached, the CLR will by default show a warning dialog window to the end user similar to the one shown in Figure 13-6.

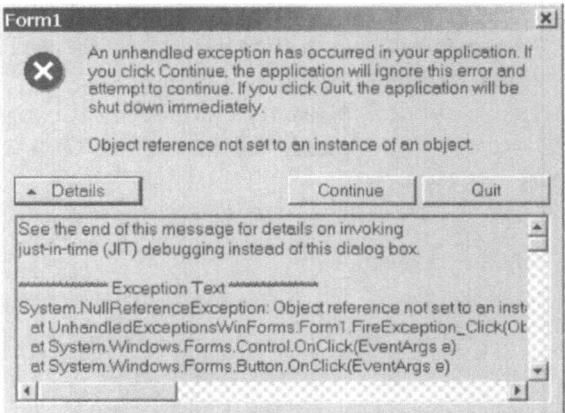

Figure 13-6. A Windows Forms unhandled exception dialog window

This dialog window is shown because an unhandled exception that occurs while a window message is processed ends up invoking **Application.OnThreadException**. Unless you override this method, it displays the dialog window shown in Figure 13-6. This dialog window informs the end user about the exception and asks whether the application should continue or quit. If the user does choose to continue, it's probably advisable for the user to save his or her work and quit the application as soon as possible.

After this dialog window is shown to the end user, the exception has been handled, so your unhandled exception filter discussed in the previous section won't be called. This means that the exception won't be logged unless the end user does so, which often means never! If this is a problem for you or for the support team, Listing 13-13 shows how you can override this default behavior in order to define your own behavior, which might include logging the unhandled exception and perhaps displaying your own "improved" dialog window.

*Listing 13-13. Overriding the Windows Form Built-in Unhandled Exception
Dialog Window*

```vb
Option Strict On
Imports System
Imports System.Windows.Forms

Module UnhandledExceptions

    Sub Main()

        'In a Windows Form app, if a managed exception occurs and a debugger
        'isn't attached, the CLR will display an exception warning dialog.
        'If we want to override this dialog, we need to register a delegate
        'so that our method will be called instead.
        AddHandler Application.ThreadException, AddressOf OverrideClrDialog

        'Here's where the normal application code should appear.
        'In this case, the form will deliberately create an exception
        'so that we can test the unhandled exception filter.
        Application.Run(New FormTest())

    End Sub

    Private Sub OverrideClrDialog(ByVal sender As Object, _
                ByVal e As System.Threading.ThreadExceptionEventArgs)
        'This method will be called by any unhandled managed exception,
        'assuming that a debugger wasn't attached.
        'You should log the exception here, and maybe display your own dialog.
        MsgBox(e.Exception.ToString, MsgBoxStyle.OKOnly, "OverrideClrDialog")
    End Sub

End Module
```

This will work fine for most unhandled exceptions, but you need to be aware
that by doing this, you're ensuring that the CLR won't normally invoke your standard unhandled exception filter. This means that you should place all of the
necessary code in your **OverrideClrDialog** method.

Instead of overriding the CLR dialog window, you can stop the CLR from displaying this window by setting the following line in the XML configuration file of
your Windows Form application:

```xml
<configuration>
    <system.windows.forms jitDebugging="true" />
</configuration>
```

This line tells the CLR that you want a JIT debugger to deal with the unhandled exception rather than the CLR, and then your standard unhandled exception filter (or the JIT debugger) can catch the unhandled exception.

In some situations, you'll need to override the CLR dialog window in Windows Forms and still catch unhandled exceptions using a standard unhandled exception filter as discussed earlier. These situations occur because the **Application.ThreadException** event isn't invoked in any of the following circumstances:

- An exception is thrown before the first window is launched.

- An exception is thrown but not marshaled back to a window thread.

- An exception is thrown while a debugger is attached.

- The application configuration file specifies JIT debugging.

- The exception isn't CLS-compliant.

Because of these situations, you may want to both override the CLR dialog window and also implement a standard unhandled exception filter. This is shown in Listing 13-14.

Listing 13-14. Catering to Every Possible Type of Unhandled Exception Situation

```
Option Strict On
Imports System
Imports System.Windows.Forms


Module UnhandledExceptions

    Sub Main()


        'First register the unhandled exception filter with the AppDomain.
        'Even in a Windows Forms app, this is useful for certain situations:
        'An exception is thrown before first window launched.
        'If a debugger is attached, unhandled exception will still reach here.
        'If app config sets JIT debugging, unhandled exception still reaches
here.
        'Exceptions that are not CLS-compliant will still only be caught here.
        AddHandler AppDomain.CurrentDomain.UnhandledException, _
                AddressOf UnhandledExceptionFilter
```

```
'In a Windows Form app, if a managed exception occurs and a debugger
'isn't attached, the CLR will display an exception warning dialog.
'If we want to override this dialog, we need to register a delegate
'so that our method will be called instead.
AddHandler Application.ThreadException, AddressOf OverrideClrDialog

'Here's where the normal application code should appear.
'In this case, the form will deliberately create an exception
'so that we can test the unhandled exception filter.
Application.Run(New FormTest())

End Sub

Private Sub UnhandledExceptionFilter(ByVal sender As Object, _
                                ByVal e As UnhandledExceptionEventArgs)
    'This method deals with everything not handled by OverrideClrDialog
    MsgBox(e.ExceptionObject.ToString, MsgBoxStyle.OKOnly, _
            "UnhandledExceptionFilter: " + e.IsTerminating.ToString)

End Sub

Private Sub OverrideClrDialog(ByVal sender As Object, _
            ByVal e As System.Threading.ThreadExceptionEventArgs)
    'This method will be called by any unhandled managed exception,
    'assuming that a debugger wasn't attached.
    'You should log the exception here, and maybe display your own dialog.
    MsgBox(e.Exception.ToString, MsgBoxStyle.OKOnly, "OverrideClrDialog')
End Sub

End Module
```

Unhandled Exceptions in XML Web Services

For internal applications running over an intranet, you shouldn't need to catch an unhandled exception inside of an XML Web service. This is because there will always be a client component waiting to catch most exceptions, and if the exception has reached the stage of being unhandled, it's likely that you won't know how to deal with that exception inside your XML Web service anyway.

For a Web service that interacts with external applications over the Internet, it's often a different story. Exposing every exception could involve significant security issues and allow malicious hackers to probe your Web service for weaknesses. In this case, you usually want to catch and record every unhandled exception and then throw a generic exception saying that the method call failed.

The first step is to realize that the **Application_Error** event in the global.asax file that you normally use to catch unhandled exceptions in ASP.NET doesn't work for unhandled exceptions within a Web service. This is because the HTTP handler for XML Web services catches any unhandled exception and turns it into a SOAP fault before the **Application_Error** event is called. This SOAP fault then becomes a **SoapException** or a **SoapHeaderException**, depending on whether the exception was thrown while processing a SOAP header or not. This exception is serialized and passed to the Web service's client. The **SoapException** (or **SoapHeaderException**) provides no direct information about the original exception, although the text of the original exception is contained in the exception's **Message** property.

To catch an unhandled exception in a Web service, you need to build a SOAP extension to catch unhandled exceptions in a global exception handler. Within your SOAP extension, you can check for SOAP exceptions in the **AfterSerialize** stage of the **ProcessMessage** method. For full details on how to do this, please refer to Chapter 8, which covers the debugging of XML Web services.

Exception Management Application Block

The Exception Management Application Block is a free customizable exception-handling framework written by a team from Microsoft. This framework aims to make your application more robust, reduce the amount of custom error-handling code that you have to write, and be flexible enough so that you can easily extend its functionality.

The framework comes as source code with considerable documentation, and it consists of two assemblies. The **ExceptionManagement** assembly contains the primary class, **ExceptionManager**, through which you publish exceptions. It also contains two other classes: **DefaultPublisher** for writing exception details to the Windows event log and **ExceptionManagerInstaller** for creating event log sources during installation. The **ExceptionManagement.Interfaces** assembly contains interfaces that are implemented by exception publisher classes, including optionally your own custom publishers.

To use the Exception Management Application Block from within your application, perform the following steps:

1. Build the two assemblies.

2. Set a reference in your project to the **ExceptionManagement.dll** assembly.

3. Add an **Imports** statement to reference the
   Microsoft.ApplicationBlocks.ExceptionManagement namespace.

4. Publish any exception by calling the static **ExceptionManager.Publish**
   method from within a **Catch** or **Finally** block, as shown in Listing 13-15.

Listing 13-15. Publishing an Exception Using the Exception Management
Application Block

```
Catch ex As Exception
    ExceptionManager.Publish(ex)
```

I have used this framework and recommend it highly. The two major benefits
for me were the ability to configure the framework's behavior very easily using
the standard .NET XML configuration files and the ease of creating and configuring custom exception publishers.

There are some caveats of which you should be aware. First, the Exception
Management Application Block only works on Windows 2000 and Windows XP.
Second, it only deals with exception publishing, so you still need to understand
how to deal with unhandled exceptions and how to create custom exceptions.
Finally, you need to come to grips with the copious documentation and understand how the framework works before implementing it in a production
application.

Analyzing Exception Behavior

If you run the Performance Monitor application as discussed in Chapter 6, you
can see that .NET provides some performance counters specifically for measuring the effects that exceptions are having on your application. You can use
these counters to monitor application performance and stability metrics, and to
spot situations where an unusual number of exceptions might indicate that
something is wrong.

Figure 13-7 shows the .NET exception performance counters displayed using
Performance Monitor. If you don't see these counters when you run Performance
Monitor, you may be a victim of a known bug where upgrading from .NET Beta 2
to RTM trashes some performance counters. To correct this, you should use the
procedure described in the Microsoft Knowledge Base article Q306722.

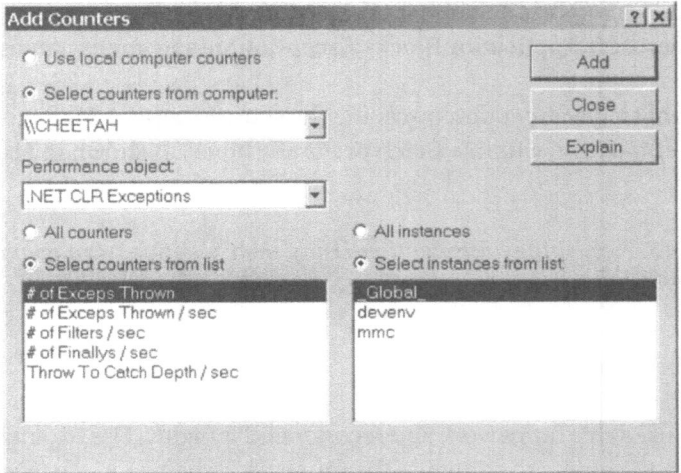

Figure 13-7. The .NET exception performance counters

Note that none of the "per second" exception performance counters are an average over time. Instead, each one displays the difference between the values produced by the last two samples divided by the number of seconds between the two sample times.

- *# of Exceps Thrown:* This counter displays the total number of exceptions thrown since your application started running, including both handled and unhandled exceptions. It also includes exceptions that are rethrown. This counter isn't really of much use except as a general guideline.

- *# of Exceps Thrown / sec:* This counter displays the number of exceptions thrown per second, including handled and unhandled exceptions. This is more useful than the previous counter, and you can use it to detect significant bursts of exceptions.

- *# of Filters / sec:* This counter displays the number of **Catch** block exception filters evaluated each second. Note that this is the number of exception filters tried, not the number actually triggered. I can't see an interesting use for this performance counter, except maybe for a comparison of the same application executed several times.

- *# of Finallys / sec:* This counter displays the number of **Finally** blocks executed each second as a result of exceptions being thrown. This number doesn't include **Finally** blocks executed on the normal code path. Once again, I can't see the use of this performance counter in most situations, except maybe as a general guideline.

- *Throw To Catch Depth / sec:* This counter displays the number of stack frames (methods) traversed each second from where each exception is thrown to where it's caught. You could use this counter to understand variations in your application's performance, but it's probably more of a curiosity.

These performance counters are more useful for understanding subtleties in performance behavior rather than for diagnosing performance problems. They can be used to explain "why" rather than "what."

Exceptions Sample Solution

If you want to investigate some more code that demonstrates how to deal with exceptions, you can find a small example application in the Technologies\ Exceptions subfolder of the .NET Framework SDK samples folder.

Summary

This chapter really went to town on exception management because this is such an important subject if you want to build stable applications. You started by looking at some of the strategic concepts that are essential to understand before you start constructing your error-handling code. Then you looked at the mechanics and management of exceptions in exhaustive detail, including exception debugging within the IDE, the use of custom exceptions, and how to deal with unhandled exceptions. Finally, you dealt with some of the more advanced situations, such as cross-thread exceptions, remoting exceptions, and using performance counters to analyze exception behavior within your application.

Possibly the most important lessons to take away from this chapter are that you need to have a strategy for your application's exception handling and you need to follow that strategy closely to make your application as solid and reliable as possible.

INTERLUDE

In 1998, the excellent online magazine Salon (`http://www.salon.com`) published the results of a competition that asked readers to write Windows error messages in the form of haikus. A *haiku* is a form of Japanese poetry where the poem must be three lines only. The first line must have five syllables, the second line seven syllables, and the third line five syllables. Within this strict framework, a haiku poem is usually a little gem of philosophy. With the kind permission of Salon magazine, here are some of the haiku poems that Salon readers produced. The world would be more entertaining if developers were as creative as this in designing their error messages.

A file that big?
It might be very useful.
But now it is gone.
—David Liszewski

Yesterday it worked
Today it is not working
Windows is like that.
—Margaret Segall

Three things are certain:
Death, taxes, and lost data.
Guess which has occurred.
—David Dixon

You step in the stream,
but the water has moved on.
This page is not here.
—Cass Whittington

Out of memory.
We wish to hold the whole sky,
But we never will.
—Francis Heaney

Chaos reigns within.
Reflect, repent, and reboot.
Order shall return.
—Suzie Wagner

ABORTED effort:
Close all that you have.
You ask way too much.
—*Mike Hagler*

First snow, then silence.
This thousand dollar screen dies
so beautifully.
—*Simon Firth*

With searching comes loss
and the presence of absence:
"My Novel" not found.
—*Howard Korder*

Windows NT crashed.
I am the Blue Screen of Death.
No one hears your screams.
—*Peter Rothman*

A crash reduces
your expensive computer
to a simple stone.
—*James Lopez*

Everything is gone;
Your life's work has been destroyed.
Squeeze trigger (yes/no)?
—*David Carlson*

I'm sorry, there's—um—
insufficient—what's-it-called?
The term eludes me...
—*Owen Matthews*

The code was willing,
It considered your request,
But the chips were weak.
—*Barry Brumitt*

Printer not ready.
Could be a fatal error.
Have a pen handy?
—Pat Davis

Errors have occurred.
We won't tell you where or why.
Lazy programmers.
—Charlie Gibbs

Server's poor response
Not quick enough for browser.
Timed out, plum blossom.
—Rik Jespersen

There is a chasm
of carbon and silicon
the software can't bridge.
—Rahul Sonnad

No keyboard present
Hit F1 to continue
Zen engineering?
—Jim Griffith

Hal, open the file
Hal, open the damn file, Hal
open the, please Hal.
—Jennifer Jo Lane

I ate your Web page.
Forgive me. It was juicy
and tart on my tongue.
—Anonymous

CHAPTER 14

Debugging Multithreaded Applications

"Multithreading" is a word that strikes fear into the hearts of many VB.Classic developers. Although VB 5.0 introduced a restricted type of multithreading called *apartment* threading, VB .NET is the first version of Visual Basic to have proper *free* threading. This means that you've been given a very powerful tool to make your application faster and more responsive to its users. As with any powerful technology, it requires that you have a good understanding of the benefits and drawbacks in order to use it properly and safely.

When I started skydiving many years ago, I never forgot the sign above the clubhouse door. It read simply "Knowledge dispels fear." In no area of software development is this saying more true than multithreading. Most Visual Basic developers are relatively unfamiliar with the subject, and even those programmers who tried VB.Classic development using apartment threading will be worried when faced with free threading. The key to avoiding threading bugs lies in a good knowledge of what can go wrong and why it goes wrong.

This chapter looks at how and why multithreading is so difficult, and gives you some knowledge and tools that will help you to tackle this subject safely. It starts with a quick look at how multithreading works and why it's so difficult to do correctly. Then it examines when multithreading is, and isn't, useful. Knowing when *not* to use multithreading is important because it can save you a lot of time in testing and debugging.

The next section of this chapter looks in more detail at the sorts of bugs that can be introduced when writing multithreaded programs. It demonstrates why it's necessary to design your multithreaded applications to avoid bugs rather than trying to remove the bugs later. The elusive nature of many multithreading bugs means that the normal code ➢ test ➢ debug cycle doesn't work well when writing multithreaded programs.

I'll show you the four main types of threading problems in some detail, using small example applications to illustrate the issues and some possible solutions. The final example application shows you how to use multithreading safely in a typical graphical user interface (GUI) program. It looks at debugging a relatively simple multithreaded application that uses messages to pass information between a user interface thread and a background thread, thus avoiding thread synchronization problems. You'll also learn how to propagate an exception across thread boundaries, even when using asynchronous threads.

Multithreading Basics

Figure 14-1 shows a simple multithreaded program using two threads that access a single instance of three separate classes.

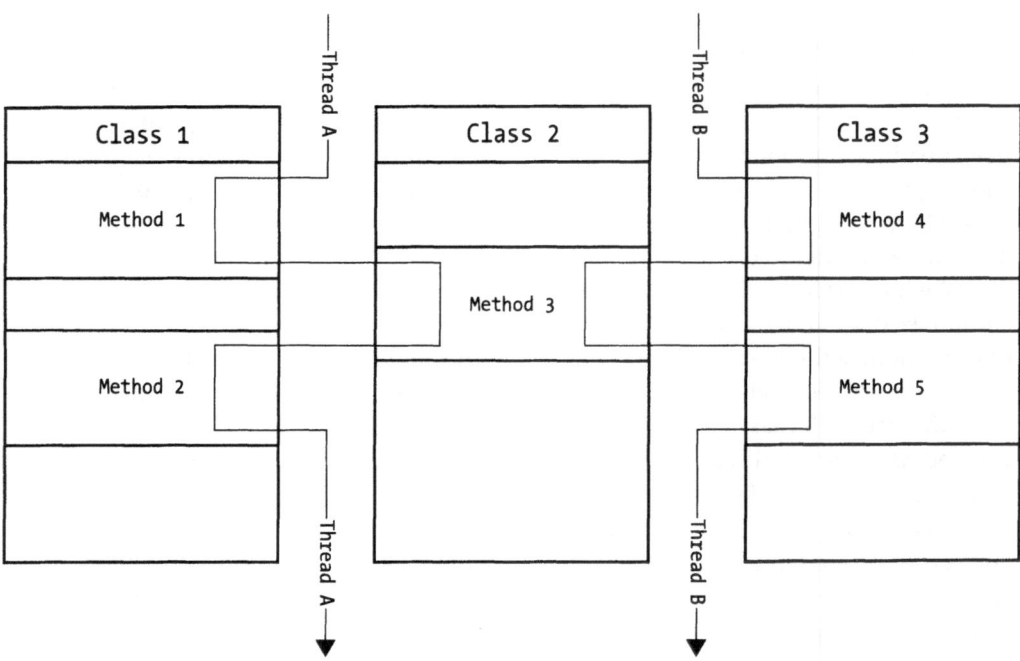

Figure 14-1. A simple multithreaded application

Thread A executes the code in class objects 1 and 2, and thread B runs through the code in class objects 2 and 3. Both threads access a common method in the instance of class 2, thereby sharing the code and data that this method uses.

Why Multithreading Is So Difficult

Of course, on a single-processor machine, the two threads don't actually execute simultaneously. What happens is that the operating system interleaves instructions from the two threads to give the impression that the threads are executing together. Whenever control is switched from thread A to thread B, the processor saves the context of thread A, restores the context of thread B, and then starts running it. As soon as an instruction from thread A is reached, the same process happens in reverse. Because this all happens so fast, you receive the impression that both threads are executing simultaneously.

Say that you have two threads containing just ten source code instructions. How many ways can these ten instructions be interleaved together? The answer, in case you haven't got a calculator handy, is 184,756! This starts to look worrying. How can you possibly test 184,756 possible code paths? Unfortunately, the situation is actually much worse than this. Threads aren't interleaved together at the level of source code, or even CIL, but at the assembly code level. When a single source statement can translate to dozens of native code instructions, you can see the impossibility of using execution testing to verify that your multithreaded application is working correctly.

So if you can't test a multithread program using code coverage tools, how about trying to desk-check it? Is it possible to examine the source code thoroughly enough to be able to predict problems resulting from multiple threads? Well, it's a nice idea that combining lots of brainpower with lots of multithreading experience can help you to find and remove the problems. The truth is that hard-earned evidence gained from very experienced developers has demonstrated that this doesn't work. Developers' brains simply aren't equipped to cope with understanding how multiple execution threads can interact with each other.

Because multithreading involves a nonlinear process, and a developer is unable to establish the exact flow of execution because the interleaving of threaded code happens at the level of assembly code, many of the bugs occur rarely and seemingly at random. Even moving a multithreaded program from a machine with a slow processor to one with a much faster processor can cause bugs to appear and disappear, because the processor speed can prevent or cause "racing" between threads.

Before looking at "racing" and other bug types that can be caused by the use of multiple threads, it's worth examining when multithreading can be useful to you, and when it doesn't give you the benefits that you might think.

Multithreading Advantages

One of the best and most common uses of multithreading is to keep the user interface of your program responsive to the user while also performing one or more background tasks. For instance, the end user might ask your application to calculate the current market value of a sophisticated financial derivative instrument. During this lengthy calculation, you want the user to be able to cancel the operation if it's taking too long, perhaps by clicking a Cancel button. This chapter's last example application shows a very similar scenario to this, and multithreading done properly works very well for this type of situation.

Another good use of multithreading is to keep the user interface updated with the intermediate results of a background task that's running. For instance, in the scenario just discussed, you might want to display intermediate results from the option valuation on the user interface while the calculation continues. If you don't use multithreading and the option calculation runs on the same thread as the user interface, you'll find that the application's window will go blank and won't be repainted. This is because the single thread can't cope with performing both tasks simultaneously.

An associated advantage of multithreading comes when you have a task that's going to take a long time to complete. In this case, you can fire off a background thread to perform the task and forget about it until the task completes at some time in the future. In the case of a background thread, this thread will be terminated automatically if the process that launched it is finished. Some dangers are associated with this automatic termination of a background thread because the termination is done through the CLR calling **Thread.Abort**. For a discussion of the dangers associated with **Thread.Abort**, please see the section titled "Terminating a Managed Thread" later in this chapter.

Yet another advantageous use of multithreading is to spawn a new thread for each user request to a server application. This allows multiple users to be serviced without the delay that might happen if the user requests are serialized and processed just one at a time. The built-in thread pool supplied by .NET is often an excellent solution to this situation.

If your application is doing input/output (I/O) work, such as accessing a disk, a printer, or the network, these resources can have unpredictable delays. Multiple threads can help to prevent I/O latency affecting other parts of your application.

You can use threads to isolate critical subsystems of your application from noncritical subsystems. Because most thread exceptions won't propagate out of the thread, this prevents an error in, say, the printing subsystem of your application affecting the radiation dosage monitoring subsystem.

A final reason for using multithreading is to establish the priority of an application's competing tasks. You can set the priority of a thread when it's created, so an important task can be assigned a high priority while less important tasks can be given a lower priority.

Multithreading Disadvantages

This section presents some of the disadvantages of writing multithreading code. There's certainly no need to use multithreading just because it's there and it's cool.

Using multithreading on a single-processor machine to process multiple tasks where each task takes approximately the same time isn't always very effective. For example, you might decide to spawn ten threads within your program in order to process ten separate tasks. If each task takes approximately 1 minute to process, and you use ten threads to do this processing, you won't have access to any of the task results for the whole 10 minutes. If instead you processed the same tasks using just a single thread, you would see the first result in 1 minute, the next result 1 minute later, and so on. If you can make use of each result without having to rely on all of the results being ready simultaneously, the single thread might be the better way of implementing the program.

If you launch a large number of threads within a process, the overhead of thread housekeeping and context switching can become significant. The processor will spend considerable time in switching between threads, and many of the threads won't be able to make progress. In addition, a single process with a large number of threads means that threads in other processes will be scheduled less frequently and won't receive a reasonable share of processor time.

If multiple threads have to share many of the same resources, you're unlikely to see performance benefits from multithreading your application. Many developers see multithreading as some sort of magic wand that gives automatic performance benefits. Unfortunately multithreading isn't the magic wand that it's sometimes perceived to be. If you're using multithreading for performance reasons, you should measure your application's performance very closely in several different situations, rather than just relying on some nonexistent magic.

Coordinating thread access to common data can be a big performance killer. Achieving good performance with multiple threads isn't easy when using a coarse locking plan, because this leads to low concurrency and threads waiting for access. Alternatively, a fine-grained locking strategy increases the complexity and can also slow down performance unless you perform some sophisticated tuning.

Using multiple threads to exploit a machine with multiple processors sounds like a good idea in theory, but in practice you need to be careful. To gain any significant performance benefits, you need to learn about thread balancing. For instance, imagine an application that receives incoming price information from the network, aggregates and sorts that information, and then displays the results on the screen for the end user. With a dual-processor machine, it makes sense to split the task into, say, three threads. The first thread deals with storing the incoming price information, the second thread processes the prices, and the final thread handles the display of the results. After implementing this solution, you find that the price processing is by far the longest stage, so you decide to rewrite that thread's code to improve its performance by a factor of three. Unfortunately, this performance benefit in a single thread may not be reflected across your whole application. This is because the other two threads may not be able to keep pace with the improved thread. If the user interface thread is unable to keep up with the faster flow of processed information, the other threads now have to wait around for the new bottleneck in the system.

When you have a bug in multithreading code, it's really easy to blame the multiple threads and immediately start looking for data races and deadlocking. You should remember not to overlook the possibility of bugs in the single-threaded sequential code.

As I've already discussed, controlling code execution with multiple threads can be complex and is likely to result in hard-to-find software defects. To avoid these bugs by the use of good design, you need to understand them in some detail. The next section looks at typical bug types related to multithreading.

Multithreading Problems

Several bug types are associated with multithreading. The ones that you're most likely to meet are as follows:

- *Data races:* A data race occurs when multiple threads are allowed simultaneous access to read from and write to the same data area. This is likely to result in inconsistency or even corruption of that data. Using synchronization locks to serialize thread access to the common data area is the usual way of combating this problem.

- *Deadlock:* A process deadlock happens when two or more threads are unable to proceed because each is waiting for one of the others to proceed. The most common type of deadlock involves one thread issuing a synchronization lock on resource A and then trying to access resource B while another thread locks resource B and then tries to access resource A. The result is that the two threads are in a deadly embrace and each thread will wait forever for the opposing thread to relinquish its lock.

- *Livelock:* Process livelock occurs when two or more threads become caught in a circular loop. For example, thread A sends an error message to thread B, which responds by sending an error message back. This can result in a never-ending stream of error messages from one thread to the other.

- *Starvation:* Thread starvation happens when a thread grinds almost to a halt because of lack of processor time or a continuing failure to access some resource being used by other threads.

The next section looks at each of these problems in more detail and suggests ways of dealing with each problem.

Understanding Data Races

A data race happens when two or more threads race each other to read from and write to common data shared between the threads. The adverse effects of a data race happen when the reading and writing occur in a sequence not anticipated by the developer of the multithreaded code, and the common data then becomes corrupted.

The **ThreadSynch** console application demonstrates how a data race can occur. This program uses multiple worker threads to perform the very simple task of incrementing a shared counter from its starting value to a specified end value. Listing 14-1 shows the **Sub Main** of the application and the **CountCoordinator** class that launches the worker threads and coordinates the shared count.

Listing 14-1. The CountCoordinator Class

```
Option Strict On
Imports System.Threading

Module CountMonitor
    Sub Main()
        Dim CountTest As New CountCoordinator(5)
        Console.ReadLine()
    End Sub
End Module

Class CountCoordinator
    Private Const MAX_COUNT As Integer = 99
    Private m_Counter As Integer = 0

    Public Sub New(ByVal NumberOfCounters As Integer)
        Dim EachWorker As Integer, NewThread As Thread, _
            Worker As CountWorker
        'Show starting conditions
        Console.WriteLine( _
          "Count started at {0} with max value of {1}.", _
          CStr(Me.CurrentCount), CStr(Me.MaxCount))
        Console.WriteLine( _
          "{0} worker threads are doing the counting.", _
          CStr(NumberOfCounters))
        'Start specified number of worker threads
        For EachWorker = 1 To NumberOfCounters
            Worker = New CountWorker(Me, EachWorker)
            NewThread = New Thread(AddressOf _
                                     Worker.IncrementCount)
```

```
            NewThread.Start()
        Next EachWorker
    End Sub

    Public Property CurrentCount() As Integer
        Get
            Return m_Counter
        End Get
        Set(ByVal Value As Integer)
            m_Counter = Value
        End Set
    End Property

    Public ReadOnly Property MaxCount() As Integer
        Get
            Return MAX_COUNT
        End Get
    End Property

End Class
```

The application creates the **CountCoordinator** class and passes 5 as the number of worker threads required to the class constructor. The class constructor starts each of the specified number of threads, and these worker threads then compete for processor time to increment the shared counter from 0 to its maximum value, in this case 99. The worker threads are given access to this counter and its maximum value through the **CurrentCount** and **MaxCount** properties of the **CountCoordinator** class.

Listing 14-2 shows the **CountWorker** class, which represents each of the worker threads. This class stored the reference to the **CountCoordinator** class that it receives in its constructor and then uses this to increment the **CountCoordinator.CurrentCount** property.

Listing 14-2. The CountWorker Class

```
Class CountWorker
    Private m_Coordinator As CountCoordinator
    Private m_WorkerId As Integer

    Public Sub New(ByVal Coordinator As CountCoordinator, _
                ByVal WorkerId As Integer)
        m_Coordinator = Coordinator
        m_WorkerId = WorkerId
    End Sub
```

```
Public Sub IncrementCount()

    'Increment shared counter until equal to maximum allowed
    With m_Coordinator

        Do While .CurrentCount < .MaxCount
            Select Case .CurrentCount
                Case Is < (.MaxCount - 10)
                    Thread.Sleep(0)
                    .CurrentCount += 10
                Case Is < .MaxCount
                    Thread.Sleep(0)
                    .CurrentCount += 1
                Case Else
            End Select
            'Show current thread and counter value
            Console.WriteLine( _
                "Worker {0} current count {1}", _
                CStr(m_WorkerId), CStr(.CurrentCount))
        Loop

    End With

End Sub

End Class
```

The **IncrementCount** method takes one of three actions, depending on the current value of the shared counter. If the counter value is within 10 of the maximum, it adds 1 to the counter. If the counter value is not within 10 of the maximum, it adds 10 to the counter. If the counter value is equal to or greater than the maximum value, the thread simply finishes running, as no more counting is required.

Given this relatively simple code, it's hard to see what could go wrong. But if you run the **ThreadSynch** program, you can see that the counter is always incremented well beyond its maximum value before all of the worker threads cease working. Figure 14-2 shows an example where the counter starts at 0, has a maximum value of 99, and five worker threads have been allocated to perform the counting. The final counter value of 131 is much higher than you might expect from reading the code.

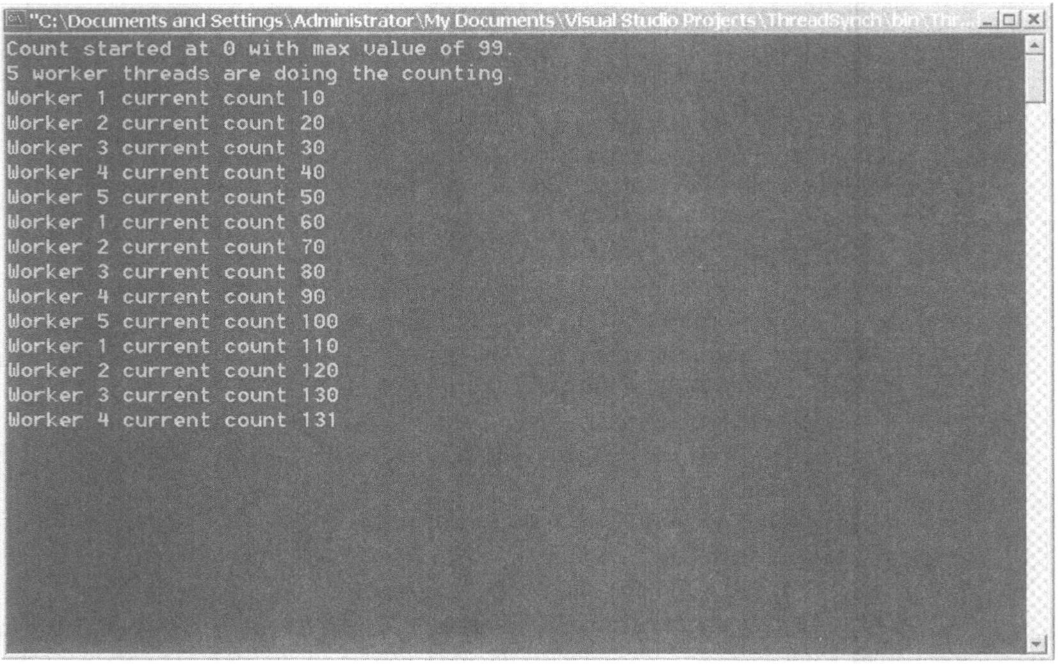

Figure 14-2. An example run of the ThreadSynch application

What's happening is that in between a thread reading the shared counter value and incrementing it, another thread has also incremented the value. The threads aren't all working with the same value of the counter, and therefore they race each other to read and increment this value.

The insidious evil is that in a real application, this final counter value could be almost any number equal to or greater than the maximum, depending on the number of allocated worker threads and when Windows decides to switch between each thread. In this example program, I deliberately made each thread give up its time slice by issuing a **Thread.Sleep(0)** instruction after reading the shared counter. This allows me to force a data race problem because sleeping one thread allows the processor to switch the execution of other threads. In the real world, where the **Thread.Sleep** instruction probably wouldn't be used in this manner, the code might work fine 99.99% of the time, and you're likely to see an inconsistent final number only when you're demonstrating the program to your boss or an important customer.

The most common way of solving a data race problem is to lock the data shared between multiple threads so that only one thread can access the shared data at any one time. One way of locking shared data is with the **SyncLock** statement. If you add the lines shown in bold in Listing 14-3 to the **CountWorker.IncrementCount** method, you'll find that the data race goes away completely.

Listing 14-3. Adding SyncLock to Synchronize Access to Shared Data

```
'Increment shared counter until equal to maximum allowed
With m_Coordinator

    Do While .CurrentCount < .MaxCount
        SyncLock(m_Coordinator)
            Select Case .CurrentCount
                Case Is < (.MaxCount - 10)
                    Thread.Sleep(0)
                    .CurrentCount += 10
                Case Is < .MaxCount
                    Thread.Sleep(0)
                    .CurrentCount += 1
                Case Else
            End Select
        End SyncLock

        'Show current thread and counter value
        Console.WriteLine("Worker {0} current count {1}", _
                    CStr(m_WorkerId), CStr(.CurrentCount))

    Loop

End With
```

In this example, **SyncLock** is used to lock access to the count coordinator object so that only one thread at a time can run code within this object for the duration of the lock. For finer synchronization, you can use the **Monitor** class. For high-performance addition or subtraction of a value type variable, you can use the **Interlocked** class. However, any locking strategy needs to beware of two potential problems. The first problem is that performance can be adversely affected if the locking is done too frequently or blocks too big a region of code from executing. The second problem is that locking exposes you to the classic deadlock situation, as discussed further in the next section.

Understanding Process Deadlock

A process deadlock happens when two or more threads are unable to proceed because each is waiting for one of the others to proceed. The most common type of deadlock occurs when one thread issues a synchronization lock on resource A and then tries to access resource B while another thread locks resource B and then tries to access resource A. The result is that the two threads are in a deadly embrace and each thread will wait forever for the opposing thread to relinquish its lock. An alternative scenario involves a cyclic chain of dependencies where multiple threads become gridlocked because they're queuing up and waiting for other threads to relinquish one or more shared resources. This is similar to the way that road traffic can become gridlocked at a very busy intersection.

The **ThreadDeadlock** console application demonstrates how a process deadlock can occur. This program consists of a **Bank** object that spawns multiple **Cashier** threads to randomly debit and credit two **Account** objects owned by the **Bank** object. Listing 14-4 shows the **Sub Main** of the application and the **Bank** class that launches the cashier threads and keeps control over the two bank accounts.

Listing 14-4. The Bank Class

```
Option Strict On
Imports System.Threading

Module DeadlockTest

    Sub Main()
        Dim TransferTest As New Bank(2, 10000)
        Console.ReadLine()
    End Sub

End Module

Class Bank
    Private m_AccountOne As New Account(1000000)
    Private m_AccountTwo As New Account(1000000)

    Public Sub New(ByVal NumberOfCashiers As Integer, _
                    ByVal NumberOfTransfers As Integer)
        Dim EachWorker As Integer, NewThread As Thread, _
            Worker As Cashier

        'Show starting conditions
        Console.WriteLine( _
          "{0} cashiers are performing {1} transfers each.", _
          NumberOfCashiers.ToString, _
                    NumberOfTransfers.ToString)
```

```
        'Start specified number of worker threads
        For EachWorker = 1 To NumberOfCashiers
            Worker = New Cashier(Me, NumberOfTransfers)
            NewThread = New Thread(AddressOf Worker.TransferMoney)
            NewThread.Name = "Cashier" & EachWorker.ToString
            NewThread.Start()
        Next EachWorker

    End Sub

    Public ReadOnly Property AccountOne() As Account
        Get
            AccountOne = m_AccountOne
        End Get
    End Property

    Public ReadOnly Property AccountTwo() As Account
        Get
            AccountTwo = m_AccountTwo
        End Get
    End Property

End Class
```

The application creates the **Bank** class and passes 2 to the class constructor as the number of cashiers required. It also passes the number of account transfers to be made, in this case 10,000. This relatively large number is used to demonstrate that a process deadlock can happen infrequently and may require some extensive execution testing to find. The **Bank** class has two instances of the **Account** class, each given an opening account balance of £1 million. When the **Bank** object is created, it then instantiates the specified number of **Cashier** objects and starts a worker thread for each of the cashiers. It also passes a reference to itself to each of the cashiers so that they can transfer money to and from the bank accounts.

One interesting point is that each of the cashier threads is given a name when it's instantiated. This really helps with debugging because the thread name is shown in the IDE Threads window, which makes each thread easier to identify. I go into more detail about the Threads window shortly, when you start to run this application.

Listing 14-5 shows the associated **Cashier** class. Each cashier is instantiated with an instruction to perform a certain number of transfers on the bank's two accounts, in this case 10,000 transfers. For each transfer, the bank accounts to credit and debit are chosen randomly from the two available. Before performing the transfer, the credit account is locked first followed by the debit account. This synchronization locking (shown in bold) prevents multiple cashiers from interfering with each other's transfers and causing a data race as seen in the previous example. Unlike the previous example, no thread sleeping is used. The sheer number of transfers happening is going to force a deadlock at some point, although thread sleeping (which allows other threads to run) will usually increase the speed at which a deadlock happens.

Listing 14-5. The Cashier Class

```
Class Cashier
    Private m_Bank As Bank, m_NumberOfTransfers As Integer

    Public Sub New(ByVal AnyBank As Bank, _
                   ByVal NumberOfTransfers As Integer)
        m_Bank = AnyBank
        m_NumberOfTransfers = NumberOfTransfers
    End Sub

    Public Sub TransferMoney()
        Dim CurrentTransfer As Integer

        With m_Bank

            For CurrentTransfer = 1 To m_NumberOfTransfers

                If TrueOrFalse() = True Then
                    SyncLock (.AccountOne)
                        SyncLock (.AccountTwo)
                            .AccountOne.CreditBalance(100)
                            .AccountTwo.DebitBalance(100)
                            Console.WriteLine( _
                                "{0}: Transfer {1}", _
                                Thread.CurrentThread.Name, _
                                CurrentTransfer.ToString)
                        End SyncLock
                    End SyncLock
                Else
                    SyncLock (.AccountTwo)
                        SyncLock (.AccountOne)
                            .AccountOne.DebitBalance(100)
                            .AccountTwo.CreditBalance(100)
                            Console.WriteLine( _
```

```
                         "{0}: Transfer {1}", _
                         Thread.CurrentThread.Name, _
                         CurrentTransfer.ToString)
                End SyncLock
            End SyncLock
        End If
    Next CurrentTransfer


    End With


End Sub


Private Function TrueOrFalse() As Boolean
    Randomize()
    Dim Test As Single = (Int((2 * Rnd()) + 1))
    Return CBool(Test = 1)
End Function
```

```
End Class
```

Finally, Listing 14-6 shows the **Account** class. This class offers functions for debiting and crediting the bank account, and a property for interrogating the current account balance.

Listing 14-6. The Account Class

```
Class Account
    Private m_AccountBalance As Decimal = 0

    Public Sub New(ByVal StartingBalance As Decimal)
        m_AccountBalance = StartingBalance
    End Sub

    Public ReadOnly Property AccountBalance() As Decimal
        Get
            AccountBalance = m_AccountBalance
        End Get
    End Property

    Public Function DebitBalance _
            (ByVal AmountToDebit As Decimal) As Decimal
        m_AccountBalance -= AmountToDebit
        Return m_AccountBalance
    End Function
```

```
Public Function CreditBalance _
        (ByVal AmountToCredit As Decimal) As Decimal
    m_AccountBalance += AmountToCredit
    Return m_AccountBalance
End Function

End Class
```

If you load the **ThreadDeadlock** solution into Visual Studio and run it using F5, you can see that it prints each transfer made by the two cashiers as it happens, along with the name of the cashier (thread) doing the transfer. At some unpredictable number of transfers, the application simply hangs, as shown in Figure 14-3. If you run the application many times, you should see that it hangs at a different point each time.

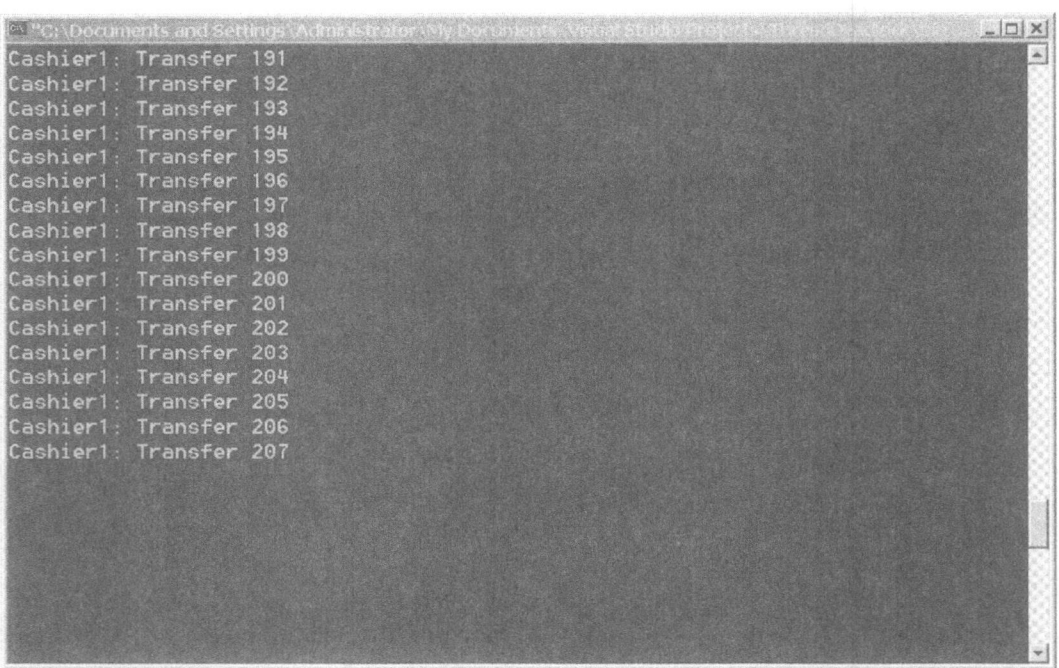

Figure 14-3. Process deadlock in the ThreadDeadlock application

To establish what's happening and why the program is hanging, press Ctrl+Break at the point where the application hangs. The debugger should break into the program at one of the four **SyncLock** statements. Select Debug ➤ Windows ➤ Threads to display the Threads window, and you can see the three managed threads within the program, as shown in Figure 14-4. The first thread is the main application thread, and the other two are the cashier threads.

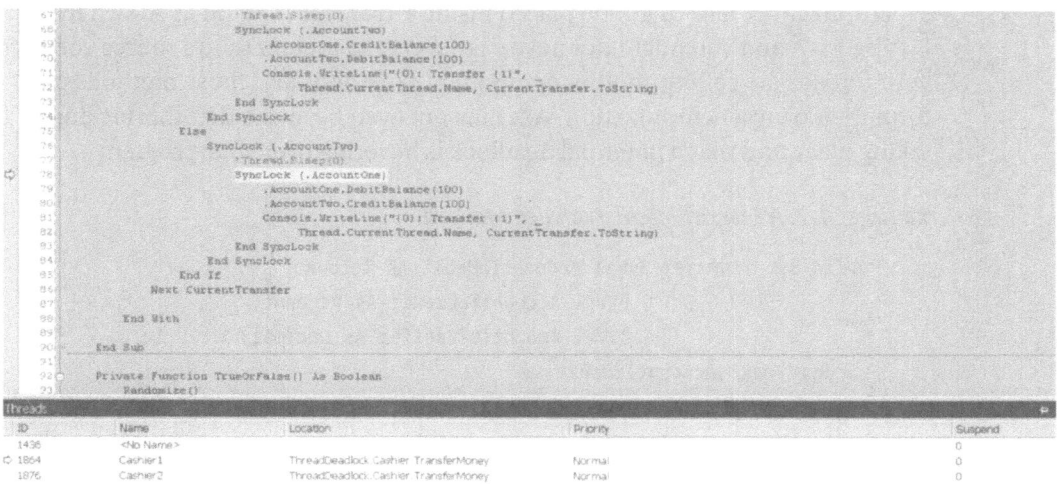

Figure 14-4. Using the Threads windows to investigate a process deadlock

The debugger should be paused on one of the **SyncLock** statements. The thread that was active when the program was suspended by the debugger is shown with a small yellow arrow next to it. If you right-click the nonactive cashier thread in the Threads window (the cashier thread without a yellow arrow next to it) and choose Switch to Thread from the context menu, you can see that the other thread is also paused at a **SyncLock** statement. If you switch between the two cashier threads in this manner, you can see that each of the threads is attempting to lock a different account. One cashier has a lock on the first account and is trying to lock the second account, and the other cashier has a lock on the second account and is trying to lock the first account. Hence the process is deadlocked and can't go any further, so the application hangs.

Notice that the program is randomly picking the order in which it locks the accounts. One way of avoiding this type of deadlock situation is always to lock your resources in exactly the same sequence within each thread. An identical sequence of synchronization locks ensures that multiple threads won't try to grab each other's resources in a nondeterministic order. This is usually easier said than done, because it's normally very hard to guarantee that code statements are executed in the same order in each thread. Depending upon thread entry, data, and timing conditions, each thread may follow a quite different execution path to its siblings. Even if you can guarantee that objects are locked in exactly the same order, you can still be caught by subtleties, as you'll see in a couple of paragraphs.

In this case, an alert developer would probably anticipate the deadlock because the synchronization is explicit, out in the open, and clearly happening in a random order. A more dangerous situation is when the synchronization locks that lead to a deadlock are implicit rather than explicit. In this example, the synchronization lock might be placed inside a **Transfer** method as shown in Listing 14-7, and you might not have easy access to that method's source code. If your threads are calling another component's methods and those methods perform their own synchronization, you may not even be aware that this locking is taking place and that a potential deadlock is hovering over your program.

Listing 14-7. A Hypothetical Transfer Method

```
Public Sub Transfer(ByVal AccountToDebit As Account, _
                    ByVal AccountToCredit As Account, _
                    ByVal AmountToTransfer As Decimal)
    SyncLock (AccountToDebit)
        SyncLock (AccountToCredit)
            'Transfer happens here
```

And here's the subtlety that I talked about a couple of paragraphs ago. In Listing 14-7, the resources are always locked in the same order, so you might think that a deadlock can't occur. However, what happens when the first thread passes account A as the debit account and account B as the credit account, while the second thread does the opposite? If both threads enter this method simultaneously, and a context switch happens after the first lock, you might well see a deadlock.

To reduce the amount of time that your application is exposed to a potential deadlock, you should acquire your synchronization locks as late as possible and release them as early as possible. You should always try to avoid lengthy operations inside code that's locked, especially operations (such as I/O) that can block indefinitely.

If your code throws an exception in a region of code protected by a **SyncLock** statement, the synchronization lock will always be released. The VB .NET compiler automatically places any synchronized region of code inside an implicit **Try...Finally** block, where the **Finally** block releases the synchronization lock. This has one interesting side effect: You can't use **SyncLock** in a method that also uses unstructured exception handling (**On Error...**), because structured and unstructured exception handling can't be combined within the same method.

A final subtlety to remember is that threads can deadlock while waiting on events as well as while waiting to acquire resources locked by other threads. This is often overlooked, especially when a developer forgets that code in an event handler is executed by the thread that raises the event, not by the thread that owns the object within which the event handler resides.

Understanding Process Livelock

Process livelock is similar to process deadlock in its external appearance, in that both situations result in the process appearing to hang indefinitely. Internally, however, livelock is quite different from deadlock. A process is considered to be in a state of livelock when thread code is still executing, but two or more threads are in a never-ending cycle with each other and no useful work is being done. One example of this was mentioned earlier, a situation where one thread throws an error message, to which a second thread, not expecting this error, responds with an error message of its own. This can result in a continuous cycle of errors being thrown.

There's no easy way to prevent process livelock, although it's often possible to detect the livelock once it's happened. In the case of a livelock produced by a cycle of exception messages, Chapter 6 discusses performance counters that you can use from Performance Monitor (or from code) to detect an excessive number of exceptions being thrown within a certain time period. Detecting a livelock internally is much easier than detecting a deadlock because thread code can continue to execute even in the presence of a livelock. However, it requires some careful design to ensure that your detection code can adequately find and stop livelocks. The best solution is to try to anticipate potential livelock situations and then design your threads to prevent them or at least make them highly unlikely to happen.

Understanding Thread Starvation

To understand thread starvation, think about approaching a road tunnel in your car. The road tunnel has only a single lane, but it has to accommodate traffic traveling in both directions. The problem is that if the oncoming stream of cars is steady enough, you won't get a chance to go through the tunnel yourself. The analogy is that each car is a thread and the tunnel is a shared resource.

Just like your car can't get through the tunnel because of the oncoming cars, a thread can be starved of a resource by multiple other threads and be unable to execute in a timely fashion. The thread might not die of starvation—it just runs very slowly. This happens when the thread can get access to the resource, but only for a limited time before competing threads grab the resource back. Going back to the car/thread analogy, think of your car managing to enter the tunnel, but having to swerve into a turnout and stop every time it meets an oncoming car.

There are at least two common reasons for thread starvation. The first reason is when you assign a lower priority than normal to a specific thread. In this case, you've explicitly requested that the thread is less important than other threads with a normal priority, and you can solve the problem by juggling and tuning thread priorities as required. The second common reason for thread starvation is sometimes called the *writer-reader* problem, where a single writer thread tries to lock some data in order to update it but is repeatedly blocked by multiple reader threads with their own synchronization locks on the same data. This situation is common enough that the .NET Framework has constructs specifically designed to help you to avoid thread starvation when it occurs.

In the writer-reader situation, you need to make sure that a writer thread isn't prevented from doing its writing for lengthy periods of time by multiple competing reader threads. To do this, you can use the Framework's **ReaderWriterLock** synchronization class. This class enforces exclusive access to a region of code for any writer thread, but it allows nonexclusive access to a code region for any reader thread. The class also coordinates thread access so that once a writer thread has requested a lock, all subsequent lock requests by reader threads are queued until the writer lock has been granted. This prevents starvation of a writer thread through any inability to grab a shared resource away from multiple reader threads.

In effect, the **ReaderWriterLock** class switches between one writer thread and a group of reader threads. In any situation where the shared resource is being updated infrequently, this class has been designed to provide better throughput than a standard one-at-a-time lock such as **SyncLock** or **Monitor**.

Listing 14-8 demonstrates this by showing a class designed for reading and writing of some hypothetical shared data. The class is completely thread-safe in that multiple reader and writer threads can use it simultaneously. Its use of the **ReaderWriterLock** class also prevents starvation of any writer threads, even in the presence of a larger number of competing reader threads. It's worth examining the code closely because, although it looks simple, it has some subtleties that may not be immediately apparent from a first reading.

Listing 14-8. A Thread-Safe Class for Reading and Writing Shared Data

```
Option Strict On
Imports System.Threading

Class ReadWrite
    'This class is thread-safe in that its methods can
    'be called safely from multiple threads simultaneously.
    Private m_Lock As New Threading.ReaderWriterLock()
```

```
Public Sub ReadData(ByVal MillisecondsToWait As Integer)
    'This procedure reads information from some source.
    'The read lock prevents data from being written until
    'the thread is done reading, while allowing other threads
    'to call ReadData.
    m_Lock.AcquireReaderLock(MillisecondsToWait)

    'We have a lock, so now try to read the data
    Try
        'Perform read operation here.
    Finally
        m_Lock.ReleaseReaderLock()
    End Try

End Sub

Public Sub WriteData(ByVal MillisecondsToWait As Integer)
    'This procedure writes information to some source.
    'The write lock prevents data from being read or
    'written until the thread has finished writing.
    m_Lock.AcquireWriterLock(MillisecondsToWait)

    'We have a lock, so now try to write the data
    Try
        'Perform write/update operation here.
    Finally
        m_Lock.ReleaseWriterLock()
    End Try

End Sub

End Class
```

Acquiring a Reader Lock

When a thread enters the **ReadData** method shown in Listing 14-8, it
attempts to acquire a reader lock using the **AcquireReaderLock** method of the
ReaderWriterLock class. The **AcquireReaderLock** will block if a different thread
has a writer lock or if any thread is waiting to acquire a writer lock. This latter
point is one of the keys to avoiding thread starvation of a writer thread. Any block
on the attempt to acquire a reader lock will last until either the reader lock is
granted or the number of milliseconds specified by the **MillisecondsToWait**

parameter of the **ReadData** method has expired. If the time-out of the reader lock attempt does expire, the **AcquireReaderLock** statement will throw an **ApplicationException** exception that can be caught by the code calling the **ReadData** method. Using a time-out in this manner prevents any possible deadlock problems.

   If the reader lock is granted, the **ReadData** method then attempts to read the data. This read attempt is placed within a **Try...End Try** block so that read lock will always be released, even if an error occurs. This is important because the number of reader locks acquired and reader locks released should always be matched.

   There is one final subtlety of the **AcquireReaderLock** method of which you should be aware. If the current thread already has a writer lock and it then attempts to acquire a reader lock, the reader lock isn't granted. Instead, the writer lock count is incremented by one and the data read then proceeds as normal. This nuance has the advantage of preventing a thread from blocking on its own writer lock. The disadvantage is that instead of calling **ReleaseReaderLock** when the data read has completed, you need to call **ReleaseWriterLock** instead. This is because every writer lock has to be matched with a writer lock release, even if the writer lock has been acquired by using the **AcquireReaderLock** method. Fortunately, you can check if the current thread already has a writer lock by checking the **IsWriterLockHeld** property and then releasing the writer lock if necessary.

Acquiring a Writer Lock

When a thread enters the **WriteData** method shown in Listing 14-8, it attempts to acquire a writer lock using the **AcquireWriterLock** method of the **ReaderWriterLock** class. This method blocks if a different thread has a reader or writer lock. If the writer lock attempt is blocked, it's placed in a queue ahead of any reader locks that are blocked. This is the final key to avoiding thread starvation of a writer thread. Once again, a time-out period is specified on the attempt to acquire the writer lock to avoid any possibility of deadlocks. If the time-out expires, the **AcquireWriterLock** statement will throw an **ApplicationException** exception that can be caught by the code calling the **WriteData** method.

   If the writer lock is granted, the **WriteData** method then tries to update the data. As with the **ReadData** method, this update is placed within a **Try...End Try** block so that writer lock will always be released, even if an error occurs. This is important because the number of writer locks acquired and writer locks released should always be matched.

   As with the **AcquireReaderLock** method, **AcquireWriterLock** also has a final subtlety that can trip you up. If a thread calls **AcquireWriterLock** while it also has a reader lock, it will block on that reader lock. If an infinite time-out is specified for the writer lock attempt, the thread will then deadlock with itself. To prevent this, you can use the **IsReaderLockHeld** property and then upgrade the reader lock to a writer lock using the **UpgradeToWriterLock** method if necessary. Remember, of course, that if you do upgrade a reader lock to a writer lock, you need to release the writer lock rather than the reader lock.

The ThreadMonitor Application

This section uses the **ThreadMonitor** application to investigate managed and unmanaged threads running within a process. If you load the **ThreadMonitor** solution into Visual Studio and execute it by pressing F5, you can see the application's user interface as shown in Figure 14-5.

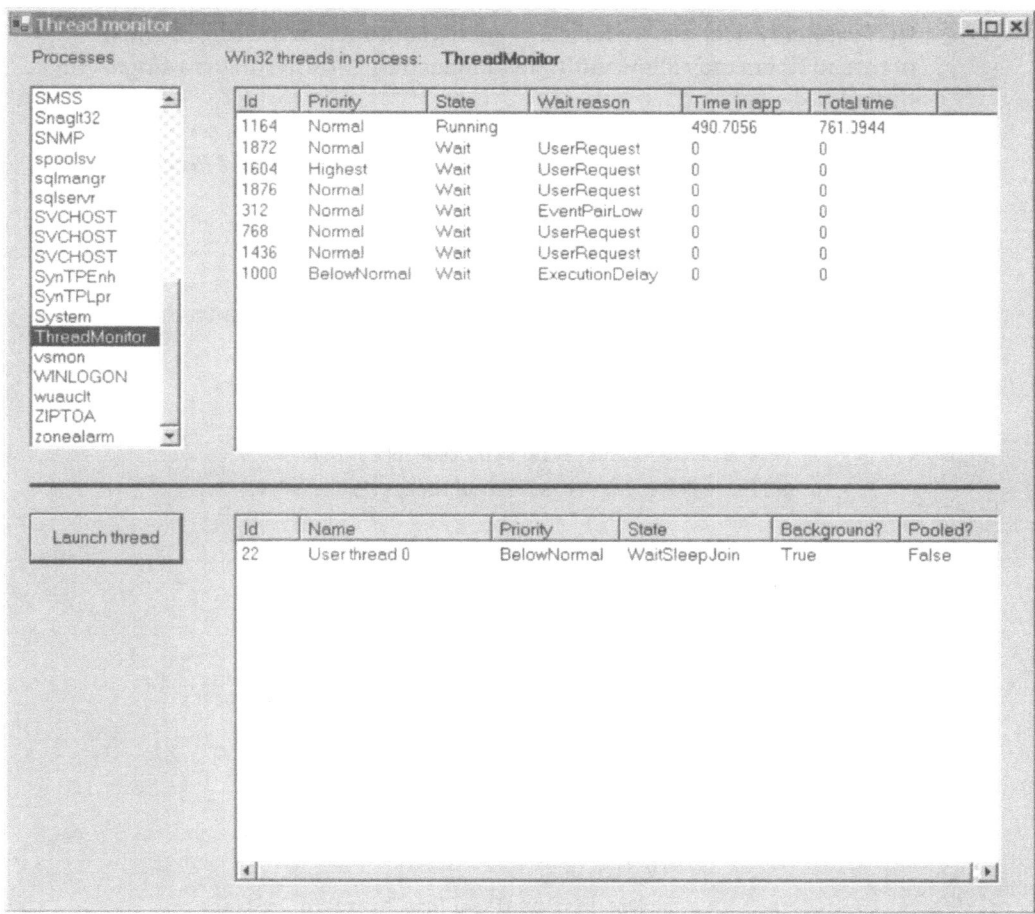

Figure 14-5. The user interface of the ThreadMonitor application

The list box on the left side of the form contains a list of the processes that are currently executing on the local machine. When you click any process, its managed and unmanaged threads are shown in the form's top list view. This list of threads is updated every second and shows details about each thread's priority, state, and processor time.

Clicking the command button underneath the list box allows you to launch a user thread. Each thread sleeps for 5 seconds and then executes a simple loop 30 million times before terminating. You can track the user threads because they're shown in the form's bottom list box as well as in the top list box.

Listing 14-9 shows the code that uses the **Process.Threads** collection to enumerate all of the Win32 threads within the selected process and display each of them in the top list box. Unfortunately, there's no direct way of knowing which of these process threads is managed and which isn't. There isn't even a guarantee that a single managed thread actually maps to a single Win32 thread, because the CLR explicitly declines to make any such guarantee. In the future, the use of thread fibers may allow multiple managed threads to run on a single Win32 thread.

Listing 14-9. Displaying All Win32 Threads Within a Specified Process

```
Private Sub UpdateWin32ThreadDisplay( _
         ByVal SelectedProcessId As Integer)
   Dim SelectedProcess As Process
   Dim ThisThread As ProcessThread, LV_item As ListViewItem

   'Get Win32 threads for this process and display them
   SelectedProcess = _
      Process.GetProcessById(SelectedProcessId)
   LabelThreadName.Text = SelectedProcess.ProcessName

   With Me.ThreadList
      .BeginUpdate()
      .Items.Clear()

      'Iterate through every Win32 thread in this process
      For Each ThisThread In SelectedProcess.Threads

         Try
            'Add thread id
            LV_item = _
               New ListViewItem(ThisThread.Id.ToString)
            'Add thread details
            With LV_item.SubItems
```

```vb
                              'Thread priority
                              .Add(ThisThread.PriorityLevel.ToString)
                              'Thread state
                              .Add(ThisThread.ThreadState.ToString)
                              'Reason for thread wait
                              If ThisThread.ThreadState = _
                                Diagnostics.ThreadState.Wait Then
                                    .Add(ThisThread.WaitReason.ToString)
                              Else
                                    .Add(vbNullString)
                              End If
                              'Thread time in app
                              .Add _
(ThisThread.UserProcessorTime.TotalMilliseconds.ToString)
                              'Thread time in OS
                              .Add _
(ThisThread.TotalProcessorTime.TotalMilliseconds.ToString)
                        End With
                        'Display the thread
                        .Items.Add(LV_item)

                    Catch Exc As InvalidOperationException
                        'Thread's disappeared - ignore

                    End Try

                Next ThisThread

                .EndUpdate()
            End With

        End Sub
```

If you choose the **ThreadMonitor** process in the list box, you can see that it contains no less than eight Win32 threads. If, however, you use Ctrl+Break to break into the program and then examine the Threads window, you'll see only two threads displayed. Make a note of the thread ID of each of the two threads shown, and then resume program execution with F5. You can use the thread IDs to locate these two managed threads in the top list box. The first thread is usually the application's main thread and will normally be the first thread in the **Process.Threads** collection, although this is also not guaranteed. The second thread shown in the Threads window is the thread that runs the message pump for the Windows Form that's being displayed.

Listing 14-10 shows the code that uses the collection of managed user threads to display every user thread in the bottom list box. This collection is maintained by the code every time a new user thread is launched or terminates. Keeping this collection solves the problem of trying to figure out which Win32 thread corresponds to which user thread. The reason for keeping track of these threads is that a managed thread object has some useful information about the thread that the standard process thread object doesn't have. Some of this extra information is displayed in the list box, including the thread name, whether it's a foreground or background thread, and whether the thread is running in the managed thread pool.

Listing 14-10. Displaying All User Threads Within a Specified Process

```
Private Sub UpdateUserThreadDisplay()
    Dim ThisThread As Threading.Thread, _
        LV_item As ListViewItem

    'Iterate through managed threads for current process
    With Me.ManagedThreadList
        .BeginUpdate()
        .Items.Clear()

        'Iterate through every thread in this process
        For Each ThisThread In UserThreads

            If ThisThread.IsAlive Then

                Try
                    'Add thread id
                    LV_item = New ListViewItem _
                        (ThisThread.GetHashCode.ToString)
                    'Add thread details
                    With LV_item.SubItems
                        'Add thread name
                        .Add(ThisThread.Name)
                        'Thread priority
                        .Add(ThisThread.Priority.ToString)
                        'Thread state
                        .Add(ThisThread.ThreadState.ToString)
                        'Thread is alive?
                        .Add(ThisThread.IsAlive.ToString)
                        'Background thread?
                        .Add(ThisThread.IsBackground.ToString)
```

```
                 'Threadpool thread?
                 .Add _
               (ThisThread.IsThreadPoolThread.ToString)
             End With
             'Display the thread
             .Items.Add(LV_item)

          Catch Exc As Threading.ThreadStateException
             'Thread's disappeared - ignore
             UserThreads.Remove _
                   (ThisThread.GetHashCode.ToString)

          End Try

       Else

          'Thread's dead - remove from collection
          UserThreads.Remove _
                (ThisThread.GetHashCode.ToString)

       End If

    Next ThisThread

    .EndUpdate()
  End With

End Sub
```

To launch and watch a user thread, click the "Launch thread" button once. A single managed thread will appear in the bottom list box, with its state set to **WaitSleepJoin**. After 5 seconds, the state will move to a state of **Running**, and then a few seconds later the thread will terminate and disappear from the display.

If you launch three threads in quick succession and then quickly press Ctrl+Break to pause the program, you can use the Threads window to examine these user threads. The thread name allocated by the code to each thread as it's launched is shown in the second column of the window. The active thread is shown with a yellow arrow next to it. To select another thread as the active thread, simply double-click it.

One interesting facility that the Threads window gives you is the ability to "freeze" or "thaw" a thread. To freeze a thread, right-click it in the Threads window and select the Freeze menu item. This prevents execution of that thread after you resume the program, which can be very useful if you want to examine the behavior of a single thread without worrying about side effects caused by other threads. To thaw a thread, right-click the thread again and select the Thaw menu item. This allows execution of that thread once the program has been resumed. Two blue bars next to a thread in the Threads window means that the thread has been frozen. Of course, this thread freezing and thawing is just a debugger artifact, and it doesn't mean anything to Windows itself. If you took away the debugger from a frozen thread, it would continue execution normally.

Multithreading in Windows Forms

The **ThreadGui** application examines some of the threading issues that you have to face in a Windows Forms program. Multithreading can be very useful in this environment because it lets you keep the user interface responsive to the end user while you're doing intensive work, and you can also use it to let the end user cancel a long-running task. The drawback is that you need to respect the single-threaded nature of a Windows Form.

If you load the **ThreadGui** solution into Visual Studio and execute it by pressing F5, you'll see the application's user interface, as shown in Figure 14-6.

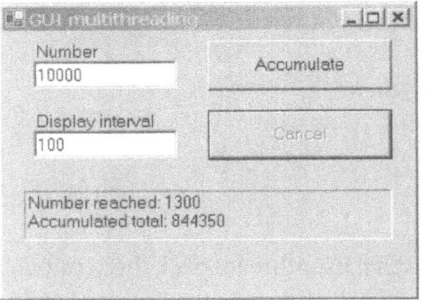

Figure 14-6. The user interface of the ThreadGui application

When you enter a number into the top text box and click the button marked Accumulate, the program accumulates a running total by adding every number together between 1 and the number entered in the text box. So if you entered **5** into the top text box, the accumulated total would be 15 (1 + 2 + 3 + 4 + 5). The Cancel button allows you to interrupt and stop the accumulation calculation at any time. The label at the bottom of the form displays the results of the calculation.

The second text box is used to allow the user to monitor progress of the calculation. After the accumulation is performed the number of times specified in this text box, the current running total is displayed in the label at the bottom of the form and the display is paused for 0.1 second so that the user can glimpse this intermediate result. Then the calculation continues accumulating until either the next display interval is reached or the calculation finishes.

The challenge is to run the potentially lengthy calculation while keeping the user interface responsive so that the user can cancel the calculation and while displaying the intermediate results of the calculation in a safe manner.

The first major problem to overcome is that you should never, ever, update a control (in this case, the label at the bottom of the form) from a thread other than the thread that created the control. If you break this Windows Forms law, your program will experience strange and difficult multithreading bugs, and you won't be able to fix these bugs except by changing your program to obey the law. The first approach that many developers experiment with when faced with this prohibition is to tell the calculation thread to raise an event that the form can handle and use to update the user interface. Unfortunately, as mentioned earlier in this chapter, this won't work. An event handler always runs on the same thread that raised the event, so the event handler also isn't allowed to update the user interface.

The second problem is for the user interface thread to find a way of telling the calculation thread that the user has canceled the calculation request. Often a developer will think about setting a class-level variable that can be accessed and shared by both threads. This is, however, difficult to do without running into the thread synchronization issues that I discussed in the previous section.

Listing 14-11 shows the code that launches the worker thread to do the calculation once the user has clicked the Accumulate button. It uses an asynchronous delegate to spawn a work request that will be handled by the .NET thread pool. The delegate's **BeginInvoke** method is used to start the calculation thread asynchronously and pass it the specified number to accumulate.

Listing 14-11. Code to Launch the Calculation Thread

```
Option Strict On
Imports System.Threading

Public Class MainForm : Inherits System.Windows.Forms.Form

    Private Delegate Sub CalcDelegate(ByVal AnyNumber As Int32)
    Private Delegate Sub _
                ProgressDelegate(ByVal CurrentTotal As Decimal, _
                                 ByVal NumberReached As Int32, _
                                 ByRef CancelRequest As Boolean)
    Private m_CancelRequested As Boolean = False
```

```
Private Sub ButtonCalc_Click(ByVal sender As System.Object, _
                              ByVal e As System.EventArgs) _
                              Handles cmdCalc.Click

    'Init calculation
    Me.cmdCalc.Enabled = False
    Me.cmdCancel.Enabled = True
    m_CancelRequested = False

    'Use asynch delegate to launch thread from thread pool
    Dim CalcAccumulation As CalcDelegate = New _
            CalcDelegate(AddressOf CalculateAccumulation)
    CalcAccumulation.BeginInvoke( _
            Convert.ToInt32(Me.txtNumber.Text), _
            AddressOf CalcComplete, Nothing)


End Sub
```

If you don't need the control that a manual thread gives you, such as setting the thread name or priority, using the thread pool spares you from the messy details of thread management and scales better in many multithreaded environments. Even better, as you'll see shortly, it's easy to propagate background thread exceptions back to the main thread when using the thread pool.

Listing 14-12 shows the method that runs the calculation thread. First place a breakpoint on line 162 (the line marked in bold in Listing 14-12) and then run the application by pressing F5. When you click the Accumulate button, the program will break as soon as it reaches your breakpoint. If you now look at the Threads window, you'll see two threads: the user interface thread and the calculation thread from the thread pool.

Listing 14-12. Performing the Accumulation Calculation

```
Private Sub CalculateAccumulation( _
            ByVal NumberToAccumulate As Int32)
    Dim CalcObject As New Calc(NumberToAccumulate), _
        CurrentTotal As Decimal = 0
    Dim CancelRequested As Boolean = False

    With CalcObject

        Do While .NumberReached <= NumberToAccumulate
            CurrentTotal = _
                .Accumulate(Convert.ToInt32(Me.txtInterval.Text))
            ShowProgress(CurrentTotal, .NumberReached, _
```

```
                    CancelRequested)
            If CancelRequested = True Then
                Exit Do
            End If
        Loop

    End With

End Sub
```

After performing each stage of the accumulation, the calculation thread calls the **ShowProgress** method, which is shown in Listing 14-13. This method is where the clever work happens. Remember that you should never update a user interface control from any thread except the one that created the control. To verify whether the user interface thread or the calculation thread is trying to update the user interface, the **ShowProgress** method checks **Me.InvokeRequired**. This will return **True** if the current thread isn't the user interface thread, and it will return **False** if it's the user interface thread. If **InvokeRequired** is **False**, then the thread is allowed to update the user interface directly, and therefore update the label with information about the progress of the calculation.

The interesting work happens when **InvokeRequired** is **True**, and therefore the user interface can't be updated directly. Every control has an **Invoke** method, and this is one control method that the CLR guarantees is safe to call from any thread. The arguments for the **Invoke** method include a delegate and a developer-defined set of arguments that are used to call the delegate's associated method. So this code calls **ShowProgress** recursively using the **ProgressDelegate** delegate. Using the **Invoke** method ensures that the recursive call happens on the user interface thread, where it's safe to update the user interface.

Listing 14-13. Updating the User Interface with Intermediate Calculation Results

```
Private Sub ShowProgress(ByVal CurrentAccumulation As Decimal, _
                    ByVal NumberReached As Int32, _
                    ByRef CancelRequest As Boolean)

    If Me.InvokeRequired = True Then

        'Transfer to GUI thread to show progress
        Dim CancelRequested As Object = False
        Dim SP As ProgressDelegate = _
            New ProgressDelegate(AddressOf ShowProgress)
        Dim Arguments() As Object = New Object() _
                {CurrentAccumulation, _
```

```
                    NumberReached, _
                    CancelRequested}
          Me.Invoke(SP, Arguments)
          CancelRequest = DirectCast(CancelRequested, Boolean)

      Else

          'We're on the GUI thread, so just show progress
          With Me.lblResult
              .Text = "Number reached: " & NumberReached.ToString
              .Text += Environment.NewLine
              .Text += "Accumulated total: " _
                      & CurrentAccumulation.ToString
          End With

          'Pause for a short time to allow user to read display
          Thread.CurrentThread.Sleep(100)

          'Return any cancellation request
          CancelRequest = m_CancelRequested

      End If

  End Sub
```

This technique for updating the user interface with progress information from the calculation thread works well and avoids any updating of the user interface from a nonuser interface thread. Instead of interacting directly, the user interface and calculation threads pass messages to each other, which means that you never have to worry about any thread synchronization or deadlock issues.

So the first problem of updating the user interface is solved, but you still need to tackle the problem of canceling the thread if the user clicks the Cancel button. The code behind the Cancel button is shown in Listing 14-14. It sets a class-level variable signifying that the user has issued a cancellation request. But how can you give the calculation thread access to this variable without running into thread synchronization issues?

Listing 14-14. Canceling the Calculation

```
Private Sub ButtonCancel_Click(ByVal sender As System.Object, _
                                ByVal e As System.EventArgs) _
                                Handles cmdCancel.Click
    'Request that calculation thread cancels itself
    m_CancelRequested = True
End Sub
```

The key to this puzzle lies in the **ShowProgress** method shown in Listing 14-13. This method has a **ByRef** argument called **CancelRequest**. When this method is called on the user interface thread, it sets this argument to the class-level request cancellation variable. Because the calculation thread regularly calls the **ShowProgress** method to update the user interface with its progress, it can read the cancellation request argument after it's called the **Invoke** method. This allows the request for cancellation to pass safely from the user interface thread to the calculation thread without having to worry about synchronization issues. Yet again, a message passing between the two threads prevents any problems that might arise if the two threads interacted directly.

Finally, once the calculation thread has completed, it invokes the callback that it was passed when it was started. This is the **CalcComplete** method shown in Listing 14-15, which simply resets the user interface so that another request can be started.

Listing 14-15. Completing the Calculation

```
Private Sub CalcComplete(ByVal CalcResult As System.IAsyncResult)
        'Called when asynch thread completes
        Me.cmdCalc.Enabled = True
        Me.cmdCancel.Enabled = False
End Sub
```

Dealing with Thread Failure

So far in this chapter, I've made the assumption that threads don't throw exceptions. Back in the real world, you need to be able to trap and deal with errors in threads launched by your applications.

Handling Thread Exceptions

An exception thrown by any thread that your application launches from its main thread is not propagated back to the main thread. The CLR simply swallows the exception and either returns the thread to the thread pool (if it came from thread pool) or just terminates the thread.

You can trap these thread exceptions by creating an unhandled exception filter and attaching this filter to the **Application.ThreadException** event. This process is described in detail in Chapter 13. An alternative possibility for threads that run in the thread pool is to add a **Try...End Try** block on the thread start delegate's **EndInvoke** method. **EndInvoke** on a thread delegate is the method used to block and wait for the thread to finish.

In the case of the **ThreadGui** application, the calculation thread is launched asynchronously, so it doesn't make sense to use **EndInvoke** after the thread has been launched. This would just force the user interface thread to block and wait for the calculation thread to finish, which defeats the point of using an asynchronous thread. Instead, you can call the **EndInvoke** method after the calculation thread has signaled its completion by calling the **CalcComplete** callback. Listing 14-16 shows you how you can modify the **CalcComplete** method shown in Listing 14-15 to catch any exception thrown by the calculation thread.

Listing 14-16. Trapping Any Calculation Thread Exception

```
Private Sub CalcComplete(ByVal CalcResult As System.IAsyncResult)
    Dim Result As AsyncResult = CType(CalcResult, AsyncResult)
    Dim MyDelegate As CalcDelegate = _
        CType(Result.AsyncDelegate, CalcDelegate)

    'Called when asynch thread completes
    Me.cmdCalc.Enabled = True
    Me.cmdCancel.Enabled = False

    Try
        'Find out if anything dodgy happened in the async thread
        MyDelegate.EndInvoke(CalcResult)
    Catch Exc As Exception
        MsgBox(Exc.Message, MsgBoxStyle.OKOnly, _
                "Async thread exception")
    End Try

End Sub
```

The first two lines in Listing 14-16 are a little confusing. Their job is to extract the original delegate from the asynchronous result returned by the calculation thread. Once the original delegate has been extracted, the line shown in bold calls **EndInvoke** on the original delegate. This has the effect of marshalling any exception that occurred in the calculation thread back to the user interface thread, where the **Catch** block shown here traps and displays the exception message.

If you throw a test exception from the **CalculateAccumulation** method shown in Listing 14-12, you should now see the displayed exception message. To throw a test exception, simply add a line such as

```
Throw ApplicationException("Test exception")
```

Terminating a Managed Thread

Explicitly terminating a managed thread should be done with some care. You can use the **Thread.Abort** method to terminate a thread, but when doing this you should be aware of exactly how the thread is terminated and the issues that this might cause. This section discusses these issues.

Using **Thread.Abort** doesn't end a thread immediately. It causes an exception of type **ThreadAbortException** to be generated in the thread to be aborted, which in turn unwinds any **Try...End Try** blocks in that thread's call stack. Code in related **Catch** and **Finally** blocks will be executed, and theoretically this code might perform long, or even infinite, calculations. This means that you can't guarantee that a thread will end when you call **Thread.Abort**.

Unlike a normal exception, an exception of type **ThreadAbortException** can't be suppressed by using a **Catch** block because it's always rethrown automatically at the end of each **Catch** block. However, a thread with sufficient privilege can call **Thread.AbortReset** to suppress this exception. This is another way in which a thread might resist being terminated.

To confirm that a thread really has terminated, you need to call **Thread.Join**. This joins your invoking thread to the thread that's been aborted and blocks your thread until either the joined thread has actually been aborted or the time-out that you specify in the **Thread.Join** has been exceeded.

If the **ThreadAbortException** caused by the call to **Thread.Abort** interrupts a thread during execution of a **Finally** block, that execution of that block of code won't be completed. This is one of the very few ways in which a **Finally** block can be bypassed.

Developers will often use **Try...Catch...Finally** to protect code where they anticipate that an exception might be thrown. The problem is that an exception of type **ThreadAbortException** can occur at any time and with no warning. This can complicate the process of writing really safe code that always unwinds itself when interrupted.

Aborting a thread with **Thread.Abort** unlocks any synchronization locks that the thread holds. This means that the data being protected by these locks may become inconsistent or corrupted, as discussed previously in the section on data race problems.

In some circumstances, attempting to abort a managed thread that's suspended by user code (as opposed to one suspended by the garbage collector or another system process) leads to that thread hanging forever and not terminating. This appears to be a known CLR bug at the time of this writing.

A better way of terminating a thread is to set a **PleaseStop** variable that the thread can check periodically. This allows a thread to terminate itself under controlled conditions. An example of using this technique safely without synchronization problems is discussed in the **ThreadGui** application earlier in this chapter.

The final fact to be aware of is that background threads are always terminated automatically when the process or thread from which they were launched is terminated. **Try...End Try** blocks are unwound normally when this happens.

Summary

Debugging a multithreaded application can be very messy and difficult. One developer memorably compared the difficulty of testing and debugging free-threaded code with performing a tonsillectomy while entering the patient from the wrong end. Understanding the common problems that can afflict a multi-threaded application is key to creating a program design that avoids the need to perform heavy debugging. The examples of problem behavior discussed in this chapter are best avoided by designing your thread interactions very carefully. The **ThreadGui** example application presents one design pattern that avoids thread interaction problems.

INTERLUDE

THE 500-MILE E-MAIL BUG

In November 2002, a system administrator named Trey Harris posted the tale of a remarkable bug that he had diagnosed and fixed. He later posted a clarification of the bug's details and a FAQ about the bug, both of which you can find at http://www.ibiblio.org/harris/500milemail.html.

While working as a system administrator for a campus e-mail system at the University of North Carolina, Trey received a phone call from the chairman of the statistics department saying that nobody in the statistics department could send e-mail farther than 520 miles from the campus! After verifying that the call wasn't a practical joke, Trey ran some tests of his own on the e-mail system. Sure enough, when he sent test e-mails to Richmond, Virginia; Atlanta, Georgia; Washington D.C.; Princeton, New Jersey; and New York City, all of which are destinations within 520 miles, the e-mails were sent successfully. When he sent a test e-mail to Memphis, Tennessee, about 600 miles away, it failed to deliver. Likewise for Boston, Massachusetts; Detroit, Michigan; and Providence, Rhode Island, the latter being 580 miles away. A minor comfort was that when he sent an e-mail to a friend in North Carolina whose ISP was in Seattle, Washington, it also failed. If the problem had been related to the geographic location of the e-mail recipient rather than the mail server, there would have been some real explaining to do.

Having duplicated the problem, he now had to figure out what was causing it. After all, it's not every day that you find such an unusual bug. He knew that a consultant had recently patched the mail server to upgrade its SunOS operating system, but the consultant hadn't touched the mail system itself. The first obvious place to look for problems was the configuration file for the sendmail utility. But the sendmail.cf file on the offending mail server looked perfectly normal.

To investigate further, Trey telnetted into the SMTP port on the mail server, and was greeted with a SunOS sendmail banner...for sendmail version 5. At this point in time, Sun shipped the tried and trusted sendmail version 5 with its operating system, even though the version of sendmail used by the university had been standardized at version 8. So when the consultant patched the OS, the sendmail utility had been downgraded from version 8 to version 5, but the sendmail.cf configuration file had not been downgraded—this was the first clue.

Although the sendmail version 5 shipped by Sun had been tweaked to cope with a version 8 configuration file, it only did so by ignoring the configuration options that it couldn't understand. One of these options was the time-out to connect to the remote SMTP server, which sendmail set to zero because it couldn't understand the version 8 setting. Some experimentation revealed that under the typical load experienced by this particular mail server, and after accounting for router delays and transmission speeds across optic fiber, a zero time-out would abort a connect call to a remote mail server in approximately 3 milliseconds.

How far does light travel in 3 milliseconds? Slightly over 500 miles.

Debugging Distributed Systems

A DISTRIBUTED SYSTEM is one where multiple processes on two or more machines cooperate with a common aim. One of the primary design goals of .NET was to make the design, development, and debugging of distributed systems significantly easier than it has been in the past. Both Web services and remoting were built with this goal in mind and have benefited from some of the hard lessons taught by technologies such as DCOM, COM+, RMI, and CORBA.

This chapter first looks at the type of problems that differentiate distributed applications from local applications and how to solve these problems. Then it examines how to set up and use remote debugging, and how to use the remote debugger to debug a distributed application that uses remoting. Finally, it covers an effective way of monitoring a distributed application.

Understanding Distributed Applications

This section takes a strategic look at the most common problems experienced by distributed applications. If you understand these problems before you start construction of your application, it's much easier to design your way around most of the problems. This can save you considerable debugging time, because debugging a distributed system can be significantly more complicated than debugging a local application. The idea driving this section is to give you sufficient information to design your distributed application properly.

Dealing with Failure

The defining difference between local and distributed applications is failure. This is because a remote method call has so many more ways of failing than a local method call. With a local method call, it normally just works. You simply don't expect it to fail, and the number of possible failures is very limited when both components are running on the same machine. When executing a remote method call, there are many possible failures, some of which appear in the following list:

- There's a problem with Windows on the sending machine that prevents the request from reaching the network stack.

- There's a problem with the network card on the sending machine.

- There's a problem with one of the network cables—the cable might be faulty, not plugged in properly, or even severed.

- There's a problem with the network itself, such as a faulty network switch or router. Switch and router issues can cause network segmentation or even complete failure.

- The receiving machine is either down or disconnected from the network for some reason.

- There's a problem with the network card on the receiving machine.

- There's a problem with Windows on the receiving machine that prevents the request from reaching the receiving component.

- There's a problem with the receiving component. The component's process has terminated or hung in some way, or the thread that's supposed to process the request has terminated with a thread exception.

- The receiving component is busy handling other requests, and therefore is unable to process the new request in a timely fashion.

- The receiving component processes the request and issues a response, but the response is lost for any of the preceding reasons.

So when you make a method call or send a message to a remote component, there are many ways (some of them quite ingenious) in which that call can fail. One of the major issues in this context is distinguishing between *partial failure* and *complete failure*. When you send a message to a remote component and don't receive a reply, what happened? Was the request lost and never received by the remote component? Or did the request reach the remote component, but the response was lost or never issued?

In the case of a lost request, this is called a complete failure. In the case of a lost response, this is called a partial failure. Distinguishing between these two types of failure is essential because if you don't know what failed, it's hard to figure out what to do about the failure. With a lost request, you can usually reissue the request without any adverse effects. With a lost response, reissuing the request may well have severe adverse effects. Figure 15-1 shows these two types of failure.

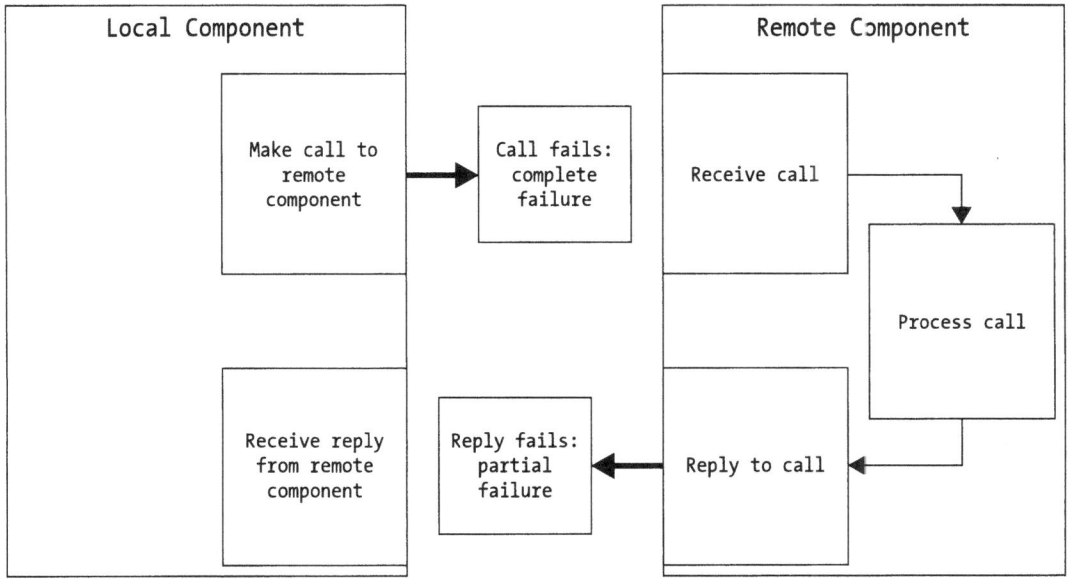

Figure 15-1. Partial failure versus complete failure

For instance, suppose you have an e-commerce Web site selling beanie babies. A customer decides to buy 2,000 beanie babies from your Web site and the Web page dutifully passes her purchase request to the remote server that processes credit cards. What happens if that server doesn't respond for 30 seconds or a minute? Has the credit card been validated and the purchase processed, but you just haven't received the purchase confirmation for some reason? Or has the purchase failed completely because the credit card server had a problem? How long should the Web page wait for a reply from the credit card server? And what should it tell the customer when no reply is forthcoming?

In order to deal with this type of situation, you need to design your distributed applications to cope with both complete and partial failures. You should have an explicit recovery strategy and you need to understand the benefits and drawbacks of each of the possible recovery strategies.

Using Distributed Transactions

The most common recovery strategy for dealing with failure in a distributed application is to use distributed transactions. You may well be familiar with transactions in a database environment. Most modern databases have the capability to roll back a sequence of database actions if a problem is encountered at some point during the sequence. In this context, a transaction says, "Something went wrong with what I was doing, so I'm going to reverse what I did and roll back to a safe situation." A distributed transaction involves communication between components to decide whether to complete the transaction in progress or to roll it back completely.

A distributed transaction therefore tries to eliminate the distinction between partial and complete failure by turning any partial failure into a complete failure. This enables you to repeat the request without worrying about adverse effects. The problem is that a distributed transaction can become very complex. It requires communication between multiple components asking, "Can I go forward? Are you ready to go forward? Please vote on going forward." All of these messages increase the complexity of the process. The more information going back and forth between the components, the more room there is for things to go wrong. Even with a sophisticated two-phase commit transaction, you still need to worry about some unlikely scenarios that can leave your application in an ambiguous state. Creating, and possibly aborting, distributed transactions gives you a significant overhead in complexity.

Using Compensatory Transactions

Another recovery strategy is to use *compensatory transactions*. When a sending component fails to receive a response to a request, it sends another request saying, in effect, "I haven't received your response to my original request, so please cancel that request if you've already acted upon it." This leverages the receiving component's knowledge of whether the failure of the original request was partial or complete. If the failure was partial, the receiving component reverses the request. If the failure was complete, the receiving component ignores the new request. In fact, in the case of a complete failure, the receiving component may not have received either request.

Compensatory transactions can also become quite complex if multiple components are involved in the transaction, although the complexity is typically less than that associated with distributed transactions. The major problem with compensatory transactions is that they rely on the ability to reverse a transaction. This isn't always possible or feasible. For instance, if the credit card has already been debited in the e-commerce scenario mentioned previously, reversing the credit card debit transparently can be difficult. You also need to cater for partial failure scenarios that can occur in the second compensating request. Just as with a two-phase commit, it's possible to come up with unlikely scenarios that leave your application in an ambiguous state.

Using Idempotent Transactions

Probably the best recovery strategy to use for many distributed applications is *idempotent transactions*. In an idempotent transaction, you simply keep on trying a request until a response to that request is received. Each request is given a unique identifier, and if the response to a request isn't received, the request is transmitted again and again until the response is received. Because the request has a unique identifier, the receiving component knows if that request has already been received and processed. If the request is new as far as the receiving component is concerned, it processes the request as normal and sends a response signifying success or failure. If the request is a duplicate of one that's already been received and processed successfully, the receiving component simply retransmits the original response to that request. If the request is a duplicate of one that failed during processing, it's reprocessed and the response is sent. In this manner, every duplicate request is filtered so that it isn't processed successfully more than once.

This is a brute force recovery strategy in that it doesn't use any clever transaction scheme or coordination between components. It simply keeps trying every request until a response (signifying either success or failure) has been received. As such, its very simplicity is a benefit. You don't need clever programming or clever developers, you just need to buy enough servers and network hardware to handle any increase in network traffic that might result from the retransmission of failed requests and responses. Nowadays, hardware is much cheaper than developers!

Swaying with the Earthquake

"Swaying with the earthquake" is a phrase that I first heard used by Ken Arnold, one of the original architects of both CORBA and Jini. It sums up very nicely the philosophy of *not* trying to build ultra-reliable components in a distributed system, because that can become very difficult and expensive. As you work toward that elusive 99.999% reliability (see Chapter 1 for a discussion on this), each extra decimal point of reliability becomes exponentially more expensive and introduces more external factors and bottlenecks. Instead of working toward a probably unattainable degree of reliability in a distributed application, it usually makes more sense to design your system so that it can function even when individual components fail. If you can design and construct your application so that it has no single point of failure, it doesn't matter so much when single components do fail. This relieves you of the tremendous burden of having to create ultra-reliable components. In effect, you design your application to continue functioning by rerouting itself around failed components.

It's similar to designing a building that needs to survive a major earthquake. Although your instinct might be to make the building as sturdy as possible, a better solution is to create a building that sways with the earthquake rather than trying to resist it. A building can survive a much bigger earthquake by swaying with the movement of the ground.

In the e-commerce scenario discussed previously, it might make more sense to have two or even three credit card components, so that if the first request fails, the Web page can direct the request to one of the other components. Your application still needs to understand and distinguish between partial and complete failure, but once again, it's much easier and cheaper to buy extra hardware and less reliable components than it is to create or find ultra-reliable components.

In a way, this mirrors the common approach of using *redundant array of inexpensive disks* (RAID) as a way of coping with the tendency of disk drives to fail at regular intervals. Instead of trying to cope with disk failure by purchasing ultra-reliable and therefore ultra-expensive drives, most companies have opted to construct hardware configurations where a good disk drive will immediately take the place of a disk drive that has failed. This approach is very effective because where a single disk may have a mean time between failures (MTBF) of 30,000 hours, the MTBF for a reasonable RAID configuration failing is something like 900 million hours. A similar approach applied to software components might be called *redundant array of inexpensive components* (RAIC).

Dealing with State

Almost every distributed system will store state somewhere, where *state* is defined as information held in one component that's needed at some point by another component. The most common storage of state is probably a database, but state is also often stored in business components and in a cache. Storing state has to be treated carefully in a distributed system because you need to understand how to keep the state consistent with reality on a continuous basis, how long the state has to be stored, and whether you need some sort of replication or backup of the state.

For example, imagine a component that acts as the cache for your trading system. This cache holds all of the current market prices, which together form the state of the market. You keep this cache because you don't want to make a lengthy interrogation of external price exchanges every time a new trader wants to look at the state of the market.

If the cache occasionally fails completely, say by going down, that doesn't worry you too much. As a last resort you can always go back to each of the price exchanges and thereby manage to reconstruct the cache. But you still need to worry about partial failure. How do you verify that the cached prices are all correct? How often should you verify that the cached prices reflect reality? How many traders can be serviced by a single cache? If a single cache isn't sufficient to service all of your traders in a timely fashion, how should you replicate the cache, and how can you verify that the replicated caches are identical to each other?

Caching strategies are well known to computer science, and if you want or need to use caches, you should certainly take the time to understand the problem that you're trying to solve and design your caching strategy properly.

Although caching generally stores information that you can reconstruct in the last resort, what happens if you store information that can't be reconstructed? For example, your application's database might hold information about all of the market trades made today by your users. In this case, you definitely need to think about questions such as "Is this component a single point of failure?" and about answers such as state replication. Be aware that replication can become very complex, especially when you start looking at everything that can go wrong and at possible recovery strategies.

Understanding Message Semantics

Chapter 1 has a short discussion on the problem of standardizing the meaning of each message passed between the components of a distributed application. The issue is that just because the different components can speak the same language (for example, XML), this doesn't mean that each component has an identical understanding of what each word in the language means. For example, two components that both see an XML attribute called **Price** many not agree on what that attribute represents. Is it *net price* or *gross price*? Is it inclusive or exclusive of sales tax? An additional problem is that different XML documents may each have an attribute with the same name, but that attribute might represent a different entity within each document.

A common communication protocol such as XML just raises this problem of semantics to a higher level—indeed a level where semantic differences may not be detected until quite late in the software development life cycle. XML can help components talk together more easily, while masking the issue of having a common understanding of what they're talking about.

This is summed up neatly in the old joke of two men walking down the road. One says to the other, "It's windy today, isn't it?" The second man replies, "No, it's Thursday." The first man comes back with, "Yes, I am too. Let's find a pub."

There's no easy answer to this problem. Careful documentation of every entity shared between components in a distributed application is essential, but even then, it's all too easy for misunderstandings to occur. If development of distributed applications was easy, everybody would be doing it and good developers wouldn't be so well paid.

Dealing with Leaky Abstractions

If you use a technology such as Web services, you can see that .NET cleverly tries to conceal the difference between a local call and a remote call. It creates a client proxy class under the hood and uses this proxy to present a convenient abstraction of the Web service and the remote call. When you make a method call to a Web service, it looks exactly as though you're calling a method on a local object. You can't even step through the client proxy code with the debugger unless you explicitly remove one of the proxy's attributes.

Unfortunately, this abstraction can sometimes leak. For instance, if you're accustomed to creating and calling local classes, and then you see the same idiom used for calling a Web service, you might expect that the Web service is an object, has a lifetime that you can control, and maintains state over its lifetime. Of course, this isn't true. A Web service is definitely not an object, it won't maintain state unless it's been explicitly developed that way, and its lifetime isn't under your control at all.

When you're debugging, you therefore need to see through the convenient abstractions that .NET offers and try to understand how the plumbing actually works. The abstractions are excellent for concealing much of the complexity of distributed programming, but don't get carried away and start to believe that the underlying mechanisms are as easy and neat as the .NET abstractions make them look.

Introduction to Remote Debugging

The Visual Studio remote debugging components allow you to debug managed and unmanaged programs running on a machine that doesn't have the full installation of Visual Studio. This means that you can use Visual Studio on your development machine to debug components running on a remote machine such as a database server, Web server, or middle-tier application server.

Probably the most common use for remote debugging is when you're investigating a production problem. The average pointy-haired boss tends to be fairly paranoid about upsetting a production machine by installing a copy of Visual Studio on it, never mind the licensing issues that this involves. With remote debugging, you can keep Visual Studio and your application's source code on your development machine and install just the remote debugging components on the production machine. You can even go further and use the remote debugging components from a network share that's accessible from the production machine, thereby leaving your production environment in an almost pristine state.

You can use the same remote debugging techniques to investigate components running on development Web servers and application servers. The only caveat with a Web server is that IIS 5.0 supports just a single developer debugging at any one time, but IIS 6.0 overcomes this restriction (for more information about this, please see Chapter 9). In addition to the debugging of Web and application servers, you can also use remote debugging to debug SQL Server stored procedures running on a remote development or production database server.

It's not unusual for a developer to have problems when running and testing a colleague's component. You can use remote debugging to reach across to your colleague's machine and see exactly why he or she is having a problem with your component. If your colleague has Visual Studio installed, you don't even need to install the remote debugging components because they're installed automatically with Visual Studio. If your colleague hasn't installed Visual Studio, the remote debugging components can be installed on his or her machine by creating a network share on your machine and connecting to that share from your colleague's machine to perform the remote debugging installation.

Finally, and if you're really ambitious, you can use remote debugging across the Internet to investigate a client's problems with your software. This requires your client's cooperation, in that the client will temporarily have to open a hole in his or her Internet firewall to allow you to use Terminal Services to log into a machine in his or her network. In addition, your client will need to install Visual Studio on the machine that you're logging into with Terminal Services. This workaround is necessary because normal remote debugging doesn't work across Windows domains that don't have two-way trust. But once your client has installed Visual Studio on one of his or her machines, you can then use Terminal Services across the Internet to reach over to that machine, and then use normal remote debugging to jump onto any other of your client's machines for problem investigation. I discuss this further in the next section.

Remote Debugging Preparation

This section looks at how to install remote debugging and at some of the choices that you need to make during the installation process.

You can install the Visual Studio remote debugging components on Windows XP, Windows 2000, Windows NT 4.0 (provided you've installed Service Pack 6a), Windows 98, and Windows ME. By default, installing remote debugging adds the Windows account that you're using for the installation of remote debugging to the Debugger Users group on the remote machine. If you're going to be debugging remotely with a different Windows user than you used for installation of the remote debugging components, you'll need to add this user account manually to the Debugger Users group on the remote machine.

If you're working within a Windows domain, you can add any individual domain user to the Debugger Users group. Alternatively, you can create a domain group containing users who wish to do debugging and then add this domain group to the Debugger Users group. A final alternative is to add the INTERACTIVE group to the Debugger Users group so that anybody who can log in will also be able to debug, but this might be a significant security risk in some environments.

Visual Studio can perform remote debugging using any of three transport protocols with .NET 1.1 (the native pipes protocol isn't available with .NET 1.0). By default, remote debugging uses DCOM as the transport protocol together with the Machine Debug Manager (MDM) service (mdm.exe). If you want to debug managed code as well as unmanaged code, this is the only remote debugging transport protocol that you can use. The second transport protocol available is *native-only TCP/IP*, but this only allows you to debug unmanaged programs, such as those written in C++ or VB.Classic. The third possibility is to use the *native-only pipe* transport protocol. As with native-only TCP/IP, this last option only allows you to debug unmanaged code. Native-only pipe is a more secure, but significantly slower, protocol than native-only TCP/IP, and it isn't available on Windows 95, 98, or ME.

Figure 15-2 shows how you can choose which of the three transport protocols you wish to use when attaching to a remote process from the Debug ➤ Processes window. Obviously, you need to choose the default DCOM protocol if you're going to be doing any remote debugging of managed code.

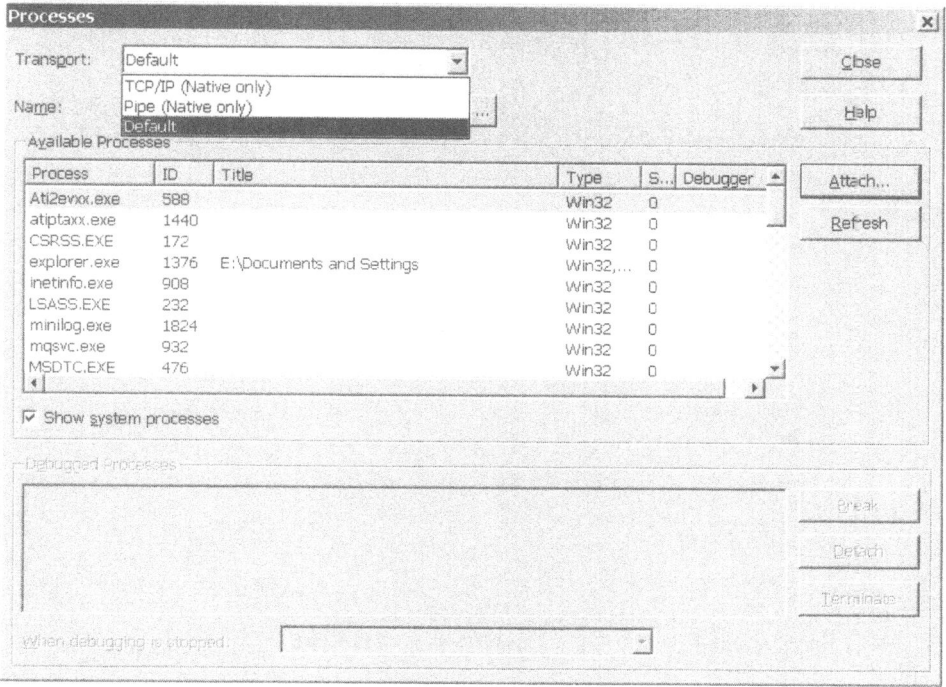

Figure 15-2. Choosing the remote debugging transport protocol

Installing Remote Debugging

Figure 15-3 shows the standard installation window for Visual Studio. The option to install remote debugging is in the bottom center of the window, and you use it to install the remote debugging components on the remote machine. No extra installation is required on the local machine. If Visual Studio is already installed on the remote machine, you won't see the option to install remote debugging because it's installed as part of Visual Studio.

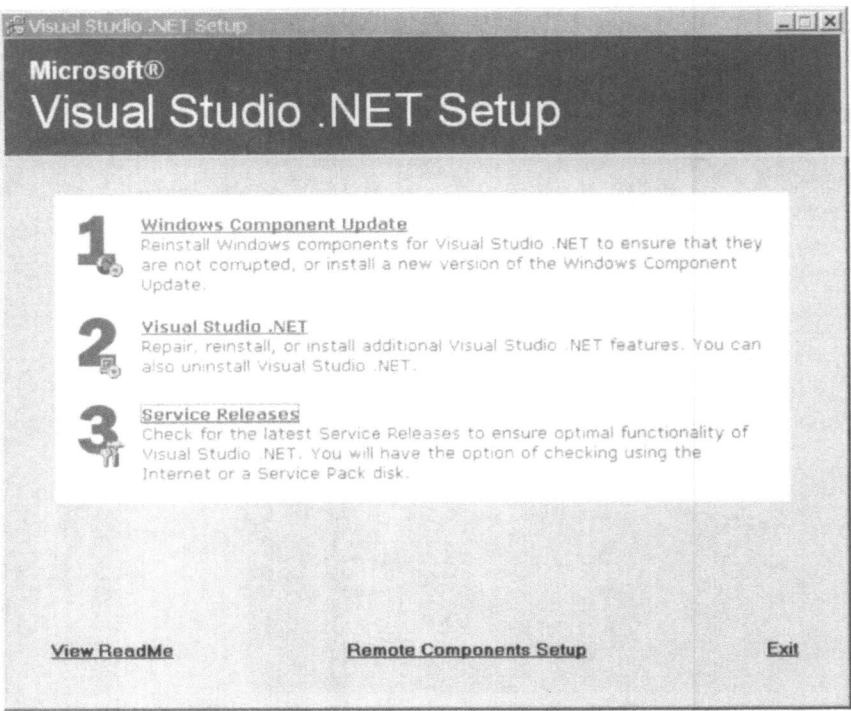

Figure 15-3. Visual Studio setup option to install remote debugging

Installing Native Remote Debugging Only

If you wish, you can opt to install just the remote components needed for debugging native Win32 programs. These are programs written using unmanaged languages such as VB.Classic and C++. The minimum components needed for remote native debugging are msvcmon.exe, msvcr70.dll, natdbgtlnet.dll, and natdbgdm.dll. If you're doing remote debugging under Windows NT, you'll also need psapi.dll, and if you need debug dump support, you'll need dbghelp.dll as well. Figure 15-4 shows the option to install native remote debugging only.

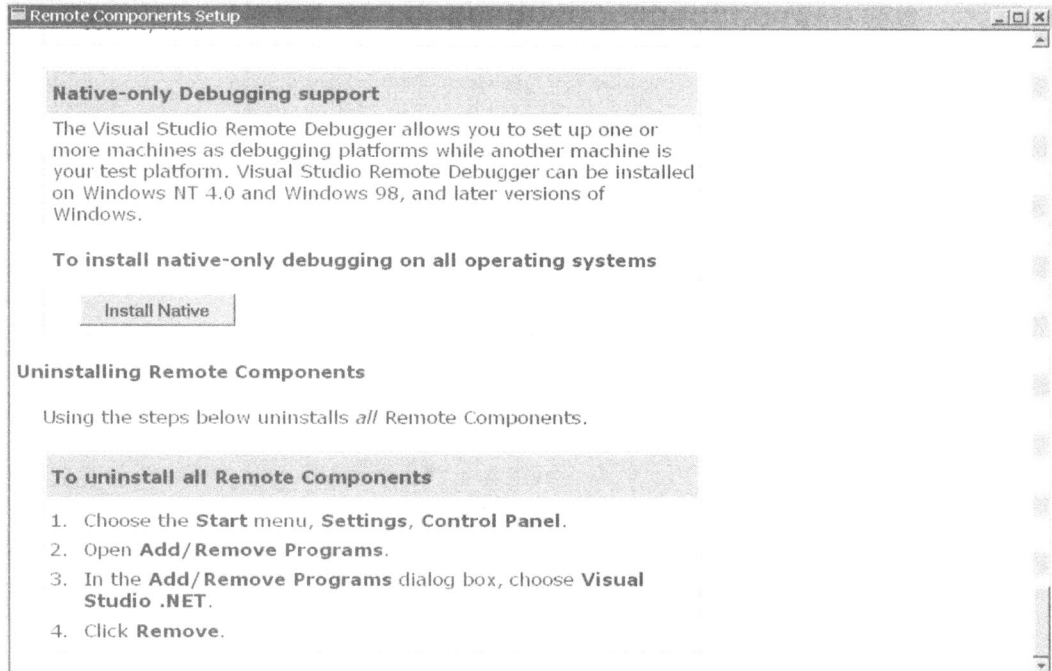

Figure 15-4. Installing native remote debugging only

You can install the native remote debugging components either directly into a single folder on the remote machine or on a local share that can then be accessed from the remote machine. This latter option is very convenient in that it allows you to do native remote debugging without installing anything at all on the remote machine. This is very useful in production environments where you may not be allowed to install any debugging components.

Installing Full Remote Debugging

Figure 15-5 shows the resulting installation instructions for setup of full remote debugging on Windows 2000. Full remote debugging allows you to debug both managed and unmanaged programs, as well as script applications. If SQL Server is detected on the remote machine, the SQL Server remote debugging components are also installed.

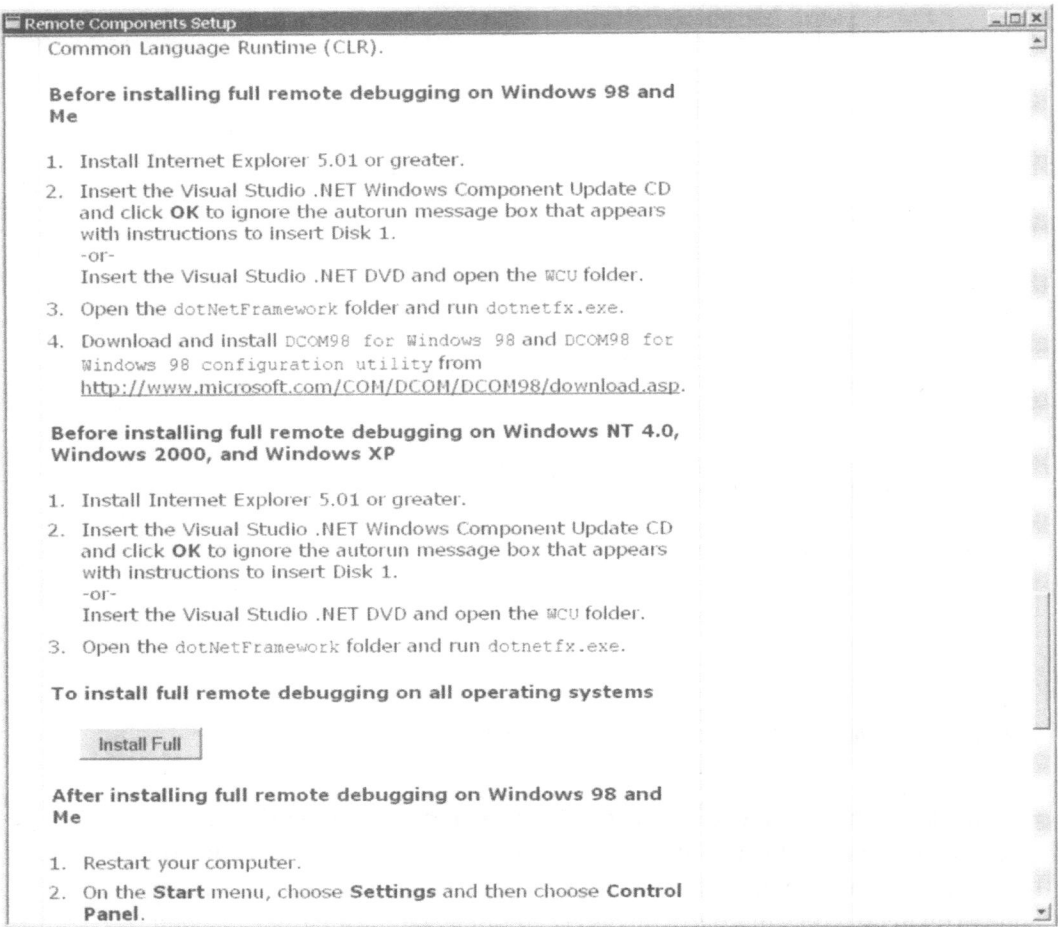

Figure 15-5. Remote debugging installation instructions

Note that each version of the operating system has its own unique instructions. For instance, when you install remote debugging on Windows ME or Windows 98, you'll probably need to install and configure DCOM because it's not installed by default on these operating systems.

Remote Debugging Restrictions

In this section I discuss the restrictions that you might encounter when using remote debugging. Most of these restrictions aren't lethal, but a couple of them can be rather troublesome. This first list includes the three most common restrictions:

- You can't use remote debugging to debug VB .NET, C#, or any other managed programs running on the Home Edition of Windows XP. This is because Windows XP Home Edition only supports TCP/IP for remote debugging, and you can only debug unmanaged (native Win32) programs remotely when using TCP/IP.

- Windows 2000 doesn't support remote debugging using Terminal Services. I haven't established why this restriction exists.

- You can't do remote debugging across Windows domains, unless those domains have two-way trust. This is a DCOM security restriction. You can use TCP/IP instead of DCOM for the remote debugging transport, but most firewalls will block the IP ports required for TCP/IP remote debugging. Note that this restriction effectively prevents standard remote debugging across the Internet.

One workaround for remote debugging across domains that don't have two-way trust is to use Terminal Services to log into a machine in the remote domain. Providing this remote machine has Visual Studio installed, you can then perform local debugging on that machine or remote debugging on another machine in the remote domain.

The next list includes some security restrictions imposed by the Visual Studio debugger. As noted after the list, these restrictions can be overcome by setting a registry key on the remote machine.

- You can't use Visual Studio to attach to, or launch, a remote process running in another user's Terminal Services session.

- Unless you're an administrator on a remote machine, you can't attach to a process started by a console (nonsystem) user on that machine. This security restriction doesn't apply if you and the console user have the same Windows account.

- You can't attach to a Windows service on a remote machine unless you're an administrator on that machine.

- You can't launch a process on a remote machine unless you're logged into that machine, either locally or using Terminal Services.

Creating or modifying the following registry key on the remote machine can overcome these security restrictions:

```
HKEY_LOCAL_MACHINE \Software\Microsoft\Machine Debug
Manager\AllowLaunchAsOtherUser
```

This registry key should be set to a DWORD value of **1**. In addition, for the last two security restrictions in this list, you need to have an administrator logged into the remote machine during the debugging session. This is an added security measure required by the Visual Studio debugger.

The HeartbeatMonitor Application

The **HeartbeatMonitor** application incorporates .NET remoting to show an effective design pattern for using "heartbeats" to monitor components in a distributed application. This section uses the **HeartbeatMonitor** distributed application to demonstrate remote debugging across machines. An understanding of .NET remoting isn't essential to follow this debugging example, but if you're new to remoting, you might want to familiarize yourself with the remoting overview contained in the Visual Studio documentation.

Introduction to HeartbeatMonitor

The **HeartbeatMonitor** solution contains the four components that make up the **HeartbeatMonitor** application. Three of the components reside on one machine, and the final component is designed for installation on another machine in the same Windows domain. If you don't have access to a second machine, the application will run in its entirety on one machine, but this approach means that you won't be able to see remote debugging in action.

The **HeartbeatMonitor** application shows how you can use *heartbeats* to monitor components running within a distributed application. A heartbeat is a signal from one component to a monitoring component confirming that the first component is alive and functioning correctly.

HeartbeatMonitor's first component consists of a single remotable class called **Heartbeat** that's shared between the other three components in the application. This class provides methods for components to generate and listen for heartbeats. It's built into its own class library called **Heartbeat.dll**.

The second component is a console application called **HeartbeatClient**. This component uses remoting and the **Heartbeat** class to emit regular heartbeats that can be heard by a local monitoring component that's listening on port 8080.

The third component is a monitoring application called **LocalMonitor**, also a console application. This component uses remoting to listen for any local component broadcasting heartbeats on port 8080. For reasons that I discuss later in the "Monitoring Distributed Applications" section, this component is designed to monitor only local components—in other words, components that are running on the same machine as the monitor. In addition, **LocalMonitor** broadcasts its own heartbeats on port 8081, which was designed for monitoring by a listener on another machine.

The final component is yet another console application, this one called **RemoteMonitor**. This component is designed to run on a separate machine from the other components, and it uses remoting and the **Heartbeat** class to listen for a regular heartbeat from any remote component broadcasting on port 8081.

In essence, the **LocalMonitor** component sits between the **HeartbeatClient** and **RemoteMonitor** components, listening to local heartbeats from **HeartbeatClient** and generating remote heartbeats for **RemoteMonitor**.

I discuss the interesting architecture considerations behind this example application later in this chapter, when I look at effective and ineffective ways of monitoring a distributed application. For the moment, you just need to understand how the separate application components cooperate, so that you install the application and then follow the remote debugging walkthrough. Figure 15-6 shows the complete architecture of the **HeartbeatMonitor** application.

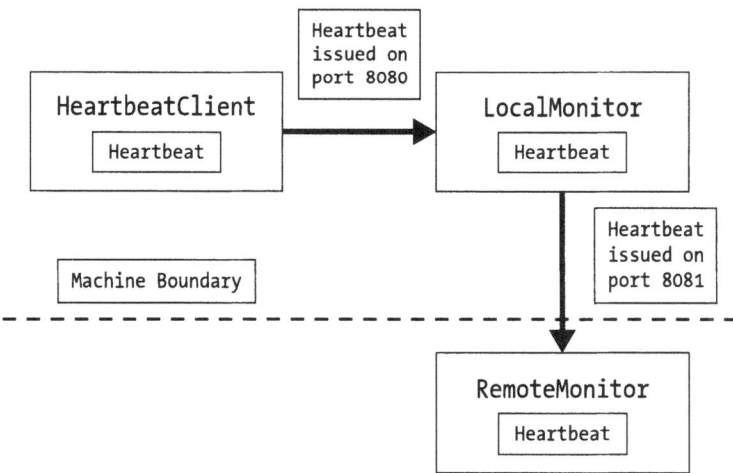

Figure 15-6. The architecture of the HeartbeatMonitor application

Installing HeartbeatMonitor

To verify that the example application is working correctly, load the **HeartbeatMonitor** solution into Visual Studio and right-click the solution in the Solution Explorer window. From the resulting context menu, go to the solution's Properties ➤ Common Properties ➤ Startup Project property page. Once there, ensure that the Multiple Startup Projects option is selected, and that the Start Action of all projects except **Heartbeat** is set to Start. Then go to the Project Dependencies property page and make sure that the project build dependencies are set correctly. The **Heartbeat** project is the base dependency and relies on none of the other projects. All of the other projects rely on just the **Heartbeat** project.

Now press Ctrl+Shift+B to build all of the projects. The Output window should show that all four projects were built without any errors or warnings. Once all of the projects in the solution have been built successfully, press Ctrl+F5 to start the solution with debugging disabled. If you're running a local firewall on your development PC, you may see some warning messages about allowing the application components to talk to each other through your firewall. The **HeartbeatMonitor** application uses remoting via two TCP channels on port 8080 and port 8081, so you may need to authorize the application to use these two ports. Alternatively, you can modify the source code and configuration files to specify different port numbers if your local firewall has any distinct preferences.

At this point, you should see three console windows opened respectively by the **HeartbeatClient**, **LocalMonitor**, and **RemoteMonitor** components. **HeartbeatClient** shows in its console window that it's started to emit a local heartbeat every 2 seconds. **LocalMonitor** shows that it's listening for local heartbeats and also generating a remote heartbeat every 10 seconds. Finally, **RemoteMonitor** shows that it's listening for remote heartbeats and prints each one that it receives. Figure 15-7 shows how the three console windows look while the **HeartbeatMonitor** application is running.

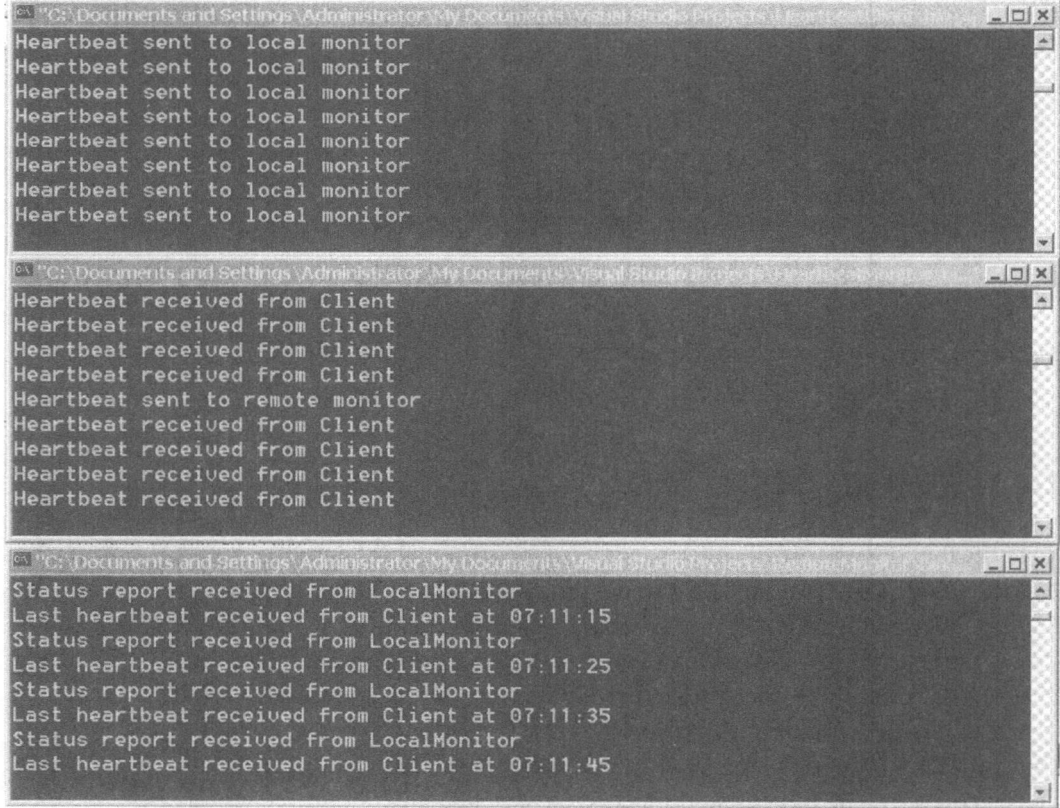

Figure 15-7. Running the HeartbeatMonitor application

Once you've confirmed that the application is up and running properly on your local development machine, you can press the Enter key in each console window to stop the related application component. First stop **HeartbeatClient**, and **LocalMonitor** should show that it has stopped receiving heartbeats. Then stop **LocalMonitor**, and **RemoteMonitor** should show that it in turn has stopped receiving heartbeats (heartbeat messages are still displayed, but the time of the last heartbeat doesn't change). Finally, you can stop **RemoteMonitor**.

Now you've seen how the application works and how its components interact, in the next section you'll look at using remote debugging to debug this application after the **RemoteMonitor** component has been moved to another machine.

Debugging HeartbeatMonitor

Before you do remote debugging of the **HeartbeatMonitor** application, you need to install the full remote debugging components on a PC other than your development machine. This process is described in the earlier section titled "Installing Full Remote Debugging." You should ensure that this second machine is in the same Windows domain as your development machine or at least on the same peer-to-peer network if that's what you have available. You should also log in using the same Windows user account on both machines before running and debugging the application, and that Windows user should be in the Debugger Users group on both machines. I discussed these restrictions earlier in the section titled "Remote Debugging Restrictions."

You also need to alter the line of code in the **LocalMonitor** component that controls the machine that the local monitor uses as the target for its remote heartbeats. To do this, change line 45 in LocalMonitor.vb to replace localhost with the IP address of your remote machine. For example, replace

```
"tcp://localhost:8081/Heartbeat.dll"
```

with

```
"tcp://192.168.254.9:8081/Heartbeat.dll"
```

You can perform either manual or automatic remote debugging of a VB .NET project. When you do automatic remote debugging, you tell Visual Studio that the project should be built, run, and debugged on a remote machine. When you do manual remote debugging, you build the project locally and then manually copy it to the remote machine. Once you've manually launched the component on the remote machine, you can manually attach the Visual Studio debugger to the remote process. I discuss these two methods of remote debugging in the next two sections.

Automatic Remote Debugging

The first step for automatic remote debugging is to set up a network share from the remote machine to your development machine, the development machine being the PC on which you're running Visual Studio. The network share should specify the remote folder where you want **RemoteMonitor** to be built and debugged. Once you've done this, go to the **RemoteMonitor** project's Configuration Properties ➤ Build property page and enter the path of this network share into the Output path field, as shown in Figure 15-8.

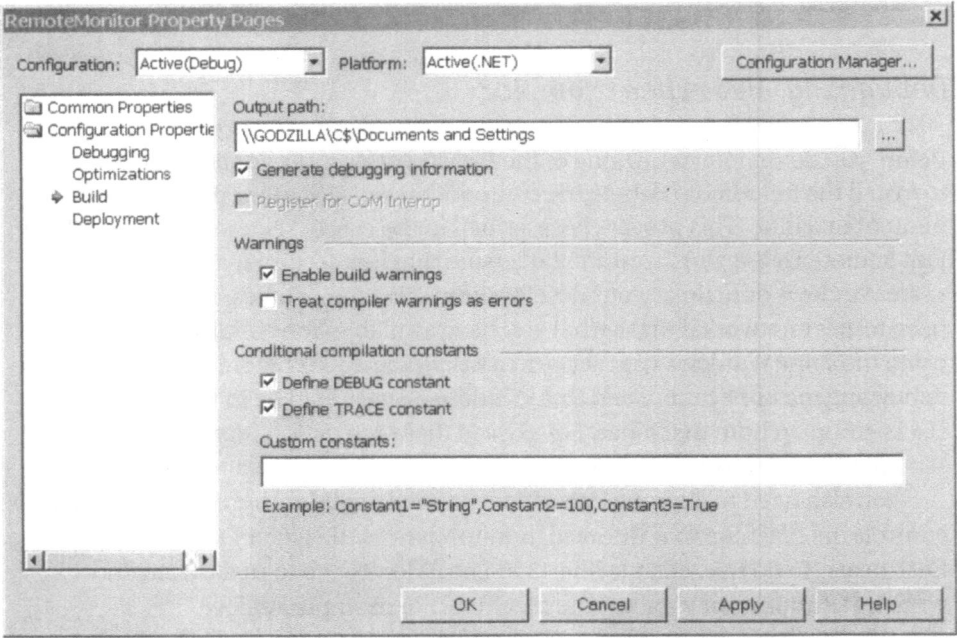

*Figure 15-8. Specifying the remote path for the **RemoteMonitor** component*

As a final step for automatic remote debugging, go to the **RemoteMonitor**'s Configuration Properties ➤ Debugging property page and select the option titled Use remote machine. In the associated text box, type the name of the remote machine.

Now when you start the solution by pressing F5, the **RemoteMonitor** project will be compiled and run on the remote machine rather than on your local machine. The debugger will automatically attach to the remote process, and you should be able to debug just as if you were debugging locally. You may find that remote debugging is somewhat slower than local debugging, but unfortunately I know of no way to speed up this process.

To check that you're debugging the remote project and not the local project, you can go to the Debug menu and select the Processes dialog window. In the Debugged Processes subwindow, you can verify that the machine name shown next to the **RemoteMonitor** process indicates the name of the remote machine. Before you close the Processes dialog window, there is one more interesting point. If you select any of the processes that are being debugged, you can see that the "When debugging is stopped" option is set to terminate the process. Unfortunately, this is the default setting that Visual Studio uses when attaching to a managed process, even though it's likely that this isn't what you normally want to do, especially in a distributed application. For instance, if you now press Enter in the **HeartbeatClient** console window to stop the client component, you'll find that Visual Studio stops the whole application, not just the client component. To prevent this behavior, you need to select each of the processes being debugged and set the "When debugging is stopped" option to detach from the process rather than terminate it. This manual procedure is a real pain when you're debugging multiple processes simultaneously.

Remote debugging can sometimes be a bit tricky to configure. For instance, if you have firewalls running on either of the two machines, you may need to change their configuration or even disable them. This is because remote debugging uses DCOM as its default transport protocol and firewalls usually don't allow DCOM by default. In fact, Microsoft claims not to support remote debugging through a firewall, although I've managed to do this without a problem.

Manual Remote Debugging

In some cases, you might not want to build, run, and debug your remote component entirely within Visual Studio. For example, you might be debugging the **RemoteMonitor** component in a production environment without wanting to recompile it at all. For this, you need to do your remote debugging manually.

Before trying this, you should revert the **RemoteMonitor** component back to its original output path and local machine settings if you experimented with automatic remote debugging as described in the previous section. Then copy the contents of the RemoteMonitor\bin folder to a folder on the remote machine. This includes the **RemoteMonitor** and **Heartbeat** executables along with their associated debug symbol files and the RemoteMonitor.config file. Then change the **HeartbeatMonitor** solution to prevent it from launching the local **RemoteMonitor** project. On the solution's Properties ➤ Common Properties ➤ Startup Project property page, modify the Start Action of the **RemoteMonitor** project to **None**. Now launch the **RemoteMonitor** component from the remote machine by double-clicking the executable, and launch the rest of the application from Visual Studio by pressing F5.

You can now go to the Debug menu and select the Processes dialog window. In the Name text box, either type in the name of the remote machine or browse to it. You should then see a list of the processes running on the remote machine, including the **RemoteMonitor** process. Click that process and then click the Attach button. When the debugger displays a dialog window asking which type of debugging you wish to do, select just the Common Language Runtime option, as shown in Figure 15-9.

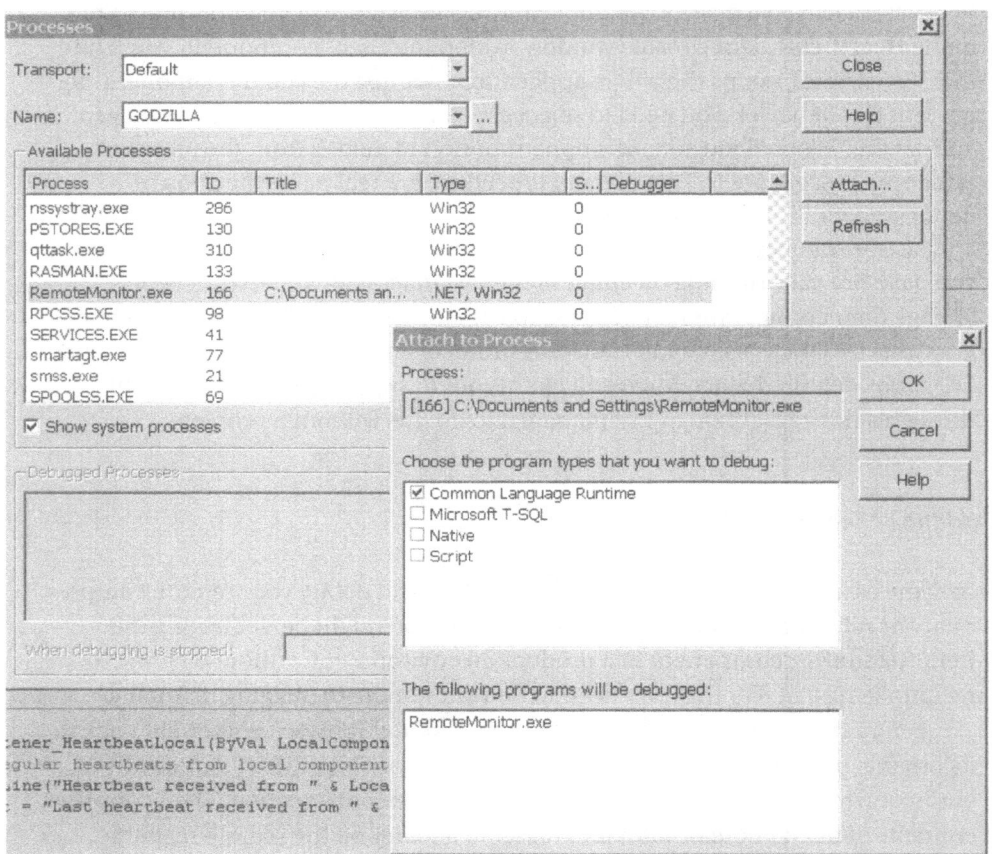

Figure 15-9. Manual remote debugging of the RemoteMonitor component

Now the Visual Studio debugger should attach to the remote process, and once again you're debugging just as if the **RemoteMonitor** component was running locally. The source stays on your local machine, but the executable and debug symbols are held remotely. One caveat with manual debugging in this fashion, whether done locally or remotely, is that you need to be really sure that the source code, executable, and debug symbols all match up exactly, otherwise you'll see strange things happen when the debugger tries to step through your source code. This is a good argument for always keeping matching debug symbols, source code, and executables together under rigorous source control, as Chapter 4 covered in more detail.

Monitoring Distributed Applications

In the previous section I discussed the **HeartbeatMonitor** application as a design pattern for monitoring distributed applications. In this section I investigate why this specific monitoring pattern is particularly effective.

One of the most common ways to monitor individual components running as part of a distributed application is to use "heartbeats." The idea behind this is that each component transmits a regular heartbeat across the local network to an associated heartbeat monitor running on another machine. Each of the heartbeat monitors has a list of components that it's supposed to watch, and it displays a status page with a "smiley" face to represent a healthy component (i.e., a component transmitting a regular heartbeat) and a "frowny" face for any component that has missed more than one heartbeat.

So now a member of your application support team phones to tell you that component ABC on server XYZ has stopped broadcasting a heartbeat. This is an application-critical component, so you need to respond fairly fast. You use Terminal Services to log into machine XYZ, but after 5 minutes you're still waiting for the login to happen because the server doesn't seem to be responding. So you phone the server support team to report a nonfunctioning server. They take 5 more minutes to respond, but then they tell you that they can log into server XYZ without a problem. Having established that you're on a different network segment than the server support team, you ring the network support team to report a possible network switch issue. After another 10 minutes, they phone you back to say that the network switches appear to be functioning normally. Sure enough, when you try to log into server XYZ again, the login works perfectly and the heartbeat status page is now showing a smiley face again for component ABC. You never do establish what went wrong, or why.

If you look back to the list of possible failures in a distributed application presented at the beginning of this chapter, you can see the problem with the debugging scenario that I just discussed. When the heartbeat monitor component is remote from the components that it's monitoring, it has no way of knowing what's really wrong. The problem could be with a component that's being monitored or with any of the software or hardware sitting between that component and the monitoring component. To perform remote diagnosis of what's really wrong would require some very sophisticated software and hardware monitoring, and introduce some serious complexity into the monitoring process.

There are two more problems with this design pattern of remote monitoring. The first is that it's not easy for a remote monitor to take any corrective action, such as restarting a component that appears to be dead in the water. The second problem is that when you have several distributed applications running on your local network, the number of heartbeat messages can rise to a significant proportion of your total network traffic. At one company where I worked, more than 50% of the application network traffic was attributed to heartbeat messages. Although this may not necessarily be a problem because heartbeat messages tend to be small and any good network should be optimized to handle many small messages, it's still a pain to explain this to the network support team. And as you can see from the debugging scenario that I've just discussed, most of these heartbeat messages are useless.

To avoid all of these problems, one very good technique is to use the local monitor design pattern, as demonstrated by the **HeartbeatMonitor** application. Because each heartbeat monitor runs locally on the same machine as the components that it's monitoring, it's able to analyze a problem in much more detail than is possible with a remote monitor. When a heartbeat is missed, the local monitor can check for problems such as low memory, low disk space, or high processor utilization. It can sometimes determine whether a problematic component is completely dead or is just hung. If necessary, it can kill and/or restart a dead component, or take some other corrective action. The local monitor can also watch the overall health of the machine on which it's running and provide advance warning about problems such as low disk space that might affect other components running on the machine. All this is possible because diagnosis of local failure is much easier and more reliable than diagnosis of remote failure.

You still need one or more remote monitors to watch the local monitors and present the aggregated results, but these remote monitors won't generate anywhere near the amount of network traffic they did in the original scenario. As an added benefit, each remote monitor doesn't need to maintain a complex and ever-changing list of application components to watch, as this list can now be kept local to each machine. Instead, each remote monitor has a much smaller list of local monitors to watch, preferably one per machine. Because the local heartbeats are aggregated before being pushed to the remote monitors, your network is no longer flooded with (mainly useless) heartbeat messages and you have much more reliable diagnostics.

I should mention, of course, that heartbeats are only part of the solution when monitoring a distributed application. You should also ensure that the server support team monitors all of your application servers for hardware faults, hardware and software warnings, and server up/down status. You should make sure that the network support team monitors the network effectively and checks the type and volume of network traffic. Finally, you must ensure that there is proper documentation that describes what should be done in the event of specific faults or warnings, including support escalation procedures.

Summary

This chapter examined debugging and monitoring distributed applications in some detail. Once you understand the major differences between debugging local and distributed applications, and especially the difficulties in trying to diagnose remote failures, it's much easier to design and implement distributed systems that can be debugged effectively. Visual Studio's remote debugging facilities are excellent, and they can help you find and diagnose a problem in-place rather than forcing you into trying to replicate the problem in your development environment. Along with allowing you to debug remotely in a nonintrusive manner and use remoting to monitor your distributed systems, .NET provides more effective distributed debugging than ever before offered by Microsoft tools.

INTERLUDE

HOW GOOD ARE YOU?

There is an interesting episode in one of the earlier *Tintin* cartoon novels where the eponymous hero travels through Russia in a car that eventually breaks down. After indulging in a frenzy of debugging by ripping out pieces of the engine and throwing them on the ground, Tintin finds that the actual problem is a flat tire. With the entire engine lying in pieces on the ground, Tintin randomly throws the pieces back into the engine bay until it's completely full. Left with a full engine bay, but still several engine sections lying on the ground, Tintin shrugs to himself and of course drives off without a problem.

As a freelance consultant who moves from corporation to corporation, I've lost count of the number of times that I've seen this scenario played out in the real world by corporate developers. For example, I was recently having a major problem when trying to use a component written by a colleague who sat next to me in the office. When I told him about the problem, I watched in amazement as he guessed the cause of the underlying bug, made a fix, recompiled the component and, without testing his fix, handed the component back to me for testing. Of course, it still didn't work. So he made another seemingly random fix and handed the component back to me, once again without doing any testing. Of course, the new fix didn't work either. This "Tintin" cycle of fix-and-failure repeated itself four or five times before my colleague eventually stopped guessing and started using a debugger to figure out what the problem actually was.

My colleague wasn't stupid; indeed, he was probably an above-average developer in a team that had several good coders. On the many occasions that I've seen this "random debugging" behavior, it rarely seems to be correlated with lack of intelligence or experience. So why is this behavior so common amongst developers?

My theory, after a couple of decades' worth of observations, is that many developers delude themselves about their own skill levels and their understanding of their own code. Most developers genuinely believe that they're well above average in debugging ability, and that their experience and brainpower allows them to make educated guesses during a debugging session.

The problem is that software development is mainly a solitary experience, which makes it very difficult to estimate exactly how good you are at understanding and debugging code, even your own code. Without the ability to compare your debugging abilities with those of other developers, it's therefore hard to judge your own skill level. It's also hard for a developer to criticize his own debugging abilities when he's devoted months and years to writing code for a living, and when his compensation is probably directly related to his ability to appear as a software expert.

One insight came from the world of professional chess, which I used to inhabit before I turned to writing software. Playing chess is somewhat similar to writing software. Both of these activities are mentally very intensive, both rely on a variety of mental skills, and both involve grandiose plans and difficult implementations. But there is one big difference between the two activities, which is that you always know exactly how good you are at playing chess.

Professional chess is a rather brutal sport because you're constantly matching yourself against other chess players in tournament games that are graded by computer. All of your chess knowledge, memory, judgment, and calculations are reduced to a single number called an *ELO grade*, and there's no shelter from this brutal truth. If you want to know how good or bad somebody is at chess, you simply have to look at his or her ELO grade.

Faced with this implacable reduction of chess skills to a single number, professional chess players tend to become very good at preventing mistakes. Either they learn not to deceive themselves or they simply fade away and don't make the grade. Developers don't often have to undergo this harsh judgment. Although a compiler will tell you when you've made a syntax mistake, your logic and semantic bugs usually aren't exposed until a later stage. Software developers are rarely beaten over the head with the results of their mistakes.

One way of simulating the feedback received by professional chess players is to make a bet with yourself every time that you fix a bug. If your bug fix fails, either immediately or at some time in the future, pay $10 (or some other nasty amount) into a "bug fund." Then see how much money the bug fund collects each week and whether the weekly amount paid into the fund goes up or down over time. What you do with the money after a year or so is up to you. Maybe give it to charity, or alternatively buy a good book on debugging.

Index